D1259709

Acousto-Optic Signal Processing

OPTICAL ENGINEERING

Series Editor

Brian J. Thompson
William F. May Professor of Engineering
and
Dean, College of Engineering and Applied Science
University of Rochester

Other Volumes in Preparation

Acousto-Optic Signal Processing

THEORY AND IMPLEMENTATION

Edited by
Norman J. Berg
Department of the Army
Harry Diamond Laboratories
Adelphi, Maryland

John N. Lee
U.S. Naval Research Laboratory
Washington, D.C.

Acousto-optic signal processing.
350

Series Introduction

Optical science, engineering, and technology have grown rapidly in the
last decade so that today optical engineering has emerged as an important discipline in its own right. This series is devoted to discussing
topics in optical engineering at a level that will be useful to those working in the field or attempting to design systems that are based on optical techniques or that have significant optical subsystems. The
philosophy is not to provide detailed monographs on narrow subject
areas but to deal with the material at a level that makes it immediately
useful to the practicing scientist and engineer. These are not research
monographs, although we expect that workers in optical research will
find them extremely valuable.

Volumes in this series cover those topics that have been a part of
the rapid expansion of optical engineering. The developments that have
led to this expansion include the laser and its many commercial and
industrial applications, the new optical materials, gradient index optics,
electro- and acousto-optics, fiber optics and communications, optical
computing and pattern recognition, optical data reading, recording
and storage, biomedical instrumentation, industrial robotics, integrated
optics, infrared and ultraviolet systems, etc. Since the optical industry
is currently one of the major growth industries this list will surely become even more extensive.

Brian J. Thompson
University of Rochester
Rochester, New York

Preface

Signal-processing requirements for applications in areas such as radar,
communications, and electromagnetic signal classification can be projected to call for ever-increasing speed, bandwidth, and dynamic range.
Many applications will also require small size and low power consump-
tion. Analog technologies continue to hold the promise of satisfying
many or all of these requirements. Two such technologies are optical
signal processing and acoustic wave filters. Heretofore, the utilization of such technologies has not been on par with their promise. For
example, optical processing in practice has been plagued by limitations
of input and output devices; acoustic wave filters often do not provide
good dynamic range. In recent years there has been much work towards
solving the problems of these technologies. Progress has been such that
the term *acousto-optics* is now being considered seriously by researchers and applications engineers looking for potential solutions to signal-
processing problems. The progress in acousto-optics has been spurred
by important technological developments in several different areas.
The first important development was the laser, which made available
sources of intense, monochromatic, coherent light. A second area of
development has been in acoustic wave devices—both bulk and surface
wave. Research in new materials and advanced transducer design
has led to the development of large-bandwidth, large-aperture delay
lines with good light-diffraction efficiency. Third, advances in the
semiconductor area have led to small, high-speed light detectors which
are available either individually or in the form of self-scanning one-
and two-dimensional arrays. The development of semiconductor-based
digital technology is also important in another way: Fast circuits are
required to handle the large data throughput on both the input and
output sides of the modern analog processor. This has naturally led
to hybrid digital/analog systems. Finally, there have been significant
advances in recent years in integrated-optics technology which have

led to the demonstration of small, near-diffraction-limited lenses and miniature laser sources with excellent spectral and mode purity. The recent work has also indicated the feasibility of full integration of all the components of an optical circuit onto a single substrate. Thus, the ultimate realization of a sophisticated acousto-optical signal processor that is ultracompact and rugged may soon be possible.

Although technological advances have been important to the maturing of acousto-optic signal-processing technology, of equal, if not greater, importance has been the development of sophisticated alternate signal-processing architectures which can overcome inherent limitations in simple architectures. A striking example of this is the time-integrating correlator, which can be used to overcome the signal-length limitation that occurs with any real delay line filter. However, implementation of a new architecture in an acousto-optic form can result in a device with some unexpected characteristics if one is not fully cognizant of the basis for the operation of the device. For this reason, the opening chapters of Part I will not only deal with general theory of the acousto-optic interaction but will also attempt to deal rigorously with the theory of acousto-optic signal-processing devices. The final chapter of Part I deals with the theory, design, and construction of acousto-optic deflectors and modulators and the extent of their current and proposed usage in signal processing.

The following two parts discuss application areas where acousto-optic devices can soon be expected to have an impact. The areas of spectrum analysis, coherent detection, and tunable filters are treated in Part II. Acousto-optic devices for RF, visible, and IR spectral analysis and filtering that are available for consideration as system components are described. Part III describes work on real-time acousto-optic signal processing of temporal signals. Processor concepts for convolvers and correlators are the main topics of discussion, although a memory device is also considered. In addition to discussing one-dimensional architectures, techniques for implementing two-dimensional signal-processing structures are also discussed. This part concludes with a chapter specifically devoted to discussing system application areas utilizing both time- and frequency-domain acousto-optic signal processors.

Although integrated optics will be an important consideration in the future development of acousto-optic signal processing, that technology must at present be considered still in its infancy. For this reason, the work described in Parts I through III deals exclusively with devices using light from a separate, discrete, source interacting with an acoustic device. Part IV, Chap. 12, will provide a description of the status of the integrated-optics technology and of the acousto-optic devices that have been realized using integrated optics. Special attention will be given to efforts to construct an integrated-optic spectrum analyzer.

We hope that the manner in which we have treated the rapidly growing field of acousto-optic signal processing will allow both the researcher and the system engineer to obtain a good overall description of the field. Without question the range of topics covered in this volume is not all-inclusive. Nevertheless, it is felt that the researcher will be able to identify further work in signal-processing and device concepts where the combination of optics and acoustics could provide an answer. For the system engineer it is intended that this volume provide sufficient detail to help understand the potential of acousto-optics in answering requirements of present and future signal-processing systems.

Norman J. Berg
John N. Lee

Contents

    Harris Corporation

    3.1   Introduction   47
    3.2   Materials and Transducer Design   49
    3.3   Acousto-Optic Modulator Design   52
    3.4   Acousto-Optic Deflectors   64
    3.5   Acoustic Focusing   75
    3.6   Outlook for Acousto-Optic Device Applications   80
          Acknowledgment   80
          References   80

PART II   FREQUENCY-DOMAIN SIGNAL PROCESSING   83
          Preface   85

4   Applications of Acousto-Optic Techniques to RF
    Spectrum Analysis   87
    John P. Lindley

    4.1   Acousto-Optic Spectrum Analyzer Applications   87
    4.2   Acousto-Optic Spectrum Analyzer Analysis   93
    4.3   Component Design Considerations   98
    4.4   Acousto-Optics and Signal Processing   104
          References   105

5   Coherent Detection and Adaptive Filtering   107
    David W. Jackson and Jerry Lee Erickson

    5.1   Introduction   107
    5.2   Processor Description   109
    5.3   Processor Transfer Function   112
    5.4   Computer Results   121
    5.5   Experimental Results   127
    5.6   Summary   136
          References   136

6   Acousto-Optic Tunable Filters   139
    I. C. Chang

    6.1   Principle of Operation   139
    6.2   Filter Characteristics   146
    6.3   Applications   156
          References   158

Contributors

IRWIN J. ABRAMOVITZ* Department of the Army, Harry Diamond Laboratories, Adelphi, Maryland

NORMAN J. BERG Department of the Army, Harry Diamond Laboratories, Adelphi, Maryland

DAVID CASASENT Carnegie-Mellon University, Pittsburgh, Pennsylvania

MICHAEL W. CASSEDAY Department of the Army, Harry Diamond Laboratories, Adelphi, Maryland

I. C. CHANG ITEK Corporation, Applied Technology Division, Sunnyvale, California

JONATHAN D. COHEN Department of Defense, Fort Meade, Maryland

JERRY LEE ERICKSON Probe Systems, Inc., Sunnyvale, California

DAVID W. JACKSON† Probe Systems, Inc., Sunnyvale, California

JOHN N. LEE U.S. Naval Research Laboratory, Washington, D.C.

JOHN P. LINDLEY‡ ITEK Corporation, Applied Technology Division, Sunnyvale, California

---

*Current affiliation: Westinghouse Defense and Electronics Center, Baltimore, Maryland
†Current affiliation: ESL Incorporated, Sunnyvale, California
‡Current affiliation: Probe Systems, Inc., Sunnyvale, California

E. C. MALARKEY Westinghouse Electric Corporation, Advanced Technology Division, Baltimore, Maryland

D. MERGERIAN Westinghouse Electric Corporation, Advanced Technology Division, Baltimore, Maryland

WILLIAM D. SCHARF Department of the Army, Harry Diamond Laboratories, Adelphi, Maryland

DON J. TORRIERI Department of the Army, Countermeasures/Counter-Countermeasures Center, Adelphi, Maryland

A Note About Notation

Acousto-optic signal processing is a new and evolving technology, and hence a standardized notation has not yet been formalized.

We have, however, attempted to use as much uniform and standardized notation throughout this book as possible. In addition, each chapter author defines the particular notation which he uses.

Presented below is a brief list of symbols:

c	speed of light
K_m	mth consitutent plane wave for a given optical mode
k_a	acoustic wave vector
L	thickness of dielectric slab
n	refractive index of medium
Q	Raman-Nath parameter
v	acoustic velocity
ΔK	momentum mismatch between optical and acoustic wave vectors
ε	dielectric constant of medium
Λ	acoustic wavelength
λ	vacuum wavelength of incident plane wave
ρ	mass density

Acousto-Optic Signal Processing

I
INTRODUCTION TO ACOUSTO-OPTICS

Preface

This part presents the basic theory of the acousto-optic interaction and the design and application of fundamental acousto-optic devices, viz., the deflector and modulator. Chapter 1 by Torrieri presents a qualitative treatment of both the isotropic and anisotropic acousto-optic interaction as well as a derivation of three basic signal-processing devices, the spectrum analyzer, the convolver, and the correlator. This chapter is fundamental to the entire book, and a proper understanding of the concepts developed therein will be extremely useful in comprehending the successive chapters. Chapter 2 by Scharf presents a more quantitative derivation of the acousto-optic interaction. This is required for a more rigorous derivation of anisotropic and high-power effects. Chapter 3 presents design criteria and examples of acousto-optic bulk-wave deflectors and modulators. It also describes a variety of applications in which these devices are utilized. In addition, it discusses acousto-optic focusing. The entire part is self-contained and complete. It serves as an appropriate stepping stone to understanding acousto-optic signal processing.

1

Introduction to Acousto-Optic Interaction Theory

DON J. TORRIERI / Department of the Army, Countermeasures/
Counter-Countermeasures Center, Adelphi, Maryland

1.1 INTRODUCTION

The interaction of light and sound can be described in terms of wave
interactions or particle collisions [1-9]. Both pictures are intuitively
appealing and can provide basic information without elaborate mathematics. In this section, a heuristic analysis is given by using an
elementary particle picture. For more precise information, such as the
dependence of the interaction on acoustic power, elaborate mathematics
is unavoidable and is presented in Chap. 2.

In the particle picture, light consists of photons and sound consists of phonons. Each photon has momentum $\hbar K$ and energy $\hbar \omega_\ell$,
where $2\pi\hbar$ is Planck's constant, K is the wave vector, and ω_ℓ is the
angular frequency. Each phonon has momentum $\hbar k_a$ and energy $\hbar \omega_a$,
where k_a is the wave vector and ω_a is the angular frequency. When a
photon and a phonon collide, one of two results is possible: Either
the phonon is annihilated, or a new phonon is created. The possibilities are illustrated in Fig. 1.1, where K' denotes the wave vector of
the scattered photon. If it is assumed that, to a good approximation,
the momentum is conserved in a collision, then phonon annihilation
implies

$$K' = K + k_a \qquad (1.1)$$

and phonon creation implies

$$K' = K - k_a \qquad (1.2)$$

We shall examine the implications of equation (1.1) in detail; the
implications of equation (1.2) are analogous. From equation (1.1) and
Fig. 1.1(a), we have

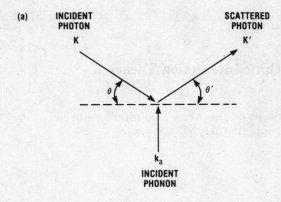

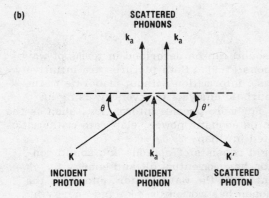

Figure 1.1 Photon-phonon interactions: (a) annihilation and (b) creation. (From Ref. 17.)

$$K' \cos \theta' = K \cos \theta \qquad\qquad\qquad (1.3)$$

$$K' \sin \theta' = k_a - K \sin \theta \qquad\qquad\qquad (1.4)$$

where K', K, and k_a are the magnitudes of the corresponding wave vectors, θ is the angle of the incident photon, and θ' is the angle of the scattered photon. If θ, k_a, and K are specified, equations (1.3) and (1.4) can be solved for θ' and K'. Dividing equation (1.4) by equation (1.3) yields

$$\theta' = \tan^{-1} \left[-\tan \theta + \left(\frac{k_a}{K} \right) \sec \theta \right] \qquad\qquad (1.5)$$

Assuming that $k_a/K \ll 1$ and $\theta \ll 1$, equation (1.5) gives

$$\theta' \simeq \frac{k_a}{K} - \theta \qquad (1.6)$$

Let v and c represent the acoustic and optical velocities, respectively. Since we know from wave theory that $v = \omega_a/k_a$ and $c = \omega_\ell/K$,

$$\frac{k_a}{K} = \frac{c\omega_a}{v\omega_\ell} \qquad (1.7)$$

Thus,

$$\theta' \simeq \left(\frac{c}{v\omega_\ell}\right)\omega_a - \theta \qquad (1.8)$$

This relation shows explicitly that the angle of the scattered photon with respect to the incident direction is proportional to the acoustic frequency. Although the acousto-optical interaction may consist of multiple collisions of photons with phonons, it turns out that equation (1.8) does hold approximately for many practical devices. Thus, a diffracted beam is deflected at an angle proportional to the acoustic frequency. If the angle is measured, the acoustic frequency can be estimated.

We define the *Bragg angle* θ_B by

$$\sin \theta_B = \frac{k_a}{2K} \qquad (1.9)$$

If $\theta = \theta_B$, equation (1.5) implies that $\theta' = \theta = \theta_B$. Equation (1.3) then gives $K' = K$. Thus, the magnitude of the photon momentum is conserved when the photon is incident at the Bragg angle. It turns out that $\theta = \theta_B$ is the condition for the most efficient diffraction of an optical wave in an isotropic medium. Figure 1.2 is a wave-vector diagram for the Bragg condition.

The conservation of energy is approximately valid for a photon-phonon collision. Thus, the freqency of a scattered photon is

$$\omega_0 = \omega_\ell + \omega_a \qquad (1.10)$$

for phonon annihilation and

$$\omega_0 = \omega_\ell - \omega_a \qquad (1.11)$$

for phonon creation. It turns out that the frequency of the principal diffracted wave satisfies equation (1.10) or equation (1.11) in many practical devices.

Birefringent diffraction, which occurs when the refractive indices for the incident and diffracted optical waves are different, exhibits

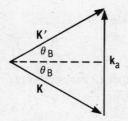

Figure 1.2 Wave vectors for Bragg angle of incidence. (From
Ref. 17.)

significantly different characteristics from isotropic diffraction. In an
anisotropic medium, a change in direction and polarization between the
incident and diffracted waves causes birefringent diffraction. Since
$\omega_a << \omega_\ell$, we have $\omega_0 \simeq \omega_\ell$ in practical cases. Thus, $K' \simeq rK$, where
r is the ratio of the refractive index associated with the diffracted
wave to the refractive index associated with the incident wave. We
expect a large principal diffracted beam if conservation of momentum
is satisfied. Using trigonometry in equations (1.3) and (1.4), we obtain the necessary conditions:

$$\sin\ \theta = \frac{k_a}{2K}\left[1 + \left(\frac{K}{k_a}\right)^2(1 - r^2)\right]$$
(1.12)

$$\sin\ \theta' = \frac{k_a}{2Kr}\left[1 - \left(\frac{K}{k_a}\right)^2(1 - r^2)\right]$$
(1.13)

With these equations, we can derive several interesting results.

To observe $\theta' = \theta$, we must have $r = 1$ or $r = (k_a/K) - 1$. The
latter equation cannot be satisfied since $k_a < K$. Thus, $\theta' = \theta$ is a
phenomenon associated with $r = 1$ and the Bragg angle of incidence.

Equations (1.12) and (1.13) do not have solutions unless the
right-hand sides have magnitudes less than or equal to unity. This
requirement and $k_a < K$ yield

$$1 - \frac{k_a}{K} \leqslant r \leqslant 1 + \frac{k_a}{K}$$
(1.14)

Thus, strong acousto-optical diffraction is usually not observed unless
equation (1.14) is satisfied.

If we specify θ, equation (1.12) gives two possible values of k_a,
and equation (1.13) gives two corresponding values of θ'. Thus, for
an incident wave vector K, there are two values of k_a that allow conservation of momentum, as illustrated in Fig. 1.3, where n_0 and n_1 are
the refractive indices for the incident and diffracted beams, respectively.

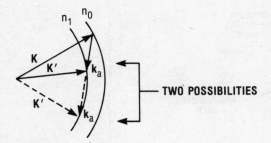

Figure 1.3 Possible wave vectors giving conservation of momentum. (From Ref. 17.)

Birefringent diffraction is important primarily because the conservation of momentum can be approximately satisfied over a wider range of acoustic frequencies or incident light directions than is usually possible with isotropic diffraction. Consequently, anisotropic materials are useful in devices requiring a large bandwidth.

1.2 BRAGG CELL INTERACTIONS

In this section, acousto-optical theoretical results are summarized and used to develop the basic theory needed for most applications.

The acoustic wave is generated from an electrical signal by a piezo-electric transducer attached to one end of a medium with an acoustic termination that suppresses reflected waves. As a result of the acousto-optical interaction, the diffracted light emerging from the medium is modulated by the information contained in the original electrical signal. Since the modulated light has a spatial variation equivalent to the time variation of the signal, parallel processing of information is possible.

The diffraction geometry associated with the acousto-optical interaction is shown in Fig. 1.4, where Λ is the acoustic wavelength. Let the angular frequency and the wave vector of the incident optical wave in the medium be denoted by ω_ℓ and K, respectively, and those of the acoustic wave by ω_a and k_a. Due to the acousto-optical interaction, the diffracted optical waves in the medium have angular frequencies $\omega_m = \omega_\ell + m\omega_a$ and approximate wave vectors $K_m = K + mk_a$, where $m = \pm 1, \pm 2, \ldots$. (The constituent plane waves of the optical field in the medium are more fully described in Chap. 2.) Special cases of diffraction can be characterized by the parameter

$$Q = \frac{k_a^2 L}{K}$$

(1.15)

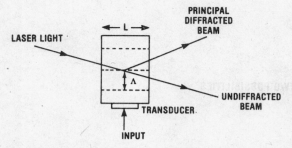

Figure 1.4 Bragg cell interaction. (From Ref. 17.)

where k_a and K are the magnitudes of the acoustic and optical wave
vectors, respectively, and L is the width of the acoustic beam. When
Q < 1, the diffraction is said to be in the *Raman-Nath regime*. When
Q >> 1, the diffraction is said to be in the *Bragg regime*. The intermediate region where 1 < Q < 10 gives a mixture of the characteristics
of the Raman-Nath and Bragg regimes.

In the Raman-Nath regime, many diffracted beams may contain significant power. This regime corresponds to ultrasonic frequencies less
than 20 MHz if L = 1 cm, the wavelength of light is approximately 0.5
μm, and the acoustic velocity is approximately 3.5×10^5 cm/s.

Most of the practical wide-bandwidth applications of acousto-optics
depend on operation in the Bragg regime. An acoustical device operating in the Bragg regime is called a *Bragg cell*. The result of the
acousto-optical interaction in a Bragg cell is the production of only two
significant beams outside the cell: the *undiffracted main beam* and the
principal diffracted beam. These beams are indicated in Fig. 1.4.

Let $\hat{K}$ and $\hat{k}_a$ represent unit vectors in the directions of K and k_a,
respectively. If $\hat{K} \cdot \hat{k}_a < 0$, the principal diffracted beam has a wave
vector $K + k_a$ and an angular frequency $\omega_\ell + \omega_a$. If $\hat{K} \cdot \hat{k}_a > 0$, the
principal diffracted beam has a wave vector $K - k_a$ and an angular
frequency $\omega_\ell - \omega_a$. For definiteness, we shall assume the latter case
in the remainder of this section and the next two sections.

Let θ denote the acute angle between $\hat{K}$ and the acoustic wave front
(perpendicular to $\hat{k}_a$). We have

$$\sin \theta = \hat{K} \cdot \hat{k}_a \tag{1.16}$$

In an isotropic medium, the Bragg angle θ_B is defined by

$$\sin \theta_B = \frac{k_a}{2K} = \frac{c\omega_a}{2nv\omega_\ell} \tag{1.17}$$

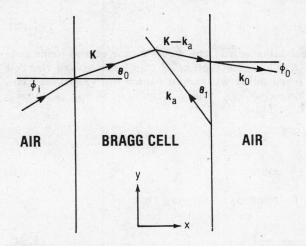

Figure 1.5 Diffraction geometry of Bragg cell for tilted acoustic wave. (From Ref. 17.)

where n is the index of refraction, v is the acoustic velocity, and c is the free-space velocity of light. The power in the principal diffracted beam varies with θ, attaining a maximum when $\theta = \theta_B$.

We shall derive the basic wave-vector relations for a Bragg cell. Consider a light wave incident upon a Bragg cell at angle ϕ_i, as illustrated in Fig. 1.5. According to Snell's law, the angle θ_0 satisfies

$$n \sin \theta_0 = \sin \phi_i \qquad (1.18)$$

The refracted light has the two-dimensional wave vector

$$\mathbf{K} = K(\cos \theta_0, \sin \theta_0) \qquad (1.19)$$

with magnitude

$$K = \frac{n\omega_\ell}{c} \qquad (1.20)$$

The acoustic wave in the cell propagates at an angle θ_1 with respect to the y axis. Thus, this tilted wave has the wave vector

$$\mathbf{k}_a = k_a(-\sin \theta_1, \cos \theta_1) \qquad (1.21)$$

with magnitude

$$k_a = \frac{\omega_a}{v} \tag{1.22}$$

After the acousto-optical interaction, the wave vector of the principal diffracted beam is $K' = K - k_a$. Refraction as this beam leaves the cell results in a diffracted beam in air with wave vector k_0. From electromagnetic theory, it follows that k_{0y}, the y component of k_0, is equal to the y component of K'. Thus,

$$k_{0y} = K \sin \theta_0 - k_a \cos \theta_1$$

$$= \frac{n\omega_\ell}{c} \sin \theta_0 - \frac{\omega_a}{v} \cos \theta_1 \tag{1.23}$$

The x component of k_0 is found by observing that

$$k_0^2 = k_{0x}^2 + k_{0y}^2 = \left(\frac{\omega_\ell - \omega_a}{c} \right)^2 \tag{1.24}$$

since the diffracted wave has frequency $\omega_\ell - \omega_a$. The angle ϕ_0 of the diffracted beam with respect to the x axis satisfies

$$\sin \phi_0 = \frac{k_{0y}}{k_0} \tag{1.25}$$

A number of special cases are of particular interest. In general, $\omega_a << \omega_\ell$ so that $k_0 \simeq \omega_\ell / c$. Thus, equations (1.18) and (1.23) to (1.25) give

$$\sin \phi_0 \simeq \sin \phi_i - \frac{k_a \cos \theta_1}{k_0} \tag{1.26}$$

In general, $k_a << k_0$. If ϕ_i and θ_1 are small, we obtain

$$\phi_0 \simeq \phi_i - \left(\frac{c}{v\omega_\ell} \right) \omega_a \qquad \phi_i, \; \theta_1 << 1 \tag{1.27}$$

This equation establishes the fundamental relation between the acoustic frequency and the deflection of the principal diffracted beam when $\hat{K} \cdot \hat{k}_a > 0$. In Fig. 1.5, $\phi_i > 0$, $\theta_0 > 0$, and $\theta_1 > 0$, but $\phi_0 < 0$.

Another special case occurs if the angles are made to satisfy $\theta_0 = 2\theta_1$. It is convenient to define the Bragg frequency ω_B by

$$\omega_B = \frac{2nv\omega_\ell}{c} \sin \theta_1 \tag{1.28}$$

Equations (1.23) and (1.28) and the relation $\sin 2\theta_1 = 2 \sin \theta_1 \cos \theta_1$ yield

$$k_{0y} = \left(\frac{\omega_B - \omega_a}{v}\right) \cos \theta_1 \qquad (1.29)$$

Thus, if $\omega_a = \omega_B$, the principal diffracted beam emerging from the Bragg cell is perpendicular to the cell-air interface ($\phi_0 = 0$). It follows from equations (1.16), (1.17), (1.19), (1.21), and (1.28) that $\theta_0 = 2\theta_1 = 2\theta_B$ and that θ, the angle between the incident light beam and the acoustic wave front, is equal to θ_B.

In the Bragg regime, the amplitude of the principal diffracted beam is approximately proportional to the amplitude of the acoustic wave if the latter has a sufficiently small amplitude. If the bandwidth of the acoustic wave is sufficiently narrow compared with its center frequency, the acoustic amplitude in the region of wave propagation can be expressed as

$$A\left(t - \frac{x}{v}\right) = A\left(t - \frac{\hat{k}_a \cdot r}{v}\right)$$

where x is the distance along the direction of the acoustic wave, r is the position vector, and v is the acoustic velocity corresponding to the center frequency of the acoustic wave. Let ω_0 and k_0 denote the frequency and the wave vector of the principal diffracted beam. Neglecting the time delay due to propagation and assuming other conditions given in Chap. 2, the principal diffracted beam is approximately represented by

$$\psi(t,r) = w(r)A\left(t - \frac{\hat{k}_a \cdot r}{v}\right)\cos(\omega_0 t - k_0 \cdot r) \qquad (1.30)$$

near the acoustic device output aperture. The weighting function $w(r)$ is the product of factors describing aperture size, acoustic attenuation, and optical amplitude profile. A heuristic derivation of equation (1.30) is obtained by assuming that the acousto-optical interaction causes a phase modulation of the incident optical wave. If the modulation is small in magnitude, the expression for the refracted optical wave can be expanded into two terms, one representing the undiffracted beam and the other representing the principal diffracted beam. The expansion indicates that the two beams are in phase quadrature.

The basic theory presented in this section leads immediately to the important applications of frequency estimation, correlation, and Fourier transformation. In the following analysis, it is always assumed that extraneous beams can be eliminated by spatial or polarization filterings.

1.3 FREQUENCY ESTIMATION

The principal components of an acousto-optical *spectrum analyzer* [10, 11] are shown in Fig. 1.6. According to equation (1.27), the principal diffracted beam is offset from the incident beam by an angle

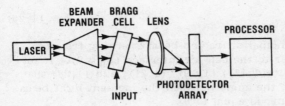

BEAM   BRAGG
EXPANDER CELL LENS

PROCESSOR

LASER

INPUT

PHOTODETECTOR
ARRAY

Figure 1.6 Acousto-optical frequency estimator. (From Ref. 17.)

$$\phi_1 = \phi_i - \phi_0 \simeq \left(\frac{c}{vf_\ell}\right)f_a \qquad (1.31)$$

where f_a and f_ℓ are the frequencies in hertz. With the Bragg cell in
the front focal plane of the lens, a Fourier transform is obtained at
the back focal plane at the photodetector array. The center of the
diffracted beam converges to a position a distance

$$F\phi_1 \simeq \left(\frac{Fc}{vf_\ell}\right)f_a \qquad (1.32)$$

from the center of the corresponding undiffracted beam, where F is
the focal length of the lens. Thus, the frequency f_a can be estimated
by measuring the relative intensities at the photodetector array elements.

The diffracted beam has an angular half-width on the order of λ/D,
where $\lambda = c/f_\ell$ is the optical wavelength in air and D is the effective
aperture of the Bragg cell, which is approximately equal to the diameter of the incident optical beam. Consequently, the diffracted beam
spreads over a half-width $F\lambda/D$ in the focal plane. The *frequency resolution* is defined to be the difference in frequency between two signals
such that the corresponding positions in the focal plane differ by the
spread of the diffracted beam in the focal plane. From this definition
and equation (1.32), the resolution is

$$R \simeq \frac{v}{D} = \frac{1}{T_c} \qquad (1.33)$$

where T_c is the time that it takes an acoustic wave to cross the effective cell aperture. To achieve this resolution in practice, the photodetector element spacing must not exceed the beam half-width.

The system of Fig. 1.6 provides an acousto-optical implementation
of a channelized radiometer. The system performance approximates
that of an ideal channelized radiometer [12] if the inherent photodetector noise is negligible compared to the noise carried by the diffracted optical beam.

1.4 CORRELATION

The acousto-optical cross correlation or convolution of signals $A_1(t)$
and $A_2(t)$ can be accomplished by either a time-integrating correlator
or a spatial-integrating correlator [10,13,14]. In this section, the operation of each of these two types of correlator is illustrated by example.
In the *time-integrating correlator*, both signals are impressed upon
diffracted optical beams. Neglecting weighting functions and spatial
dispersion during propagation for simplicity, we may represent the two
beams by

$$\psi_1(t,r) = A_1\left(t - \frac{\hat{k}_{a1} \cdot r}{v}\right) \cos(\omega_{01} t - k_{01} \cdot r) \tag{1.34}$$

$$\psi_2(t,r) = A_2\left(t - \frac{\hat{k}_{a2} \cdot r}{v}\right) \cos(\omega_{02} t - k_{02} \cdot r + \phi) \tag{1.35}$$

where ϕ is the phase of ψ_2 relative to ψ_1. The two beams strike an
array of photodiodes. If the spatial variation of the fields over the
photodiode dimensions is negligible, the output of a photodiode at
point r is a time integral of the intensity of the total radiation. Thus,
the output is proportional to

$$V(t,r) = \int_{t-T}^{t} [\psi_1(t',r) + \psi_2(t',r)]^2 \, dt' \tag{1.36}$$

where T is the duration of the integration interval. Substituting equations (1.34) and (1.35) into equation (1.36) and using trigonometry,
we obtain

$$V(t,r) = V_1(t,r) + V_2(t,r) + V_3(t,r) \tag{1.37}$$

where

$$V_1(t,r) = \int_{t-T}^{t} A_1\left(t' - \frac{\hat{k}_{a1} \cdot r}{v}\right) A_2\left(t' - \frac{\hat{k}_{a2} \cdot r}{v}\right)$$
$$\times \cos[(\omega_{01} - \omega_{02})t' - (k_{01} - k_{02}) \cdot r - \phi] \, dt' \tag{1.38}$$

$$V_2(t,r) = \frac{1}{2} \int_{t-T}^{t} \left[A_1^2\left(t' - \frac{\hat{k}_{a1} \cdot r}{v}\right) + A_2^2\left(t' - \frac{\hat{k}_{a2} \cdot r}{v}\right) \right] dt' \tag{1.39}$$

$$V_3(t,r) = \int_{t-T}^{t} \left\{ A_1\left(t' - \frac{\hat{k}_{a1} \cdot r}{v}\right) A_2\left(t' - \frac{\hat{k}_{a2} \cdot r}{v}\right) \cos[(\omega_{01} + \omega_{02})t' \right.$$
$$\left. - (k_{01} + k_{02}) \cdot r + \phi] + \frac{1}{2} A_1^2\left(t' - \frac{\hat{k}_{a1} \cdot r}{v}\right) \cos(2\omega_{01} t' \right.$$

$$-2k_{01}\cdot r) + \frac{1}{2} A_2^2 \left(t' - \frac{\hat{k}_{a2}\cdot r}{v} \right) \cos(2\omega_{02}t'$$

$$\left. -2k_{02}\cdot r + 2\phi) \right\} \; dt' \qquad\qquad (1.40)$$

The sinusoidal factors in equation (1.40) are assumed to vary much more rapidly than A_1 and A_2. Thus, if T is sufficiently large and $\omega_{01} \simeq \omega_{02}$, V_3 is negligible compared with V_1 and we may neglect V_3 in the subsequent analysis. V_2 is a measure of the sum of the intensities of the two waves. If these intensities are varying slowly in time, then V_2 can be suppressed by passing $V(t,r)$ through a bandpass filter. The effect on V_1 is small if the spectrum of V_1 is concentrated away from the spectrum of V_2. If the spectra of V_1 and V_2 are similar, the presence of the spatial carrier in V_1 facilitates the separation of V_1 from V_2. The separation is implemented by digital filtering of the photodiode outputs, which provide spatial samples of $V(t,r)$.

Alternatively, we can eliminate V_2 by using two adjacent photodiode arrays. One of the optical beams that is applied to one array is phase-shifted by π radians with respect to the corresponding optical beam that is applied to the other array. The difference between the two array outputs produces

$$V(t,r) \simeq V(t, r, \phi = \phi_1) - V(t, r, \phi = \phi_1 + \pi)$$

$$\simeq V_1(t, r, \phi = \phi_1) - V_1(t, r, \phi = \phi_1 + \pi)$$

$$= 2V_1(t, r, \phi = \phi_1) \qquad\qquad (1.41)$$

If $\omega_{01} = \omega_{02}$ and we change coordinates, equation (1.38) gives

$$V_1(t,r) = E(t,q) \cos [(k_{01} - k_{02})\cdot r + \phi] \qquad\qquad (1.42)$$

$$E(t,q) = \int_{L(t)} A_1(u)A_2(u + q) \; du \qquad\qquad (1.43)$$

$$L(t) = \left(t - \frac{\hat{k}_{a1}\cdot r}{v} - T, t - \frac{\hat{k}_{a1}\cdot r}{v} \right) \qquad\qquad (1.44)$$

$$q = \frac{(\hat{k}_{a1} - \hat{k}_{a2})\cdot r}{v} \qquad\qquad (1.45)$$

These equations indicate that $E(t,q)$ has a spatial variation that approximates the cross correlation if $\hat{k}_{a1}\cdot r \neq \hat{k}_{a2}\cdot r$ and T is on the order of the larger of the periods or durations of $A_1(t)$ and $A_2(t)$. The spatial frequency $k_{01} - k_{02}$ in equation (1.42) is related to the acoustic frequencies in the Bragg cells that generate ψ_1 and ψ_2. Thus, if the

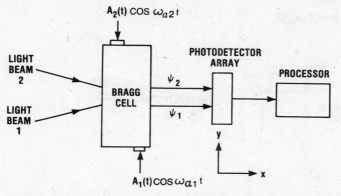

Figure 1.7 Time-integrating correlator. (From Ref. 17.)

spatial frequency is measured, we can sometimes obtain an estimate of an unknown acoustic frequency.

The photodiode noise and the bias terms may cause saturation in a photodiode if the photodiode integrates over a long interval. However, the overall integration interval T can be extended by postdetection electronic integration.

A number of acousto-optical time-integrating correlators are discussed in Chaps. 9 and 10. As an example, Fig. 1.7 displays one implementation. Light beam 1 interacts with a tilted acoustic wave generated by $A_1(t)$ to produce the diffracted beam ψ_1. The diffracted beam ψ_2 is produced analogously by light beam 2 and $A_2(t)$. If the acoustic wave vectors are given by

$$\hat{k}_{a1} = (-\sin \theta_1, \cos \theta_1)$$
$$\hat{k}_{a2} = (-\sin \theta_1, -\cos \theta_1)$$

$$(1.46)$$

then equation (1.45) for the correlation variable becomes

$$q = \frac{2 \cos \theta_1}{v} y \qquad\qquad (1.47)$$

Since $y \leqslant D$, we have $q \leqslant 2T_c$, which illustrates the limitations on the values of the correlation variable for which the cross correlation can be measured with a time-integrating correlator. In a practical configuration, lenses and stops may be needed to eliminate the various extraneous beams that are generated along with the desired ones.

In a *spatial-integrating correlator*, a beam represented by equation (1.34) interacts with an acoustic wave having frequency ω_{a2} and wave vector k_{a2} to produce a principal diffracted beam represented by

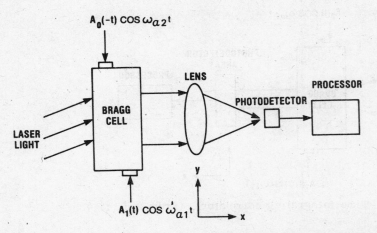

Figure 1.8 Spatial-integrating correlator. (From Ref. 17.)

$$\psi(t,r) = A_1\left(t - \frac{\hat{k}_{a1}\cdot r}{v}\right) A_2\left(t - \frac{\hat{k}_{a2}\cdot r}{v}\right) \cos\left(\omega_0 t - k_0 \cdot r\right) \qquad (1.48)$$

where $\omega_0 = \omega_{01} - \omega_{a2}$ and $k_0 = k_{01} - k_{a2}$. For noncoherent detection, a Fourier-transforming lens is placed perpendicular to k_0. At the center of the focal plane, the intensity is proportional to [15]

$$I(t) = \left|\int_R A_1\left(t - \frac{\hat{k}_{a1}\cdot r}{v}\right) A_2\left(t - \frac{\hat{k}_{a2}\cdot r}{v}\right) d^2 r\right|^2 \qquad (1.49)$$

where the region of integration R is determined primarily by the pupil of the lens and the dimensions of the acoustic devices. To simplify equation (1.49), we assume that the two acoustic wave vectors are oppositely directed and parallel to the y direction, as depicted in Fig. 1.8. To within a proportionality factor, we obtain

$$I(t) = \left|\int_0^D A_1\left(t - \frac{y}{v}\right) A_2\left(t + \frac{y}{v}\right) dy\right|^2 \qquad (1.50)$$

where D is the effective length of the Bragg cell. We change coordinates, drop a constant, and use $T_c = D/v$ to obtain

$$I(t) = \left|\int_{t-T_c}^t A_1(u) A_2(2t - u)\, du\right|^2 \qquad (1.51)$$

If $A_2(t)$ is a time-reversed version of another signal $A_0(t)$, that is, if $A_2(t) = A_0(-t)$, then

$$I(t) = \left| \int_{t-T_c}^{t} A_1(u) A_0(u - 2t) \, du \right|^2 \qquad (1.52)$$

This equation indicates that, for large enough T_c, the intensity at the center of the focal plane is proportional to the squared cross correlation of $A_1(t)$ and $A_0(t)$. If a photodetector is placed at the center point, its output is the squared cross correlation as a function of time. The limits of the integral indicate that a full cross correlation is possible only if $A_1(t)$ and $A_0(t)$ have periods or durations less than T_c.

A closely related technique for achieving cross correlation is to use a reference mask in place of one of the acoustic signals. Implementation details of some spatial-integrating correlators are presented in Chap. 7.

1.5 FOURIER TRANSFORMATION

Acousto-optical Fourier transformation can be accomplished in a number of ways [10,13,16], including the use of the time-integrating correlator. Let $A(t)$ denote the signal to be transformed. We assume that $A_1(t)$ is formed as the product of $A(t)$ and a periodic scanning waveform. Over one scan of the waveform,

$$A_1(t) = 2A(t) \cos(\omega_c t + \pi \mu t^2) \qquad 0 \leqslant t \leqslant T_s \qquad (1.53)$$

where ω_c is the scanning frequency at $t = 0$, μ is the rate of frequency change, and T_s is the scan period. Let $A_2(t)$ denote the scanning waveform; that is,

$$A_2(t) = \cos(\omega_c t + \pi \mu t^2) \qquad 0 \leqslant t \leqslant T_s \qquad (1.54)$$

Substituting equations (1.53) and (1.54) into equation (1.43), using trigonometry, and dropping a negligible integral, we obtain the output of a time-integrating correlator due to one scan:

$$E(t,q) = \int_{L_1(t)} A(u) \cos(\omega_c q + 2\pi \mu q u + \pi \mu q^2) \, du \qquad (1.55)$$

$$L_1(t) = L(t) \cap [0, T_s] \qquad (1.56)$$

We may rewrite equation (1.55) in the form

$$E(t,q) = \text{Re}[F(2\pi \mu q) \exp(j \omega_c q + j \pi \mu q^2)] \qquad (1.57)$$

where Re(x) denotes the real part of x, $j = \sqrt{-1}$, and

$$F(2\pi\mu q) = \int_{L_1(t)} A(u) \exp[ju(2\pi\mu q)]\, du \qquad (1.58)$$

is an approximation of the Fourier transform at an angular frequency equal to $2\pi\mu q$. Let $|F|$ denote the magnitude and χ the phase of F. From equation (1.57), we obtain

$$E(t,q) = |F(2\pi\mu q)| \cos[\omega_c q + \pi\mu q^2 + \chi(2\pi\mu q)] \qquad (1.59)$$

Thus, the magnitude and the phase of the Fourier transform of A(u) can be approximately produced by digital processing of the photodetector array outputs.

REFERENCES

1. A. Korpel, Acousto-optics—a review of fundamentals, *Proc. IEEE 69*:48, Jan. 1981.
2. J. Sapriel, *Acousto-Optics*, Wiley, New York, 1979.
3. I. C. Chang, Acousto-optic devices and applications, *IEEE Trans. Sonics Ultrason. 23*:2, Jan. 1976.
4. A. Yariv, *Introduction to Optical Electronics*, 2nd ed., Holt, Rinehart and Winston, New York, 1976.
5. M. Born and E. Wolf, *Principles of Optics*, 5th ed., Pergamon, Elmsford, N.Y., 1975.
6. N. Uchida and N. Niizeki, Acousto-optic deflection materials and techniques, *Proc. IEEE 61*:1073, Aug. 1973.
7. A. Korpel, Acousto-optics, in *Applied Solid State Science*, Vol. II (R. Wolfe, ed.), Academic Press, New York, 1972.
8. R. W. Damon, W. T. Maloney, and D. H. McMahon, Interaction of light with ultrasound: Phenomena and applications, in *Physical Acoustics*, Vol. 7, (W. P. Mason and R. N. Thurston, eds.), Academic Press, New York, 1970.
9. R. Adler, Interaction between light and sound, *IEEE Spectrum*, 4:42, May 1967.
10. T. M. Turpin, Spectrum analysis using optical processing, *Proc. IEEE 69*:79, Jan. 1981.
11. D. L. Hecht, Spectrum analysis using acousto-optic filters, *Opt. Eng. 16*:461, Sept. 1977.
12. D. J. Torrieri, *Principles of Military Communication Systems*, Artech House, Dedham, Mass., 1981.
13. W. T. Rhodes, Acousto-optic signal processing: Convolution and correlation, *Proc. IEEE 69*:65, Jan. 1981.
14. R. A. Sprague, A review of acousto-optic signal correlators, *Opt. Eng. 16*:467, Sept. 1977.

15. J. W. Goodman, *Introduction to Fourier Optics*, McGraw-Hill, New York, 1968.
16. D. L. Hecht and P. S. Guilfoyle, Acousto-optic spectrum and Fourier analysis techniques, in *IEE International Specialist Seminar on Case Studies in Advanced Signal Processing*, 1979, p. 216.
17. D. J. Torrieri, Signal processing theory of Bragg cells, CM/CCM-81-1, U.S. Army DARCOM, May 1981.

2
Generalized Description of Acousto-Optic Interactions

WILLIAM D. SCHARF / Department of the Army, Harry Diamond
Laboratories, Adelphi, Maryland

2.1 GEOMETRICAL DESCRIPTION

This section will present a simple geometric method of visualizing the
acousto-optic interaction in a general isotropic or anisotropic medium.
In the following section calculational methods will be outlined for obtaining amplitudes of all diffracted orders. In general, these methods
require numerical solution; however, in the case of most general interest (the linear Bragg regime, to be defined later), simple and reliable
approximate expressions are obtained.

2.1.1 Isotropic Slab

The circles in Figs. 2.1 and 2.2 represent the loci of propagating-mode
wave vectors for an unmodulated isotropic dielectric medium. In an infinite slab whose faces are perpendicular to the x direction and on
which a y-polarized plane wave is incident at a given angle, boundary
conditions (angle of incidence) will select out (through Snell's law)
two backward and forward traveling allowed propagation modes
$\exp[i(\pm K_{x_0}x + K_{z_0}z - \omega t)]$, indicated by arrows in the figures.[†] For
these two modes, K_z is equal to the wave-vector z-component of the
incident optical plane wave. If, in addition, we impose an acoustic
modulation, propagating in the z direction, of the dielectric constant,

$$\varepsilon \to \varepsilon + \alpha \cos(k_a z - \omega_a t) \qquad (2.1)$$

the propagating modes are no longer plane waves but may be expressed
as infinite (due to multiple diffraction) sums of plane waves:

[†]All symbols are defined in the symbol table at the end of this chapter.

23

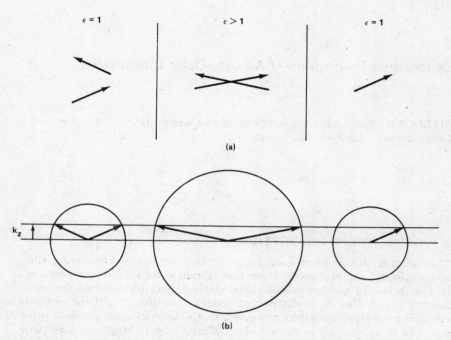

$\epsilon = 1$ $\epsilon > 1$ $\epsilon = 1$

(a)

k_z

(b)

Figure 2.1 Two views of the interaction of an optical plane wave with an infinite dielectric slab, showing incident, reflected, and transmitted waves and internal backward and forward traveling waves. (b) illustrates Snell's law, which arises from the requirement of matching K_z to satisfy boundary conditions. The two smaller circles, of radius ω/c, represent the external medium (air or vacuum). The larger circle, of radius $\omega\sqrt{\epsilon}/c$, represents the denser dielectric medium. The two parallel lines (the lower of which passes through the centers) determine the wave vectors (internal and external) present in the solution. Many more wave vectors appear upon introduction of acoustic modulation. (See Fig. 2.2.)

$$\exp(\pm iK_x x) \sum_{-\infty}^{\infty} \exp[i(K_{z_m} z - \omega_m t)] \qquad (2.2)$$

where $K_{z_m} = k_{z_0} + mk_a$ and $\omega_m = \omega_0 + m\omega_a$. This expansion is justified by the fact that, when substituted into the field equations, it yields a uniquely solvable set of recursion relations.

Figure 2.2 shows a simple geometrical way of visualizing the coupling between optical and acoustic waves. This view of the interaction involves an approximation made explicit in the following para-

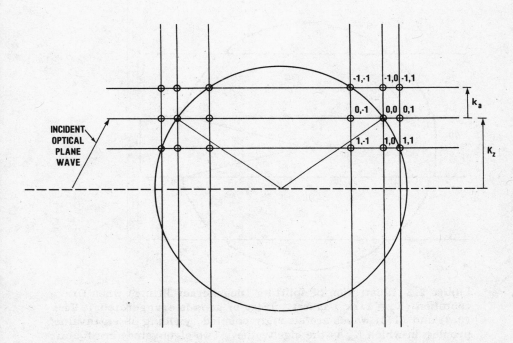

Figure 2.2 Illustration of the lattice (in wave-vector space) of plane waves composing the full optical field produced, in an infinite slab whose refractive index is sinusoidally modulated, by the passage of an optical plane wave through that medium. The acoustic signal propagates parallel to the slab faces in the z direction. Each lattice point (junction of horizontal and vertical lines) represents a plane wave. The circle, of radius $\omega\sqrt{\bar{\varepsilon}}/c$, represents the naturally propagating optical modes of the unperturbed medium. The vacuum incident wave vector, of length ω/c, is indicated at the left. All wave vectors whose first index is zero share the same z component as this incident plane wave. All others are vertically displaced by integral multiples of $|k_a|$, the magnitude of the acoustic wave vector. The vertical lines pass through the intersections of horizontal lines and circles.

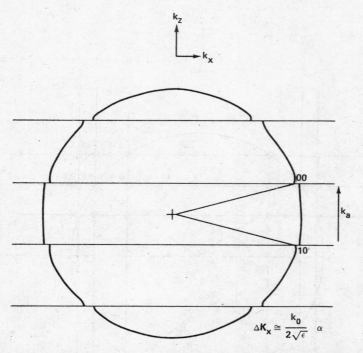

Figure 2.3 Illustration of splitting (degeneracy lifting) when Bragg condition ($K_z = 1/2k_a$) is met. (Size of gaps is exaggerated.) The (0,0) and (1,0) waves are strongly coupled, yielding an eigenvalue problem in which K_x is the eigenvalue. Two eigenvalues are found whose difference (the gap size ΔK_x) for the low-power (linear) case is proportional to acoustic modulation amplitude α.

graphs. In the figure, which represents a locus of points in wave-vector space, the circle represents the set of propagating optical wave vectors, of a given frequency, in the unperturbed medium; i.e., all wave vectors with radius $2\pi(n/\lambda)$, where n is the refractive index and λ is the free-space optical wavelength: $\lambda = c/\nu$. The coupling produces, along with the plane waves represented by the arrows of Fig. 2.2, the plane waves represented by the infinite set of points above and below, with spacing given by the acoustic wave vector. These points can be visualized as representing multiple phonon scattering. Due to this coupling it is now impossible to satisfy the electromagnetic boundary conditions (tangential field continuity) without introducing additional normal modes, also represented in Fig. 2.2 by columns of points. This process thus results in an infinite lattice (in wave-vector space) of backward and forward traveling plane waves, describing the total optical field in the medium. Thus, the acoustic modulation imposes a vertical coupling between lattice points, while the boundary conditions impose a horizontal coupling. Note that this determination of the relevant plane waves is purely kinematic and cannot determine the amplitudes of the various component waves. The amplitudes depend, for instance, on slab thickness, while the wave vectors do not.

The above discussion is, in fact, only approximate. In reality, the wave vectors, as well as the amplitudes, depend on modulation intensity. The circle from which the lattice is generated is distorted by the presence of the acoustic modulation. At a Bragg angle, defined by $K_{z_0} = (N/2)k_a$ (N an integer), there is a degeneracy in the

pattern of Fig. 2.2. The same column of points is generated by $K_{z_0} = +(N/2)k_a$ as for $K_{z_0} = -(N/2)k_a$. This degeneracy is lifted by

the periodic modulation, just as for the electron states in a perfect solid or for the propagating modes in a periodically loaded transmission line. (See Fig. 2.3.)

Without the acoustic modulation, the two modes

$$U_+ = \exp[i(K_x x + \frac{N}{2}k_a z - \omega_N t)]$$

$$U_- = \exp[i(K_x x - \frac{N}{2}k_a z - \omega_{-N} t)]$$

(2.3)

are degenerate; that is, characterized by the same K_x. An alternative representation of these degenerate solutions is in terms of the two modes:

$$U_c = \frac{1}{2}(U_+ + U_-) = \cos\left(\frac{N}{2}k_a z - N\omega_a t\right) \exp[i(K_x x - \omega_0 t)]$$

$$U_s = \frac{1}{2i}(U_+ - U_-) = \sin\left(\frac{N}{2}k_a z - N\omega_a t\right) \exp[i(K_x x - \omega_0 t)]$$

(2.4)

These two modes exhibit *standing wave* behavior in the z direction. The degeneracy of these two modes is lifted by the acoustic perturbation:

$$U_c \rightarrow ce_N\left(N\left(\frac{1}{2}k_a z - \omega_a t\right), -2\alpha\frac{\Lambda^2}{\lambda^2}\right) \exp[i(K_{c_N} x - \omega t)]$$

$$U_s \rightarrow se_N\left(N\left(\frac{1}{2}k_a z - \omega_a t\right), -2\alpha\frac{\Lambda^2}{\lambda^2}\right) \exp[i(K_{s_N} x - \omega t)]$$

(2.5)

where α is the modulation amplitude defined in equation (2.1), ce_N and se_N are the periodic Mathieu functions, and K_{c_N} and K_{s_N} are related to the Mathieu eigenvalues, a_N and b_N [1], by

$$K_{c_N}^2 = \frac{\omega^2}{c^2}\varepsilon - \frac{k_a^2}{4}a_N \qquad K_{s_N}^2 = \frac{\omega^2}{c^2}\varepsilon - \frac{k_a^2}{4}b_N$$

(The differential equations describing the z variations of a y-polarized propagating mode in a periodically modulated isotropic medium happen to reduce to the well-known Mathieu equations.) Note that $K_{c_N} = K_{s_N}$ only for $\alpha = 0$; i.e., when no acoustic modulation is present. For $\alpha \neq 0$, modes with K_x between these two values cannot exist and are said to be in a *forbidden band*. These K_x's (and hence the width of the forbidden band) are dependent on the modulation amplitude α and hence on the acoustic power. For small α (*linear* condition), the splitting is small and can be neglected for the purposes of determining the interaction bandwidth.

Physically, the change of representation from U_+ and U_- to U_c and U_s involves the change from traveling waves to standing waves. In the special (Bragg) case when the standing waves have the same z periodicity as the acoustic modulation, these two standing waves behave very differently from one another. One is in phase with the modulation, while the other is out of phase with it. In one case, the nonzero E field will predominantly "see" a large dielectric constant (large polarizability). In the other case, the nonzero E field will predominantly see a small dielectric constant (small polarizability). The dispersion curve naturally reflects this anomalous *splitting* of effective material constants for specific (Bragg) modes.

The splitting described above transforms the simple propagating mode U_+ into a double mode characterized by two distinct k's, and the same is true of U_-:

$$U_+ = \exp[i(K_x x - \omega t)]\left(\cos\frac{N}{2}k_a z + i\sin\frac{N}{2}k_a z\right)$$

$$\rightarrow \exp(-i\omega t)\left[\exp(iK_{c_N}x)ce_N\left(\frac{N}{2}k_a z, -2\Delta\right)\right.$$

$$\left. + i\exp(iK_{s_N}x)\ se_N\left(\frac{N}{2}k_a z, -2\Delta\right)\right] \tag{2.6}$$

$$U_- = \exp[i(K_x x - \omega t)]\left(\cos\frac{N}{2}k_a z - i\sin\frac{N}{2}k_a z\right)$$

$$\rightarrow \exp(-i\omega t)\left[\exp(iK_{c_N}x)\ ce_N\left(\frac{N}{2}k_a z, -2\Delta\right)\right.$$

$$\left. -i\exp(iK_{s_N}x)\ se_N\left(\frac{N}{2}k_a z, -2\Delta\right)\right] \tag{2.7}$$

where $\Delta = \alpha(\Lambda^2/\lambda^2)$ and $\omega_a/\omega_0 \ll 1$.

2.1.2 Anisotropic Slab

The plane-wave mode coupling described above for an isotropic slab applies also for an anisotropic slab. Here we shall discuss a uniaxial medium, where the free wave-vector surface is a double surface—a sphere for the ordinary waves and an ellipsoid for the extraordinary waves. The two surfaces meet tangentially in the direction of the optic axis. The effect of the acoustic modulation on this double-surface dispersion curve (shown in Fig. 2.4 for a negative uniaxial crystal, e.g., lithium niobate, with acoustic propagation along the optic axis) is essentially the same as that discussed above for the isotropic case.

In addition, a new effect—acoustic coupling between ordinary and extraordinary modes—arises when there are off-diagonal terms in the modulation tensor α_{ij}, where the dielectric tensor is

$$\varepsilon_{ij} + \alpha_{ij} \cos(k_a z - \omega_a t) \tag{2.8}$$

This cross coupling can become very strong when the acoustic modulation scatters a plane wave from one surface to another. Figure 2.5 shows this diagrammatically for lithium niobate, for acoustic propagation along the optic axis, when an acoustic frequency of several gigahertz is needed to produce strong cross-mode coupling for visible light. Figure 2.6 shows cross-mode coupling for the case of acoustic propagation perpendicular to the optic axis (collinear case), where

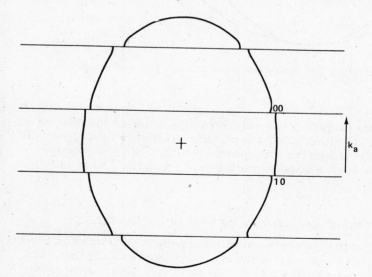

Figure 2.4 Bragg splitting for extraordinary modes in an anisotropic medium. (Size of gaps is exaggerated.)

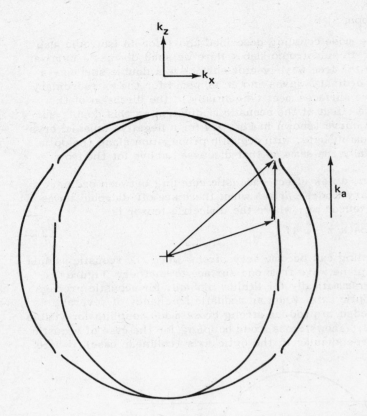

Figure 2.5 Splitting for cross-mode coupling. (Size of gaps is exaggerated.)

a lower acoustic frequency will suffice (on the order of 500 MHz for visible light). In either case, the coupling is observed experimentally as a Bragg-type scattering with polarization flip. An x-z-polarized incident wave emerges after scattering as a y-polarized wave and vice versa.

2.2 QUANTITATIVE TREATMENT OF SPECIFIC EXAMPLES

A thorough quantitative treatment of acousto-optic diffraction is beyond the scope of this discussion; however, it can be shown [2] that, with certain approximations, the transmitted diffracted orders have amplitudes T_m^S given by

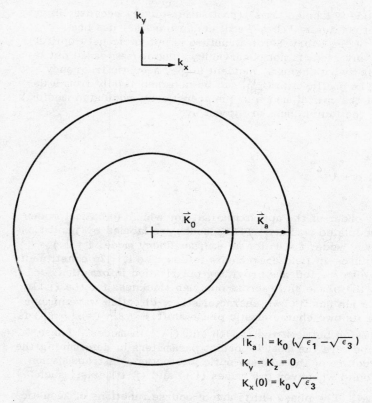

$$|\vec{k}_a| = k_0 (\sqrt{\epsilon_1} - \sqrt{\epsilon_3})$$
$$K_y = K_z = 0$$
$$K_x(0) = k_0 \sqrt{\epsilon_3}$$

Figure 2.6 Collinear cross-mode coupling. Acoustic signal propagates in same direction as optical signal (x direction in this figure). Signal emerges with opposite polarization. Note that, for a uniaxial crystal with optic axis in the z direction, the wave-vector surfaces in the x-y plane are concentric circles, while the surfaces in the x-z plane are a circle and an ellipse meeting tangentially on the z axis. (See Fig. 2.5.)

$$T_m^{s2}(\text{rms}) \simeq w^{-1} \sum_{\substack{jj' \\ tt'}} C_{mjj'}^{stt'} \cos \Delta \beta_{jj'}^{tt'} \left[1 + \left(\frac{w^2 - 1}{2w} \right)^2 \sin^2 \Delta \beta_{jj'}^{tt'} \right]^{-1}$$

(2.9)

where $w \simeq (1/2)[\sqrt{\epsilon} + (1/\sqrt{\epsilon})]$ and $\epsilon = (1/3)(2\epsilon_1 + \epsilon_3)$. The transmission amplitude is labeled "rms" (root mean square) because, in the formula, structure due to Fabry-Perot etalon lines [3] has been averaged out. (The Fabry-Perot structure is not an acousto-optical effect and, in any case, is not observable, since it is smeared out by uncertainties in slab thickness, incident angle, acoustic frequency, and so on.) The coefficients $C_{mjj'}^{stt'}$ can be determined only from a detailed study of the optical modes in the acoustically modulated medium. The ranges of the four indices are given by

$$-p \leqslant m \leqslant p + 1$$

$$0 \leqslant s \leqslant 1$$

$$-p \leqslant j \leqslant p + 1$$

$$0 \leqslant t \leqslant 1$$

where p is the order of the approximation, for which 4p optical modes exist in the modulated medium. These modes are labeled by j and t. (For an ordinary mode, t = 0; for an *extraordinary* mode, t = 1.) Each mode requires 4p field components to describe it: 2p constituent plane waves, with the index s providing polarization information. β_j^t (= $K_{xj}^t L$) is the phase shift across one slab thickness for the (j,t)th mode. (Each mode has its own characteristic x-direction wavenumber K_{xj}^t and hence its own characteristic phase shift.) $\Delta \beta_{jj'}^{tt'}$ (= $\beta_j^t - \beta_{j'}^{t'}$) is the phase mismatch between the (j,t)th and (j',t')th modes. These phase mismatches are the most important parameters in determining the resonance structure of the acousto-optic interaction. A transmission peak will be found whenever two modes (j,t) and (j',t') exist, such that $\Delta \beta_{jj'}^{tt'} = 2\pi N$. The phase shifts are of course functions of acoustic frequency and of optical incidence angle. (For the zero-order approximation, in an isotropic medium, the familiar Bragg peak is found when $\Delta \beta_{01} = 0$.)

The approximations made in the derivation of equation (2.9) for the transmitted amplitudes are

1. $\omega_a/\omega_c \ll 1$ (always a good approximation, comparing microwave frequencies with optical frequencies).   (2.10)
2. $\Lambda \gg \lambda$ (a more restrictive approximation).   (2.11)
3. Infinite number of diffracted orders approximated by a finite number.
4. $Q = k_a^2 L/K \gg 1$.   (2.12)

For the case of acousto-optical devices operating at low acoustic power near the Bragg angle, the zero-order (p = 0) approximation, implying only one diffracted transmitted ray, is quite good. In the following, this approximation, which yields analytic solutions, will be made.

Mention should be made of the Raman-Nath case, in which condition 4 does not hold, and the acoustic disturbance acts merely as a *phase lattice.* Each internal ray can be regarded as traveling in a straight line and being phase-shifted according to the dielectric properties of the medium along its path. This is a reliable approach only if the interaction length is short enough that the ray crosses the interaction region without experiencing much change in refractive index, i.e., if $L \tan \theta \ll \Lambda$. Since $\tan \theta \simeq k_a / k_0 \sqrt{\epsilon}$, the dimensionless parameter is

$$Q = \frac{k_a^2 L}{k_0 \sqrt{\epsilon}} = \frac{k_a^2 L}{K} \tag{2.13}$$

A small value of Q implies Raman-Nath phase-lattice conditions. A large value of Q implies Bragg conditions, which rely on a relatively long interaction length, so that, when the phase relations are right, there will be considerable energy exchange between the acoustic wave and a particular diffracted wave. (In the Raman-Nath case, many diffracted beams appear, so that the $p = 0$ approximation described above is not appropriate.)

The following pages treat systems of varying complexity which share the property that all physical quantities are independent of the y coordinate. Thus, in particular, no propagation vector has a y component. In each case, the zero-order ($p = 0$) approximation is used.

Case I: Isotropic, y polarized The amplitude of the transmitted Bragg-diffracted wave is

$$T_m \; (rms) = B(x) \; \frac{k_0 L}{4 \sqrt{\epsilon}} \; \alpha \; \frac{\sin x}{x} \tag{2.14}$$

where

$$x = \frac{1}{2} \Delta \beta_{01} = \frac{1}{2} L(K_{x_0} - K_{x_1}) = \frac{1}{2} L(\Delta K_x) \tag{2.15}$$

and where B(x) is a *boundary factor* given by

$$B(x) = \left\{ \frac{w^4 + 1}{2w^2} \; \frac{1 - [(w^2 - 1)^2 / (w^4 + 1)] \sin^2 x}{1 + [(w^2 - 1)/2w]^2 \sin^2 2x} \right\}^{1/2} \tag{2.16}$$

Note that $B(x) \rightarrow 1$ as $w \rightarrow 1$ ($\epsilon \rightarrow 1$). $B(x)$ contains all boundary effects which are acousto-optic in origin, the Fabry-Perot effect having been averaged out. All dependence on angle, acoustic frequency, and acoustic power is contained in the important phase-mismatch parameter x. The ΔK_x is sometimes referred to in the literature as *momentum mismatch* [4] and is seen from the expression

$$\Delta\beta_{01} = \frac{k_0 L}{2\sqrt{\epsilon}}\sqrt{\gamma^2 + \alpha^2} = \sqrt{(\Delta\beta_g)^2 + (\Delta\beta_{n\ell})^2} \tag{2.17}$$

where $\gamma = k_0^{-2}(K_{z_0}^2 - K_{z_1}^2)$, to depend on

1. The purely geometric mismatch γ, which can be determined directly from the undeformed wave-vector surfaces (circles and ellipses: see Fig. 2.7):

$$\text{Geometric } \Delta\beta_{01} = \Delta\beta_g \simeq \frac{L}{2\sqrt{\epsilon}k_0}(K_{z_0}^2 - K_{z_1}^2) \tag{2.18}$$

2. The amplitude of the acoustic disturbance (and hence microwave power), which distorts the wave-vector surfaces by opening up forbidden bands at the Bragg angles:

$$\text{Nonlinear } \Delta\beta_{01} = \Delta\beta_{n\ell} \equiv \frac{k_0 L}{2\sqrt{\epsilon}}\alpha \tag{2.19}$$

At low microwave power, the interaction is linear [since $x \simeq (k_0 L/4\sqrt{\epsilon})\gamma$ is independent of power], and the diffracted power is proportional to the acoustic *pump* power. Of course, when the Bragg condition ($\gamma = 0$) is met, $x = (k_0 L/4\sqrt{\epsilon})\alpha$, placing a nonzero lower bound on x, so that $\sin x/x$ never quite achieves its limiting value of unity. However, if α is large enough so that this lower bound is significantly larger than zero, the $p = 0$ approximation itself becomes questionable, and more expansion terms must be included.

The crucial parameter γ can be expressed in terms of acoustic frequency or angle of incidence:

$$\gamma = k_a(2k_z - k_a)k_0^{-2} \tag{2.20}$$

$$\gamma = 4\sin\theta_p(\sin\theta - \sin\theta_p) \tag{2.21}$$

$$\gamma = \frac{k_a}{k_0^2}(k_{a_p} - k_a) \tag{2.22}$$

where peak angle $= \theta_p = \sin^{-1}(k_a/2k_0)$ and the peak $k_a = k_{a_p} = 2K_z = 2K_0\sin\theta$. Thus, the mismatch $\Delta k_{g_{01}}$ of Fig. 2.7 could be eliminated (and the Bragg condition achieved) either by decreasing the angle of incidence or increasing the acoustic frequency.

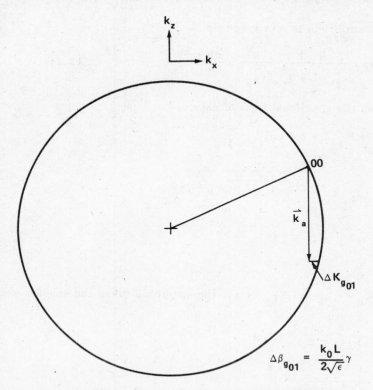

Figure 2.7 Illustration of geometric momentum mismatch $\Delta K_{g_{01}}$ and of geometric phase mismatch $\Delta \beta_{g_{01}}$. Diffracted amplitude T_1 is maximum when Bragg condition is met—when $\Delta K_{g_{01}} = 0$. Note that $\Delta K_{g_{01}} = 0$ does not imply $\Delta K_{01} = 0$. The degeneracy is lifted by the modulation, and $\Delta K_{01} = \Delta K_{n\ell_{01}} \simeq (k_0/2\sqrt{\epsilon})\alpha$. (See Fig. 2.3.)

Case II: Uniaxial, x-z polarized (see Fig. 2.4)

$$\epsilon = \begin{bmatrix} \epsilon_1 & & \\ & \epsilon_1 & \\ & & \epsilon_3 \end{bmatrix} \qquad \alpha = \begin{bmatrix} \alpha & & \\ & \alpha & \\ & & \alpha \end{bmatrix} \qquad (2.23)$$

The diffracted amplitude is now given by

$$T_m \text{ (rms)} = B(x) \frac{\sqrt{\Delta_0 \Delta_1}}{\varepsilon_1^2 - 1/4\, \alpha^2} \frac{k_0 L}{4\sqrt{\varepsilon_3}} \alpha \frac{\sin x}{x} \qquad (2.24)$$

where $B(x)$ has the functional form of case I,

$$\Delta_m = \varepsilon_1 (\varepsilon_1 - \tilde{K}_{z_m}^2) + \varepsilon_3 \tilde{K}_{z_0} \tilde{K}_{z_1} - \frac{1}{4}\alpha^2$$

$$x \simeq \frac{k_0 L}{4(\varepsilon_1^2 - 1/4\,\alpha^2)\sqrt{\varepsilon_3}} \sqrt{\varepsilon_1^2 \varepsilon_3^2 \gamma^2 + \alpha^2 \Delta_0 \Delta_1}$$

$$\tilde{K}_{z_m}^2 = \frac{K_{z_m}^2}{k_0^2}$$

Note that if $\tilde{K}_{z_0}^2 \ll \varepsilon_1$ and $\tilde{K}_{z_1}^2 \ll \varepsilon_1$, the amplitude takes the simple form

$$T_m \text{ (rms)} = B(x) \frac{k_0 L}{4\sqrt{\varepsilon_3}} \alpha \frac{\sin x}{x}$$

$$x \simeq \frac{k_0 L}{4\sqrt{\varepsilon_3}} \sqrt{\frac{\varepsilon_3^2}{\varepsilon_1^2}\gamma^2 + \alpha^2}$$

Case III: Uniaxial (see Fig. 2.5)

$$\varepsilon = \begin{bmatrix} \varepsilon_1 & & \\ & \varepsilon_1 & \\ & & \varepsilon_3 \end{bmatrix} \qquad \alpha = \begin{bmatrix} 0 & 0 & 0 \\ 0 & 0 & \alpha \\ 0 & \alpha & 0 \end{bmatrix}$$

For an incident x-z-polarized wave diffracted to a y-polarized wave, the mismatch parameter is given by

$$x \simeq \frac{k_0 L}{2\varepsilon_1 [\sqrt{(\varepsilon_3/\varepsilon_1)(\varepsilon_1 - \tilde{K}_{z_0}^2)} + \sqrt{\varepsilon_1 - \tilde{K}_{z_1}^2}]}$$

$$\times \sqrt{[\varepsilon_3(\varepsilon_1 - \tilde{K}_{z_0}^2) - \varepsilon_1(\varepsilon_1 - \tilde{K}_{z_1}^2)]^2 + \varepsilon_1(\varepsilon_1 - \tilde{K}_{z_0}^2)\alpha^2} \qquad (2.25)$$

and for an incident y-polarized wave diffracted to a x-z-polarized wave by

$$x \simeq \frac{k_0 L}{2\varepsilon_1 [\sqrt{(\varepsilon_3/\varepsilon_1)(\varepsilon_1 - \tilde{K}_{z_1}^2)} + \sqrt{\varepsilon_1 - \tilde{K}_{z_0}^2}]}$$

$$\times \sqrt{[\varepsilon_3(\varepsilon_1 - \tilde{K}_{z_1}^2) - \varepsilon_1(\varepsilon_1 - \tilde{K}_{z_0}^2)]^2 + \varepsilon_1(\varepsilon_1 - \tilde{K}_{z_1}^2)\alpha^2} \qquad (2.26)$$

Case IV: Collinear (see Fig. 2.6)

$$\varepsilon = \begin{bmatrix} \varepsilon_1 & & \\ & \varepsilon_1 & \\ & & \varepsilon_3 \end{bmatrix} \qquad \alpha = \begin{bmatrix} 0 & 0 & 0 \\ 0 & 0 & \alpha \\ 0 & \alpha & 0 \end{bmatrix}$$

The acoustic wave vector $k_a = (k_a, 0, 0)$. The eigenvalues (values of K_{xj}^t) are the solutions of a quartic which cannot be solved analytically. However, in the linear regime, the purely geometrical mismatch parameter can be used:

$$x \simeq \frac{k_0 L}{2}\left(\sqrt{\varepsilon_3 - \tilde{K}_z^2} - \sqrt{\varepsilon_1 - \tilde{K}_z^2} + \frac{k_a}{k_0}\right) \qquad (2.27)$$

Note that this mismatch is first order in acoustic frequency k_a, whereas it is second order in angle of incidence $\tilde{K}_z$.

As shown above, for the linear Bragg interaction, the diffracted amplitude is proportional to the amplitude of the acoustic perturbation of the dielectric tensor. If a modulation waveform is imposed on the acoustic traveling wave,

$$\varepsilon \rightarrow \varepsilon + \alpha(t) \cos(k_a z - \omega_a t) \qquad (2.28)$$

then the diffracted amplitude also becomes time dependent. If the modulation changes slowly (i.e., the fractional frequency bandwidth is small), the diffracted amplitude will follow the modulation waveform:

$$T_m \text{ (rms)} \simeq B(x) \frac{k_0 L}{4\sqrt{\varepsilon}} \frac{\sin x}{x} \alpha(t) \qquad (2.29)$$

The function $\sin x/x$ achieves 95% of its maximum value at $x \simeq 0.55$. [For simplicity, we ignore $B(x)$ here.] Thus with a 5% uncertainty in diffracted amplitude (10% uncertainty in power) a fractional half bandwidth for an isotropic interaction given [see equations (2.15), (2.17), and (2.22)] by

$$\left(\frac{\Delta k_a}{k_p}\right)_{5\%} \simeq \left(\frac{k_0^2}{k_a k_p}\right) \frac{4\sqrt{\varepsilon}}{k_0 L}(0.55) \qquad (2.30)$$

can be tolerated. For instance, for $LiNbO_3$ ($\sqrt{\varepsilon} \approx 2.22$) with an optical wavelength of 0.6 µm, an acoustic aperture of 1 cm, a carrier (acoustic) frequency of 200 MHz, and assuming no acoustic dispersion $(\partial v/\partial \omega_a = 0)$,[†]

$$\left(\frac{\Delta \nu}{\nu}\right)_{5\%} \approx 4\%$$

Thus a modulation frequency of 8 MHz could be tolerated. That is, if the 200-MHz carrier is modulated by an 8-MHz signal, the transmitted Bragg-diffracted amplitude has 95% the magnitude of the unmodulated carrier. Thus, a signal (e.g., a pulse with a 50-ns rise time) whose Fourier spectrum contains nothing significant above 8 MHz can be used to modulate a 200-MHz acoustic carrier without fear of violating equation (2.29)—at least to within 5% accuracy. The frequency bandwidth is shown for two interaction widths in Fig. 2.8.

Of course, any uncertainty in frequency implies an uncertainty in diffraction angle ($\theta_{out} \approx (\lambda/v)[(1/2)\nu_a] \rightarrow (\lambda/v)[(1/2)\nu_a \pm \Delta \nu_a]$), and the size and position of the photodetector or focusing lens must be chosen with this in mind. It is within these constraints that equation (2.29) is justified.

Similarly, a 5% tolerance in angle of incidence can be derived. For the parameters used in the previous paragraph,

$$\left(\frac{\Delta \theta}{\theta_p}\right)_{5\%} \approx \frac{1}{4}\frac{\gamma}{\theta_p^2} \approx \left(\frac{\Lambda}{\lambda}\right)^2 \frac{4\sqrt{\varepsilon}}{k_0 L} (0.55) \approx 4\%$$

The angle bandwidth is shown for two interaction widths in Fig. 2.9.

The above treatment for the isotropic case can be generalized to include anisotropic linear interactions by using the appropriate expressions for $\Delta \beta_{01_g}$.

A brief treatment of the physical origin of the modulation of the refractive index is given in the following paragraphs [5]. The first-order tensor expression for this modulation is

$$\Delta \left(\frac{1}{n^2}\right)_{ij} = P_{ijk\ell} u_{k,\ell} + r_{ijk} E_k \qquad (2.31)$$

$$= P_{ijk\ell} (S_{k\ell} + \omega_{k\ell}) + r_{ijk} E_k \qquad (2.32)$$

where $(1/n^2)_{ij} = (\varepsilon^{-1})_{ij}$

$u_{k,\ell} = \partial u_k/\partial x_\ell$

[†]The sound velocity in $LiNbO_3$ is about 3.5×10^5 cm/s.

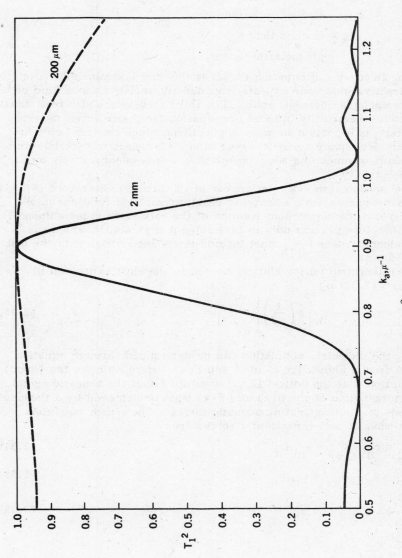

Figure 2.8 Transmitted diffracted power $|T_1|^2$ as a function of k_a (acoustic wave vector). Solid curve shows L = 2 mm (Q = 69.3). Dashed curve shows L = 200 µm (Q = 6.93).

u_k = displacement in the k direction

$S_{k\ell} = (1/2)(u_{k,\ell} + u_{\ell,k})$ = (symmetric) strain tensor

$\omega_{kq} = (1/2)(u_{k,\ell} - u_{\ell,k})$ = rotation tensor

r_{ijk} = electro-optic tensor

E_k = electric field

$P_{ijk\ell}$ = photoelastic tensor

The first term of equation (2.32) is the simple strain-induced shift in refractive index one expects from density variations in a fluid or a nonpiezoelectric isotropic solid. The third term arises also from density variation—electrically induced compressions in piezoelectric material. This term is important in many applications, since electric fields inevitably accompany acoustic waves in any piezoelectric material—and the means of launching acoustic waves in solids generally rely on piezoelectricity.

The second term does not appear in the pre-1970 literature [6]. It is called the roto-optic effect and results from local rotations in the medium and the consequent rotation of the refractive index ellipsoid. It is therefore present only in birefringent crystals, in which the photoelastic tensor $P_{ijk\ell}$ must include terms antisymmetric in the last two indices.

The dielectric tensor shift is related to the shift expressed in equation (2.32) by

$$\alpha_{ij} = \Delta\,\varepsilon_{ij} \simeq -\varepsilon_{ik}\left[\Delta\left(\frac{1}{n^2}\right)\right]_{k\ell}\varepsilon_{\ell j} \qquad (2.33)$$

Thus, the dielectric modulation can be determined through equation (2.32) from a knowledge of $u(x)$ and $E(x)$. Here we make the (good) assumption that the optical signal does not affect the acoustic signal.

Determination of the $u(x)$ and $E(x)$ must be achieved by a thorough analysis of the propagating acoustic modes. The tensor equations which must be self-consistently solved are

$$T_{ij} = c_{ijk\ell}S_{k\ell} - e_{nij}E_n \qquad (2.34)$$

$$D_m = e_{mk\ell}S_{k\ell} + \varepsilon_{mn}E_n \qquad (2.35)$$

$$\frac{\partial D_i}{\partial x_i} = 0 \qquad (2.36)$$

$$\frac{\partial T_{ij}}{\partial x_i} = \rho\,\frac{\partial^2 u_j}{\partial t^2} \qquad (2.37)$$

where $c_{ijk\ell}$ is the elasticity tensor and e_{ijk} is the piezoelectric tensor.

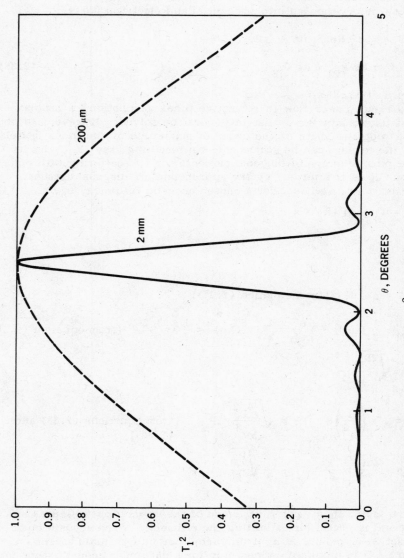

Figure 2.9 Transmitted diffracted power $|T_1|^2$ as a function of angle of incidence. Solid curve shows L = 2 mm (Q = 69.3). Dashed curve shows L = 200 μm (Q = 6.93).

The above equations, together with the symmetry (for bulk modes) or boundary (for surface modes) conditions, determine the propagating modes. These modes are in general very complicated, involving dilation, distortion, and local rotations. Time-averaged power flow density can be decomposed into mechanical and electrical parts:

$$\langle P_i \rangle = -\frac{1}{2} \operatorname{Re}(T_{ij}\dot{u}_j^*) + \frac{1}{2} \operatorname{Re}(\phi\dot{D}_i^*)$$

$$= \operatorname{Re} P_{iM} + \operatorname{Re} P_{iE} \tag{2.38}$$

where $E_i = -\partial\phi/\partial x_i$.

To relate power flow to refractive index modulation, a complex set of tensor equations must in general be solved. However, to obtain a *rough* estimate of the order of magnitude of the index modulation, the tensors can be *scalarized*—representing, say, $P_{ijk\ell}$ by its scalar part (average of diagonal elements) or (if scattering with polarization flip is of interest) by the appropriate off-diagonal element. In scalar form, we have, for a chosen acoustic frequency ω_a,

$$u = u_0 \exp[i(k_a \cdot x - \omega_a t)]$$

$$k_a = \frac{\omega_a}{v_a}$$

$$kT \approx \rho\omega^2 u \quad \text{[from equation (2.37)]}$$

$$P_M \approx \frac{1}{2} T\omega u \approx \frac{\rho\omega^3 u^2}{2k} = \frac{1}{2}\rho v^3 (ku)^2 = \frac{1}{2}\rho v^3 S^2 \quad \text{[from equation (2.38)]}$$

$$S = \sqrt{\frac{2P_M}{\rho v^3}}$$

$$\alpha = \epsilon^2 \Delta\left(\frac{1}{n^2}\right) \approx \epsilon^2 PS = \sqrt{\frac{\epsilon^4 P^2}{\rho v^3}}\sqrt{2P_M} \quad \text{[from equations (2.33) and (2.32)]}$$

$$\Delta n = \frac{\Delta n^2}{2n} = \frac{\alpha}{2n} = \sqrt{\frac{\epsilon^3 P^2}{\rho v^3}}\sqrt{\frac{P_M}{2}}$$

The factor $M_2 = \sqrt{\epsilon^3 P^2/\rho v^3}$ is one of the *acousto-optic figures of merit* and is useful for estimating the efficiency of the acousto-optic diffraction (intensity of light diffracted per unit acoustic microwave power). It is uniquely defined only for a particular acoustic mode in an isotropic nonpiezoelectric material.

Two further cautions are in order regarding the use of the above-mentioned figure of merit:

1. Transducer insertion loss must be considered.
2. For surface waves, the ratio of mechanical power density $P_M (W/m^2)$ to power is roughly proportional to frequency, since the depth of penetration of the surface wave is proportional to the acoustic wavelength.

Symbol Table

Symbol	Definition
a_N	Mathieu eigenvalue
b_N	Mathieu eigenvalue
$B(x)$	Boundary factor
c	Speed of light
$C_{ijk\ell}$	Elasticity tensor
D_m	Electric displacement
E_k	Electric field
$e_{mk\ell}$	Piezoelectric tensor
K	Wave vector normalized to $k_0 (= \omega_0/c)$
k_a	Acoustic wave vector
K_m	mth constituent plane wave for a given optical mode
k_p	Acoustic wave number at Bragg peak
k_0	Vacuum optical wave number
L	Thickness of dielectric slab
n	Refractive index of medium
p	Order of approximation
P	Scalarized photoelastic tensor
P_i	Acoustic power flow density
P_{iE}	Electric part of P_i
$P_{ijk\ell}$	Photoelastic tensor
P_{iM}	Mechanical part of P_i
Q	Raman-Nath parameter, determines width of resonance peak
r_{ijk}	Electro-optic tensor

$S_{k\ell}$	Strain tensor
T_{ij}	Stress tensor
T_m	Amplitude of mth transmitted wave
U	Eigenvectors representing optical modes
U_k	Displacement in k direction
v	Acoustic velocity
w	Dielectric-mismatch parameter
x	Phase-mismatch parameter
α	Amplitude of acoustic perturbation of dielectric constant
β	Phase shift ($= k_x L$)
γ	Dimensionless geometric mismatch parameter
Δ_m	$\varepsilon_1(\varepsilon_1 - \tilde{K}_{z_m}^2) + \varepsilon_3 \tilde{K}_{z_0} \tilde{K}_{z_1} - (1/4)\alpha^2$
ε	Dielectric constant of medium
θ	Angle of incidence
Λ	Acoustic wavelength
λ	Vacuum wavelength of incident plane wave
ν	Acoustic frequency
ω_a	Acoustic radian frequency
$\omega_{k\ell}$	Rotation tensor
ω_m	Radian frequency of K_m plane wave
ω_0	Radian frequency of incident plane wave

REFERENCES

1. N. W. McLachlan, *Theory and Application of Mathieu Functions*, Oxford Press, Oxford, 1947.
2. N. Karayianis, W. D. Scharf, and F. J. Crowne, *The Isotropic Acousto-Optic Interaction in a Dielectric Medium*, Harry Diamond Laboratories Internal Report DELHD-R-RT-CA-80-8, Sept. 1980.
3. M. Born and E. Wolf, *Principles of Optics*, fifth ed., Pergamon Press, 1975.
4. I. C. Chang, Acousto-optic devices and application, *IEEE Trans. Sonics and Ultrasonics 23* (January 1976), 2.

5.   J. Sapriel, *Acousto-Optics*, Wiley, 1979.
6.   D. F. Nelson, *Electric, Optic, and Acoustic Interactions in Dielectrics*, Chap. 13, Wiley, New York, 1979.

ADDITIONAL REFERENCE MATERIAL

R. Adler, Interaction between light and sound, *IEEE Spectrum*, May 1967.

M. V. Berry, *The Diffraction of Light by Ultrasound*, Academic Press, New York, 1966.

M. Born and E. Wolf, *Principles of Optics*, 5th ed., Pergamon, Elmsford, N.Y., 1975.

I. C. Chang, Acoustooptic devices and applications, *IEEE Trans. Sonics Ultrason.*, Jan. 1976.

R. W. Dixon, Acoustic diffraction of light in anisotropic media, *IEEE J. Quantum Electron.*, Feb. 1967.

S. Fukuda, T. Karasaki, T. Shiosaki, and A. Kawabata, Photoelasticity and acousto-optic diffraction in piezoelectric semiconductors, *Phys. Ref. Sect. B*, Nov. 1979.

Yu. V. Gulyaev, V. V. Proklov, and G. N. Shkerdin, Diffraction of light by sound in solids, *Sov. Phys. Usp.*, Jan. 1978.

W. R. Klein and B. D. Cook, Unified approach to ultrasonic light diffraction, *IEEE Trans. Sonics Ultrason.*, July 1967.

A. Korpel and T. Poon, Explicit formalism for acousto-optic multiple plane-wave scattering, *J. Opt. Soc. Am.*, July 1980.

N. W. McLachlan, *Theory and Applications of Mathieu Functions*, Oxford University Press, London, 1947.

D. F. Nelson, *Electric, Optic, and Acoustic Interactions in Dielectrics*, Wiley, New York, 1979.

O. Nomoto, Diffraction of light by ultrasound: Extension of the Brillouin theory, *Jpn. J. Appl. Phys.*, May 1971.

J. M. Rouvaen, M. G. Ghazaleh, E. Bridoux, and R. Torguet, On a general treatment of acousto-optic interactions in linear anisotropic crystals, *J. Appl. Phys.*, Aug. 1979.

J. Sapriel, *Acousto-Optics*, Wiley, New York, 1979.

V. V. Soroka, A method for calculating the efficiency of acoustooptical interaction, *Sov. Phys. Acoust.*, March 1980.

3

Bulk Acousto-Optic Device Technology

HARRIS CORPORATION* / Melbourne, Florida

3.1 INTRODUCTION

In this chapter we shall describe the design and application of bulk-wave acousto-optic modulators, beam deflectors, and traveling-wave focusing devices. A brief review of the fundamental acousto-optic interaction design equations are given in this section.

In Sec. 3.2 we shall examine materials used in acousto-optic devices and the piezoelectric transducer design. Once this groundwork is laid, we shall analyze and survey applications for acousto-optic modulation, deflection, and focusing in Sec. 3.3, 3.4, and 3.5, respectively.

When an acoustic wave is generated in an optical medium, there is a corresponding perturbation in the refractive index of the material. The optical effect of this refractive index change is very similar to that of a diffraction grating, with an *acoustic grating* spacing equal to the acoustic wavelength Λ. When monochromatic incident light passes through an acousto-optically active medium, the light is diffracted by an amount equal to [1]

$$2\theta_b = \frac{\lambda}{n\Lambda} \qquad (3.1)$$

with respect to the incident light beam.

In the above expression θ_b is the Bragg angle, λ is the optical wavelength in the free space, and n is the refractive index of the optical medium. For modulators and deflectors, it is generally desirable to have a high interaction efficiency and hence a large modulation index. The acousto-optic interaction is then generally known as Bragg interaction or a thick grating phenomenon. In this case, the incident optical vector K_i and the acoustic wave vector k_a must obey the phase

---

*This chapter represents technology developed by the Optical Systems Department of Harris Corporation, Melbourne, Florida © 1983.

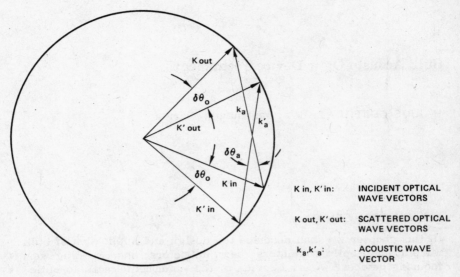

Figure 3.1 Acousto-optic wave-vector diagram. (From Ref. 15, © 1981 IEEE.)

diagram shown in Fig. 3.1. A measure of the Bragg interaction condition is given by the parameter [2]

$$Q = \frac{2\pi}{n} \frac{\lambda L}{\Lambda^2} \tag{3.2}$$

where L is the acousto-optic interaction length.

For $Q \geqslant 7$ the interaction is in the Bragg region [2]. Since Q is directly proportional to the interaction length L, a higher Q will require less drive power for a given interaction efficiency. However, the tradeoff lies in the bandwidth of the acoustic frequency (Δf_a or Δk_a) and the input optical wave-vector dispersion (ΔK_i). These considerations will be discussed in detail when we review the design of modulators and deflectors. The diffracted light intensity is given by

$$\frac{I_1}{I_0} = \eta \ \mathrm{sinc}\left[\eta + \left(\Delta K \frac{L}{2}\right)^2\right]^{1/2} \tag{3.3}$$

where I_1 and I_0 represent the diffracted and incident light intensity and ΔK is the momentum mismatch of the light and acoustic wave vectors.

The efficiency parameter η is given by

$$\eta = \frac{\pi^2}{2\lambda^2}\left(\frac{n^6 p^2}{\rho v^3}\right)\frac{L}{H} \ P_a \tag{3.4}$$

where p is the photoelastic coefficient, ρ is the mass density, v is the acoustic velocity, H is the height of the acoustic beam, P_a is the acoustic power, and the quantity $n^6 p^2/\rho v^3$ is the acoustic figure of merit M_2, which is one of the key fundamental parameters in materials selection.

While the actual diffraction efficiency is given by equation (3.3), η as defined in equation (3.4) provides a reasonable answer in the case of low modulation index or when a quick check of interaction efficiency is required.

3.2 MATERIALS AND TRANSDUCER DESIGN

3.2.1 Material Selection

Acousto-optic device technology has matured to the point that performance is chiefly limited by material parameters, particularly the figure of merit and acoustic attenuation. Nature has arranged that materials with high figures of merit usually have high attenuation and vice versa. The widely used acousto-optic materials are fused quartz, tellurium dioxide, and lithium niobate. Development work [3] on new infrared materials has been reported recently. A list of commonly used acousto-optic materials is given in Table 3.1.

For materials with a low figure of merit, a higher drive power can be used to obtain the required efficiency. Experience has indicated that a practical limit for small devices (active area ~ 0.1 mm^2) is a drive power density of 100 to 500 W/mm^2, provided there is proper heat sinking to transfer the heat energy. At the high drive power levels, the acoustic attenuation may cause significant optical distortion, which is especially bad in an interferometric system.

3.2.2 Piezoelectric Transducer Material Selection and Design

The widely used acoustic transducer materials are single-crystal lithium niobate (LiNbO$_3$) with two crystal orientations for the longitudinal or the shear-wave generation and thin-film zinc oxide (ZnO). LiNbO$_3$ transducers are more adapted for devices operating below 1 GHz because of a higher coupling coefficient and low electrical Q factor. At 1 to 2 GHz, LiNbO$_3$ and ZnO have similar performance parameters. For frequencies much beyond 2 GHz, the thin-film ZnO transducers have been in use for over 10 years, whereas work with the LiNbO$_3$ transducers is still in development. However, based on analysis and results at the lower frequencies, LiNbO$_3$ transducers should be able to outperform ZnO transducers below 5 GHz.

Table 3.2 lists the essential parameters for LiNbO$_3$ and ZnO.

Table 3.1 Acousto-Optic Properties of Selected Crystalline Materials

Material	Density, ρ (10^3 kg/m^3)	Velocity, v (10^3 m/s)	Index, n
LiTaO$_3$	7.45	6.19	2.18
LiNbO$_3$	4.64	6.57	2.20
TiO$_2$	4.23	8.03	2.584
Sr$_{0.75}$Ba$_{0.25}$Nb$_2$O$_6$	5.40	5.50	2.299
GaP	4.13	6.32	3.31
TeO$_2$	6.00	4.20	2.26

3.2.3 Transducer Design and Electrical Equivalent Circuit

Transducer design has to be optimized so that it can efficiently transfer electrical power into acoustic power in the acousto-optic materials.
The theory of transducer design was treated by Sittig [4] and Meitzler
and Sittig [5]. The important task in transducer design is the matching of the source and load impedance and the mechanical impedance of
the electrode layers, the transducer, and acousto-optical material. The
two-port network developed by Sittig [4] and Mietzler and Sittig [5]
connecting the electrical and mechanical circuits describes totally the

Table 3.2 Piezoelectric Transducer Material Parameters

Material mode orientation	Coupling constant	Relative dielectric constant	Frequency constant, $f_0 t$ (MHz m)
LiNbO$_3$ longitudinal Y cut $\angle 36°$	$(0.49)^2$	39	3700
LiNbO$_3$ shear X cut $\angle 41°$	$(0.68)^2$	44	2400
ZnO longitudinal	$(0.25)^2$	8.8	3200

	Figures of merit	
Attenuation, Γ (dB/μs GHz^2)	M_2 (10^{-15} s^3/kg)	M_3 (10^{-15} m s^2/kg)
0.062	1.37	1.84
0.098	7.00	10.1
0.566	3.93	7.97
2.20	38.6	48.8
3.80	44.6	93.5
6.30	34.5	32.8

performance of the transducer. Figure 3.2 shows the equivalent circuit derived for an input-output transducer pair. The load voltage is then given by

$$\frac{V_s}{V_\ell} = \frac{1}{2R_\ell Z_t}[(AZ_t + B) + R_s(CZ + D)][A(Z_t + B) + R_\ell(CZ_t + D)]$$

(3.5)

where $Z_\ell = Z_s$ and is purely resistive and A, B, C, and D are transducer two-port parameters; in the simplest form the two-port matrix is given by

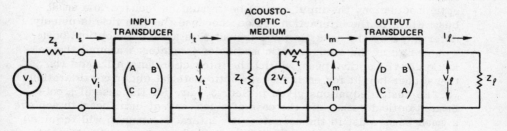

Figure 3.2 Acoustic transducer equivalent circuit. (From Ref. 15, © 1981 IEEE.)

$$\begin{pmatrix} A & B \\ C & D \end{pmatrix} \tag{3.6}$$

where

$$A = \cos\left(\pi\,\frac{f}{f_0}\right) - \frac{k^2}{\pi f/f_0}\sin\left(\pi\,\frac{f}{f_0}\right)$$

$$B = j\left[Z_0\sin\left(\pi\,\frac{f}{f_0}\right)+ 2\,\frac{k^2 Z_0}{\pi f/f_0}\cos\left(\pi\,\frac{f}{f_0}\right)\right]$$

$$C = j\,\frac{f}{f_0}\,(2\pi f_0 C_0)\cos\left(\pi\,\frac{f}{f_0}\right)$$

$$D = -2\pi f_0 C_0\,\frac{f}{f_0}\sin\left(\frac{\pi f}{f_0}\right)$$

where k^2 is the coupling constant.

For a one-transducer system, the insertion loss (IL) is given by

$$IL = 10\,\log\,\frac{P_s}{P_\ell} \tag{3.7}$$

The acousto-optic device has only one input transducer, and its in-sertion loss is therefore half the value given in equation (3.7).

When the network is complicated, a computer matrix program is set up to compute the bandwidth and conversion loss of the acoustic trans-ducer.

3.3 ACOUSTO-OPTIC MODULATOR DESIGN

3.3.1

The general design equations covered in Sec. 3.1 are the starting point for the design of acousto-optic modulators. For high-speed acousto-optic modulation, the input optical beam must be focused to a small beam width in the interaction region, because the rise time is usually determined by the acoustic wave transit time across the optical beam. The design of the acousto-optic modulator is centered around the se-lection of the optical beam width, the interaction length L, and the transducer height for each acousto-optic material under consideration.

The design equations given in Sec. 3.1 are for the case of a col-limated optical beam, and the case of a convergent light beam to achieve a small beam waist in the acousto-optic interaction region will require a more elaborate analysis. The input light momentum vector K_{inc} of constant magnitude is distributed over an angular range $\delta\theta_0$ (see Fig. 3.3).

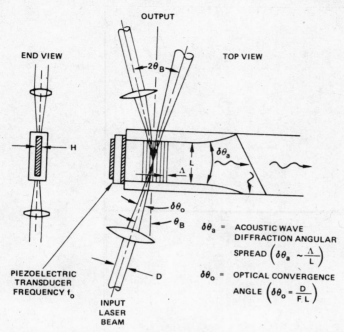

Figure 3.3 Acousto-optic modulator configuration. (From Ref. 15, © 1981 IEEE.)

The diffracted light beam wave vector is given by the relation

$$K_d = K_{inc} \pm k_a \tag{3.8}$$

To have a perfect phase match, the acoustic vector must have a corresponding angular range $\delta\theta_a$ to match the optical wave vector, as shown in Fig. 3.1.

In the nonideal situation when $\delta\theta_a > \delta\theta_0$, the portion of acoustic energy whose angular spread is outside the range of $\delta\theta_0$ is not used in the acousto-optic interaction and will be wasteful. On the other hand, when $\delta\theta_a < \delta\theta_0$, a momentum cannot be conserved for all the optical wave components, which results in an elliptical output beam. We define a parameter R, the beam spread ratio, as

$$R = \frac{\delta\theta_a}{\delta\theta_0} \tag{3.9}$$

The effect of the parameter R on the eccentricity of the diffracted beam is shown in Fig. 3.4. From the figure it is seen that if the cross section of the diffracted beam is to depart from the circular case by no

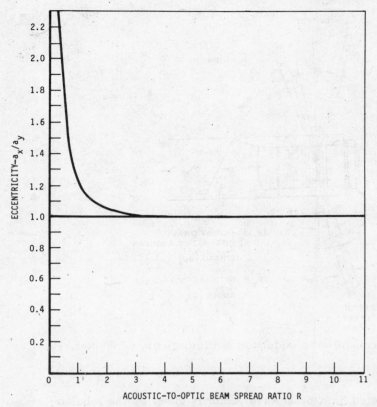

Figure 3.4 Effect of the beam spread ratio R on refocused spot shape.

more than 10% then the beam spread ratio R must be equal to or larger than 1.5. The maximum optical efficiency of an acousto-optic modulator is dependent on both the beam spread ratio R and the acousto-optic interaction Q [equation (3.2)]. By using partial wave analysis, the dependence of the optical efficiency on the parameters Q and R can be determined. The results are summarized in Figs. 3.5 and 3.6. Figure 3.5 shows the maximum optical efficiency for values of Q ranging from 2 to 100. In these calculations R is taken to be infinity. When a finite value of R is used, the maximum efficiency is reduced. The dependence of the efficiency on the beam spread ratio is shown in Fig. 3.6 for several values of Q between 50 and 100. The modulation frequency response can be determined under the assumption that R >> 1 in the following manner. Let E(x) describe the laser beam amplitude profile at the center of the modulator where x is the acoustic wave propagation direction. The optical wave front can be described by a collection of optical plane-wave components given by [6]

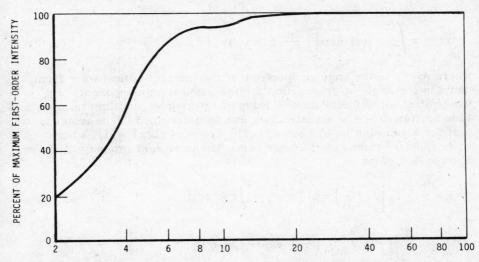

Figure 3.5 First-order intensity as a function of the parameter Q.

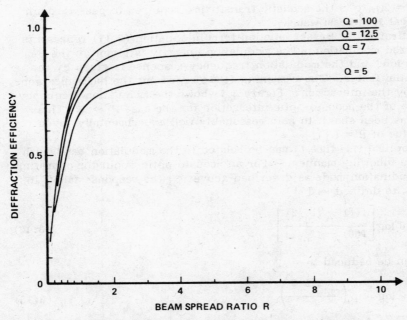

Figure 3.6 Diffraction efficiency as a function of the beam spread
ratio. (From Ref. 15, © 1981 IEEE.)

$$E(x) = \int_{-\pi}^{\pi} A_f(\theta) \exp\left[j \frac{2\pi n}{\lambda} [(\sin \theta)x] \right] d\theta \tag{3.10}$$

where $A_f(\theta)$ is the angular spectrum of the incident optical wave front and θ is the angle of propagation for the plane-wave component. By using Kirchhoff's formulation of Huygens' principle, the light ampli-tude scattered by the acoustic field can be determined. The result is that for a gaussian input beam $|E(x)|^2 = I_0 \exp[-2(x^2/w_0^2)]$, where w_0 is the $1/e^2$ radius of the laser beam, the total light intensity I can be represented as

$$I = \frac{I_0}{2} + I_0 \left[J_1\left(\frac{\alpha\pi}{2}\right) \exp\left(\frac{-\pi^2 f^2 \tau^2}{8}\right) \cos 2\pi ft \right.$$

$$+ \sum_{n=1}^{\infty} (-1)^n J_{2n+1}\left(\frac{\alpha\pi}{2}\right) \exp[-(2n + 1)^2$$

$$\left. \times \frac{\pi^2 f^2 \tau^2}{8}]\cos(2n +1) \ 2\pi ft \right] \tag{3.11}$$

where $\tau = 2w_0/v$ is the acoustic transit time required to pass through the optical $1/e^2$ beam waist.

The first-order Bessel function term in equation (3.11) represents the desired modulation. The modulation linearity is given by the Bes-sel function, and the modulation frequency response is given by the exponential factor. The remaining terms represent the harmonics gen-erated by the interaction. Figure 3.7 shows the modulation frequency response of the acousto-optic interaction for the case R >> 1. This result has been shown to hold reasonably well experimentally, even for a value of R = 1 [7].

The optical rise time t_r can be related to the modulation bandwidth δf in the following manner.[†] For an acousto-optic modulator operating in the modulation mode as described above, β, the response falloff in decibels, is defined as [7]

$$\beta = 10 \log\left[\frac{I(f) - (I_0/2)}{I(0) - (I_0/2)} \right] \tag{3.12}$$

which can be reduced to

$$\beta \simeq 10 \log \exp\left(\frac{-\pi^2 f^2 \tau^2}{8}\right) \tag{3.13}$$

_____
[†] $\delta f = 2\Delta f$, where δf is video bandwidth in a single-side-band modula-tion system. Δf is the RF bandwidth of the acousto-optic modulator.

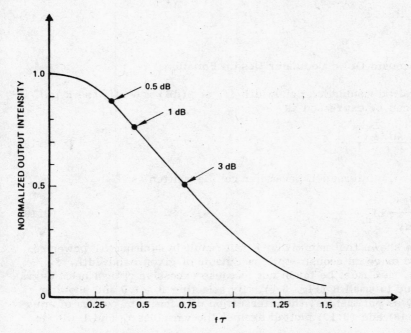

Figure 3.7 Modulation frequency response for analog acousto-optic modulation ($\delta \theta_a \gg \delta \theta_0$). (From Ref. 15, © 1981 IEEE.)

The modulation bandwidth δf associated with a response falloff in decibels of β is simply the value of the modulation frequency f which satisfies equation (3.13):

$$\delta f = \frac{c}{\pi} \frac{\sqrt{\beta}}{\tau} \qquad \tau = \frac{2w_0}{v} \qquad (3.14)$$

$$c = \sqrt{0.8 \ln 10} \simeq 1.4$$

The optical beam waist can thus be expressed as

$$2w_0 = \frac{1.4 v \sqrt{\beta}}{\pi \delta f} \qquad (3.15)$$

The optical rise time t_r for an acousto-optic modulator with a gaussian input beam profile is given by [8]

$$t_r = \frac{\tau}{1.5} \qquad (3.16)$$

where t_r is the 10 to 90% rise time. By combining the above equations the relationship between the modulation bandwidth and the rise time is

$$\delta f = \frac{0.29\sqrt{\beta}}{t_r} \qquad\qquad (3.17)$$

3.3.2 Acousto-Optic Modulator Design Equations

For a desired modulation bandwidth δf, at β(dB) roll-off, the R parameter can be expressed as

$$R = \frac{1.4n\sqrt{\beta}\ v^2}{4\delta f\ \lambda}\ \frac{1}{f_0 L} \qquad\qquad (3.18)$$

Likewise, the interaction parameter can be written as

$$Q = \frac{2\pi\lambda}{nv^2}\ Lf_0^2 \qquad\qquad (3.19)$$

It can be shown that minimizing R will result in minimum RF power required to drive an acousto-optic modulator of given bandwidth δf. However, care must be taken not to cause excessive optical beam degradation due to small R (Fig. 3.5). By selecting R = 1.5 and allowing δf and Q as parameters, the intersection of a family of curves of equations (3.18) and (3.19) plotted against the variables f_0 and L will de-

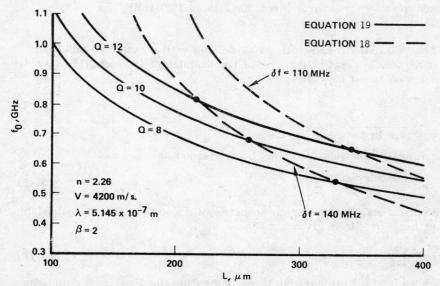

Figure 3.8 Acousto-optic modulator design; R = 1.5. (From Ref. 15, © 1981 IEEE.)

termine the operating frequency f_0 and the interaction length L. As
an example, the design for a TeO_2 modulator is shown in Figure 3.8.
The parameters for the TeO_2 material are shown in the insert. The
family of curves are plotted for the Q values of 8, 10, and 12, and
they intersect a second family of curves for the bandwidths of 110 and
140 MHz. For the 140-MHz bandwidth modulator, the lowest operating
frequency is about 570 MHz for a Q value of 8, which will be the optimum choice. There is no advantage in choosing a higher value of Q as
it is evident from Fig. 3.5 that the interaction is decreased at higher
operating frequencies and requires more drive power. This design
procedure has been proven to be very practical.

The acoustic transducer height is usually chosen to be 2 to 3 times
the optical beam waist ($2w_0$) expressed in equation (3.15). Dixon [9]
has shown that the material efficiency parameter M_3 ($M_3 = M_2nv$) is
most appropriate for consideration of optimum modulator selection, and
equation (3.4) is reduced to

$$\eta = 9M_3(\lambda^3 f_0)^{-1}P_a \qquad\qquad (3.20)$$

3.3 Acousto-Optic Modulator Applications

Acousto-optic modulators are widely used in a large number of applications, such as laser modulation in laser printers, Q switching for industrial processing lasers; laser ranging, mode locking, and cavity
dumping for ultrashort light pulses; and many other applications. A
list of some of the acousto-optic modulator parameters are shown in
Table 3.3.

Table 3.3 Representative Acousto-optic Modulator

Material	Laser wavelength (μm)	Center frequency (MHz)	Rise time (MHz)	Efficiency (%)
SF-8	0.633	40	15 (RF)	> 85
TeO_2	0.633	80	40 (RF)	> 85
SiO_2	0.5	400	150 (RF)	> 20
TeO_2	0.633	500	170 (AM) 300 (RF)	50
TeO_2	0.633	750	250 (AM) 600 (RF)	25

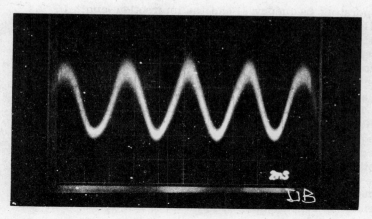

Figure 3.9 Modulated light.

   The acousto-optic modulator transfer function is sinusoidally dependent on the input voltage and therefore is nonlinear. For on-off modulation, this presents no special difficulty, and the maximum modulation rate is determined by the rise time of the modulation system. For
analog modulation, it is necessary to bias the modulator at a carrier
frequency so that the operating point is in an approximately linear region. For high frequency modulation, care must be exercised to control the bias and ensure proper phasing in the electrical network. A
photograph of a 200-MHz modulation is shown in Fig. 3.9.
   An example of an advanced modulator development is the multichannel acousto-optic modulator consisting of 32 channels on a single optical
substrate. A large transducer is bonded to the optical medium, and
an interdigital electrode pattern is deposited on the transducer. Each
electrode is individually driven, thus forming the multichannel modulator. A schematic of the multichannel modulator is shown in Fig. 3.10.
The parameters for the 32-channel modulator are as follows:

Number of contiguous channels   32
Transducer size   100 μm
Center-to-center spacings   250 μm
Rise time   18 ns
Diffraction efficiency   60% at 50 mW RF
System cross-talk isolation   30 dB

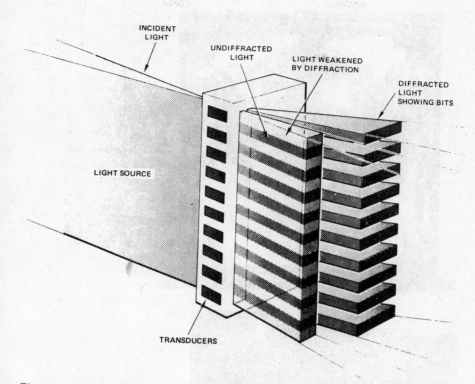

Figure 3.10 Multichannel acousto-optic modulator configuration.

Channel-to-channel variation	±1.3 dB
Optical transmission at 0.514 μm	94%
Center RF frequency	150 MHz

A photograph of the assembled unit is shown in Fig. 3.11. The most challenging parameter to meet is in the cross talk between physically adjacent elements. Careful design in the microstrip line feed, impedance matching, and grounding of the transducers were key in reducing the cross talk. Cross-talk measurements were made in the following manner. A portion of the diffracted spot of the channel under observation was centered on a photodetector. As evidence of the cross-talk phenomenon, variations in the intensity of the center of the diffracted spot were recorded as a function of the phase between the RF drives of a given channel and those channels adjacent to it. The phase relation was varied with a *line-stretching* device. The cross-

(a)

(b)

Figure 3.11 Multichannel acousto-optic modulator. (a) Rear view,
showing connectors, PC card microstrip lines, air cooling valves; (b)
output view, showing TeO_2 crystal, toroidal impedance matching in-
ductors.

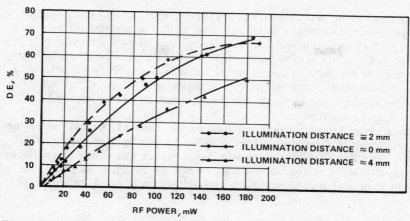

Figure 3.12 DE as a function of RF drive power using spot illumination—channel A3.

talk figure in decibels is $20 \log(\sqrt{1 + \Delta x} - 1)$, where Δx is half of the total observed variation in optical power of the diffracted spot, normalized to the mean optical power of the diffracted spot. The measurement of cross-talk in this manner represents a specification on the bit height fluctuations of the digital data retrieved from the acousto-optic modulator. The worst cross talk measured was 31.6 dB.

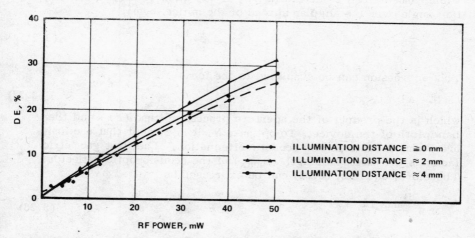

Figure 3.13 DE as a function of RF drive power using line illumination (seven channels driven).

When used in an actual recording system, the acousto-optic modulator was illuminated with a line source of light. Standard diffraction
efficiency (DE) measurements on single-channel devices, however, are
typically made with a single beam (spot illumination). To provide comparison values for both types of data, DE was measured with both spot
and line illumination. The approximate diameter of the spot or width
of the line as it passes beneath the transducers is predetermined (from
resolution and rise-time considerations) to be 90μm.

Diffraction efficiency was calculated as the ratio of the optical power
diffracted into the first-order spot divided by the optical power in the
dc beam. For line illumination it was desired that the width of the laser
beam perpendicular to the acoustic k_a vector be roughly 90 μm. The
results of spot and line illumination are plotted in Figs. 3.12 and 3.13.

3.4 ACOUSTO-OPTIC DEFLECTORS

The acousto-optic interaction deflects the optical beam linearly as a
function of the input acoustic frequency; this phenomenon is a suitable
application for a medium-resolution high-speed optical beam deflector.
The basic design equations for acousto-optic beam deflectors will be
discussed together with specific considerations for beam deflection and
signal-processing devices. The single most important parameter for
acousto-optic deflectors and signal processors is the number of resolvable elements. The number of resolvable elements can be related to
resolvable frequencies or spots either in the Fourier transform plane or
in the image plane of the acousto-optic devices. The number of resolvable elements can be determined by the relation of the maximum deflection angle over the angular spread of the optical beam:

$$N = \frac{\Delta\theta}{\delta\theta_0} \qquad\qquad (3.21)$$

This expression can be simplified to the form

$$N = \Delta T \,\Delta f \qquad\qquad (3.22)$$

which is the product of the aperture processing time (ΔT) and the
bandwidth of the device. To optimize N, it is evident that the limits
are geometric factors and acoustic attenuation. The first geometric
factor is the maximum length (D_{max}) of the acousto-optic deflector.
Therefore, equation (3.22) can be expressed as

$$N \leq \frac{D_{max}}{2} \frac{1}{\Lambda_0} \qquad\qquad (3.23)$$

where Δf is assumed to be $f_0/2$. The second constraint on the number
of resolvable spots can be obtained from the consideration of geometric
acoustic beam spreading and the interaction parameter Q; these requirements give the condition

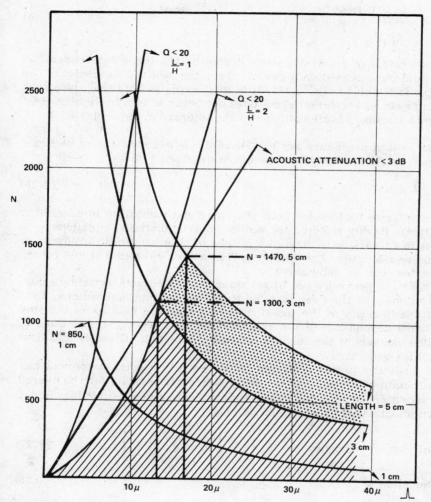

Figure 3.14 Acousto-optic deflector optimization plots. (From Ref. 15, © 1981 IEEE.)

$$N \leqslant \left(\frac{nQ}{4\pi}\right)^2 \Lambda_0^{\,2}$$

(3.24)

The final fundamental limit is the acoustic attenuation in the deflector. By assuming a frequency square dependence on acoustic attenuation γ, equation (3.22) can be expressed as

$$N \leqslant \frac{1.5}{\gamma \Lambda^2_{1GHz}} \Lambda_0 \tag{3.25}$$

The number of resolvable spots limited by the three independent constraints are plotted on a graph versus the acoustic wavelength. An example is shown in Fig. 3.14. It is interesting to note that the maximum number of resolution spots does not occur at extremely high frequencies because of attenuation and the interaction parameter limitations.

The design procedure for acousto-optic deflectors can now be summarized. As a helpful guide Gordon has defined [10]

$$M_1 = M_2 n v^2 \tag{3.26}$$

as the optimum balance for both efficiency and bandwidth in material selection. Having selected the acousto-optic substrate, equations (3.23) to (3.25) are used to plot graphs of time bandwidth product versus wavelength. The operating frequency (wavelength) and other parameters can be determined.

There are generally two broad categories of acousto-optic deflector applications. In the first case for signal-processing applications, the amplitude linearity of the signal must be preserved because of the *sine* functional dependence of the light modulation. Hecht [11] has made a detailed analysis of the relation between diffraction efficiency and non-linearities generated.

In a multifrequency deflector, where each frequency component has a diffraction efficiency η_ℓ, the approximate expressions for the overall diffraction efficiency, depletion, compression, cross-modulation, and intermodulation terms are given as [11]

Diffraction efficiency $\approx$ $\quad \eta_1 \left(1 - \frac{1}{3}\eta_1 + \sum\limits_{\ell=2} \frac{2}{3}\eta_\ell \right) \tag{3.27}$

Depletion $\approx$ $\quad\quad\quad \sum\limits_{\ell=1} \eta_\ell \tag{3.28}$

Compression $\approx$ $\quad\quad \frac{1}{3}\left(\eta_1 + 2\sum \eta_\ell \right) \tag{3.29}$

Cross modulation $\approx$ $\quad \frac{2}{3}\eta_2^2 \tag{3.30}$

Third-order modulation $\approx \frac{1}{36}\eta_1^2\eta_2 \tag{3.31}$

Depletion is the reduction of the incident light intensity due to the diffracted frequencies. Compression is the fractional reduction to one frequency due to the presence of other frequency components. Cross modulation is the change in one signal intensity due to the presence of a second frequency. The third-order intermodulation is a spurious output due to the presence of two signals. To calculate the dynamic range (DR) of a power spectrum analyzer system, the following formula can be used [12]:

$$DR = \left[\frac{1 + 2N_1}{1 - (1/3)(\eta_1 + 2\Sigma_\ell \eta_\ell)} \right]^2 \tag{3.32}$$

where N_1 is the number of frequency components that saturate the detector array.

Another important consideration for wide-bandwidth signal-processing devices is the spatial resolution of the modulation optical wave front (E_d); it is a convolution of the signal bandwidth with the interaction aperture length and in general can be shown to be [13]

$$E_d \propto \int_{-\tan \theta(L/2)}^{\tan \theta(L/2)} E(y - y' - vt) \exp[2jK_0(\sin\theta) y'] \, dy' \tag{3.33}$$

Assuming a single frequency input, this integral reduces to

$$E_d \propto \text{sinc}\left(\frac{Q}{4} \frac{\Delta f}{f_0} \right) \tag{3.34}$$

For broadband applications Q is chosen to be in the range of 12 to 16 and is generally satisfactory. In certain applications, two acousto-optic devices are placed in an optical path so that the signal in one cell is either correlated or convolved against the reference cell. In these cases, the spatial resolution of both cells must be considered; it is necessary to image one cell directly onto the second cell employing optics, or else the following expression on bandwidth needs to be considered:

$$E_d \propto \sin\left(\frac{\Delta K \, L}{2} \right) \cos\left[\frac{\Delta K}{2} (L + S) \right] \tag{3.35}$$

where S is the separation between the two cells. The analysis is identical to the diffraction of light from a double slit. The net result is that the bandwidth is degraded, and L and S must be chosen to allow sufficient bandwidth for the system.

The second major type of application for acousto-optic deflectors is medium-efficiency optical beam deflection. In this case, equation (3.3) is plotted for the efficiency versus the normalized drive power term η in increments of $\pi/16$ at three different frequency bandwidths $\Delta f = 0$, $\Delta f = 0.25$, and $\Delta f = 0.5$ (Fig. 3.15).

It is most interesting to note that when $\eta = \pi/4$ the bandwidth remains essentially flat at 50% efficiency. Therefore, for broad-bandwidth deflectors it is best to make a compromise and choose 50% diffraction

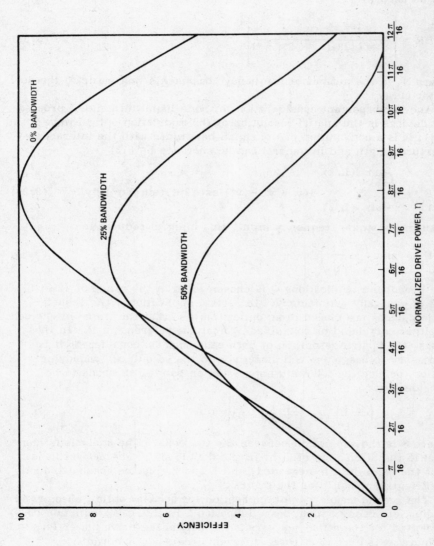

Figure 3.15 Wide-bandwidth acousto-optic deflector efficiency. (From Ref. 15, © 1981 IEEE.)

efficiency in order to obtain a wider bandwidth. When the bandwidth
is broad, it would be futile to drive the acoustic power over $\eta > 5\pi/16$.
Although the Bragg interaction bandwidth can be chosen to be essentially flat, acoustic attenuation and transducer bandwidth will contribute
to the total bandwidth of the deflection system; these effects will be
discussed in later sections.

In many of the applications, the acousto-optic deflector is used in
the swept frequency mode; i.e., a linear FM signal is fed into the
acoustic cell of the form

$$A(t) = \cos\left[2\pi\left(f_0 t + \frac{1}{2} f't^2\right)\right] \tag{3.36}$$

and the traveling acoustic wave signal will be of the form

$$S(x,t) = \cos\left\{2\pi\left[f_0\left(t + \frac{x}{v}\right) + \frac{1}{2} f'\left(t + \frac{x}{v}\right)^2\right]\right\} \tag{3.37}$$

By rearranging the phase terms,

$$S(x,t) = \cos 2\pi\left[\left(f_0 t + \frac{1}{2} f't^2\right) + \left(f_0 + f't\right)\frac{x}{v} + \frac{1}{2} f'\frac{x^2}{v^2}\right] \tag{3.38}$$

The first term in the cosine argument is a phase shift. The second
term is the linear change in deflection of the incident beam as the frequency is varied linearly in time f't. The last term is the focal power
of the acousto-optic deflector. The amount of wave-front phase curvature within a cell length D is then equal to $(\pi/4)f'(\Delta T)^2$. For a good
lens formed by the linear FM signal, the requirement is that the total
phase error be less than 1/8 wave; then

$$\frac{\pi}{4}\left|\Delta f'\right|(\Delta T)^2 \leqslant \frac{2\pi}{8}$$

or   (3.39)

$$\left|\Delta f'\right|(\Delta T)^2 \leqslant 1$$

where $\left|\Delta f'\right|$ is the deviation of the frequency slope. By using equation
(3.22) and the definition

$$f' = \frac{\Delta f}{S} \tag{3.40}$$

where S is the total FM sweep time, equation (3.39) reduces to

$$\frac{\left|\Delta f'\right|}{f'} \leqslant \frac{S}{\Delta T} N \tag{3.41}$$

Acousto-optic deflectors have been found to possess extremely good
linearity; therefore, the linearity requirement is imposed on the input
electronic oscillator circuit. Dickson has a more detailed and accurate

analysis of the spot size and linearity requirement for the swept frequency mode [14].

Attenuation of the acoustic wave generally occurs across the deflector, resulting in a nonuniform spatial distribution. The far-field
intensity distribution of a uniformly illuminated acousto-optic deflector
is thus expressed as

$$\frac{I}{I_0} = C_1 e^{-\gamma D} \left| \frac{\sin(\pi Dx/\lambda F - j\gamma D/2)}{\pi Dx/\lambda F - j\gamma D/2} \right|^2 \qquad (3.42)$$

where C_1 is a constant, F is the lens focal length, D is the optical
aperture, γ is the acoustic wave amplitude attenuation factor in nepers
per centimeter, and x is the displacement in distance on the far-field
output plane. The far-field intensity pattern in Fig. 3.16 has a slightly larger half-power beam width and somewhat larger sidelobe intensity
as the acoustic wave attenuation increases. An acoustic attenuation of

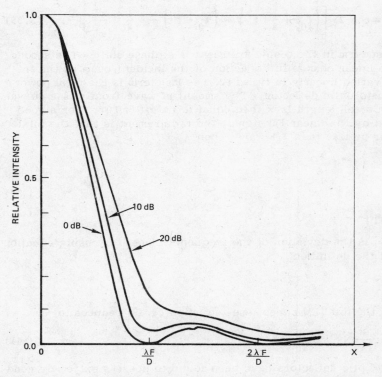

Figure 3.16 Acousto-optic deflector spot profile degradation due to
attenuation. (From Ref. 15, © 1981 IEEE.)

12 dB across the optical aperture is sometimes considered tolerable. The exponential factor in equation (3.42) indicates a reduced optical intensity due to reduced average acoustic wave power in the interaction, thus requiring more driver power to achieve a given efficiency.

Another aspect of interest is the effect of apodized optical illumination on the acousto-optic spatial modulator. With a gaussian input optical distribution to the acoustically lossy acousto-optic device, the far-field intensity can be derived and becomes

$$\frac{I}{I_0} = C_2 \exp\left[-\gamma D + \frac{(\gamma D)^2}{8}\right]\left\{\frac{D^2}{4}\exp\left[-2\left(\frac{\pi D x}{2\lambda F}\right)\right]\right\} \qquad (3.43)$$

where D is the e^{-2} width of the gaussian optical input beam. It is important to note that the factor in braces in equation (3.43) is identical to the far-field intensity distribution of the gaussian input. Therefore, even though the device output does suffer a loss in intensity, the far-field intensity distribution, i.e., the spot shape in the Fourier transform plane, of an acousto-optic spatial modulator remains unchanged regardless of the presence of acoustic wave attenuation, provided that the optical input wavefront is gaussian.

Two alternatives can be considered for the reduction of the Bragg angle deviation [ΔK in equation (3.3)] in an acousto-optic beam deflector for better efficiency or reduction in drive power.

The anisotropic interaction in TeO_2 crystals offers a tremendous advantage in acousto-optic deflectors because of the high figure of merit ($M_2 > 700$) and an effective interaction length (L'), given by [15]

$$L' = 4.4\left(\frac{f_0}{\Delta f}\right)L \qquad (3.44)$$

which is about 8 times the normal interaction length. Results of TeO_2 deflectors will be discussed later.

Another technique is to use a phased array to track the Bragg acousto-optic interaction, allowing a longer interaction length for the same interaction bandwidth. Step array transducers have been analyzed and demonstrated [16], but they are difficult to fabricate. Planar arrays have two main lobes, and consequently the effective interaction length gain only offers a power reduction of less than 2. Papers on the phased array work are given in the References [16].

A summary of some of the deflectors is shown in Table 3.4. For scanning applications, the most useful deflectors are the slow-shear TeO_2 devices. A recording system employing the TeO_2 deflector is shown in Fig. 3.17. In applications for parallel recording and angle of arrival measurements multichannel deflectors are required. A six-channel deflector is shown in Fig. 3.18, and a "freeze" snap-shot of the information in the device is shown in Fig. 3.19.

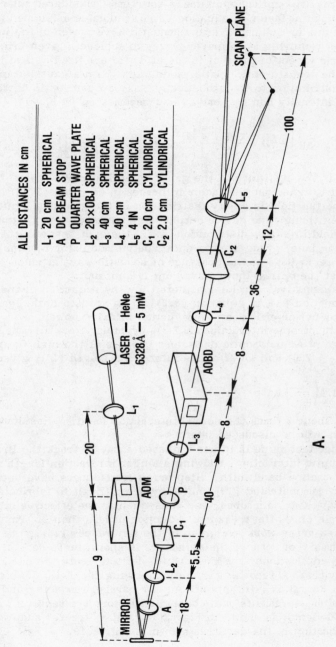

ALL DISTANCES IN cm

L_1 20 cm   SPHERICAL
A   DC BEAM STOP
P   QUARTER WAVE PLATE
L_2 20×OBJ SPHERICAL
L_3 40 cm   SPHERICAL
L_4 40 cm   SPHERICAL
L_5 4 IN   SPHERICAL
C_1 2.0 cm CYLINDRICAL
C_2 2.0 cm CYLINDRICAL

LASER — HeNe
6328 Å — 5 mW

Figure 3.17a AOBD laser scanner optical layout. (From Ref. 17 © SPIE.)

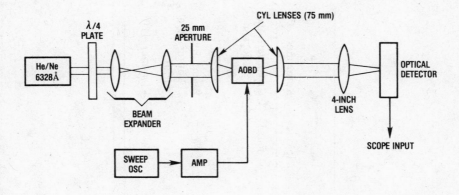

B.

Figure 3.17b AOBD diffraction efficiency measurement system. (From Ref. 17 © SPIE.)

Figure 3.18 Six-channel acousto-optic deflector.

Table 3.4 Acousto-optic Deflectors

Device type	Material	Laser wavelength (μm)	Center frequency (MHz)	Bandwidth (MHz)	Aperture (μs)	Efficiency	Reference
Deflector	TeO_2 slow shear	0.633	75	50	40	80% max.	Grossman and Reddersen [17] Merry [18]
Deflector	$LiNbO_3$	0.633	1600	1050	1.0	1.0%/W	Hecht [11] Young et al. [19]
Deflector	$LiNbO_3$	0.633	2500	1600	2.4	1.8%/W	Kirchner [20]

Figure 3.19 Recording of six-channel multibeam deflector.

3.5 ACOUSTIC FOCUSING

Acoustic focusing makes use of the portion of a traveling acoustic stress wave that has an increase in the index of refraction and therefore possesses focusing power. The device coupled with an input predeflector can enhance the resolution of the predeflector by a factor up to 40. We shall concentrate on the properties of the focusing lens. The block diagram showing the acoustic traveling-wave lens is shown in Fig. 3.20. An acoustic strain wave with wavelength Λ travels in the x direction. A light beam impinges on the acoustic wave at a prescribed time such that it travels through a region with a localized increase in the refractive index. The refractive index in the medium is expressed as

$$n = n_0 \left[1 + \frac{\Delta n}{n_0} \cos \left(\omega t - \frac{2\pi x}{\Lambda} \right) \right] \tag{3.45}$$

The central portion of the positive half cycle of this pressure wave produces a refractive index profile that focuses the incident light beam in the same manner as a cylindrical lens. Foster [21] has shown that the focal length (FL) of the traveling lens created by this acoustic wave is given by

$$FL = \frac{\Lambda}{4} \sqrt{\frac{n_0}{\Delta n}} \tag{3.46}$$

and the spot size produced may be written as

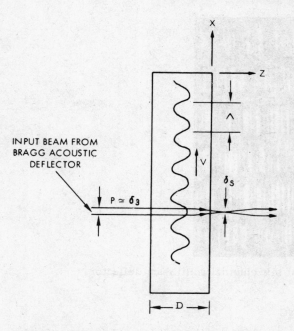

Figure 3.20 Geometry of the acoustic traveling lens device. (From Ref. 21 © SPIE.)

$$\alpha \sqrt{n_0} \, \Delta n \, \sin \left(\frac{2\pi}{\Lambda} \sqrt{\frac{\Delta n}{n_0}} \, L \right) \tag{3.47}$$

where α is the ratio of the incoming optical beam diameter (FWHM) to the acoustic wavelength; typically $\alpha = 0.25$. The peak change in the index of refraction created by the acoustic power P_a is given by

$$\Delta n = \sqrt{\frac{M_2 P_a}{2HL}} \tag{3.48}$$

The drive voltage for the focusing device consists of a properly shaped RF pulse such that its frequency spectrum coincides with the transducer bandwidth

We also define a gain parameter G as the ratio of the input optical beam size over the focused spot size δs:

$$G = 0.3 \, \frac{\Lambda}{\lambda} \left(\frac{\Delta n}{n_0} \right)^{1/2} \tag{3.49}$$

An application of the acoustic focusing lens is the acoustic traveling-wave lens (ATWL) recorder system. A block diagram of the system is

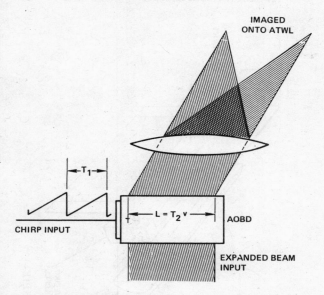

Figure 3.21 Block diagram of ATWL system.

shown in Fig. 3.21. In this system an acousto-optic beam deflector illuminates the focusing devices. The input optical beam must be synchronized and travel at the same speed as the acoustic wave in the
focusing device. The advantage of the acoustic traveling lens system
is the high scan rate of up to 2×10^8 pixels/s and the high resolution
of up to 20,000 pixels/line scan. These parameters are at least one
order of magnitude better than a single-stage acousto-optic beam deflector.

An experimental setup of the traveling-wave lens recorder is shown
in Fig. 3.22. The laser pulses from the cavity-dumped mode-locked
laser are coded such that they represent the data to be recorded. The
light beam goes through beam-forming optics and is properly shaped to
match the aperture of the predeflector, which is an acousto-optic beam
deflector. The scan beam output from the predeflector again goes
through beam-forming optics such that it properly illuminates that
focusing lens cell. The tracking requirement of the predeflector and
focusing cell is most critical; typical linearity of 10^{-4} or better is imposed on the RF chirp for the predeflector. The focused spots of information are then recorded on the film in the focal plane. The smallest
spot size achieved is on the order of 6.5 μm with a gain of 45 over the
input spot. The spot profile is shown in Fig. 23.

The effect of the focused spot over the input spot is shown on a
multiexposure photograph in Fig. 3.24, and a recording of the spot on
32-μm centers is shown in Fig. 3.25.

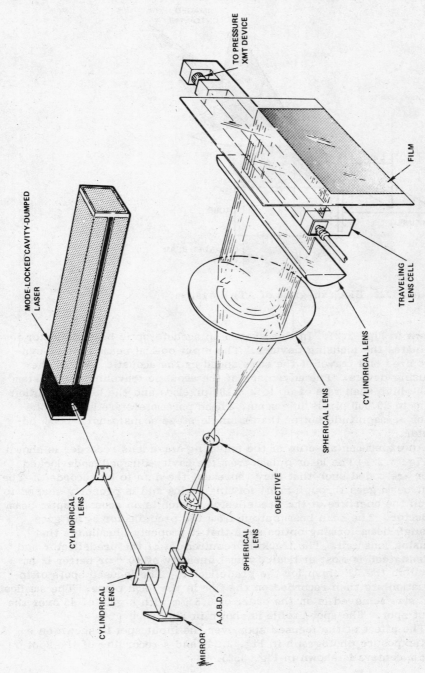

Figure 3.22 Traveling-wave lens recorder. (From Ref. 21 © SPIE.)

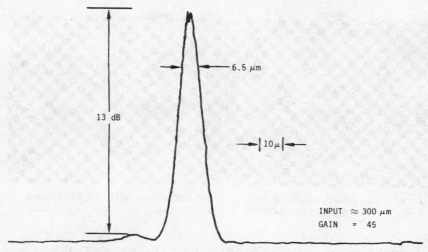

Figure 3.23 Spot profile produced by ATWL.

Figure 3.24 Effect of acoustic lens.

Figure 3.25 Checkerboard test pattern recorded with ATWL bread-
board. (From Ref. 21 © SPIE.)

3.6 OUTLOOK FOR ACOUSTO-OPTIC DEVICE APPLICATIONS

Acousto-optic device technology has matured to be applied in many industrial and military applications. In particular the new advances in
signal-processing systems to be discussed in subsequent chapters will
offer further development and application of acousto-optic devices.

ACKNOWLEDGMENT

The work reported here was the result of several colleagues, namely,
E. H. Young, Jr., S. K. Yao, J. R. Boyd, M. L. Shah, and B. G.
Grossman.

REFERENCES

1. A. Korpel, Acousto-optics, in *Applied Solid State Science*,
    Vol. 3 (R. Wolfe, ed.), Academic Press, New York, 1972, pp.
    73-179.

2. W. R. Klein and B. D. Cook, Unified approach to ultrasonic
    light diffraction, *IEEE Trans. Sonics Ultrason. SU-14*:723-733,
    July 1967.

3. M. Gottlieb and G. W. Roland, Infrared acousto-optic materials:
    Applications, requirements and crystal development, *Proc. SPIE
    214* (acousto-optic bulk wave devices):88-95, Nov. 1979.

4. E. K. Sittig, Design and technology of piezoelectric transducers
    for frequencies above 100 MHz, in *Physical Acoustics*, Vol. IX
    (W. P. Mason and R. N. Thurston, eds.), Academic Press,
    New York, 1972.

5. A. H. Meitzler and E. K. Sittig, Characterization of piezoelectric transducers used in ultrasonic devices operating above 0.1 GHz, *J. Appl. Phys.* *40*:4341-4352, Oct. 1969.
6. J. W. Goodman, *Introduction to Fourier Optics*, McGraw-Hill, New York, 1968.
7. J. R. Boyd, *Technical Report 6035*, Harris Corp., 1978.
8. D. Maydan, Acousto-optical pulse modulators, *IEEE J. Quantum Electron.* *QE-6*:15-24, Jan. 1970.
9. R. W. Dixon, Photoelastic properties of selected materials and their relevance for applications to acoustic light modulators and scanners, *J. Appl. Phys.* *38*:5149-5153, Dec. 1967.
10. E. I. Gordon, A review of acousto-optical deflection and modulation devices, *Proc. IEEE 54*:1391-1401, Oct. 1966.
11. D. L. Hecht, Acousto-optic device techniques—400 to 2300 MHz, in *1977 Ultrasonics Symp. Proc.* (IEEE Cat. #377CH1264-ISU), 1977.
12. A. Vander Lugt, private communications, Feb. 1980.
13. E. H. Young, Jr., private communications, 1974.
14. L. D. Dickson, Optical considerations for an acousto-optic deflector, *Appl. Opt. 11*(10), Oct. 1972.
15. E. H. Young, Jr., and S. K. Yao, Design considerations for acousto-optic devices, *Proc. IEEE 69*:54-64, Jan. 1981.
16. D. A. Pinnow, Acousto-optic light deflection: Design consideration for first order beam steering transducers, *IEEE Trans. Sonics Ultrason. SU-18*:209-214. Oct. 1971.
17. B. G. Grossman and B. R. Reddersen, High speed laser facsimile scanner, *Proc. SPIE*, Aug. 1979.
18. J. B. Merry, High resolution acousto-optic deflector demonstrated in a laser scanner, *CLEOS*, Feb. 1978.
19. E. H. Young, Jr., J. R. Boyd, and B. G. Grossman, private communications.
20. E. K. Kirchner, Deposited transducer technology for use with acousto-optic bulk wave devices, *Proc. SPIE 214* (acousto-optic bulk wave devices), Nov. 1979.
21. R. H. Johnson and R. M. Montgomery, Optical beam deflector using acoustic-traveling-wave technology *Proc. SPIE*, Aug. 1976.

II
FREQUENCY-DOMAIN SIGNAL PROCESSING

Preface

The acousto-optic deflector is the basis for frequency-domain signal processing. Combining this device with a Fourier transform lens produces the frequency spectrum of an RF signal at the focal plane of the lens. If a detector array is placed at the focal plane, the spectrum of the signal can be determined quite rapidly. This configuration is referred to as a Bragg cell spectrum analyzer and is the topic of discussion of the first chapter of this part (Chap. 4). A full discussion is given of various factors which affect Bragg cell performance, and experimental results are presented which illustrate some of the diverse uses of this powerful structure. The second chapter (Chap. 5) considers the case where coherent light detection is used in conjunction with a Bragg cell. Reconstruction of the original signal and adaptive filtering are possible using this approach. A theoretical and experimental presentation of this innovative approach together with some application areas is given in the chapter. The final chapter (Chap. 6) discusses an entirely different application of acousto-optics, viz., the area of tunable optical filtering. In this architecture the input light beam can be considered the unknown with the RF acoustic source the controllable variable. The anisotropic acousto-optic interaction is used to obtain maximum efficiency, with large acceptance angle and fine resolution. A variety of applications is presented illustrating the power of this approach.

4

Applications of Acousto-Optic Techniques to RF Spectrum Analysis

JOHN P. LINDLEY[†] / ITEK Corporation, Applied Technology Division, Sunnyvale, California

The acousto-optic (AO) spectrum analyzer is probably the simplest optical processor with practical value. It performs a single dimensional real-time Fourier transform of hundreds of data points with only four active components, a light source, a Bragg cell, a transform lens, and a photodetector array. This chapter will discuss the basic operating parameters of the spectrum analyzer when used for radio-frequency (RF) signal analysis.

4.1 ACOUSTO-OPTIC SPECTRUM ANALYZER APPLICATIONS

The applications for acousto-optic spectrum analyzers often include monitoring a wide band of the electromagnetic spectrum, providing the ability to recognize desired characteristics of any signal which may appear in that band, and, by using this information, identifying the source and nature of the signal. Severe problems arise when the band of interest contains a large number of signals of different amplitudes and types of modulation. The difficulties are compounded if the signals are pulses of relatively short duration. Also, modulation methods have been devised specifically to make detection and identification more difficult, e.g., frequency-jump and spread spectrum techniques. These modulations severely limit the capability of traditional measurement techniques.

The choices of systems to detect and sort these signals is further limited by the need to achieve a high probability of intercept of transi-

[†]Current affiliation: Probe Systems, Inc., Sunnyvale, California

ent signals over a broad frequency band, in a wide field of view, and with an environment crowded with many continuous wave (CW) and pulsed signals.

The value of simultaneous processing of signals in frequency has long been recognized. However, the use of conventional receiver systems to make such measurements can be expected to become increasingly unsatisfactory due to low probability of intercept resulting from scan-on-scan effects. In contrast, a receiver system incorporating acousto-optic signal processing can provide continuous simultaneous detection of RF over a wide dynamic range with 100% probability of intercept.

Optical processing techniques have enormous potential for handling these large volumes of information. The appearance of the laser as a coherent source of light during the last decade has stimulated the development of a wide range of special-purpose systems capable of performing functions previously accomplished by microwave and lower-frequency systems but with orders-of-magnitude greater speed and capacity.

The Bragg receiver produces the power density spectrum for all signals in its input band simultaneously. The signals can be inter-mixed, pulsed, or CWs, and include broadband signals such as jammers or intrapulse modulated radars. Figure 4.1 shows some signals observed in the San Francisco Bay Area. The signals shown are an example of broadband signals in the presence of CW carriers. The six signals between 2.5 and 2.55 GHz are television microwave links. Four noise-modulated signals can be identified, each with a different modulation characteristic. Three of the four are between 2.45 and 2.5 GHz, and the fourth is superimposed on the lowest frequency TV carrier. The signals were first thought to be jammers but were later found to be microwave ovens.

This set of signals would be nearly impossible to analyze with conventional equipment. The modulation rates, signal excursion, and periods of transmission of four overlapped noise-modulated carriers have been measured in the presence of six CW signals. This is an excellent demonstration of the power of optical processing techniques to analyze simultaneous signals.

4.1.1 The Use of the AO Spectrum Analyzer in Radio Astronomy

One of the earliest applications for the AO spectrum analyzer was in the field of radio astronomy. It replaced banks of filters constructed with conventional electronic components. Because of the cost of constructing these filters and tuning them individually to adjacent frequencies, the number of filters were limited, as was the operational bandwidth. The optical techniques made possible bandwidths up to 500 MHz at relatively low cost.

One radio astronomy application is in studying the bursts of energy emitted by pulsars. The broad bandwidth of the AO device enables

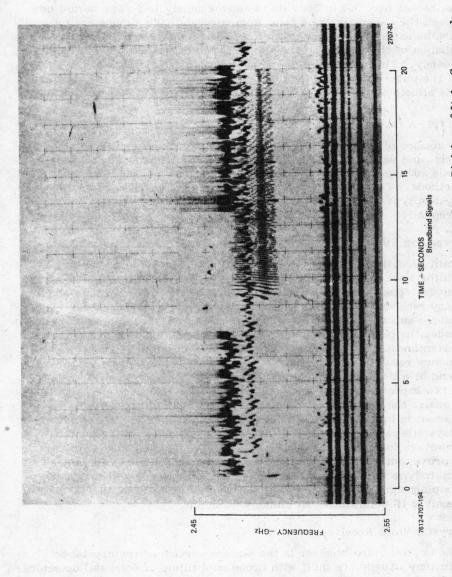

Figure 4.1 Broadband RF signals. (Courtesy of Applied Technology, Division of Itek, Sunnyvale, California.)

measurements of the dispersion of the interstellar medium in which the
higher-frequency components arrive at the receiver before the lower-
frequency ones. These emissions have been observed [3] to sweep
downward from 500 to 300 MHz in approximately 1 s. The period between the sweeps is 1/3 s, and thus several of the signals are present
simultaneously. Another application is in the measurement of the scintillation of the radio star and the variation of the scintillation with frequency. This permits improved accuracy in the estimate of the energy
of the pulse by summing over a large bandwidth and thereby reducing
the effects of the scintillation and other propagation effects.

4.1.2 A Comparison of AO Spectrum Analyzers with Other Receivers

A number of new technologies have been developed for RF signal analysis, and each can be used to advantage in particular applications.
This section will compare the optical spectrum analyzer to the other
methods. Table 4.1 shows typical performance parameters of the major
system types, which are described in detail in the following paragraphs.

Sweeping Superheterodyne Receivers or Spectrum Analyzers

Until recently, the only choices of equipment to monitor broad bandwidths were the scanning superheterodyne or the crystal video receiver. The superheterodyne receiver is the basis of all home and military receivers because it has high sensitivity, good frequency resolution, and low cost. However, when used in a sweeping or scanning
mode, the probability of intercepting a pulsed signal is poor, since the
instantaneous bandwidth must be narrow in order to achieve the frequency resolution, and thus the receiver detects only one frequency
band at a time.

   To improve the probability of intercept for fixed-frequency pulsed
signals, the sweep rate is slowed so that the dwell time on a frequency
element is longer than the pulse interval, and digitally refreshed displays are used to remove the flicker in the oscilloscope presentation.
However, for single pulses of frequency-unstable signals there is no
improvement in intercept by increasing the dwell time. The superheterodyne receiver has virtually no capability against frequency
hopping signals unless the total hop range of the signal lies within the
receiver IF bandwidth—an unlikely situation.

Crystal Video Receivers

The crystal video receiver is the modern version of the crystal set,
and they usually are built with broadband filters and crystal detectors
which detect any signal which is within the input filter width. Crystal
video is the inverse of the superheterodyne. It has poor sensitivity

Table 4.1 Receiver Technique Comparison

	Superheterodyne	Crystal video	Microscan compression	IFM	Channelized SAW	Channelized Optical
Equivalent number of channels	1	1	1	1	8 to 32	500 to 2000
Observation bandwidth	2 GHz	2 to 4 GHz	2 GHz	2 to 4 GHz	100 MHz	500 to 2000 MHz
Instantaneous bandwidth	0.1 to 10 MHz	2 to 4 GHz	1 to 100 MHz	2 to 4 GHz	100 MHz	500 to 2000 MHz
Frequency resolution	0.1 to 10 MHz	2 to 4 GHz	1 MHz	10 MHz	10 MHz	1 MHz
Sweep time	1 to 10 s	No sweep	1 to 10 μs	No sweep	No sweep	No sweep
Measure frequency of simultaneous signals?	Yes; signal duration > 1 to 10 s	No	Yes; signal duration > 1 to 10 μs	No	Yes	Yes
Measure CW?	Yes	No	Yes	Sometimes	Yes	Yes
Data rate	Low	High	Very high	High	High	Variable digital controlled integration
Cost	Low	Low	High	Low	Moderate	Moderate

Source: Courtesy of Applied Technology, Division of Itek, Sunnyvale, California.

and frequency resolution, but the instantaneous bandwidth can be very
large so that the entire band is detected at one time, and the probability of intercept is high. Special techniques (such as pulse parameter measurement) are used to separate the signals, since frequency
information is not available. The crystal video has been used primarily for warning applications and only rarely for reconnaissance,
also due to the poor frequency resolution.

Receivers Using Compressive Filters

To increase the probability of intercept of the scanning superheterodyne receiver, the microscan or compressive receiver was developed.
Both sweep rate and bandwidth can be increased so that near-unity
probability of intercept can be achieved. In some receivers, a 1-GHz
band is swept in less than 1 µs. A dispersive filter is used to remove
the chirp introduced by the sweeping local oscillator, and the frequency resolution can approach that of a standard superheterodyne.
However, the local oscillator and dispersive filter must be extremely
linear to maintain the resolution. In the microwave region, the output
data rate is high due to the large bandwidth and fast sweep. The
major disadvantage of microwave compressive receivers is the high cost
due to the need to handle high data rates and the precision of the local
oscillator and filters.

Instantaneous Frequency Measurement Receivers

The crystal video receiver also has been improved by using discrim-
inator techniques to provide a frequency reading. This is called instantaneous frequency measurement (IFM). Most units have a broad
input band with one or more frequency measurement channels. Several
techniques are used, but most are based on phasing methods to produce a detected voltage output which is proportional to frequency and
are similar to a conventional FM receiver. Multiple channels are used
to remove ambiguities and improve measurement accuracy. Like an FM
receiver, limiters are often used to capture the strongest signal so
that unambiguous measurements can be obtained. Accurate readings
on the strongest signal can be achieved with only 1 to 2 dB difference
between the two signals. The IFM generally reads a weighted frequency
average for noise signals, such as jammers, has difficulty with multiple
strong CW signals, and cannot read the weaker of time overlapping signals. These are serious disadvantages in reconnaissance situations
where measurements of broadband emitters in a crowded environment
are required.

Channelized Receiver Techniques

All the above receivers are basically single-channel devices. Another
class of receivers known as multichannel systems is now being devel-

oped. In principle, with a multichannel approach, any frequency bandwidth and resolution can be achieved with unity probability of intercept by merely increasing the number of channels. Previously, this
has been extremely costly and has only been implemented for special
purposes. New developments in surface wave filter design and optical
processing have greatly reduced the cost and made possible the wide
deployment of channelized systems.

SAW Filters

Surface-acoustic-wave (SAW) filters are now being used for channel
separation. A single device can have one input with a number of parallel output ports. SAW filters have been built in the 100 to 500 MHz
range with 100-MHz input bandwidth. The number of channels is dependent on the physical size of the substrate crystal and the operating wavelength.

The output bandwidth and frequency are set by the number and
spacing of the interdigital finger pairs in the transducer. Thus, to
achieve multiple outputs at different frequencies, each output transducer must be scaled for that frequency. As the number of channels
is increased, the number of transducers and the Q of the transducers
must be increased in proportion; thus, the size and complexity of the
filter increase rapidly. These considerations limit the number of channels that can be built on one substrate.

A significant advantage of the SAW filter is that is can be produced
using photolithography methods. After a photomask is developed for
the filter, additional filters can be made at low cost. However, this
cost advantage cannot be maintained when multiple similar filters are
used to increase bandwidth, since the cost must include the multiple
RF converters which are required to heterodyne the input bands down
to the SAW filter input frequency.

Optical Processing

A Fourier transform optical processor is one method of constructing a
channelized system with a large number of channels at low cost. Since
500 to 2000 channels can be realized in one system, the cost per channel is extremely low. The decision as to which system to use depends
on the application and the environment in which it is to work. In general, if a large number of channels is required, then the optical techniques are appropriate, but if only a few are required, 5 to 10, then
discrete filters would probably be best. In between these limits,
the other factors must be considered.

4.2 ACOUSTO-OPTIC SPECTRUM ANALYZER ANALYSIS

The acousto-optic spectrum analyzer makes use of a Bragg cell as the
electrical input transducer. A typical optical processor with 500-MHz

Figure 4.2 Optical RF spectrum analyzer. (Courtesy of Applied Technology, Division of Itek, Sunnyvale, California.)

bandwidth and 1-MHz resolution is shown in Fig. 4.2. It can be
analyzed in many different ways. In this section a classical ray trace
approach and a mathematical analysis will be compared with an electrical equivalent circuit. Each will reveal different aspects of the
spectrum analyzer.

4.2.1 Ray Trace Analysis of the Optical Components

The basic apparatus in the spectrum analyzer is shown in the ray
trace diagram in Fig. 4.3. The laser beam is expanded to match the
cell aperture and recollimated by lenses L1 and L2. As described in
Chap. 1, the acousto-optic cell acting as a moving diffraction grating
diffracts a portion of the laser light at an angle proportional to the frequency of the electrical input frequency and with intensity proportional
to the signal power. The Fourier transform lens produces the frequency transform one focal length from the lens, and the information
is read out using a self-scanned photodetector array.

   In this application the transform lens can be placed adjacent to the
cell rather than one focal length away since the phase of the signal is
not detected. The ray trace diagram shows that performance of the
spectrum analyzer can be predicted without considering a Fourier
transform.

   Since the collimation of the expanded beam is not affected by the
diffraction process and the rays from a given grating remain parallel,
the ray trace shows that the lens forms a point image at a distance
equal to the lens focal length. Also, the ray trace confirms that for
each beam angle out of the Bragg cell there is a discrete point focus
in the frequency plane, and, since the angle is proportional to the frequency, there is a one-to-one correspondence of the light image in
the frequency plane to the input signal.

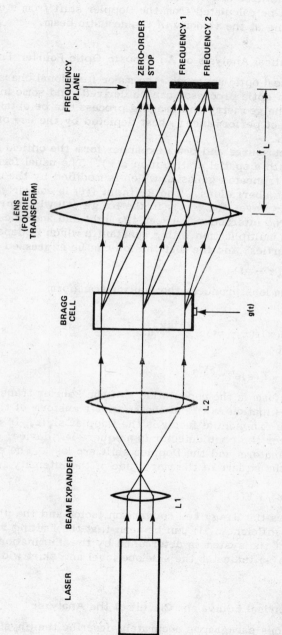

Figure 4.3 Bragg analyzer ray trace diagram. (Courtesy of Applied Technology, Division of Itek, Sunnyvale, California.)

The light in the first-order beam is shifted in frequency by an amount which can be calculated from the Doppler shift from a diffraction grating moving at the velocity of the acoustic beam.

4.2.2 A Mathematical Analysis of An Acousto-Optic Fourier Transform

By using a classical optic approach, the major functional characteristics of an acousto-optic processor can be derived, and some intuitive presentation of the geometry and imaging process can be obtained. However, the exact performance is best depicted by the use of a mathematical approach.

The laser light source and beam expander form the optical input to the Bragg cell with a spatial distribution $a(x)$. The usual form of the distribution is a truncated gaussian which is modified by the cell aperture and lens aberrations. The RF input $f(t)$ is converted to a traveling acoustic wave, $f(x - vt)$, in the Bragg cell which propagates at velocity v. The interaction between the light and acoustic wave is a point-by-point multiplication with a constant c which is dependent on the cell properties, and the distribution can be expressed as

$$i(x) = ca(x)f(x - vt)$$

The transform lens produces the Fourier transform

$$I(s) = \int_0^\infty ca(x)f(x - vt)e^{-2\pi isx} \, dx$$

$$= cA(s) * F(s)e^{i2\pi svt}$$

Thus, the transform is the convolution $*$ of the Fourier transform of the illumination function $A(s)$ and the Fourier transform of the acoustic wave $F(s)$. The exponential factor is the Doppler shift. In a simple spectrum analyzer the photodetector is a square law device, and the phase of the transform and the Doppler shift are lost. The electrical output is then the square of the magnitude of the intensity function,

$$E(s) = C |A(s) * F(s)|^2$$

where C includes the Bragg cell conversion factor and the photodetector quantum efficiency. It can be seen that the limiting resolution (or spot size) of the system is determined by the illumination $a(x)$, and the transform $A(s)$ indicates the sidelobe level and skirt width of the spot.

4.2.3 The Electrical Equivalent Circuit of the Analyzer

While the previous paragraphs accurately describe the physical interaction in the optics, a better understanding of the electrical performance

and, in particular, the data rates can be obtained from the electrical
equivalent circuit.

The electrical equivalent circuit of the Fourier transform can be
considered to be a channel bank filter. The circuit shown in Fig. 4.4
is the equivalent when a self-scanned photodetector array is used as
the output; this is the equivalent of a multiple-channel IF filter with a
second detector and followed by a commutating switch. The bandwidth
and Q of the filters are determined jointly by the resolution of the optical
system and the number of photodetectors per resolution element. The
energy in each channel is detected and stored as charge in the junction capacity of the detector. When the array element is accessed, the
charge is read out and the capacitor reset.

The input bandwidth is the Bragg cell bandwidth, and it can be
seen that any signal within the band will be detected and a charge
proportional to the signal energy stored. The output bandwidth is
determined by the digital circuitry which determines the rate at which
the switch is stepped.

When the stepping frequency is f, the dwell time on each step is $1/f$.
Thus the time to read out N detectors is N/f, which is the time the sig-

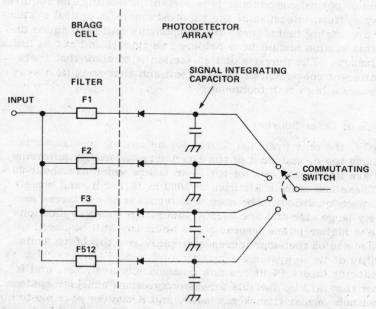

Figure 4.4 Optical processor electrical equivalent circuit. (Courtesy
of Applied Technology, Division of Itek, Sunnyvale, California.)

nal is integrated, and f/N is the sampling rate. Sampling theory predicts the maximum signal modulation that can be measured to be less
than one-half of the sampling rate. The output bandwidth of the system
is equal to one-half of the clock frequency, and the digital data rate
is equal to the clock frequency. Thus the number of photodetectors
and the clock frequency must be chosen carefully to meet the system
operating goals. These factors are discussed in the section on system
components.

By using the equivalent circuit, it can easily be seen that the input
bandwidth is determined by the Bragg cell parameters and the output
bandwidth by the photodetector array parameters. The optical spectrum analyzer reduces the data rate so that subsequent digital processors can be used effectively. Typically the compression is about 1000
times, 500-MHz input bandwidth versus 500-kHz output bandwidth.
However, there is a corresponding reduction in the information due to
the signal integration. The electrical equivalent circuit is the best
representation for discussing the output data rates and the sampling
problems, but it does not accurately represent the optical and acoustic
processes.

4.3 COMPONENT DESIGN CONSIDERATIONS

The selection of optical components is important in meeting the requirements of any system. Because of the rapid advances in optical systems
and optical processing techniques, the components and techniques described in this section should be considered as typical and not as limits
of the technology. The purpose of this section is to show that there
are many different components to select from and that an optical system is no longer a high risk technology.

4.3.1 Choice of Laser Sources

Until recently, the only practical source for an optical spectrum analyzer was a gas laser, and most of the Fourier transform RF spectrum
analyzers have used small 1- or 2-mW HeNe lasers which are about 30
cm long. These lasers have lifetimes of 2000 to 10,000 h, and some
have been space-qualified. The main disadvantage of gas lasers are
the relatively large size and low output power. In those applications
which require higher-power lasers, a gas laser may still be used;
however, the size of the laser increases rapidly and therefore limits
the portability of those systems.

Semiconductor lasers [4,6] are now commerically available, and it
appears that they will be suitable for many spectrum analyzer systems.
The size is much smaller than a gas laser, and it may be possible to obtain over 10 to 40 mW of optical power in the near future in the size of
a TO-5 transistor case. The main disadvantage of semiconductor lasers

is that the spectral width of the laser is not as pure as a gas laser and the wavelength changes appreciably with temperature. At present, this limits the use to low-resolution applications; however, the size of the optical processor is greatly reduced.

In 1979 an operable spectrum analyzer was constructed using a semi-conductor laser, shown in Fig. 4.5. The laser, a Hitachi HLP 1600, is visible on the right-hand side of the bench. It is mounted in a round metal carrier and has a prism mounted on the end to direct the beam into the Bragg cell. The Bragg cell is mounted in the center of the bench and is followed by two pentaprisms. Pentaprisms were used instead of right-angle prisms because of the additional path length in the prism which reduced the overall length of the optical bench. The photodetector array was mounted on the second pentaprism and is visible to the rear of the bench on the left-hand side. The unit acheived 5-MHz resolution in a 500-MHz RF bandwidth. Similar small analyzers are now under development using integrated optic technology [5].

4.3.2 Typical Bragg Cell Performance

Table 4.2 shows typical measured performance data for a variety of materials and frequency ranges [1,2]. The insertion loss values are the total loss from the RF input to the acoustic beam and include all mismatch and tuning losses. One can see with $LiNbO_3$ the various tradeoffs involved in using any single material.

In choosing a cell for a particular application, the desire is to match the bandwidth and resolution to the requirement without overdesigning the cell. In general as the bandwidth is made narrower, the center

Table 4.2   Acousto-optic Cells

	Material			
	$LiNbO_3$	$LiNbO_3$	GaP	TeO_2
Bandwidth, MHz	1050	530	630	90
Resolution, MHz	1.0	0.7	1.8	0.08
Time-bandwidth	1050	760	350	1125
Dynamic range, dB	36	46	58	> 70
Efficiency, %/W	1.0	4.6	16	770
Insertion loss, dB	2.4	2.2	4.6	0.25

Source: Courtesy of Applied Technology, Division of Itek, Sunnyvale, California.

MINIBENCH ASSEMBLY

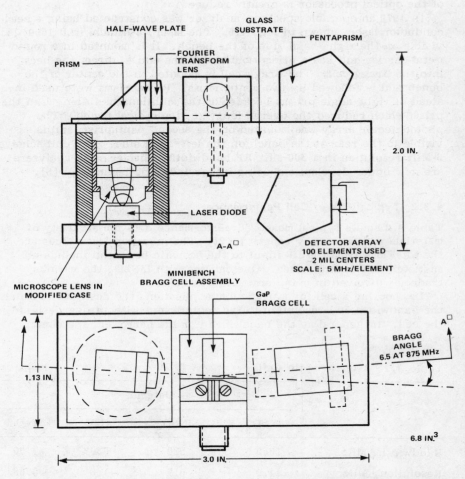

Figure 4.5 Miniature spectrum analyzer. (Courtesy of Applied Technology, Division of Itek, Sunnyvale, California.)

frequency can be reduced, and the conversion efficiency will be increased. A high conversion efficiency is desirable for signal sensitivity. In most systems with integrating detectors, excess aperture, and therefore excess resolution, will not affect system performance. However, if it is desired to use a fast detector in the Fourier trans-

Figure 4.5 (Continued)

form plane to recover the signal modulation, an aperture in excess of
that required to meet the resolution requirements will limit the frequency response of the system. As discussed above, the image in the
transform plane is the convolution of the illumination and the signal
time function; thus the signal modulation response is reduced for modulation periods shorter than the cell transit time. Another viewpoint
is to consider a short pulse traveling through the cell. Even though
the pulse may be shorter than the transit time, light is diffracted into
the first order during the time for the pulse to traverse the cell and
stretch the pulse length. Of course, the spectral width will be com-
mensurate with the temporal width of the pulse.

4.3.3 The Effect of the Photodetector on Performance

There are a number of different photodetectors which can be used in
this application. In this section, the detectors are classified by the
number of output connections and whether the switching circuits are
contained on the silicon substrate.

4.3.4 Self-Scanned Serial Output Arrays

A self-scanned array is one in which there are fewer output terminals
than photodetector elements, and the detectors are connected to the
output by semiconductor switching networks contained on the same substrate. Common switching methods include charge-coupled devices
(CCD) in which the electron flow is controlled by potential barriers and
MOS devices where FET switches are controlled by shift registers.

Table 4.3 shows the configurations of some currently available detector arrays. (These detectors can be obtained from a number of
sources including Fairchild Semiconductor, General Electric, RCA, and
Reticon Corp.)

The choice of the best detector depends on the application. It is
possible to generalize that the CCD detectors seem to have slightly
higher dynamic range than the MOS, but they are not as good for saturating signals. The output of the CCD detectors tends to "bloom" or
spread nonuniformly in saturation. The output of the MOS detectors
is hard limited, and it is more useful in high-signal environments.

Table 4.3 Photodetector Arrays

Number of elements	
Linear	Two dimensional
64	32 × 32
128	50 × 50
256	90 × 244
384	100 × 100
500	320 × 512
512	380 × 244
768	
936	
1024	
1728	
1872	
2048	

Source: Courtesy of Applied
Technology, Division of Itek,
Sunnyvale, California.

These are not hard and fast rules, and systems have been built using both types of detectors.

The advantage of the self-scanned arrays is that all the switching circuitry is contained on the silicon substrate, and it is not necessary to connect a wire to each of the detector elements. The major disadvantage is that the access time to connect to any one detector is limited by the digital circuits on the chip. Although special designs have been built, it is difficult to obtain multiple outputs with large signal bandwidths.

The choice of the length of the detector is determined by tradeoffs between the desired resolution and the permissible output data rate, which are the key factors. To achieve the best resolution, the optical spot should be oversampled so that the peak frequency and spot width can be determined. To achieve this, a large number of detectors is desirable. However, the more detectors that are used, the longer it takes to return to a detector using a given output data rate. The re-visit time, or sample time, sets the maximum modulation rate that can be detected. This parameter is also called integrating time since it is the period in which signal energy is collected on the detector. Another disadvantage of oversampling is that the sensitivity is reduced. The maximum sensitivity results when all the energy from the signal is collected by one photodetector. When additional detectors are used, each detector receives correspondingly less light, and the detector output is reduced. This can be a significant effect when the amount of light is limited by Bragg cell drive restrictions. This often occurs when short pulses are to be measured and the transform of the pulse is broader than one photodetector.

Many applications involve the measurement of short pulses, and the detectors that would be suitable for CW signals or noise jammers are not sensitive to a pulsed signal. The only detector arrays previously available for continuous readout were ones which integrate the signal for a period which is determined by the number of photodetectors times the clock period. For example, a 512-element photodetector clocked at 1 MHz would integrate for 512 μs. The sensitivity of a detector to a single short pulse is inversely proportional to the square root of the integration time.

The detector integrates the energy from the signals present during the integration period. A pulsed signal has a fixed energy, and thus the response does not change as the integration period is changed as long as the time is longer than the pulse length. Unfortunately, the background noise continues to be integrated during the period, and longer integration periods decrease the pulsed signal-to-noise ratio. Thus for best short pulse response it is desirable to use the shortest integration period and a detector width equal to the transform width.

Most linear photodetectors can be operated at clock rates that exceed 1 MHz. The integration period is equal to the clock period multiplied by the number of detectors in the array. Thus, the shortest

integration period is usually about 0.25 to 1 ms. The integration time
can be reduced by increasing the clock rate, using detectors with
parallel output ports or random-access-addressed detector arrays.

The data rate can be set to be compatible with a wide variety of
auxiliary equipment. It is changed by varying the photodetector
clock frequency. The range of practical values is from a few kilohertz
to a few megahertz; however, changing the clock rate affects some of
the operating parameters. For example, slowing the clock frequency
increases the integration time and can increase the integrated dark
current or background noise.

4.3.5 Self-Scanned Parallel Output Arrays

By dividing the detector array into a number of segments, the revisit
time can be correspondingly reduced. Tradeoffs between the number
of taps and the permissible output data rate are the key factors. To
minimize complexity, a large number of detectors per tap is desirable.
However, the more detectors that are used, the longer it takes to return to a detector using a given output data rate. A 5-μs integration
time has been demonstrated in a 480-element detector array with 10
taps built by Reticon Corp. and operated at a clock rate of 10 MHz.
The detector outputs are combined so that multiple simultaneous signals are detected. The electronics necessary for this approach are
more costly than for a single-channel system due to the higher clock
speed and the parallel channels.

4.3.6 Discrete Photodetector Arrays

Discrete arrays have the advantage that the integration time can be
set to correspond to the system needs without consideration of the output switching limitations on self-scanned arrays. An additional advantage is that arrays can be built from individual detectors. This
gives additional design flexibility because of the many detectors from
which to choose [7]. Of course, the disadvantage of discrete detectors
is the cost and complexity of a large number of duplicate amplifier
channels for each of the detectors.

4.4 ACOUSTO-OPTICS AND SIGNAL PROCESSING

Throughout the course of electro-optic processor development the per-
ception of the role of the optical processor has changed. Originally,
the optical processor was thought to be a stand-alone unit which had
little interaction with other pieces of equipment. Little thought was
given to the utilization of the data output of the processor other than
to view it on an oscilloscope or TV. Now it is recognized that the
optical unit will be a part of a system which will be digitally controlled.

The optical processor is a high-speed, special-purpose, parallel computing device. The program of the processor is fixed once the physical placement of the optical components is determined. Once the program is set, the processor can make an extremely high number of calculations per second.

For example, in an acousto-optic spectrum analyzer, the program is one to Fourier-transform the time sample in the Bragg cell and produce the spectrum of the input RF signal. The program can only be changed by rearranging the lenses, but the processor can make 1 billion Fourier transforms per second. Thus, an optical processor can be considered to be a computer peripheral device programmed to do specific mathematical functions at high speed. Besides the Fourier transform, the functions include all types of multipoint mathematical multiplication of real and complex variables. These include correlations, convolutions, and combinations of these with Fourier transforms. One, two, three, or more functions may be inputted, and the output may be in one or two dimensions. A number of these schemes have been demonstrated and have shown time-bandwidth products of over a million.

Optical processing is useful where a specific mathematical function is to be performed that has a large data base. In the examples above, a 1000-point Fourier transform is calculated in 2 ns, which is the time for the light to pass through the processor. In essence, the transform is calculated continuously on the time sample contained in the Bragg cell. In contrast, a fast Fourier transform in a digital computer is a batch process. The digital computer has the advantage that it can easily be reprogrammed, whereas the "program" of the optical processor is set when the optics are positioned. However, the optical processor does what it is designed to do at an extremely high speed.

The main feature of optical processors is that they process a large signal bandwidth in parallel. This is at the same time the biggest advantage and the biggest problem. An optical processor produces so much information it is difficult to use it all.

REFERENCES

1. I. C. Chang, Acoustooptic devices and applications, *IEEE Trans. Sonics Ultrason. SU-23*:1-22, Jan. 1976.
2. David L. Hecht, Multifrequency acoustooptic diffraction, *IEEE Trans. Sonics Ultrason. SU-24*:7-18, Jan. 1977.
3. T. W. Cole, The AOS: Widening the radio sky, *Sky and Telescope 60*(2): 108-110, Aug. 1980.
4. Dan Botez, CW high-power single-mode operation of constricted double-heterojunction AlGaAs lasers with a large optical cavity, *Appl. Phys. Lett. 36*(3): 190-192, Feb. 1, 1980.

5. M. K. Barnoski, B. Chen, T. R. Joseph, J. Y. Lee, and O. G.
    Ramer, Integrated optic spectrum analyzer, *IEEE Trans. Circuits
    Syst. CAS-26*:113, 1979.
6. A. A. Bergh, and J. A. Copeland, Optical sources for fiber trans-
    mission systems, *IEEE Proc. 69*(10):1240-1247, Oct. 1980.
7. R. G. Smith, Photodetectors for fiber transmission systems, *IEEE
    Proc. 69*(10):1247-1253, Oct. 1980.

5

Coherent Detection and Adaptive Filtering

DAVID W. JACKSON[†] and JERRY LEE ERICKSON / Probe Systems,
Inc., Sunnyvale, California

5.1 INTRODUCTION

This chapter describes an acousto-optic signal-processing technique
that can be used to filter radio-frequency electronic signals. Of particular interest is the ability of this technique to remove or excise narrowband interference from broadband signals. When compared to electronic filtering with either analog or digital techniques, the acousto-
optical filter offers unique capabilities and new standards of performance.

Recent advances in acousto-optic technology now make possible the
development of rugged, compact optical processors capable of solving
significant problems posed by modern broadband signals and complex
electromagnetic environments. The optical excisors developed [1,2,3]
have demonstrated several orders-of-magnitude improvement in the detection of broadband signals. These optical processors have been made
much smaller and lower in cost than what would be required if one used
an alternate technology.

A significant characteristic of the optical excisor is that it has
an RF (radio-frequency) signal input and and RF signal output
(Fig. 5.1). The excisor takes the broadband signal input and continuously forms the complex spectrum of the signal as a spatial distribution of light. By using apertures and/or spatial modulators, the undesired portions of the spectrum can be blocked. The optical excisor
then continuously reconstructs the broadband output signal from the
remaining portions of the spectrum. If one does not block any portions of the spectrum, the optical excisor continuously reconstructs
an exact replica of the original time-domain input signal.

[†]Current affiliation: ESL Incorporated, Sunnyvale, California

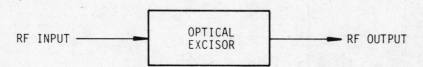

Figure 5.1 An optical excisor (1) takes a broadband RF input from an antenna, preamplifier, or downconverter; (2) forms the spectrum of the input signal; (3) removes undesired portions of the spectrum; and (4) reconstructs the spectrum into a broadband time-domain waveform to produce an RF output. The RF output can then directly feed a spectrum analyzer, correlator, or conventional receiver.

It should be noted that the optical excisor is a predetection signal processor, and it has a continuous and coherent output suitable as the input to detectors such as spectrum analyzers, correlators, and superheterodyne or crystal video receivers. For example, an optical excisor having a filter resolution of only 0.5 MHz has been used to remove interference from signals that are subsequently analyzed to a resolution of 0.1 Hz.

Alternate technologies have been evaluated for performing the excision of narrowband signals, and none show sufficient promise to compete effectively with the performance capabilities of an optical excisor. Although digital excisors have been developed, the maximum bandwidth for reasonable size systems is less than 50 MHz, even for digital circuits forecast to be available within the next decade. Surface acoustic wave (SAW) processors have been analyzed, and the predicted performance is not fully satisfactory due to a lack of broadband phase coherence and difficulties in matching a large number of SAW devices for continuous I and Q channel processing. Transversal filters constructed from charge-coupled devices (CCDs) can be very compact and economical, but they currently lack the speed and accuracy to process wideband signals with sufficient resolution.

It should also be noted that the digital, SAW (chirp), and CCD (chirp) approaches to excision require time framing of the input signal. When the central lobe of a narrowband interference signal is excised in the frequency domain, the remaining sidelobe energy is converted to an undesirable broadband signal [4] for these time-framing excisors. This spectral broadening of narrowband interference can have degrading effects on the detection of low-level, broadband signals. This spectral broadening does not occur in the optical excisor because it utilizes a continuous, sliding transform rather than a time-framed transform.

The optical excisor has the inherent ability to automatically adapt to changes in the signal spectrum. If a narrowband interference signal appears in the spectrum, its high-power spectral density can permit a device within the optical excisor to automatically attenuate only that portion of the spectrum while leaving the remaining portions relatively unaffected.

Section 5.2 is an overall description of a generalized optical excisor and is intended to give an intuitive insight to the optical excision technique. Section 5.3 presents a mathematical description of the optical excisor and shows the results of computer model testing of the analytical description. Section 5.4 gives experimental verification of the processor transfer function and shows laboratory results of narrowband interference rejection using optical excision.

5.2 PROCESSOR DESCRIPTION

The optical excisor continuously forms the spectrum of a broadband electrical signal and reconstructs from that spectrum an exact replica of the input signal. The important feature of this process is that the spectrum is spatially distributed and is available for editing or removing undesired portions of the spectrum. A typical example is to excise narrowband interference from broadband signals.

A general description of an optical excisor can be based on the arrangement shown in Fig. 5.2. The electrical input signal $s(t)$ can be nearly an octave in bandwidth and is typically derived from a broadband antenna, downconverter, and amplifiers. This signal excites an electrical-to-acoustical transducer in the acousto-optic modulator. The acoustical signal travels down the modulator and is absorbed at the end opposite the transducer. The acousto-optic modulator may be of the bulk-wave [1,2,3] or surface-acoustic-wave [8] variety.

When the modulator is illuminated with spatially coherent light, the acoustical signal $s(t,z)$ modulates the phase of the light passing through the acousto-optic modulator. The resulting spatial phase distribution can be considered equivalent to a superposition of plane waves of various phases and amplitudes. By using a lens to focus the various diffracted plane waves, each wave can be separated, and the amplitude and phase of each spectral component of the original input signal can be measured. As described so far, the optical excisor appears similar to a conventional Bragg cell spectrum analyzer.

In addition to diffracting the plane waves in accordance to the spectrum of the input signal, the acousto-optic modulator also Doppler-shifts the diffracted plane waves. The amount of Doppler shift is exactly equal to the frequency of the input signal, and therefore if the amount of Doppler shift can be measured, the frequency of the input signal can be determined.

A straightforward technique for measuring an optical Doppler shift is to add some unshifted light from the optical source and square-law-detect the sum signal (i.e., optical heterodyne detection). The resulting beat signal frequency will be equal to the frequency difference be-

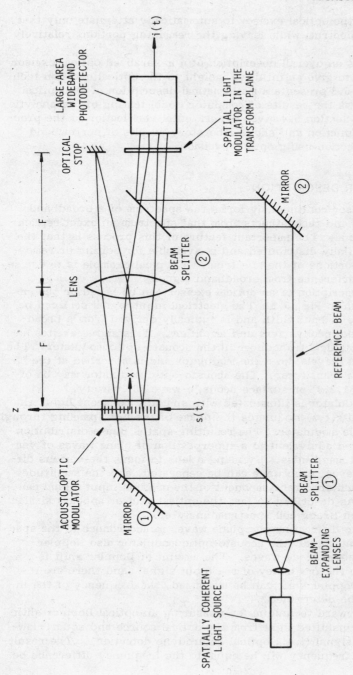

Figure 5.2 Optical layout. The electrical input s(t) travels through the acousto-optic modulator and is coherently illuminated by a spatially coherent light source such as a laser. The light diffracted by the acoustical signal is brought to a focus by the lens and forms the spectrum of the signal on a spatial light modulator. By selectively passing only the desired portions of the spectrum, interference signals can be rejected. By coherently illuminating the photodetector with the remaining spectrum and an optical reference beam, the photomixing and signal summing by the detector reconstructs the time-domain waveform of the desired portions of the input signal and provides a coherent continuous output i(t).

tween the two optical signals and hence be equal to the amount of Doppler shift.

In Fig. 5.2 the unshifted reference beam is derived from the spatially coherent optical source by using optical beam splitter 1 (partially reflecting mirror) to send some light to mirror 1, which then reflects the light to the acousto-optic modulator. The light transmitted by the beam splitter is reflected by mirror 2 up to beam splitter 2. The second beam splitter reflects some of the reference beam to the large-area, wideband photodetector and passes some of the light diffracted by the acousto-optic modulator. By carefully adjusting the mirrors and beam splitters, both the reference beam and the diffracted beams appear to come from the same direction and to be added together on the photodetector surface.

For example, if the input signal s(t) is a continuous tone at a frequency of 70 MHz, the light diffracted by the acousto-optic modulator will be Doppler-shifted by 70 MHz, and the lens will focus the light to a small spot on the photodetector surface. The addition of the reference beam will cause this spot to appear to blink on and off at a 70-MHz rate, and hence the electrical signal out of the photodetector will vary at a 70-MHz rate. If the amplitude of the input signal changes by a certain amount, then the amplitude of the light diffracted by the acousto-optic modulator must change by a proportionate amount. This optical amplitude change will result in a proportionate change in the heterodyne component of the output signal i(t). In general (see Sec 5.3) there is a linear relationship between the input signal s(t) and the heterodyne component of the output signal i(t) for weak acousto-optic diffraction.

Since the transfer function between s(t) and i(t) is linear, one can add a second signal at another frequency, and it also will appear at the detector output i(t). As many signals as desired can be superposed, and all will appear at the detector output.

So far, the optical excisor appears to be a complicated way to construct a short circuit. However, each input frequency will be in a different location on the front of the photodetector, and the ability to resolve two closely spaced signals is limited only by the optical quality and apertures of the optics and the acousto-optic modulator. The total number of resolvable frequency cells depends on the time-bandwidth product and optical apodization of the acousto-optic modulator. As an example, a 40-MHz-bandwidth acousto-optic modulator at a center frequency of 70 MHz having a rectangular optical aperture equivalent to 10 μsec of the input signal will produce 400 (the time-bandwidth product) frequency resolution cells, each 100-kHz wide.

If two input signals are sufficiently different in frequency to be resolved in the back focal plane, a spatial light modulator can be placed in this location and turn off either one or both of the input signals. Another technique would be to block the light due to one signal by using an aperture or small wire in the focal plane, thereby passing only the desired signal. By placing a material such as photochromic glass or photodichroic crystal in the focal plane, narrowband signals, because of their relatively high intensity, will be attenuated automatically.

If the reference beam is adjusted to have the same wave-front curvature as the spectrum of the signal, the phase response of the optical excisor can be essentially free of distortion, and broadband signals will be passed coherently. This means that a short pulse at the input will appear as a short pulse at the output. A single pulse is a continuum of frequencies of various amplitudes, and the optical spectrum of the pulse is displayed in the back focal plane, while at the same time there is also an output that is an exact electrical replica of the input pulse.

A broadband signal that has in its spectrum a narrowband interference signal can be placed at the input of the optical excisor, and the narrowband signal will form a small spot of light, while the broadband signal will extend over a relatively large area. By placing a small wire in the focal plane to block the light from the narrowband interference, the strength of the interference can be significantly reduced while only blocking a small portion of the broadband signal. The bigger the wire, the more the interference will be blocked, and therefore the more it will be attenuated at the output $i(t)$. However, a larger wire will also remove more of the broadband signal and perhaps begin to cause significant changes in the broadband output waveform.

The obvious task for the designer of an optical excisor is to optimize the transfer function to achieve a useful amount of attenuation for narrowband signals without removing significant portions of a broadband signal. The following section describes a mathematical model of an optical excisor that shows the relationships among the aperture illumination, the size of the blocking apertures, and the phase tilt of the reference beam. By using these relationships, a design can be developed that can provide several orders of magnitude of attenuation for narrowband signals while only removing a few percent of a broadband signal.

5.3 PROCESSOR TRANSFER FUNCTION

To obtain an understanding of the linear filtering capabilities of the optical processor shown in Fig. 5.2, a simple mathematical model for the processor transfer function has been derived. This model assumes a weak acousto-optic interaction for the acousto-optic (AO) modulator so that the diffracted light amplitude is linearly related to the input signal amplitude $s(t)$. Also, the model assumes that the optical transmission of the transform-plane spatial light modulator is independent of the incident optical intensity. This assumption corresponds to a programmable spatial light modulator. The results for an adaptive spatial light modulator whose optical transmission is a function of the incident optical intensity may be approximately inferred from this analysis. The resulting mathematical description of the processor transfer function has been studied extensively using computer calculations as well as experimental results.

To derive this mathematical model, assume in Fig. 5.2 that the acoustic wave of the AO modulator is propagating in the +z direction and imposes a dielectric modulation ϵ' proportional to $s[t - (z/v)]$. Also assume that the optical beam incident on the AO modulator propagates in the x-z plane with a y polarization and that all spatial variations in the y direction may be ignored. Finally, assume that the incident optical beam propagates through free space at an angle ϕ_i to the x axis such that the diffracted energy of the modulated optical beam is concentrated in the $m = -1$ diffraction order with a negative Doppler shift. With these assumptions, the diffracted optical amplitude E_{-1} in the $m = -1$ diffracted order has a free-space representation which can be described in the plane $x = 0$ as

$$E_{-1}\big|_{x=0} = Cw(z)s_+\left(t - \frac{z}{v}\right)e^{j(2\pi/\lambda)(\sin\,\phi_i)z - j2\pi f_\ell t} \tag{5.1}$$

In this expression, C is a complex constant, $w(z)$ is the spatial apodization of the acousto-optic modulator window, λ is the free-space wavelength of the optical source, and f_ℓ is the time frequency of the optical source. The plus subscript for the signal s_+ is used to signify that the diffracted optical beam has a negative Doppler shift. The analytic signal $s_+[t - (z/v)]$ may be expressed in terms of the Fourier transform $S(f_a)$ of the input signal as

$$s_+\left(t - \frac{z}{v}\right) = \int_{-\infty}^{\infty} S_+(f_a)e^{j2\pi f_a[t-(z/v)]}\, df_a \tag{5.2a}$$

where

$$S_+(f_a) = \begin{cases} S(f_a) & f_a > 0 \\ \frac{1}{2}S(0) & f_a = 0 \\ 0 & f_a < 0 \end{cases} \tag{5.2b}$$

It can be clearly seen that equation (5.1) contains a negative Doppler shift when equation (5.2) is substituted into equation (5.1) to derive

$$E_{-1}\big|_{x=0} = Cw(z)e^{j(2\pi/\lambda)(\sin\,\phi_i)z}$$

$$\times \int_{-\infty}^{\infty} S_+(f_a)e^{-j2\pi f_a(z/v)-j2\pi(f_\ell-f_a)t}\, df_a \tag{5.3}$$

Notice that the optical time frequencies in this expression are given by $f_\ell - f_a$, where $f_a > 0$ so that the Doppler shift is indeed negative.

The signal beam optical amplitude E_{-1} described by equation (5.3) is located in the front focal plane of a lens. In the back focal plane or Fourier transform plane of the lens, the signal beam optical amplitude E_{SF} is described by the spatial Fourier transform [5] of equation (5.3) yielding

$$E_{SF}(z') = \int_{-\infty}^{\infty} (E_{-1}\big|_{x=0}) e^{-j2\pi(z'/\overline{\lambda}F)z} \frac{dz}{\overline{\lambda}F} \qquad (5.4)$$

In this expression, z' is the spatial coordinate in the Fourier transform plane, $\overline{\lambda}$ is the average optical wavelength, and F is the lens focal length. By inserting equation (5.1) into equation (5.4) and substituting the normalized and displaced Fourier transform variable $\gamma = [-(z'/\overline{\lambda}F) + (\sin\phi_i)/\lambda]$, the signal beam optical amplitude E_{SF} in the Fourier transform plane can be expressed as

$$E_{SF}(\gamma) = CW(\gamma) * [vS_+(\gamma v)e^{j2\pi\gamma vt}]e^{-j2\pi f_\ell t} \qquad (5.5)$$

where $W(\gamma)$ is the spatial Fourier transform of the window apodization $w(z)$, while the $*$ symbol denotes convolution over the variable γ. Since the variable γ is proportional to z' or the spatial distance in the lens focal plane, the convolution of equation (5.5) acts to spread each Doppler-shifted, spectral component $vS_+(\gamma v)\exp(j2\pi\gamma vt)$ of the input signal s(t) over a spatial width in the transform plane determined by $W(\gamma)$. The number of spatially resolvable spots in the Fourier transform plan is thus limited by $W(\gamma)$, and it is straightforward to show that the number of spatially resolvable spots is roughly equal to the time-bandwidth product of the apodized acousto-optic modulator.

The signal beam optical amplitude of equation (5.5) is coherently detected by adding an optical reference beam which is typically not Doppler-shifted. The optical reference beam amplitude E_{RF} in the Fourier transform plane is in general a function of spatial position and may also be expressed in terms of the normalized and displaced Fourier transform plane variable γ:

$$E_{RF} = R(\gamma)e^{-j2\pi f_\ell t} \qquad (5.6)$$

Assuming that the spatial light modulator at Fig. 5.2 is located just after the Fourier transform plane, the optical intensity $I(\gamma,t)$ in the Fourier transform plane just before the spatial light modulator may be expressed as

$$I(\gamma,t) = \frac{1}{2}|E_{SF} + E_{RF}|^2 \qquad (5.7)$$

This optical intensity distribution is then passed through the spatial
light modulator located in the Fourier transform plane, and the transmitted optical power is collected by a large-area photodetector as in
Fig. 5.2. If the optical *intensity* transmittance of the spatial light modulator is defined by $A_0(\gamma)$, then the photocurrent i(t) of the large-
area photodetector is given by.

$$i(t) = \int_{-\infty}^{\infty} A_0(\gamma)I(\gamma,t)\ d\gamma \qquad (5.8)$$

It is important to note that $A_0(\gamma)$ is a real-valued intensity transmittance rather than a complex-valued amplitude transmittance. One important consequence of this is that the optical phase distortions of the
spatial light modulator have no effect on the output photocurrent i(t).
Another important consequence is that the filtering dynamic range is
limited by the intensity contrast ratio c of the spatial light modulator
rather than the much smaller amplitude contrast ratio $\sqrt{c}$.

By combining equations (5.5), (5.6), (5.7), and (5.8), the output
photocurrent can be expressed as the sum of three terms:

$$i(t) = i_R + i_S(t) + i_{HET}(t) \qquad (5.9a)$$

where i_R, i_S, and i_{HET} may be written as

$$i_R = \frac{1}{2}\int_{-\infty}^{\infty} A_0(\gamma)\left|R(\gamma)\right|^2\ d\gamma \qquad (5.9b)$$

$$i_S(t) = \frac{1}{2}|C|^2 \int_{-\infty}^{\infty} A_0(\gamma)\left|\int_{-\infty}^{\infty} W\left(\gamma - \frac{f}{v}\right)S_+(\gamma)e^{+j2\pi ft}\ df\right|^2\ d\gamma$$

$$(5.9c)$$

$$i_{HET}(t) = \mathrm{Re}\int_{-\infty}^{\infty}\int_{-\infty}^{\infty} A_0(\gamma)R^*(\gamma)W\left(\gamma - \frac{f}{v}\right)CS_+(f)e^{j2\pi ft}\ d\gamma\ df$$

$$(5.9d)$$

The i_R component of the photocurrent represents the total reference
beam optical power collected by the photodetector. This component
is independent of time. The $i_S(t)$ component of the photocurrent
represents the total diffracted signal beam optical power collected by
the photodetector. One can show [6] that $i_S(t)$ is a low-frequency
term with the majority of its power near dc and whose absolute maximum temporal frequency is less than $f_{max} - f_{min}$, where f_{max} and f_{min}
are the maximum and minimum frequencies of the input signal s(t). The
$i_{HET}(t)$ component of the photocurrent is the desired, linear, RF output of the heterodyne detection process. One can see from equation

(5.9) that each spectral component $S_+(f)$ of the input signal $s(t)$ contributes a temporal frequency component $\exp(j2\pi ft)$ to the output signal $i_{HET}(t)$. This is a linear filter process. To more clearly define the linear filter response, one may rewrite equation (5.9d) as

$$i_{HET}(t) = \text{Re} \int_{-\infty}^{\infty} 2H_+(f)S_+(f)e^{j2\pi ft}\, df \tag{5.10a}$$

where

$$H_+(f) = \frac{1}{2} C\{W(-\gamma) \ast [A_0(\gamma)R^*(\gamma)]\}\Big|_{\gamma=f/v} \tag{5.10b}$$

Equation (5.10a) implies that the filter response for positive frequencies $f > 0$ is defined by $H_+(f)$. From equation (5.10b) one can see that the filter response $H_+(f)$ is basically equal to $A_0(f/v)R^*(f/v)$ convolved with the inverted window transform $W(-f/v)$.

Equation (5.10a) is not quite in the final form of a linear filter response due to the Re operator (real part of) and the restriction to positive frequencies $f > 0$. To clearly express the linear filter response for positive and negative frequencies, one may rewrite equation (5.10a) using the fact that $s(t)$ is real, so that $S(f) = S^*(-f)$. This yields

$$i_{HET}(t) = \int_{-\infty}^{\infty} H(f)S(f)e^{j2\pi ft}\, df \tag{5.11a}$$

where

$$H(f) = \begin{cases} H_+(f) & f \geqslant 0 \\ \\ H_+^*(-f) & f < 0 \end{cases} \tag{5.11b}$$

One can see that the linear frequency response of the optical system from the input signal $s(t)$ to the heterodyne component $i_{HET}(t)$ of the photocurrent is defined by $H(f)$. Furthermore, $H(f) = H^*(-f)$, as is required of real-valued input and output signals.

Since the heterodyne component of the photocurrent is a linear-filtered version of the input signal, the temporal frequencies f of $i_{HET}(t)$ are band-limited to the frequency range $f_{min} < f < f_{max}$. As before, f_{max} and f_{min} are the maximum and minimum frequencies of the input signal $s(t)$. Thus, if the input signal has less than an octave bandwidth so that $f_{max} - f_{min} < f_{min}$, then $i_{HET}(t)$ may be electronically separated from i_R and $i_S(t)$ by the use of a high-pass filter. Typically, a band-pass filter is used at the output instead of a high-pass filter since this minimizes the wideband shot noise and rejects signal harmonics that can be present when multilongitudinal mode lasers are used as the optical source.

The linear filter response characteristics of the optical processor may be best understood by a close examination of $H_+(f)$ from equation (5.10b). The simplest situation occurs with a plane-wave optical reference beam and a "transparent" spatial light modulator so that $R(\gamma) = A_0(\gamma) = 1$. In this case, one may see from equation (5.10b) that

$$H_+(f) = \frac{1}{2} Cw(0) \quad \text{for } R(\gamma) = A_0(\gamma) = 1 \tag{5.12}$$

In other words, the filter response $H(f)$ is constant, independent of frequency, so that the system acts like an electrical short circuit from the input to output. In actual practice, with $R(\gamma) = A_0(\gamma) = 1$, there is a constant time delay from the input $s(t)$ to the output $i_{HET}(t)$ caused by the constant acoustic transit time from the acoustic transducer boundary to the middle of the AO modulator window at $z = 0$.

The next step in complexity is to consider a reference beam amplitude with a linear phase tilt of the form $R(\gamma) = \exp(-j2\pi z_0\gamma)$ and a transparent spatial light modulator with $A_0(\gamma) = 1$. For this case, one may derive the filter response $H_+(f)$ from equation (5.10b) as

$$H_+(f) = w(z_0)e^{j2\pi(z_0/v)f} \quad \text{for } R(\gamma) = e^{-j2\pi z_0\gamma}, \; A_0(\gamma) = 1 \tag{5.13}$$

One can see that the filter response $H_+(f)$ in this case has a linear phase shift versus frequency f. This linear phase shift translates to a constant time delay $t_D = -z_0/v$ so that the system acts like a delay line whose amplitude is proportional to window function $w(z_0) = w(vt_D)$. If the phase tilt parameter z_0 is increased beyond the window width so that $w(z_0) = 0$, then the output signal disappears. One may intuitively understand this variable time delay phenomenon by realizing that a tilted plane-wave optical reference beam $R(\gamma) = \exp(-j2\pi z_0\gamma)$ in the back focal plane of the Fourier transform lens is equivalent to a point optical source reference beam at $z = z_0$ in the front focal plane of the lens. The large-area heterodyne photodetection causes this point source reference beam to produce a *heterodyne sampling* of the diffracted signal beam amplitude in the plane of the AO modulator at the location $z = z_0$. Since different values of $z = z_0$ represent different time delays from the acoustic transducer boundary, the time delay varies with z_0. If z_0 becomes too large, the point source falls outside of the AO modulator window so that $w(z_0) = 0$, and no heterodyne sampling may occur.

More complex filter functions $H_+(f)$ may be obtained by manipulating the intensity transmittance $A_0(\gamma)$ of the spatial light modulator to block or pass various spectral components of the signal. An example of a

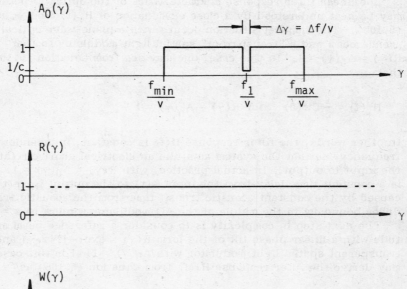

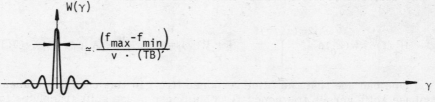

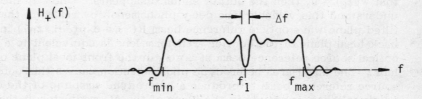

Figure 5.3 Filter response derivation for a simple band-pass filter with a narrow frequency rejection notch.

band-pass filter with a narrow frequency rejection notch is shown in Fig. 5.3. This example assumes a plane-wave optical reference beam with $R(\gamma) = 1$ so that the product $R^*(\gamma)A_0(\gamma) = A_0(\gamma)$. The intensity transmission $A_0(\gamma)$ in Fig. 5.3 is designed to pass the spatial frequen-

cies in the range $f_{min}/v < \gamma < f_{max}/v$ except for a narrow frequency
rejection notch of width $\Delta\gamma = \Delta f/v$ located at $\gamma \doteq f_1/v$. The depth of
the rejection notch in $A_0(\gamma)$ is limited by the intensity contrast ratio
c of the spatial light modulator. The window transform $W(\gamma)$ shown in
Fig. 5.3 has some sidelobe structure caused by the finite truncation
width of the window apodization $w(z)$. By assuming that $f_{max} - f_{min}$
equals the bandwidth of the acousto-optic modulator, the width of the
main lobe of $W(\gamma)$ is narrower than the overall width of the function
$A_0(\gamma)$ by a factor of approximately $(TB)'$, where $(TB)'$ is an effective
time-bandwidth product of the apodized acousto-optic modulator. The
filter response $H_+(f)$ for this case is determined by the convolution
$W(-\gamma) * A_0(\gamma)$ and leads to the result depicted in Fig. 5.3. Note
that the sidelobe structure of $W(\gamma)$ creates ripple in $H_+(f)$ near the
sharp transitions of $A_0(\gamma)$. Also note that for a narrow spatial frequency rejection notch in $A_0(\gamma)$, the depth of the frequency rejection notch in $H_+(f)$ will be limited by the convolution with $W(\gamma)$.
However, if the rejection notch in $A_0(\gamma)$ is very wide, then the depth
of the rejection notch in $H_+(f)$ will be limited to the contrast ratio c
at the spatial light modulator.

It should be apparent that the window transform $W(\gamma)$ plays a key
role in limiting the filter resolution of the optical processor. It is
desirable that the central lobe width of $W(\gamma)$ be as narrow as possible
to maximize the frequency resolution. It is also desirable that the
sidelobes of $W(\gamma)$ be as low as possible to avoid ripple and maximize
excision depth. These two properties are contradictory because the
window apodization $w(z)$ is limited in width by the AO modulator window. There must be a compromise between central lobe width and
ripple by controlling the window apodization $w(z)$.

If the optical source is a laser with a single, near gaussian transverse spatial mode, then the window apodization $w(z)$ may be expressed
approximately as a truncated gaussian of the form

$$w(z) = \frac{1}{\pi^{1/4}G^{1/2}}e^{-(1/2)(z/Gz_1)^2}\;\mathrm{rect}\left(\frac{z}{z_1}\right) \qquad (5.14)$$

This expression assumes that the full AO modulator window is of width
z_1 in the z direction. The gaussian width parameter G may be controlled by varying the focal lengths of the collimation optics. Plots
of $w(z)$ for several values of G are shown in Fig. 5.4.

From Fig. 5.4, one can see that values of G greater than 2.0 create
approximately rectangular window apodizations so that $W(\gamma)$ is proportional to $\mathrm{sinc}(z_1\gamma)$. For G less than roughly 0.25, the window apodization is approximately gaussian and provides a much lower sidelobe
window transform $W(\gamma)$ with a wider central lobe width than produced
by rectangular apodization. A compromise between ripple and the
central lobe width (i.e., filter resolution) can be obtained by controlling G.

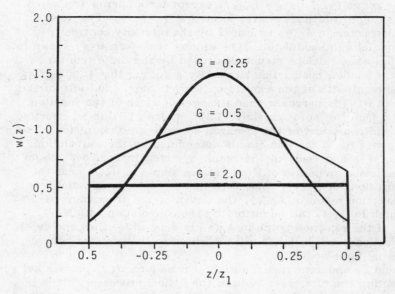

Figure 5.4 Truncated gaussian window apodization w(z) for several
values of the width parameter G. (From Ref. 6.)

Finally, it should be noted that the form of equation (5.14) for the
window apodization has the property that the integral of $|w(z)|^2$ is
constant, independent of G, if the rectangular truncation is ignored.
This is in correspondence with a fixed amount of optical power incident
on the acousto-optic modulator, independent of the focal lengths of the
collimation optics. As G is increased, more signal beam light is wasted,
and the amplitude of w(z) at z = 0 drops, thereby decreasing the amplitude of the detected output signal for a plane-wave reference beam.

A few general comments regarding the complex phase of the filter
response $H_+(f)$ from equation (5.10b) can also be made. Assuming
that the window apodization w(z) is an even function, both $W(-\gamma)$ and
$A_0(\gamma)$ are real functions. This implies that any variations in the
complex phase of $H_+(f)$ can only be created by spatial variations in the
complex phase of the reference beam amplitude $R(\gamma)$.

Suppose that the optical reference beam is a plane wave with $R(\gamma) =$
C_2, where C_2 is a complex constant. Then the phase of $H_+(f)$ from
equation (5.10b) is equal to the phase of the complex product $C_1 C_2$.
In other words, the phase of $H_+(f)$ is constant, independent of its
magnitude or the frequency f. Thus, by manipulating the intensity
transmission $A_0(\gamma)$ of the spatial light modulator, narrow band-pass
or band-stop filters can be created with no phase dispersion or distortion in the filter response H(f). This is impossible with conventional

electrical filtering elements (L, C, R) which have causal filter responses. The acousto-optic processor can effectively create noncausal filter responses in a manner similar to a tapped transversal filter whose tap weights are symmetric about a fixed time delay.

More general phase variations for the optical reference beam amplitude $R(\gamma)$ may also be considered. Complex phase variations in $R(\gamma)$ create similar phase variations in the frequency response $H_+(\gamma)$. This property was utilized by Whitman et al. [7] to develop a dispersive (i.e., chirp) type of filter response using a curved-wave-front reference beam formed with a lens.

Unfortunately, the phase modulation capability of the reference beam can create undesirable phase modulation of the output signal due to microphonic vibrations of the Mach-Zehnder interferometer of Fig. 5.2. These microphonic vibrations modulate the phase of the output signal *carrier* but have no effect on the group delay from the input signal to the output signal. In many applications, the phase of the signal carrier frequency is unimportant. In any event, this carrier phase modulation can be minimized by using a well-designed interferometer structure.

5.4 COMPUTER RESULTS

A computer program was developed for calculating the filter response $H(f)$ for optical excision applications. The most important filter parameters for this program are shown in Table 5.1. As in the previous discussion, the window apodization was assumed to be a truncated gaussian of width z_1 as in equation (5.14). A plane-wave optical reference beam with a normalized phase tilt parameter z_0/z_1 was also assumed. The spatial light modulator was assumed to be programmable with an intensity transmittance $A_0(\gamma)$ similar to that of Fig. 5.3 with excision

Table 5.1 Filter Parameters

TB	Time-bandwidth product of the full, unapodized AO modulator
G	Gaussian width parameter for the window apodization
z_0/z_1	Normalized phase tilt parameter for the optical reference beam
$z_1 \Delta\gamma$	Normalized frequency width of the excision notch(es) in the spatial light modulator transmittance function $A_0(\gamma)$
c	Contrast ratio of the spatial light modulator

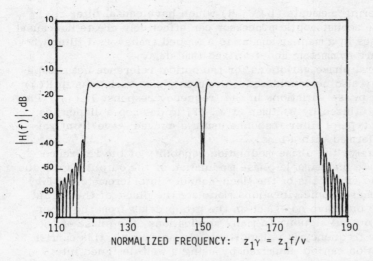

Figure 5.5 Filter magnitude response: TB = 64, $z_0/z_1 = 0$, $z_1 \Delta \gamma = 1.5$, $c = \infty$. (From Ref. 6.)

notches of normalized frequency width $z_1 \Delta \gamma = z_1 \Delta f/v$. Note that an excision notch width of $z_1 \Delta \gamma = 1.0$ is equal to the width between the nulls of a window transform $W(\gamma) \simeq \text{sinc}(z_1\gamma)$ obtained with a rectangular window apodization $w(z)$. The total number of adjacent excision notches of width $z_1 \Delta \gamma$ which can fit in the total bandwidth of the AO modulator is given by $TB/(z_1 \Delta \gamma)$, where TB is the time-bandwidth product of the AO modulator.

   For all the computer-generated filter response examples that follow, the time-bandwidth product TB is set to 64, while the contrast ratio c is assumed to infinite. The infinite contrast ratio is a valid approximation for most cases since the filter response magnitude is typically dominated by the sidelobe structure of $W(\gamma)$ for reasonable contrast ratios c of 100 or more.

   Figure 5.5 shows an example of the filter response obtained with rectangular apodization (G = 2.0), no phase tilt of the reference beam ($z_0/z_1 = 0.0$), and an excision notch of width $z_1 \Delta \gamma = 1.5$ located near the center of the passband. Notice that there is a significant amount of ripple or ringing in the filter magnitude response near its transitions. This is caused by the high sidelobe content of the window transform $W(\gamma) \simeq \text{sinc}(z_1\gamma)$ obtained with the rectangular window apodization. For window apodizations which are more gaussian in shape, this ringing disappears, and the filter attenuation of the passband is much greater.

   An expanded view of the filter excision notch of Fig. 5.5 is shown in Fig. 5.6. The "bump" in the middle of this excision notch is created

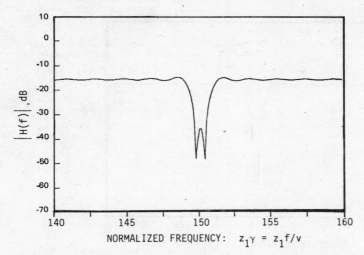

Figure 5.6 Filter magntidue response, expanded view: TB = 64, $G = 2.0$, $z_0/z_1 = 0$, $z_1 \Delta \gamma = 1.5$, $c = \infty$. (From Ref. 6.)

by the sidelobe content of the window transform $W(\gamma)$. This bump limits the excision depth to approximately 20 dB, which is not very satisfactory. The shape of the excision notch can be manipulated by controlling the parameter triplet $(z_1 \Delta \gamma, G, z_0/z_1)$ to obtain a deeper and more satisfactory excision notch.

For example, the same rectangular apodization $(G = 2.0)$ and phase tilt $(z_0/z_1 = 0.0)$ can be used, but the width of the excision notch is reduced to $z_1 \Delta \gamma = 1.25$. The resultant filter rejection notch is shown in Fig. 5.7. The bump at the bottom of the excision notch has disappeared. At first thought, this selection of the parameter triplet $(z_1 \Delta \gamma, G, z_0/z_1)$ appears optimum in that it provides one of the narrowest possible excision notches, as provided by rectangular apodization, while simultaneously providing large excision depth. However, there is a serious drawback to this approach for selecting $(z_1 \Delta \gamma, G, z_0/z_1)$ because the rectangular apodization causes poor rejection of interference over a wider bandwidth.

An example of a wider-bandwidth excision notch is shown in Fig. 5.8 for rectangular apodization, no phase tilt, and a notch width of $z_1 \Delta \gamma = 5.625$. The ripple of the window transform limits the amount of guaranteed signal rejection to 20 to 25 dB. By changing the window apodization to be slightly gaussian with $G = 0.35$, a much better signal rejection with wider notches can be obtained, as illustrated in Fig. 5.9. Here the excision depth to the top of the bumps is approximately 37 dB, a significant improvement. The lower sidelobes of $W(\gamma)$ with the more gaussian apodization provide this improvement.

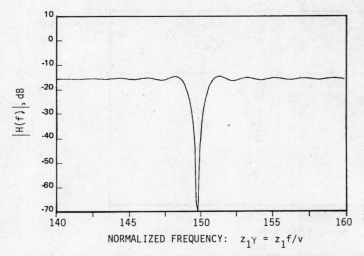

Figure 5.7 Filter magnitude response, expanded view: TB = 64, G = 2.0, $z_0/z_1 = 0$, $z_1 \Delta\gamma = 1.25$, c = ∞.

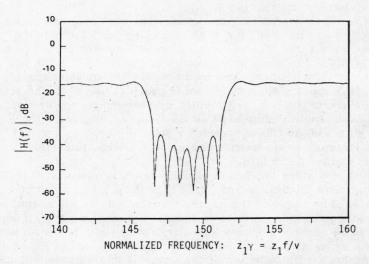

Figure 5.8 Filter magnitude response, expanded view: TB = 64, G = 2.0, $z_0/z_1 = -$, $z_1 \Delta\gamma = 5.625$, c = ∞.

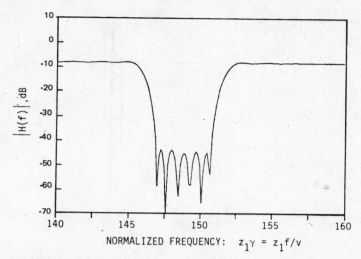

Figure 5.9 Filter magnitude response, expanded view: $TB = 64$, $B = 0.35$, $z_0/z_1 = 0$, $z_1 \Delta \gamma = 5.625$, $c = \infty$.

While the gaussian apodization decreases sidelobe problems, it has the drawback of less resolution than can be obtained with rectangular apodization. This is evident from the excision notch of Fig. 5.10, which is obtained with a gaussian apodization of $G = 0.35$ and no phase tilt. The excision notch width of $z_1 \Delta \gamma = 1.875$ for Fig. 5.10 is much wider than the excision notch width of $z_1 \Delta \gamma = 1.25$ for Fig. 5.7, yet the excision depth is less. This gaussian apodization requires a much wider notch to create a null in the filter response than does rectangular apodization. This general rule always holds when the phase tilt parameter z_0/z_1 is zero.

When the phase tilt parameter z_0/z_1 is not restricted to be zero, the above rule is not always satisfied so that low-sidelobe gaussian apodization can be used simultaneously obtaining deep excision with very narrow excision notches. This is in apparent defiance of conventional filtering theory. An example of this effect is shown in Fig. 5.11 for a strongly gaussian window apodization with $G = 0.20$, a phase tilt of $z_0/z_1 = 0.25$, and an excision notch of width $z_1 \Delta \gamma = 1.125$. The resulting frequency excision notch contains a null at its center and is much narrower than any notch which can be obtained with rectangular apodization. Unfortunately, this interesting result obtained with this particular choice of the triplet ($z_1 \Delta \gamma$, G, z_0/z_1) does have some drawbacks for realistic excision applications. First, the excision depth of the notch of Fig. 5.11 is extremely sensitive to small variations in the parameters $z_1 \Delta \gamma$, G, and z_0/z_1. For example, changing the phase tilt parameter z_0/z_1 from 0.25 to 0.20 causes the frequency rejection

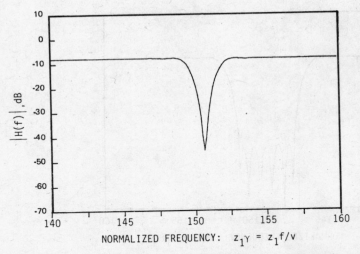

Figure 5.10 Filter magnitude response, expanded view: TB = 64, $G = 0.35$, $z_0/z_1 = 0$, $z_1 \Delta \gamma = 1.875$, $c = \infty$.

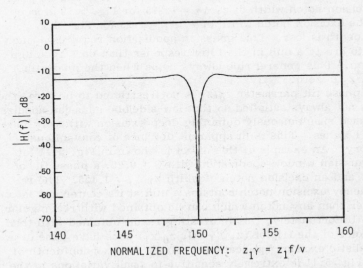

Figure 5.11 Filter magnitude response, expanded view: TB = 64, $G = 0.20$, $z_0/z_1 = 0.25$, $z_1 \Delta \gamma = 1.125$, $c = \infty$.

at the notch center to be reduced to a mere 13 dB as opposed to the 60 dB shown in Fig. 5.11. This extreme sensitivity to variations in the parameters $z_1 \Delta\gamma$, G, and z_0/z_1 suggests that the excision depth in this case would be very sensitive to optical scatter noise so that deep excision for all frequencies could not be guaranteed. Furthermore, moderately wider excision notches in the range $1.25 < z_1 \Delta\gamma < 3.0$ produce very limited excision depth so that interference of moderate bandwidth would require disproportionately wide excision notches for adequate rejection. Finally, this approach is suitable only for a programmable type of spatial light modulator since a spatial light modulator which adapts to the diffracted signal spectrum cannot create such a narrow notch, $z_1 \Delta\gamma = 1.125$, in $A_0(\gamma)$ since the adaptation resolution is determined by the much wider central lobe width of $W(\gamma)$.

In summary, the selections of the parameters $z_1 \Delta\gamma$, G, and z_0/z_1 interact in a fairly complex way to determine the excision performance of the optical processor. For further discussion of the tradeoffs involved in selecting these parameters, the reader is directed to Ref. 6.

5.5 EXPERIMENTAL RESULTS

A number of experimental results have been obtained in the laboratory to verify the linear filtering capabilities of the optical excisor. These experiments utilized various components in the optical Fourier transform plane to create excision notches. In one set of experiments, thin opaque wires of known diameter were placed in the transform plane to create narrow excision notches. In another set of experiments [1], a PROM[†] spatial light modulator was placed in the transform plane in a fashion which automatically attenuated narrowband interference. The results of other investigators [8] using a programmable lead lanthanum zirconate (PLZT) ceramic spatial light modulator in the transform plane are also briefly discussed.

The wire and PROM experiments utilized a 5-mW HeNe laser for the optical source. For the large-area photodetector, a five-stage photomultiplier tube (Varian VPM 152-D) with a frequency range of dc to 2 GHz was used. Two different acousto-optic modulators were utilized in these experiments. One acousto-optic modulator was an IntraAction AOD-70 which has a time-bandwidth product of 400 and a frequency range of 50 to 90 MHz. The other acousto-optic modulator was an Andersen Laboratories BD-125 which has a time-bandwidth product of 125 and a frequency range of 28 to 52 MHz. Both of these modulators use glass as the acousto-optic medium.

The first experiment utilized the IntraAction AO modulator with a thin bare copper wire in the transform plane. The copper wire acts

---

[†]Pockel's Readout Optical Modulator is produced by Itek Corporation.

to block a portion of the diffracted signal spectrum, thereby creating
an excision notch. The filter magnitude response as a function of frequency was then measured using a network analyzer. For this experiment, the filter parameters of Table 5.1 were adjusted to match
the filter parameters of the computer plots shown in Fig. 5.5 and 5.6
To do this, the time-bandwidth product of the acousto-optic modulator
was reduced to 64 by masking the AO modulator window to a time width
of 2.18 μsec and utilizing a Fourier transform plane aperture to limit
the frequency range to 54.5 to 83.8 MHz. The copper wire was chosen
to have an effective diameter of $z_1 \Delta \gamma = 1.5$ and was placed in the approximate middle of the Fourier transform plane aperture at 69.5 MHz.
The illumination of the AO modulator was made rectangular, and the
phase tilt parameter z_0/z_1 was set to zero.

The measured filter magnitude response for this first experiment is
shown in Fig. 5.12. A comparison of (a) and (b) of Fig. 5.12 with the
computer plots of Figs. 5.5 and 5.6, respectively, shows that there is
very close agreement between the experimental results and theory. In
particular, the level of the bump in the excision notch is approximately
20 dB below the passband level for both the experimental and computer
results. The ripple pattern near the passband edges is also closely
matched between the experimental and theoretical results. The main
discernible difference between the experimental and theoretical results
is that the level of the passband for the results of Fig. 5.12(a) is not
quite flat. This effect is caused primarily by the unevenness in the
diffraction efficiency of the acousto-optic modulator as a function of
frequency.

The above experiment shows very close correspondence between
theory and practice when a shallow excision notch is constructed.
When attempting to construct much deeper excision notches, the excision depth becomes limited by optical scatter noise. As an example
of this optical scatter limit, a second experiment was performed which
utilized a strongly gaussian window apodization (G = 0.22) with a relatively wide wire ($z_1 \Delta \gamma = 3.83$) in the transform plane. This second
experiment utilized the Andersen Laboratories Bragg cell so that the
window apodization G = 0.22 corresponds to a 1/e amplitude time-
bandwidth product of roughly 79. The measured filter magnitude response for this second experiment is shown in Fig. 5.13.

The results of Fig. 5.13 show very little frequency response ripple
due to the low-sidelobe gaussian window apodization, and the excision
notch is very deep, in excess of 40 dB. Furthermore, the excision
depth near the notch center is very jagged and varies from 40 to 48
dB in depth. This jaggedness is believed to be caused by optical scatter. A theoretical calculation based on a window apodization G = 0.22
and notch width $z_1 \Delta \gamma = 3.83$ predicts 50 dB of excision depth at the
notch center.

The discrepancy between theory and practice for the deep excision
notch shown in Fig. 5.13 is primarily due to optical scatter. When much

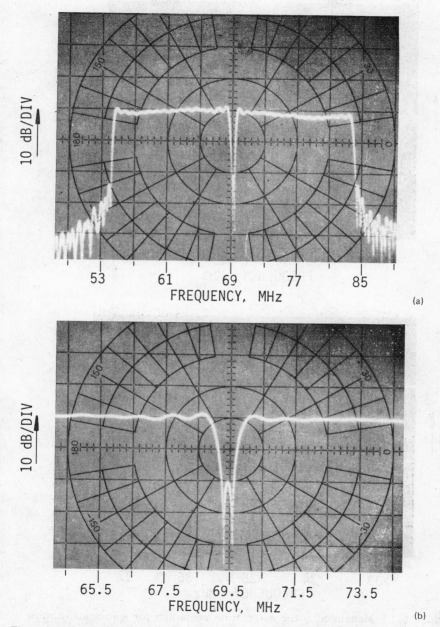

Figure 5.12 Measured filter magnitude response for rectangular window apodization. (From Ref. 6.) (a) Magnitude response. (b) Magnitude response, expanded view.

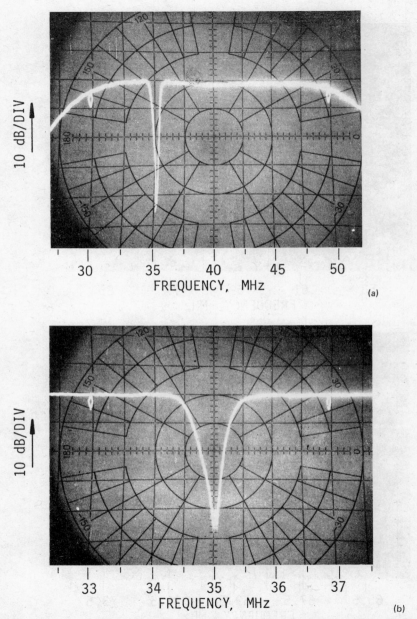

Figure 5.13 Measured filter magnitude response for gaussian window apodization. (a) Magnitude response. (b) Magnitude response, expanded view.

wider wires with $z_1 \Delta\gamma \gg 3.83$ were placed in the Fourier transform
plane, the excision depth remained at approximately 40 dB. It is believed that excision depths much greater than 40 dB can be attained
with cleaner, lower-scatter lenses. This laboratory demonstration of
40-dB excision depth was performed in a relatively dirty environment
with inexpensive lenses.

In another set of experiments [1], a PROM spatial light modulator
was placed in the transform plane to demonstrate the concept of a self-
adaptive spatial light modulator which automatically attenuates intense,
narrowband interference. The PROM is intended to be utilized as an
image storage device which is written on with blue light and read out
with red light. However, the experiments reported here utilized the
red HeNe light in the Fourier transform plane of the optical excisor
for both the writing and reading functions. For this mode, a strong
narrowband interference signal will create a bright red spot in the
transform plane which effectively acts to write a *dark spot* on the
PROM. This dark spot in turn effectively prevents the bright optical
spot corresponding to the narrowband interference from being passed
to the photodetector. Thus the strong narrowband interference signal
effectively attenuates itself. However, weak broadband signals are
not attenuated because they are below the nonlinear threshold for writing on the PROM.

The PROM experiments utilized the Andersen Laboratories Bragg cell
with strongly gaussian window apodization G = 0.22. The optical intensity spot in the Fourier transform plane created by a single-frequency input with diffraction efficiency DE was given approximately
by

$$I(z',y) = \left(\frac{DE}{100\%}\right)(0.56)e^{-(y/0.1)^2 - [(z'-z_0)/0.0027]^2} \text{ W/cm}^2 \qquad (5.15)$$

In this expression, the distances z' and y are in centimeters. For the
input signal frequency range of $\Delta f = 24$ MHz for the input signal, the
deflection range in the Fourier transform plane was given by $\Delta z' = 0.46$
cm.

With the above-described beam shapes and the PROM in the Fourier
transform plane, a single-frequency signal was applied to the input
of the optical excisor. The PROM was then erased using a flash from
a UV lamp. Approximately 2 sec after this erasure, the RF power level
from the photodetector was measured and compared against the input
RF power level. The 2 sec of time after the PROM erasure allowed the
PROM ample time to adapt to intense signal levels. The measured output RF power level versus the input RF power level for this experiment
is plotted in Fig. 5.14.

From Fig. 5.14 it can be seen that the PROM has a nonlinear *clipping*
characteristic which attenuates intense signals, while weaker signals

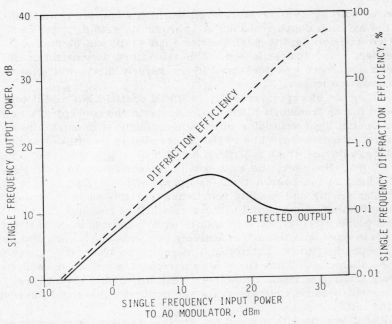

Figure 5.14 Experimental data for PROM clipping characteristics with a single-frequency input. (From Ref. 1.)

are passed unaffected. In fact, a strong signal can be attenuated below the level of a weak signal. Broadband signals should be relatively unattenuated compared to narrowband signals because their power spectrum distribution in the optical Fourier transform plane will be below the clipping threshold of the PROM.

To graphically demonstrate the automatic excision capabilities of the PROM-based excisor, a strong continuous-wave (CW) interference signal with some weak broadband noise was added to a broadband, pulsed RF signal. This combined signal was used as the input to the optical excisor. The weak broadband noise simulates the receiver front-end noise of a communications or radar system. The CW interference acts as a jamming signal which prevents examination of the broadband signal in any detail. The PROM-based excisor acts to reject the CW interference, leaving only the pulsed signal and background noise as the optical processor output. The results of this experiment are shown in Fig. 5.15 in the time domain via a scope and in the frequency domain via a spectrum analyzer.

Figures 5.15(a) and (b) show the combined input signal in the time and frequency domains, respectively. The input time waveform of Figure 5.15(a) was obtained by carefully adjusting the trigger level of the scope to trigger off the pulsed signal. From Fig. 5.15(a), it is difficult to ascertain the exact modulation of the pulsed waveform due to the narrowband interference. From the input spectrum in Fig. 5.15(b), it is seen that the narrowband interference signal is approximately 20 dB above the peak of the pulse spectrum. The pulse spectrum is centered at 40 MHz, and only the central lobe of the pulse spectrum is visible above the broadband noise. The combined input spectrum is filtered to a bandwidth of 25 MHz using a bandpass electronic filter.

The output of the PROM-based optical excisor is shown in Figs. 5.15(c) and (d) in the time and frequency domains, respectively. The photographs for Figs. 5.15(c) and (d) were taken approximately 2 sec after the PROM erasure flash, and Fig. 5.15(d) shows that the narrowband interference is roughly 8 dB below the peak of the pulse spectrum. Thus the PROM-based excisor has attenuated the narrowband signal by 28 dB relative to the broadband pulsed signal. The output time-domain waveform of Fig. 5.15(c) clearly shows that the braodband signal is a simple RF pulse of 200 nsec duration. Since the input broadband signal was also an RF pulse of 200 nsec duration, the clearly constructed pulse at the processor output demonstrates that the optical processor does not introduce severe phase distortion over relatively wide bandwidths. The slight amount of magnitude distortion shown in the spectrum of Fig. 5.15(d) is attributable to dust on the PROM surface and could be alleviated by using a cleaner PROM.

While the PROM-based optical excisor demonstrated encouraging results, its utility in a practical system is limited by the fact that the PROM is an image storage device which must be cycled through an erase phase followed by a read/write phase. Variations of the PROM [1] are being considered which will avoid the image storage properties of the current PROM so that time-framing and cycling problems may be avoided.

Other types of optical spatial light modulators have also been examined in the Fourier transform plane of the optical excisor. One example is a programmable PLZT ceramic spatial light modulator [8] which will allow the filter magnitude response to be controlled by electronic means. By applying a transverse electric field to the PLZT ceramic, the polarization of a transmitted optical beam can be rotated. By placing the PLZT ceramic between crossed optical polarizers, the intensity of the transmittal optical beam can be electronically controlled. Spatial control of the transmitted optical intensity can be obtained by having separately addressable electrodes across the aperture of the PLZT ceramic.

Such a PLZT ceramic spatial light modulator was constructed and consisted of 300 individually addressable elements, each of width 0.25 mm. This spatial modulator was placed in an optical excisor which used a surface-acoustic-wave device for the acousto-optic modulator. Gaussian window apodization was used for illumination of the SAW device,

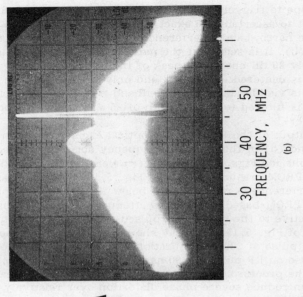

10 dB/DIV →

FREQUENCY, MHz

(b)

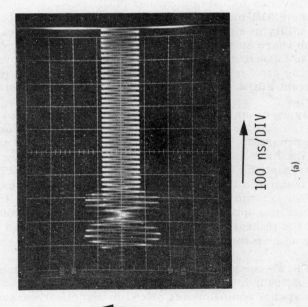

VOLTS →

100 ns/DIV

(a)

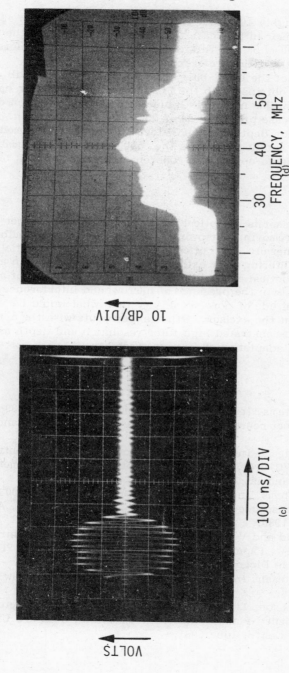

Figure 5.15 Excision of narrowband interference from a broadband pulsed signal using a PROM-based excisor. (From Ref. 1.)

resulting in roughly 100 resolvable spots over a bandwidth of 30 MHz. The optical excisor in this case was configured such that the transformed signal beam passed through the PLZT modulator before being combined with the optical reference team.

The results of the PLZT-based excisor showed that 18 dB of excision could be obtained with the PLZT modulator, while an opaque wire having a similar notch width obtained 23 dB of excision depth. Theory in this case predicted 24 or 25 dB of excision depth. The moderate excision depth of the PLZT ceramic spatial light modulator is encouraging and demonstrates the concept of a programmable, linear filter using acousto-optics with coherent detection.

5.6 SUMMARY

The optical excisor is an optical processor developed to meet the requirement for removing narrowband interference from broadband signals. More generally, the optical excisor offers the potential of real-time adaptive filtering over extremely wide bandwidths. In actual experiments, an optical excisor has permitted the detection of spread spectrum signals in the presence of narrowband interference with two orders of magnitude of more sensitivity than what would have been possible without the excisor. Other experiments with the optical excisor have demonstrated high filter resolution and depth as well as filter response adaptation and programmability.

REFERENCES

1. Probe Systems, Inc., Optical Clippers, Contract N00039-79-C-0141. Defense Documentation Center, Cameron Station, Alexandria, Va., May 1980.
2. Probe Systems, Inc., Holographic Local Oscillator, Contract N00039-79-C-0141, Defense Documentation Center, Cameron Station, Alexandria, Va., May 1980.
3. Probe Systems, Inc., Electronic Clipper, Contract N00039-79-C-0141, Defense Documentation Center, Cameron Station, Alexandria, Va., May 1980.
4. G. W. Judd and V. H. Estrick, Applications of SAW chirp filters—an overview, Paper 239-33, presented at the Annual SPIE Symposium, San Diego, Calif., July 28-Aug. 1, 1980.
5. J. W. Goodman, *Introduction to Fourier Optics*, McGraw-Hill, New York, 1968.
6. J. E. Erickson, Linear Acousto-Optic Filtering with Heterodyne and Frequency-Plane Control, Ph.D. thesis, Stanford University, Stanford, Calif., June 1981.

7. R. Whitman, A. Korpel, and S. Lotsoff, Applications of acoustic Bragg diffraction to optical processing techniques, in *Proceedings of the Symposium on Modern Optics*, Polytechnic Press, New York, pp. 243-256, 1976.

8. J. N. Lee, N. J. Berg, M. W. Casseday, and P. S. Brody, High-speed adaptive filtering and reconstruction of broadband signals using acousto-optic techniques, in *1980 IEEE Ultrasonics Symposium Proceedings* (80CH1602-2), p. 488 (1980).

6

Acousto-Optic Tunable Filters

I. C. CHANG / ITEK Corporation, Applied Technology Division, Sunnyvale, California

This chapter describes an acousto-optic device that is capable of performing spectrum analysis of optical signals. The device, called an acousto-optic tunable filter (AOTF), is an electronically tuned optical filter that operates on the principle of acousto-optic diffraction in an anisotropic medium. The spectral bandpass of the filter can be rapidly tuned over large spectral regions simply by changing the frequency of the applied RF signal. Some of the salient features of the AOTF include a large angular aperture while maintaining high spectral resolution, electronic tuning with a fast scan rate, a wide tuning range without secondary passbands, and the capability of operating in sequential, random-access, and multiwavelength modes. In addition, the all-solid-state AOTF is rugged and has no moving parts. These features make the AOTF attractive for a variety of applications.

The first AOTF was proposed by Harris and Wallace [1] utilizing collinear acousto-optic interactions. Later, the AOTF concept was enlarged by Chang [2] in a noncollinear interaction configuration. The theory and practice of the AOTF have been previously discussed [3].

The operating physical principle of the AOTF will first be discussed, followed by an analysis of its device characteristics and a short summary of its applications.

6.1 PRINCIPLE OF OPERATION

The principle of acousto-optic diffraction is similar to that of a transmission diffraction grating. As such, it is possible to use an acousto-optic Bragg cell as the dispersive element in an optical spectrometer. One obvious advantage of the *acousto-optic* grating spectrometer is that the grating constant (which is equal to the acoustic wavelength) can be electronically changed, thus providing a capability of rapidly scanning the spectral region. The spectral resolution (at optical wave-length λ) of the spectrometer is defined by

$$R = \frac{\lambda}{\Delta \lambda} \qquad (6.1)$$

where $\Delta \lambda$ is the difference in wavelength between two equal-intensity spectrum lines that are just resolved. Consider the Bragg cell as a traveling wave grating; the spectral resolution is then equal to the number of acoustic wavelengths across the optical aperture. Referring to Fig. 6.1, which shows a two-dimensional model of an acousto-optic Bragg cell, the maximum spectral resolution is given by [3]

$$R = \left(\frac{D}{\Lambda}\right) \cos \psi = f_a \left(\frac{D}{v_a}\right) \cos \psi \qquad (6.2)$$

where f_a is the acoustic frequency and v_a is the acoustic velocity. Since $(D/v_a) \cos \psi$ is the acoustic transit time across the light beam τ, it follows from equation (6.2) that

$$R = f_a \tau \qquad (6.3)$$

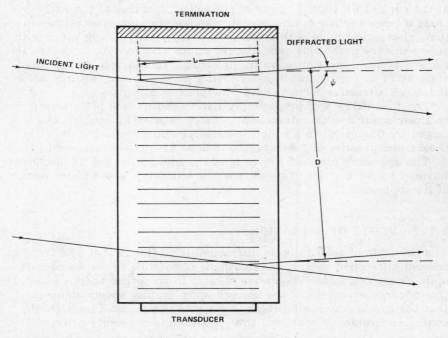

Figure 6.1 Acousto-optic Bragg cell.

To obtain large spectral resolution, the operating acoustic frequency must be sufficiently high. The maximum achievable resolution is thus limited by the acoustic attenuation at the high-frequency end and the spatial constraint of the optical aperture. The preceding results assumed that the light beam is a well-collimated plane wave; otherwise, the resolution will drop sharply from its maximum value. Thus, this type of acousto-optic grating spectrometer has an exceedingly small angular aperture, which in turn limits the throughput of the instrument.

The basis of the acousto-optic grating spectrometer described above is the angular dispersion characteristics of the acousto-optic diffraction. The acousto-optic device is operated as a transverse spatial modulator, or deflector, in which the angular spread of the optical beam is much smaller than that of the acoustic beam; $\delta \psi_o << \delta \psi_a$. To achieve proper spectrometer operation, additional spatial filtering (e.g., aperture stops) must be used. An entirely different approach is to utilize the spatial modulation along the interaction direction (longitudinal modulation) associated with the acousto-optic diffraction. The appropriate geometry in this case is that the angular divergence of the optical beam is much greater than that of the acoustic beam; i.e., $\delta \psi_o >> \delta \psi_a$. The acousto-optic device is operated as a longitudinal spatial modulator, or a spectral filter. The resolving power of the spectral filter is now given by the number of acoustic wavelengths along the interaction lengths; i.e.,

$$R = \left(\frac{L}{\Lambda}\right)\sin \psi \tag{6.4}$$

where L is the interaction length. In contrast to the previous case of the acousto-optic grating (deflector) spectrometer, where the spectral resolution is determined by the optical beam divergence, it is now determined by the interaction bandwidth. High spectral resolution is obtained by increasing the number of longitudinal modulation periods accumulated along the interaction length.

The angular aperture of this type of spectral filter is, in general, proportional to the width of the passband and is quite small. This is best illustrated using wave-vector diagrams. Figure 6.2(a) shows the construction of wave vectors for acousto-optic diffraction in an optically isotropic medium. The wave vectors satisfy the momentum matching condition; i.e.,

$$K_d = K_i + k_a \tag{6.5}$$

where k_a is the acoustic wave vector and K_i and K_d are the wave vectors for the incident and diffracted light, respectively. Notice that a change of the angle of incident light will introduce a momentum mismatch ΔK and a corresponding decrease of diffraction efficiency, resulting in a small angular aperture for the spectral filter.

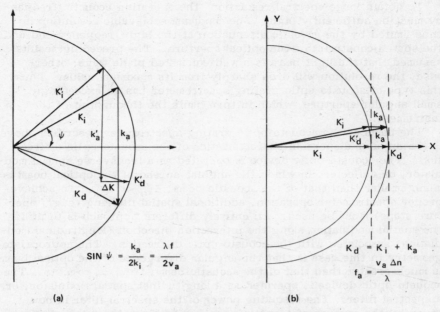

$$\text{SIN } \psi = \frac{k_a}{2k_i} = \frac{\lambda f}{2v_a}$$

$$K_d = K_i + k_a$$

$$f_a = \frac{v_a \, \Delta n}{\lambda}$$

(a)   (b)

Figure 6.2 Wave-vector diagram for acousto-optic interaction.

Dixon [4] analyzed acousto-optic diffraction in an optically anisotropic medium. Figure 6.2(b) describes the birefringent diffraction in
a uniaxial crystal when the wave vectors are normal to the optic axis.
The figure also shows a special case where the interacting acoustic and
optical waves are collinear. For this case, the momentum-matching
condition [equation (6.5)] reduces to

$$\lambda = \frac{v_a \, \Delta n}{f_a} \qquad (6.6)$$

where v_a is the acoustic velocity, $\Delta n = |n_e - n_o|$ is the birefringence,
and n_o and n_e are the refractive indices for the ordinarily and ex-
traordinarily polarized light, respectively.

The collinear acousto-optic interaction was first demonstrated by
Dixon using crystal quartz as the interaction medium. In the experiment, a linearly polarized HeNe laser beam ($\lambda = 633$ nm) incident
to the crystal interacts collinearly with a longitudinal acoustic wave
along the [100] crystalline axis. A significant portion of the incident
light was coupled into the orthogonal polarization as the frequency of
the driving signal approached the value given by equation (6.6).
Separation of the incident and diffracted light was achieved by the use
of a beam-splitting polarizer.

Two years after Dixon reported this work on the collinear acousto-optic interaction, Harris and Wallace [1] published a paper proposing a new type of electronically tunable optical filter utilizing collinear acousto-optic interaction. They analyzed in detail the collinear acousto-optic interaction in a birefringent medium and pointed out that the diffraction of light into its orthogonal polarization occurs only for a small band of optical frequencies centered about the wavelength determined by equation (6.6). By changing the acoustic frequency, it is thus possible to tune the passband of the filter over a wide spectral region. The spectral resolution of the filter is given by equation (6.4) (with $\psi = 90°$), and then by using equation (6.6),

$$R = \frac{L \, \Delta n}{\lambda} \qquad\qquad\qquad (6.7)$$

A more significant feature of this type of electronically tunable filter is that the spectral resolution is maintained over a relatively large angular distribution of incidence light. The large angular aperture characteristic is illustrated in Fig. 6.2(b). Since the tangents to the loci of the light wave vectors are parallel (in a collinear interaction), to a first-order change of incidence angle the momentum-matching condition [equation (6.5)] is still approximately maintained. This forms the principle of collinear acousto-optic tunable filters. Hereafter, the acousto-optic tunable filter (AOTF) will be used to describe spectral filters with large angular aperture based on anisotropic acousto-optic interaction.

The experimental demonstration of the collinear AOTF was described in a series of papers by Harris and co-workers [5-7]. Figure 6.3(a) shows the schematic of a transmission-type collinear AOTF. The filter consists of a birefringent crystal, calcium molybdate, and a pair of polarizers and analyzers. A longitudinal acoustic wave, launched by the piezoelectric transducer, is converted into a shear wave at the prism interface, propagates down the crystalline medium, and is absorbed by the acoustic terminations. The incident light wave passes through the input polarizer. At a given frequency, a small band of optical wavelengths satisfying equation (6.6) is cumulative diffracted into the orthogonal polarization and transmitted through the output analyzer. As the acoustic frequency is changed, the passband wavelength of the AOTF is changed. The tuning curve (i.e., the acoustic frequency-optical wavelength relation) of a $CaMoO_4$ AOTF is shown in Fig. 6.3(b).

The important feature of large angular aperture while maintaining high resolution was also demonstrated with the collinear AOTF [6,7]. The width of the filter passband was found to be relatively insensitive to the angular divergence of the incident light beam until the total external angular aperture reaches the value [1]

$$\Delta \psi = 2n \sqrt{\frac{\lambda}{\Delta n L}} \qquad\qquad\qquad (6.8)$$

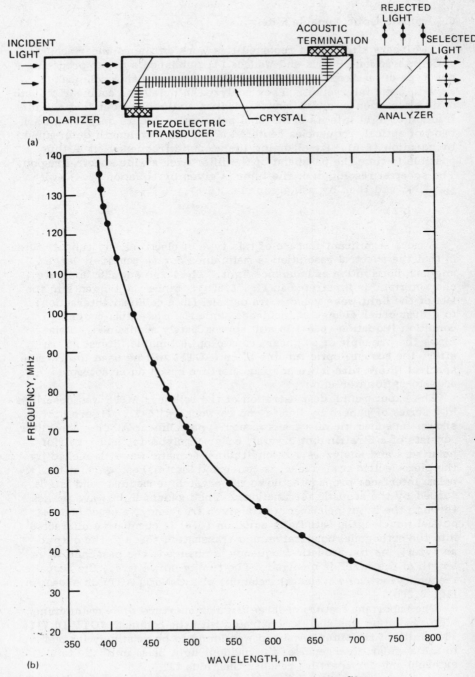

Figure 6.3 Collinear CaMoO$_4$ acousto-optic tunable filter.

144

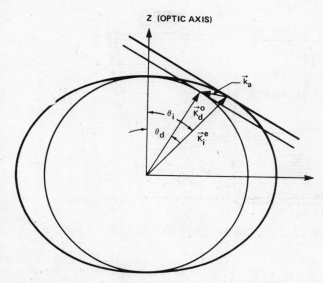

Figure 6.4 Wave-vector diagram for noncollinear acousto-optic filter. (From Ref. 2.)

where n is the refractive index for the incident light wave. In the experiment of the CaMoO$_4$ AOTF [6], a half-power bandwidth of 8 Å was measured at an f/6 aperture. This angular aperture is at least one order of magnitude larger than that of a grating for the same spectral resolution.

In the early work on collinear AOTFs, operation was reported in the visible spectral region using LiNbO$_3$ [5] and CaMoO$_4$ [6,7]. Later development extended the operating wavelength range into the ultraviolet region using crystal quartz [8,9], and into the infrared region using Tl$_3$AsSe$_3$ [10,11].

The collinearity requirement limits the AOTF materials to rather restricted classes of crystals. Some crystals with a large acousto-optic figure of merit (e.g., TeO$_2$) are excluded because of symmetry considerations. To utilize such materials, Chang [2] described a method to obtain a wide-angle filter operation in a noncollinear interacting configuration. The concept of the noncollinear AOTF is based on the compensation of momentum mismatch due to the change of angle of the incident light by the angular change of birefringence. As shown in Fig. 6.4, the acoustic wave vector is chosen so that the tangents to the incident and diffracted light wave vectors' loci are parallel. When the condition of *parallel tangents* is satisfied, the phase-matching relation will be approximately maintained for a light beam having a range of incident angles. This concept of parallel tangents, which implies

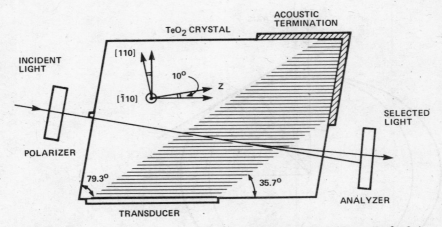

Figure 6.5 Schematic of noncollinear TeO$_2$ AOTF. (From Ref. 2.)

that the rays (i.e., group velocity) for the incident and diffracted light are collinear, is a generalization of the collinear AOTF.

Figure 6.5 shows the schematic of the noncollinear AOTF using TeO$_2$ as the filter medium [2]. The AOTF was tunable from 700 to 450 with a half-power bandwidth of 40 Å at an f/4 aperture. Nearly 100% transmission was obtained with a drive power of about 120 mW. The filtered beam is spatially separated from the incident beam with an angle of about 6°.

Noncollinear AOTFs have also been demonstrated in the ultraviolet [12] and in the infrared regions [11,13,14].

6.2 FILTER CHARACTERISTICS

The various characteristics of AOTFs will be discussed in the following paragraphs. These characteristics include filter tuning relation, bandpass response, spectral resolution and angular aperture, transmission and drive power, out-of-band rejection, and sidelobe suppression. An analysis of the AOTF was given in an earlier paper [15].

6.2.1 Filter Tuning Relation

To derive the device characteristics of AOTFs, one needs to solve the problem of anisotropic acousto-optic diffraction involving a well-collimated acoustic wave and a cone of convergent light beams. One way to accomplish this is to decompose the incident light beam into plane waves and superimpose the results of plane-wave analysis. It is thus useful to first consider the interaction of perfect plane waves in an anisotropic medium.

The acoustic diffraction of light can be viewed as a parametric interaction. A coupled mode analysis of acousto-optic interaction in an anisotropic medium was discussed in a previous paper [15]. Via the elasto-optic effect, an incident optical wave may be coupled into the orthogonally polarized wave. The ratio of the intensities of the diffracted to incident optical waves is [3]

$$H = H_0 \, \text{sinc}^2\left(\frac{\Delta KL}{2\pi}\right) \tag{6.9}$$

where H_0 is the peak transmission, $\text{sinc}(x) = \sin(\pi x)/\pi x$, ΔK is the momentum mismatch, and L is the interaction length. Maximum transmission occurs when the momentum is matched ($\Delta K = 0$). Consider the anisotropic acousto-optic diffraction in a uniaxial crystal. In the constant azimuth plane of acoustic wave propagation, the momentum-matching condition [equation (6.5)] becomes [4,15]

$$\cos(\theta_a - \theta_i) = \frac{n_d}{2n_i}\left[\frac{\lambda}{n_d\Lambda} + \frac{n_d\Lambda}{\lambda}\left(\frac{n_i^2}{n_d^2} - 1\right)\right] \tag{6.10}$$

where θ_i and θ_a are the polar angles of the incident light beam and the acoustic wave, respectively; n_i is the refractive index for the incident optical wave; and n_d is the refractive index for the diffracted wave. Assume that the diffracted light is ordinarily polarized, $n_d = n_o$. It is convenient to define a normalized optical wavelength $a = \lambda/n_o\Lambda$. The angular dependence of the anisotropic acousto-optic diffraction [equation (6.10)] is shown in Fig. 6.6, where the normalized wavelength a is plotted as a function of incident light angle θ_i for a few choices of acoustic angle θ_a (a fractional birefringence of 0.07 in assumed). At the wavelength when the angular variation becomes zero, the acousto-optic diffraction is relatively insensitive to the angular deviations of incident light. This condition, which is referred to as *noncritical momentum matching*, occurs when the tangents to the incident and diffracted optical wave-vector loci are parallel. The acousto-optic diffraction is then applicable for proper AOTF operation. One special solution, shown in Fig. 6.6, is the collinear acousto-optic interaction ($\theta_i = \theta_a = 90°$). For the general case of noncollinear interaction, two solutions of θ_i (one minimum and the other maximum) exist for a selection of θ_a. Near the inflection point where the minimum and maximum approximately coincide, the variation of passband wavelength is zero to second-order changes of θ_i, resulting in extremely large angular aperture.

For most birefringent crystals the fractional birefringence is small; thus, the appropriate choice of θ_i for a given θ_a is approximately independent of the birefringence. The center wavelength of the AOTF passband is then given by [3,15]

$$\lambda = \frac{v_a \Delta n}{f_a}(\sin^4\theta_i + \sin^2 2\theta_i)^{1/2} \tag{6.11}$$

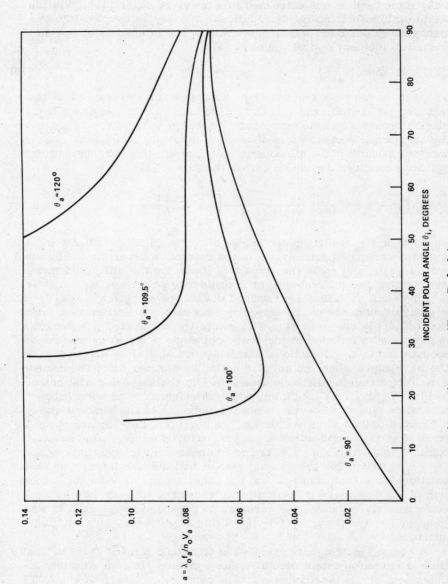

Figure 6.6 A versus θ_i for various θ_a. (From Ref. 3.)

which is the tuning relation of AOTFs for an incident angle θ_i. When $\theta_i = 90°$, it reduces to equation (6.6), the expression for collinear AOTFs.

6.2.2 Bandpass Response

When the noncritical momentum-matching condition is satisfied, the momentum mismatch ΔK is dependent on angular deviation in the second order. Under the assumption that the optical wavelength is smaller than the acoustic wavelength, an approximate expression for ΔK as a function of incident light angular variations ($\alpha_i = \Delta\theta_i$, $\beta_i = \sin\theta_i \, \Delta\phi_i$) is [15]

$$\Delta K = -b \sin^2 \theta_i \left(\frac{\Delta\lambda}{\lambda^2} \right) + \frac{\pi\,\Delta n}{\lambda} (F_\theta \alpha_i^2 + F_\phi \beta_i^2) \tag{6.12}$$

where

$$b = 2\pi \left(\Delta n - \lambda \frac{\partial\,\Delta n}{\partial\lambda} \right)$$

is the dispersive constant and

$$F_\theta = 2\cos^2\theta_i - \sin^2\theta_i \qquad F_\phi = 2\cos^2\theta_i + \sin^2\theta_i \tag{6.13}$$

Since b is positive, equation (6.12) shows that a deviation of azimuth angle $\Delta\phi_i$ shifts the filter passband toward a longer wavelength, while the effect of deviation of polar angle $\Delta\theta_i$ depends on the sign of F_θ; when $F_\theta > 0$, the passband shifts to a longer wavelength, and when $F_\theta < 0$, the passband shifts toward a short wavelength.

The plane-wave analysis described above can now be applied to an AOTF geometry involving an incident cone of light. The filter transmission for normalized light distribution $I(\alpha_i,\beta_i)$ is obtained by integrating the plane-wave transmission [equation (6.9)] over the solid angle aperture

$$T(\Delta\lambda) = \int_{\alpha_i,\beta_i} H(\Delta\lambda, \alpha_i, \beta_i) I(\alpha_i,\beta_i) \, d\alpha_i \, d\beta_i \tag{6.14}$$

Figure 6.7 plots the bandpass response of a noncollinear TeO_2 AOTF, assuming a uniformly divergent incident light beam (f/2.5). The measured results (shown in the figure as circles) were obtained at 3.39 μm.

6.2.3 Resolution and Angular Aperture

Approximate expressions for the spectral resolution and angular aperture can be obtained from equation (6.12). For collimated incident

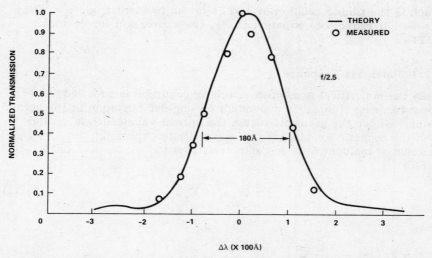

Figure 6.7 Spectral bandpass of the TeO_2 AOTF. (From Ref. 13.)

light, the half-peak transmission occurs when $\Delta KL \simeq 0.9\pi$. The full width at half maximum (FWHM) of the AOTF passband is then

$$\Delta\lambda = \frac{1.8\pi\lambda^2}{bL\sin^2\theta_i} \tag{6.15}$$

The internal half-angular aperture of the AOTF is approximately given by $(\lambda/L\,\Delta n\,|F_\theta|)^{1/2}$ and $(\lambda/L\,\Delta n\,|F_\phi|)^{1/2}$ for a uniformly divergent beam in the polar and azimuth plane, respectively. The total solid angle external to the filter medium is

$$\Delta\Omega \simeq \frac{n^2\pi(\lambda/\Delta n\,L)}{\sqrt{|F_\theta F_\phi|}} \tag{6.16}$$

Equations (6.15) and (6.16) establish the tradeoff relationship between resolving power and solid angle of AOTFs:

$$\frac{\lambda}{\Delta\lambda}\,\Delta\Omega \simeq \frac{n^2\pi}{\sqrt{|F_\theta F_\phi|}} \tag{6.17}$$

It is instructive to compare the performance of AOTFs and diffraction gratings. Consider, for example, a $CaMoO_4$ AOTF (n = 2) with a resolving power of 1000. The solid angle estimated from equation (6.16) is about 1.3×10^{-2} sr. Assuming equal aperture size, the entendue of the AOTF is greater than a grating with comparable resolution by one to two orders of magnitude.

6.2.4 Transmission and Drive Power

An important parameter in the design of an AOTF is the required drive power. The peak transmission of an AOTF is given by [13]

$$T_0 = \sin^2 \left(\frac{\pi^2}{2\lambda^2} M_2 P_d L^2 \right)^{1/2} \tag{6.18}$$

where P_d is the acoustic power density and M_2 is the acousto-optic figure of merit. Maximum transmission occurs when the power density reaches the value

$$P_d = \frac{\lambda^2}{2 M_2 L^2} \tag{6.19}$$

As an example, the acoustic power density of an infrared TeO_2 AOTF is estimated using a $\theta_i \approx 20°$ design ($M_2 \approx 10^{-12}$ m^2/W) and an interaction length of 1 cm. At $\lambda = 4$ μm, the required acoustic power density is estimated to be 8 W/cm^2. This relatively high power requirement is probably the most serious disadvantage of the AOTF and limits its use for certain important system applications (such as focal plane sensors). One technique to reduce the drive power is to utilize acoustic resonance enhancement [16]. In an acoustic resonator structure, the peak acoustic field at resonance can be orders of magnitude greater than that of a traveling acoustic wave. Naturally, the resonant AOTF must be operated at the discrete resonant acoustic frequencies. For collinear AOTFs, the passband response (in acoustic frequency) consists of two to three modes. For noncollinear AOTFs, the passband response consists of many resonant modes. The passband response between successive resonant peaks will be sufficiently overlapped. Thus, the scanning response to the resonant AOTF is essentially the same as the conventional traveling-wave case.

The drive power of the resonant AOTF is reduced by the enhancement of diffraction efficiency due to acoustic resonance. The enhancement factor can be derived by considering the buildup of acoustic waves in a resonator. At resonance the enhancement factor, under an impedance-matching condition, can be shown to be equal to the reciprocal of one-way acoustic loss. The total acoustic loss includes losses due to acoustic attenuation in the filter medium and reflection loss at the boundaries.

The reduction of drive power was demonstrated in a collinear $CaMoO_4$ AOTF. There are two discrete acoustic resonances within the passband of the AOTF. Operating the filter at the peak of the acoustic resonance, a reduction of drive power of 22 dB was achieved. Acoustic resonance enhancement was also demonstrated using a noncollinear TeO_2 AOTF operated in the infrared region of 2 to 5 μm.

About nine resonant modes were observed within one filter passband.
Due to the relatively high acoustic attenuation in TeO_2, a power reduction factor of 16 was obtained.

6.2.5 Out-of-Band Rejection and Sidelobe Suppression

The dynamic range of an AOTF spectrometer is determined by the peak
transmission and out-of-band rejection of the AOTF. The out-of-band
rejection for an AOTF is determined by two factors. Overall out-of-
band rejection is determined by the contrast ratio, i.e., the fraction
of (undiffracted) light leakage through crossed polarizers. In the infrared, this is limited by the poor contrast ratio of the wire grid polarizers. In the visible, where calcite polarizers with a good extinction
ratio (> 40 dB) are available, the limiting factor is caused by residual
strain of the filter medium. In crystals such as quartz and TeO_2, de-
polarization due to optical activity severely degrades the spectral
purity. An increase of contrast ratio is achieved in the noncollinear
AOTF, where the incident and diffracted light are spatially separated.
It can be shown [15] that the angle between the incident and diffracted
light at the exit face of the AOTF is approximately given by

$$\Delta \theta = \Delta n \sin 2\theta_1 \qquad\qquad (6.20)$$

The filter can be operated without the use of polarizers if the angular
aperture is less than the deflection angle.

Near the filter band, out-of-band rejection is determined by the
sidelobe structure of the filter band-pass response. Improved out-of-
band rejection can be obtained by techniques of amplitude apodization
[17]. In the collinear AOTF, an acoustic pulse apodized in time is
launched into the filter medium. By utilizing a triangular window, the
first sidelobe was reduced by −22 dB with a collinear quartz AOTF.
For the noncollinear AOTF, the apodization can be realized by weighted
acoustic excitation at a transducer array. This was demonstrated in a
noncollinear TeO_2 AOTF. A maximum sidelobe of −26 dB was achieved
using a Hamming-type window. Similar results were obtained with
electronically programmable apodizations [16].

6.2.6 Typical AOTF Performance

The performance of AOTFs is primarily limited by the availability of
superior materials. To qualify as a candidate for use as the interaction medium for an AOTF, the material must be optically birefringent
and transparent in the operating range of interest; it must have a low
acoustic attenuation in the acoustic frequency range and a large
acousto-optic figure of merit. The acoustic-optic figure of merit for
an AOTF is $M_f = n^8 p^2 / \rho v_a^3$, where n is the index of refraction, ρ is
the density, v_a is the acoustic velocity, and p is the relevant elastooptical coefficient for the filter interaction.

Table 6.1 Performance of Acousto-optic Tunable Filters

MATERIAL	CONFIGURATION	TUNING RANGE (μm)	MEASURED WAVELENGTH (μm)	BANDWIDTH	ANGULAR APERTURE	OPTICAL APERTURE	EFFICIENCY
QUARTZ	COLLINEAR	0.23-0.7	0.325	1.5Å	5°	7 mm x 7 mm	10%/W
QUARTZ	NONCOLLINEAR	0.23-0.7	0.325	10Å	10°	4 mm x 30 mm	10%/W
TeO_2	NONCOLLINEAR	0.45-0.75	0.633	$50 cm^{-1}$ (20Å @ 0.633 μm)	10°	5 mm x 5 mm	95% MAX. @ 0.5W
TeO_2	NONCOLLINEAR	0.45-0.75	0.633	$7 cm^{-1}$ (3Å @ 0.633 μm)	5°	3 mm x 8 mm	70% MAX. @ 1.5W
TeO_2	NONCOLLINEAR	2.0-5.0	3.39	$5 cm^{-1}$ (57Å @ 3.39 μm)	10°	5 mm x 10 mm	7%/W
Tl_3AsSe_3	COLLINEAR	7.0-11	10.6	$0.7 cm^{-1}$ (78Å @ 10.6 μm)	10°	3 mm x 3 mm	—
Tl_3AsSe_3	NONCOLLINEAR	7.0-11	10.6	0.6 μm (@ 10.6 μm)	35°	4 mm x 15 mm	6%/W

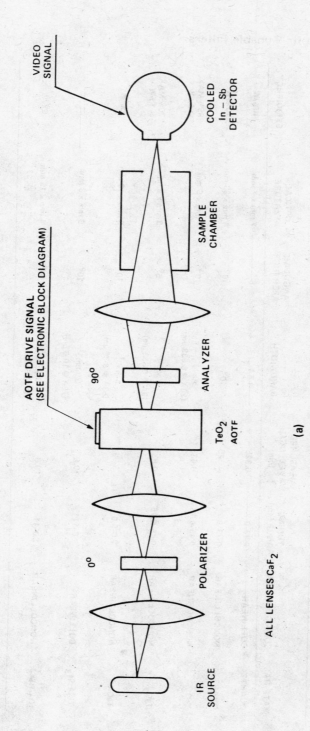

IR
SOURCE

POLARIZER

0°

TeO₂
AOTF

AOTF DRIVE SIGNAL
(SEE ELECTRONIC BLOCK DIAGRAM)

90°

ANALYZER

SAMPLE
CHAMBER

COOLED
In – Sb
DETECTOR

VIDEO
SIGNAL

ALL LENSES CaF₂

(a)

154

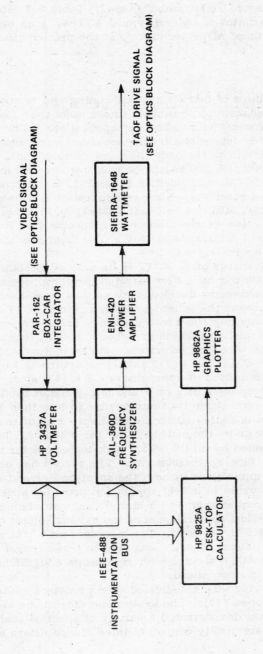

Figure 6.8 Computer-controlled infrared AOTF spectrometer. (From Ref. 21.)

155

AOTFs using the following materials have been demonstrated: $LiNbO_3$, $CaMoO_4$, quartz, TeO_2, and Tl_3AsSe_3. Table 6.1 lists the performance characteristics of several typical AOTFs. It is believed to represent the status of AOTF technology at the present time (1981).

6.3 APPLICATIONS

The combined capabilities of fast electronical tuning and relatively large throughput of acousto-optic tunable filters make them favorable for rapid-scan spectrometer and radiometer applications. The time response of an AOTF is determined by the acoustic transit time across the optical beam, which is on the order of a few microseconds. The rapid-scanning capability of AOTFs can be used for spectral analysis applications where a fast data acquisition is needed, for instance, in the studies of chemical reactions. Such an application was demonstrated by Shipp et al. [18]. Using a collinear $CaMoO_4$ AOTF, these workers measured the time-resolved absorption spectra from oxidation of formaldehyde by acid dichromate at 25°C. The filter was scanned between 462 and 667 nm in 11.7 ms.

One significant advantage of an AOTF is its easy adaptability for computer control. This has been demonstrated in microprocessor-controlled AOTF spectrometers developed by various co-workers [19-21]. Figure 6.8 shows the schematic of an infrared AOTF spec-trometer-radiometer covering the 2 to 5 μm range [21]. The optical system consists of a tungsten carbide gray body, a CaF_2 lens, an AOTF between crossed wire grid polarizers, and an indium antimonide cooled detector. The AOTF has an f/3 angular aperture of 3 by 20 mm, resulting in a throughput of approximately 5×10^{-2} sr cm^2. The filter has a spectral resolution of 7 cm^{-1} and is capable of randomly accessing any wavelength within its tuning range in less than 10 μs. The actual scan speed is limited either by the sweep rate of the RF frequency synthesizer or by the sensitivity of the detector. The AOTF spectrometer is controlled by an HP 9825A desk-top calculator through several IEEE-488 interfaceable instruments. The system has been evaluated in various applications in both the spectrometer and radiometer mode. A test of the system in a field application provided spectral information on a test rocket engine in a high-altitude simulation chamber. Figure 6.9 shows a typical spectral scan of the exhaust plume having an oxygen/fuel ratio of 4.5 at sea level. The measurement of the entire scan was performed in about 20 ms. Compared to a mechanical grat-ing spectrometer, the AOTF spectrometer represents a significant in-crease in the data acquisition speed.

An AOTF spectrometer with a dedicated microprocessor control (Z-80) was also developed [20]. The system operates in the visible (400 to 700 nm) and has demonstrated a variety of spectral analysis applications that include quality control of interference filters and

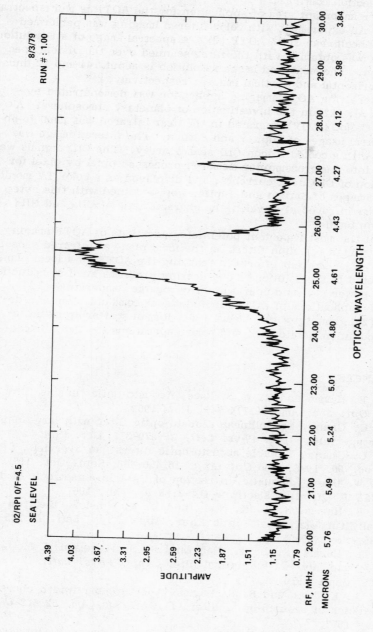

Figure 6.9 Spectra scan of rocket exhaust plume radiation.

light-emitting diodes, thin-film monitoring, and real-time evaluation
of antireflection coatings.

Another important area of application for the AOTF is multispectral
imaging. An experiment with color filtered imaging was performed
using a noncollinear TeO_2 AOTF [3]. A spectral image of a resolution
test chart was obtained with the filter scanned over the visible spectral region. The measured image resolution is about 144 and 72 lines/
mm for horizontal and vertical images, respectively.

An interesting AOTF imaging application was demonstrated by
Watson et al. [22] in the investigation of planetary atmosphere. A
collinear $CaMoO_4$ AQTF operated in the near infrared was used to obtain spectral images of Jupiter and Saturn. The filtered image was
detected with a cooled silicon CID sensor array. The CID signals were
read out into a microcomputer memory, processed pixel by pixel for
subtraction of CID dark currents, and displayed on a color TV monitor.
Spectral images of Saturn and Jupiter were obtained with this sytem
in the near infrared at wavelengths characteristic of CH_4 and NH_3
absorption bands.

One of the most important potential applications of AOTF imaging is
for background rejection filters on the focal plane of infrared sensor
systems [23]. Present efforts in realizing the AOTF on a focal plane
are directed to the solution of engineering problems such as reduction
of drive power [16] and operating at cyrogenic temperatures [24].

Other applications of AOTFs include laser communication and detection [25], tuning of dye lasers [26], Raman scattering measurements, pollution monitoring, and color separations.

REFERENCES

1. S. E. Harris and R. W. Wallace, Acousto-optic tunable filter,
    J. Opt. Soc. Am. 59:774-747, June 1969.
2. I. C. Chang, Noncollinear acousto-optic filter with large angu-
    lar aperture, *Appl. Phys. Lett.* 25:370-372, Oct. 1974.
3. I. C. Chang, Tunable acousto-optic filters, an overview, *SPIE
    Proc. 90*, 1976; also *Opt. Eng.* 16:455-460, Sept.-Oct. 1977.
4. R. W. Dixon, Acoustic diffraction of light in anisotropic media,
    IEEE J. Quantum Electron. QA-3:85-93, Feb. 1967.
5. S. E. Harris, S. T. K. Nieh, and D. K. Winslow, Electron-
    ically tunable acousto-optic filter, *Appl. Phys. Lett.* 15:325-
    326, Nov. 1969.
6. S. E. Harris, S. T. K. Nieh, and R. S. Fiegelson, $CaMoO_4$
    electronically tunable optical filter, *Appl. Phys. Lett.* 17:223-
    225, Sept. 1970.
7. S. T. K. Nieh and S. E. Harris, Aperture-bandwidth charac-
    teristics of acousto-optic filter, *J. Opt. Soc. Am.* 62:672-676,
    May 1972.
8. J. A. Kusters, D. A. Wilson, and D. L. Hammond, Optimum

crystal orientation for acoustically tuned optic filters, *J. Opt. Soc. Am.* *64*:434-440, April 1974.

9. I. C. Chang, Tunable acousto-optic filter utilizing acoustic beam walkoff in crystal quartz, *Appl. Phys. Lett.* *25*:323-324, Sept. 1974.

10. J. D. Feichtner, M. Gottlieb, and J. J. Conroy, A tunable collinear acousto-optic filter for the intermediate infrared using crystal Tl_3AsSe_3, in *IEEE Conf. Laser Engineering and Applications*, Washington, D.C., May 1975.

11. I. C. Chang and P. Katzka, Tunable acousto-optic filters at 10.6 microns, *IEEE Ultrason. Symp. Proc.* Sept. 1978.

12. P. Katzka and I. C. Chang, Noncollinear acousto-optic filter for the ultraviolet, *SPIE Symp. Proc.* Aug. 1979.

13. I. C. Chang, Development of an infrared tunable acousto-optic filter, *SPIE Proc.* *131*:2-10, Jan. 1978.

14. J. D. Feichtner, M. Gottlieb, and J. J. Conroy, Tl_3AsSe_3 noncollinear acousto-optic filter operation at 10 micrometers, *Appl. Phys. Lett.* *34*:1-3, Jan. 1979.

15. I. C. Chang, Analysis of the noncollinear acousto-optic filter, *Electron. Lett.* *11*:617-618, Dec. 1975.

16. I. C. Chang, P. Katzka, J. Jacob, and S. Estrin, Programmable acousto-optic filter, in *IEEE Ultrason. Symp. Proc.* Sept. 1979.

17. I. C. Chang and P. Katzka, Tunable acousto-optic filters and apodized acoustic excitation, *J. Opt. Soc. Am.* *68*:1449, Oct. 1978.

18. W. S. Shipp, J. Biggins, and C. W. Wade, *Rev. Sci. Instrum.* *47*:565, 1976.

19. J. Jacob and I. C. Chang, Development of an AOTF spectrometer, *SPIE Symp. Proc.* *202*, Aug. 1979.

20. J. J. Conroy, M. Gottlieb, and J. D. Feichtner, Microcomputer controlled tunable acousto-optic filter, *SPIE Symp. Proc.* *202*, Aug. 1979.

21. P. Kataka, S. Estrin, I. C. Chang, and G. Petrie, Computer controlled infrared AOTF spectrometer, *SPIE Symp. Proc.* *246*, July 1980.

22. R. B. Watson, S. A. Rappaport, and E. E. Frederick, *Icarus* *27*:417, 1976.

23. I. C. Chang, Tunable spectral filters, *SPIE Symp. Proc.* *244*, July 1980.

24. M. Khoshnevisan and E. Sovero, Development of a cryogenic infrared acousto-optic tunable spectral filter, *SPIE Symp. Proc.* *245*, July 1980.

25. I. C. Chang, Laser detection utilizing tunable acousto-optic filters, *J. Quantum Electron.* *14*:108-111, Feb. 1978.

26. D. J. Taylor, S. T. K. Neih, and T. W. Hansch, Electronic tuning of a dye laser using the acousto-optic filter, *Appl. Phys. Lett.* *19*:269-271, Oct. 1971.

III
TIME-DOMAIN SIGNAL PROCESSING

Preface

The ultrasonic delay line which performs the spatial light modulation extends physically over an interval of time, and hence manipulations and processing of the RF signal in the time domain as well as the frequency domain are feasible with acousto-optics. Indeed, some of the most powerful applications of acousto-optics are found in the area of time-domain signal processing. The first chapter of this part (Chap. 7) considers integration of signals along a space coordinate (e.g., the length of the delay line) and shows how this leads to convolution and correlation. The second chapter (Chap. 8) discusses a novel approach for storing an index of refraction pattern in lithium niobate and hence obtaining a memory correlator. The next two chapters Chaps. 9 and 10) discuss the area of one- and two-dimensional time-integrating correlators. Chapter 9 discusses incoherent approaches to realizing these structures, whereas Chap. 10 considers coherent schemes. The attractions of the convolver and correlator structures herein discussed are relatively large processing gains (10^3 to 10^7) with simultaneous maintenance of large instantaneous bandwidths (approximately 50 to 500 MHz). A discussion of these factors as well as those affecting signal-to-noise performance and dynamic range is included in these chapters, as well as a number of illustrative applications. The concluding chapter of this part (Chap. 11) discusses various system applications and shows how the signal-processing functions, both frequency- and time-domain, achievable with acousto-optics can be advantageously used. Chapters 7, 8, and 10 also introduce the surface-acoustic-wave (SAW) delay line to the acousto-optic signal-processing field. The general architectures discussed still use conventional bulk optics; however, the addition of SAW devices should portend even more powerful signal-processing algorithms and capabilities for the future.

7

Space-Integrating Acousto-Optic Signal Processors Using Surface-Acoustic Wave Delay Lines

MICHAEL W. CASSEDAY, NORMAN J. BERG, and IRWIN J. ABRAMOVITZ[*]/ Department of the Army, Harry Diamond Laboratories, Adelphi, Maryland

The signal-processing requirements of such diverse systems as advanced radars, very large sonar arrays, spread spectrum communication networks, and electronic warfare receivers severely tax presently available analog and digital signal processors. Advanced radar systems, for example, require large-dynamic-range matched filters to optimally detect the wideband FM (chirp) or direct-sequence-coded pulse signals used in these systems. The signals from large sonar arrays, on the other hand, might be best processed by frequency-azimuth (ω-k) beam forming on the sensor outputs, while electronic warfare systems may need rapid spectrum analysis for threat detection. Spread spectrum communication networks using wideband direct-sequence or wideband frequency-hopped signals are usually designed for optimum detection and demodulation with a correlator. All these systems require real-time processing of wideband signals over a large dynamic range, and these requirements have been the stimulus for the development of several acousto-optic signal processors.

Acousto-optic signal processors are based on the interaction of light and sound. This interaction results in diffraction of the light and is due (at least in part) to periodic variations in the index of refraction of the medium induced by the sound. Thus, a time segment of an electrical signal may be converted to a spatial distribution of diffracted light if the signal is used to generate sound waves propagating in an illuminated transparent medium. The diffracted light may then be manipulated with optical elements, such as lenses and mirrors, and converted back into an electrical signal with a photodetector. Under certain conditions, mathematical operations involving time variations in the signal may be accomplished by spatial operations; in particular, a time variable may be integrated over a spatial variable. The acousto-

[*]Current affiliation: Westinghouse Electric Corporation, Advanced Technology Division, Baltimore, Maryland

optic signal processors discussed in this chapter make use of this possibility and thus are referred to as *space-integrating* processors.

Originally, the acousto-optic interaction was experimentally verified in 1932 by Debye and Sears in the United States and by Lucas and Biquard in France; however, more recent technological advances (such as the invention of the laser, refinements in synthetic crystal-growing techniques, and the development of acoustic delay lines made of transparent materials) have greatly accelerated the development of acousto-optic devices. For example, several of the acousto-optic signal processors described in this chapter depend on the Bragg diffraction of coherent laser light by Rayleigh waves propagating in a lithium niobate (LiNbO$_3$) surface-acoustic-wave (SAW) delay line.

7.1 THE ACOUSTO-OPTIC INTERACTION IN SAW DELAY LINES

7.1.1 Bragg Diffraction by SAWs

Figure 7.1 shows the basic acousto-optic interaction in a y-cut, z-propagating LiNbO$_3$ SAW delay line. Coherent light from a linearly polarized laser (s polarization) is expanded, collimated, and shaped into a beam of sufficient width to illuminate the required length (time-delay aperture) of the delay line. The light is then focused by a high-F-number cylindrical lens, and the sheet beam formed near the back focal plane of the lens is projected through the surface region of the delay line. The SAW propagating in the delay line (generated by an electrical signal applied to the delay-line transducer) diffracts a portion of the light incident upon it. Operation is in the Bragg diffraction

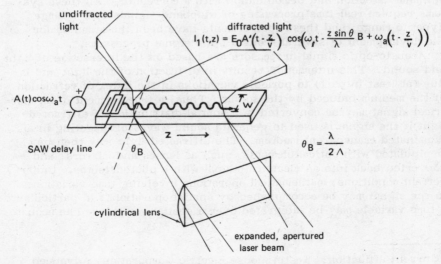

$$I_1(t,z) = E_0 A'\left(t - \frac{z}{v}\right) \cos\left(\omega_t t - \frac{z \sin\theta}{\lambda} B + \omega_a\left(t - \frac{z}{v}\right)\right)$$

$$\theta_B = \frac{\lambda}{2\Lambda}$$

Figure 7.1 Acousto-optic interaction in a SAW delay line.

regime, so the angle of incidence of the light with the acoustic wave phase fronts is set to Θ_{Bn}, the Bragg angle in the material, where

$$\Theta_{Bn} = \sin^{-1} \frac{\lambda}{2n\Lambda} \tag{7.1}$$

Here λ is the free-space light wavelength, n is the index of refraction of the delay-line material, and Λ is the SAW wavelength. Outside the delay line, the angle changes in accord with Snell's law, and in air the angle Θ_B is defined as

$$\Theta_B = \sin^{-1} \frac{\lambda}{2\Lambda} \tag{7.2}$$

This is not necessarily the angle of incidence of the light with the delay line, unless the acoustic phase fronts are perpendicular to the sides of the delay line (which by design is often the case). For y-z LiNbO$_3$ illuminated with 0.6328-μm wavelength HeNe laser light, $n = 2.24$; at 100-MHz acoustic frequency $\Lambda = 34.88$ μm. This yields a Θ_{Bn} of 0.232° and a Θ_B of 0.520°.

To ensure operation in the Bragg diffraction regime, the SAW phase fronts must be of sufficient width W that the quantity Q defined as

$$Q \equiv \frac{2\pi}{n} \frac{\lambda W}{\Lambda^2} \tag{7.3}$$

is greater than 10 [1]. An acousto-optic device typical of those discussed in this section might use a delay line having a transducer acoustic aperture of 175 acoustic wavelengths. For a center frequency of 300 MHz, this yields a Q of about 27.

In Bragg diffraction, a single first-order diffraction term contains most of the diffracted light, and its intensity I_1 is [2,3]

$$I_1 = I_0 \eta \, \mathrm{sinc}^2 \left[\eta + \left(\frac{\Delta K \, W}{2} \right)^2 \right]^{1/2} \tag{7.4}$$

Here I_0 is the intensity of the incident light, η is defined as

$$\eta = \frac{\pi^2}{2\lambda^2} M_2 \frac{W}{\Lambda} P_a \tag{7.5}$$

and ΔK is the momentum mismatch between the incident light and the acoustic propagation vectors. P_a is the acoustic power, and M_2 is an acousto-optic figure of merit [4] which depends on the elasto-optic coefficient of the delay-line material. This figure of merit M_2 is not so easily determined for SAW acousto-optic interaction in LiNbO$_3$ because the electro-optic effect [5] and the corrugation effect [6] contribute to the diffraction of the light. However, the acousto-optic interaction for SAWs has been observed to follow the form of equation (7.4) quite closely for s-polarized incident light.

For perfectly plane acoustic and light waves, the momentum mismatch ΔK is zero at the exact Bragg frequency, and equation (7.4) reduces to

$$I_1 = I_0 \sin^2\left[\frac{\pi}{\lambda}\left(\frac{M_2 W P_a}{2\Lambda}\right)^{1/2}\right] \qquad (7.6)$$

Thus for sufficiently small P_a, I_1 may be considered to be linearly proportional to P_a. If the acoustic and/or light waves are not perfectly plane, then ΔK is not zero even at the Bragg frequency, the diffraction term is reduced, and the linearity is degraded. For near-field acoustic propagation in the SAW delay line, and for coherent light collimated in high-quality optical systems, plane-wave conditions are approached quite closely, and ΔK can be reduced to acceptably small values.

When the operating frequency differs from the Bragg frequency, ΔK may no longer be small, and the term $(\Delta K \, W/2)^2$ indicates the bandwidth limit for the acousto-optic interaction. From scalar diffraction theory, the 3-dB bandwidth Δf for isotropic interaction may be estimated to be [5]

$$\Delta f = f_0 \frac{2\Lambda^2}{\lambda W} \qquad (7.7)$$

To increase this bandwidth, it is necessary to reduce the acoustic phase-front width W, at the expense of reduced diffraction (interaction efficiency).

This bandwidth limit seems to hold rather well for SAW acousto-optic interaction in y-cut, z-propagating $LiNbO_3$ with s-polarized (vertical polarization) light. However, for p-polarized light (horizontal polarization), this is not the case. Figure 7.2 shows the measured diffraction power versus angle of incidence for two different delay lines for both s- and p-polarized light. Diffraction occurs over nearly twice as large a range of angles for p- as for s-polarization, indicating that twice the bandwidth can be obtained. It is speculated that this increased bandwidth is due, at least in part, to the optical anisotropic properties of $LiNbO_3$ in the z direction, parallel to the polarization vector for p-polarized light.

The frequency of the diffracted light is shifted by an amount equal to the acoustic frequency in accordance with the laws of conservation of momentum and energy. When the diffraction is in the direction of the sound propagation, the frequency of the light is increased, and vice versa for diffraction away from the acoustic K vector.

To return to Fig. 7.1, consider that a finite-duration, band-limited band-pass electrical signal represented by $A(t) \cos(\omega_a t + \phi_1)$ is applied to the interdigitated transducer of the pictured delay line. This generates an acoustic signal $A'(t,z)$ which propagates along the z axis, where it may be described as

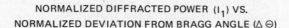

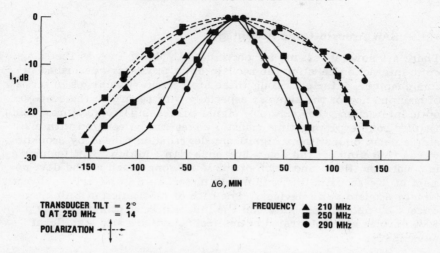

Figure 7.2 SAW acousto-optic interaction vs. incidence angle for vertically and horizontally polarized light.

$$A'(t,z) \backsim A'\left(t - \frac{z}{v}\right) \cos\left[\omega_a\left(t - \frac{z}{v}\right) + \phi_1\right] \tag{7.8}$$

and v is the acoustic propagation velocity. For uniform, coherent, collimated monochromatic illumination, the light incident on the z axis can be described as E_{inc}, where

$$E_{inc}(t,z) = E_0 \cos\left(\omega_\ell t + \frac{z \sin \Theta_{Bn}}{\lambda} + \phi_2\right) \tag{7.9}$$

and ω_ℓ is the incident light frequency. If ω_a is at the Bragg frequency and the acoustic wave amplitude is sufficiently small, the diffracted light E_{dif} can be described by

$$E_{dif}(t,z) \backsim E_0 A'\left(t - \frac{z}{v}\right) \cos\left[(\omega_\ell + \omega_a)t - \frac{\omega_a z}{v}\right.$$
$$\left. - \frac{z \sin \Theta_{Bn}}{\lambda} + \phi_1 + \phi_2\right] \tag{7.10}$$

Thus the diffracted light contains the amplitude, frequency, and phase information of the original electrical signal, and at some given instant of time t_0, the spatial distribution of the light between z_1 and z_2 contains the signal information between the times $t = t_0 - z_1/v$ and $t = t_0 - z_2/v$.

7.1.2 SAW Acousto-Optic Advantages

There are several reasons for choosing SAW delay lines as the acousto-optic interaction cells for the acousto-optic processors described in this chapter. Principal among these are certain advantages in terms of manipulation of the signals, especially with regard to the acousto-optic interaction. For example, signal-processing architectures which require counterpropagating acoustic waves can be realized with a single delay line, without significant degradation caused by acoustic waves reflecting off the delay-line ends. In addition, SAW technology is a maturing field, and much of the work done, such as the development of low-acoustic-diffraction cuts in certain SAW materials, directly benefit acousto-optic devices. The ease of fabrication of SAW transducers by photolithography and the inherent compatibility of the planar SAW devices with integrated optics technology are also significant advantages.

7.1.3 Practical Limitations

At this point some practical considerations which tend to limit this SAW acousto-optic interaction should be noted. To maximize the interaction, it is necessary to maximize the portion of the incident light which actually illuminates the SAW. This is a most difficult problem, as most of the energy in the SAW is in a region which extends only one acoustic wavelength below the delay-line surface. This places rather severe restrictions on the flatness of the surface of the delay line (to match the very thin sheet beam of light), on the quality of the edges of the delay line (through which the sheet beam must pass), and the quality and F number of the cylindrical lens (which forms the sheet beam). In addition, to obtain operation in the Bragg diffraction regime, the SAW must be illuminated uniformly across the phase-front width W. Thus the optical system must produce a sheet beam which must both be thin and have a large depth of field, which are conflicting requirements. The alignment of all the optical elements (including the delay line) is also a nontrivial task. However, operation with 5% diffraction ($I_1/I_0 \times 100\%$) for 30-mW acoustic power has been achieved in typical experimental setups. Since only about half of the light was actually incident on the acoustic region, the actual diffraction efficiency was somewhat greater.

7.2 SAW ACOUSTO-OPTIC CONVOLVERS AND CORRELATORS

As mentioned earlier, correlators are one of the types of signal processors which we hope to realize in acousto-optic form. The (cross) correlation of two signals A(t) and B(t) may be defined as

$$r_{12}(t) = \int_{\tau} A(\tau)B(\tau - t) \, d\tau \qquad (7.11)$$

and may also be defined as

$$R_{12}(\tau) = \int_{t} A(t)B(t - \tau) \, dt \qquad (7.12)$$

In equation (7.11) the integration variable is a time delay τ, and the correlation is a time variable, while in equation (7.12), the integration variable is time, and the correlation is a variable in the delay τ. From equation (7.10), we observe that the light diffracted in the acousto-optic interaction depicted in Fig. 7.1 is a function of both time and time delay ($z/v = \tau$).

One should be able to build a correlator by finding some acousto-optic method of multiplying two signals over a range of time delays and then integrating the product either over the delay range or in time (as appropriate). And of course, acousto-optic architectures exist which realize either equation (7.11) or (7.12). Those which realize equation (7.11) are called *space-integrating* correlators, be-cause the integration variable τ is a spatial variable, z/v. Those which realize equation (7.12) use a light detector that charges a ca-pacitor to do the integration and are called *time-integrating* correla-tors.

Each type of correlator has unique advantages and disadvantages. Time-integrating acousto-optic correlators sample the spatial distribu-tion of the diffracted light with photodetector arrays. The spatial distribution of this light varies with input signal frequency, and the Nyquist sampling theorem sets a definite limit on the variation that the array can resolve. This limits the bandwidths of the signals which can be processed. However, the time-integrating feature of these arrays allows the processing of very long-duraction signals, and thus very large time-bandwidth products (a figure of merit) may be achieved.

Space-integrating acousto-optic correlators (which may actually be realized with a convolver), on the other hand, are restricted in band-width primarily by the bandwidth limitations of the acousto-optic inter-action [see equation (7.7)]. Techniques exist to avoid this and other bandwidth restrictions, and very large (> 500 MHz) instantaneous bandwidths have been achieved. However, because the integration is performed over a spatial variable (which is limited by the practically attainable size of the delay line and by acoustic attenuation limits on the acousto-optic interaction), these correlators are limited to relatively short-duration signals. Still, relatively large time-bandwidth products can be obtained. Several space-integrating acousto-optic signal processors are examined in detail in this chapter.

Figure 7.3 illustrates the operation of a SAW acousto-optic convolver. Two finite-duration, band-limited band-pass signals, $B(t) \cos \omega_a t$ and $C(t) \cos \omega_a t$, are applied to the interdigitated transducers at

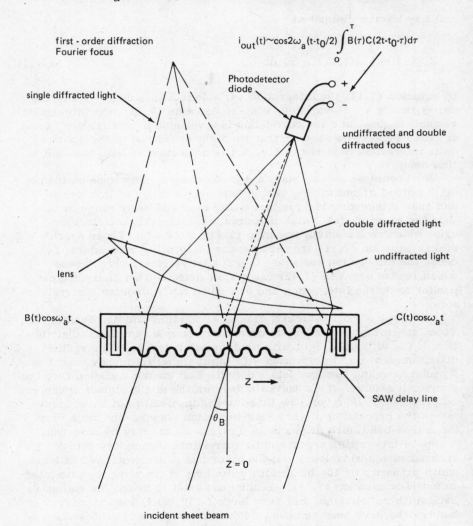

Figure 7.3 SAW acousto-optic convolver.

opposite ends of a y-cut, z-propagating $LiNbO_3$ SAW delay line. The transducer fingers are perpendicular to the crystal z axis (the z direction in the figure), a pure-mode propagation direction for SAWs [7] in this acoustically anisotropic material. For this particular transducer orientation, the phase fronts of the SAWs will be perpendicular to the direction of propagation. This is not necessarily the case for other orientations of the transducers because of the acoustic anisotropy [7].

The electrical signals generate counterpropagating SAWs, which may be described as standing waves in the delay line. That is,

$$B(t) \cos \omega_a t \rightarrow B'\left(t - \frac{d}{v}\right) \cos \omega_a\left(t - \frac{d}{v}\right) \qquad (7.13a)$$

and

$$C(t) \cos \omega_a t \rightarrow C'\left(t - \frac{d}{v}\right) \cos \omega_a\left(t - \frac{d}{v}\right) \qquad (7.13b)$$

where d is the distance from the transducer associated with the particular SAW to the observation point in the delay line and B' and C' are the acoustic wave magnitudes which are assumed to be linearly proportional to B and C. By defining the midpoint between the transducers as z = 0 and suitably rewriting equation (7.13), the description of the two acoustic standing waves can be put into a common coordinate system, yielding

$$B(t) \cos \omega_a t \rightarrow B'\left(t - \frac{L}{2v} - \frac{z}{v}\right) \cos \omega_a\left(t - \frac{L}{2v} - \frac{z}{v}\right) \qquad (7.14a)$$

and

$$C(t) \cos \omega_a t \rightarrow C'\left(t - \frac{L}{2v} + \frac{z}{v}\right) \cos \omega_a\left(t - \frac{L}{2v} + \frac{z}{v}\right) \qquad (7.14b)$$

where L is the distance between the transducers (i.e., L/2v is the propagation time from either transducer to the z = 0 location).

A sheet beam of coherent light is incident on the propagating SAWs at the Bragg angle, illuminating the region L between the transducers. Along the z axis, this light can be described as in equation (7.9). The light interacts with both SAW waves, and a small amount of light (linear operation requires small diffraction) is diffracted by each. For the geometry shown, the diffracted light may be described by

$$B(t) \cos \omega_a t \rightarrow A_1 B'\left(t - \frac{L}{2v} - \frac{z}{v}\right) \cos\left[\omega_\ell t + \frac{z \sin \Theta_{Bn}}{\lambda}\right.$$
$$\left. - \omega_a\left(t - \frac{L}{2v} - \frac{z}{v}\right)\right] \qquad (7.15a)$$

and

$$C(t) \cos \omega_a t \rightarrow A_1 C' \left(t - \frac{L}{2v} + \frac{z}{v} \right) \cos \left[\omega_\ell t + \frac{z \sin \Theta_{Bn}}{\lambda} \right.$$

$$\left. + \omega_a \left(t - \frac{L}{2v} + \frac{z}{v} \right) \right] \tag{7.15b}$$

where A_1 includes the diffraction efficiency proportionalities.

Each of these first-order diffractions is incident upon the other SAW at the Bragg angle, and a small portion of each will undergo a second diffraction. This doubly diffracted light may be described by

$$B_1 C_2 \rightarrow A_2 B' \left(t - \frac{L}{2v} - \frac{z}{v} \right) C' \left(t - \frac{L}{2v} + \frac{z}{v} \right) \cos \left[\omega_\ell t \right.$$

$$\left. - \frac{z \sin \Theta_{Bn}}{\lambda} - 2\omega_a \left(t - \frac{L}{2v} \right) \right] \tag{7.16a}$$

and

$$C_1 B_2 \rightarrow A_2 C' \left(t - \frac{L}{2v} + \frac{z}{v} \right) B' \left(t - \frac{L}{2v} - \frac{z}{v} \right) \cos \left[\omega_\ell t \right.$$

$$\left. - \frac{z \sin \Theta_{Bn}}{\lambda} + 2\omega_a \left(t - \frac{L}{2v} \right) \right]$$

Here $B_1 C_2$ and $C_1 B_2$ indicate the order of diffraction of the doubly diffracted light, and A_2 includes the double-diffraction efficiency proportionalities. It can be seen that this doubly diffracted light is collinear with that portion of the incident light which has not been diffracted.

A lens is used to focus the undiffracted and the doubly diffracted light onto a large-area square law photodetector diode, where heterodyne detection of the doubly diffracted light takes place (the undiffracted light serves as the local oscillator). The singly diffracted light leaves the delay line with an angle $\Theta = 2\Theta_B$ between it and the undiffracted and doubly diffracted light. The lens focuses this light to a spot well removed from the photodiode, so it does not contribute to the detected signal.

Since only a small fraction of the incident light is diffracted (linear operation is at low diffraction efficiency), the output current of the square law detector may be approximated as

$$I(t) \sim \int_{z=-L/2}^{L/2} \left\{ E_0 \cos \omega_\ell t + A_2 B' \left(t - \frac{L}{2v} - \frac{z}{v} \right) \right.$$

$$\times C' \left(t - \frac{L}{2v} + \frac{z}{v} \right) \cos \left[\omega_\ell t + 2\omega_a \left(t - \frac{L}{2v} \right) \right]$$

$$+ A_2 C' \left(t - \frac{L}{2v} + \frac{z}{v} \right)$$

$$\times \ B'\left(t - \frac{L}{2v} - \frac{z}{v}\right) \ \cos\left[\omega_\ell t - 2\omega_a\left(t - \frac{L}{2v}\right)\right]\Bigg\}^2 \ dz \qquad (7.17)$$

The spatial phase term $z \sin \theta_{Bn}/\lambda$ is dropped for the sake of simplification, as it makes no measurable contribution to the output. Taking the square yields the following terms:

$$I(t) \sim \int_{z=-L/2}^{L/2} E_0^2 \cos^2(\omega_\ell t) \ dz \qquad (7.18a)$$

$$+ \int_{-L/2}^{L/2} A_2^2 B'^2\left(t - \frac{L}{2v} - \frac{z}{v}\right) C'^2\left(t - \frac{L}{2v} + \frac{z}{v}\right)$$

$$\times \ \cos^2\left[\omega_\ell t - 2\omega_a\left(t - \frac{L}{2v}\right)\right] \ dz \qquad (7.18b)$$

$$+ \int_{-L/2}^{L/2} A_2^2 C'^2\left(t - \frac{L}{2v} + \frac{z}{v}\right) B'^2\left(t - \frac{L}{2v} - \frac{z}{v}\right)$$

$$\times \ \cos^2\left[\omega_\ell t - 2\omega_a\left(t - \frac{L}{2v}\right)\right] \ dz \qquad (7.18c)$$

$$+ \ 2\int_{-L/2}^{L/2} E_0 A_2 B'\left(t - \frac{L}{2v} - \frac{z}{v}\right) C'\left(t - \frac{L}{2v} + \frac{z}{v}\right) \ \cos(\omega_\ell t)$$

$$\times \ \cos\left[\omega_\ell t + 2\omega_a\left(t - \frac{L}{2v}\right)\right] \ dz \qquad (7.18d)$$

$$+ \ 2\int_{-L/2}^{L/2} E_0 A_2 C'\left(t - \frac{L}{2v} + \frac{z}{v}\right) B'\left(t - \frac{L}{2v} - \frac{z}{v}\right) \ \cos(\omega_\ell t)$$

$$\times \ \cos\left[\omega_\ell t - 2\omega_a\left(t - \frac{L}{2v}\right)\right] \ dz \qquad (7.18e)$$

$$+ \int_{-L/2}^{L/2} A_2^2 B'^2\left(t - \frac{L}{2v} - \frac{z}{v}\right) C'^2\left(t - \frac{L}{2v} + \frac{z}{v}\right)$$

$$\times \ \cos\left[\omega_\ell + 2\omega_a\left(t - \frac{L}{2v}\right)\right] \cos\left[\omega_\ell - 2\omega_a\left(t - \frac{L}{2v}\right)\right] \ dz \quad (7.18f)$$

The first term in equation (7.18) simply yields a steady-state current, while the second and third terms yield much lower-level currents with frequency components extending to the bandwidth of $B^2(t)$ and $C^2(t)$. The fourth term may be manipulated using the cosine-product-identity to yield the following sum and difference terms:

$$\text{Sum} \sim \int_{-L/2}^{L/2} A_2 E_0 B' \left(t - \frac{L}{2v} - \frac{z}{v}\right) C' \left(t - \frac{L}{2v} + \frac{z}{v}\right) \cos \left[2\omega_\ell t \right.$$

$$\left. + 2\omega_a \left(t - \frac{L}{2v}\right)\right] \, dz \qquad (7.19)$$

$$\text{Difference} \sim \int_{-L/2}^{L/2} A_2 E_0 B' \left(t - \frac{L}{2v} - \frac{z}{v}\right) C' \left(t - \frac{L}{2v} + \frac{z}{v}\right)$$

$$\times \cos \left[2\omega_a \left(t - \frac{L}{2v}\right)\right] \, dz \qquad (7.20)$$

The sum term is at such a high frequency that it will be filtered out by the detector-diode self-capacitance and lead inductance. The difference term is a band-limited band-pass signal with center frequency $2\omega_a$.

The fifth term may be manipulated in the same way as the fourth, and since the order of diffraction is unimportant $[B(t)C(t) = C(t)B(t)$ and $\cos(-2\omega_a t) = \cos(2\omega_a t)]$, the two difference terms may be combined, yielding a term at $2\omega_a$ of

$$I(t)_{2\omega_a} \sim 2 \int_{-L/2}^{L/2} E_0 A_2 B' \left(t - \frac{L}{2v} - \frac{z}{v}\right) C' \left(t - \frac{L}{2v} + \frac{z}{v}\right)$$

$$\times \cos \left[2\omega_a \left(t - \frac{L}{2v}\right)\right] \, dz \qquad (7.21)$$

The final term in the expansion of the square is much smaller than the other terms, and any component of interest is centered at the frequency $4\omega_a$ and will be filtered from the output, and so will be ignored. Rearranging terms yields

$$I(t)_{2\omega_a} \sim 2E_0 A_2 \cos \left[2\omega_a \left(t - \frac{L}{2v}\right)\right] \int_{-L/2}^{L/2} B' \left(t - \frac{L}{2v} - \frac{z}{v}\right)$$

$$\times C' \left(t - \frac{L}{2v} + \frac{z}{v}\right) \, dz \qquad (7.22)$$

Substituting $\tau = t - z/v - L/2v$, $L/v = t_0$, and $d\tau = -dz/v$ into equation (7.22) yields

$$I(t)_{2\omega_a} \sim -2vE_0 A_2 \cos[\omega_a(2t - t_0)] \int_{\tau=t-t_0}^{t} B'(\tau)C'(2t - t_0 - \tau) \, d\tau$$

$$(7.23)$$

If the duration of the input signals $B(t) \cos \omega_a t$ and $C(t) \cos \omega_a t$ are less than the time aperture L/v of the interaction region and if both signals occur entirely within the same time span (which also cannot exceed L/v), then the integration limits in equation (7.23) can be extended to infinity without error.

This output is recognized as the convolution of $B(t)$ and $C(t)$ in a compressed time frame, delayed by a time t_0 in the compressed frame. In real time, the convolution is output at twice the input signal frequency with double the bandwidth in half the usual time, with output beginning after a delay equal to half the interaction time.

If $B^2(t)$ and $C^2(t)$ have the same frequency range and this range does not exceed one octave bandwidth centered at ω_a, then the convolution may be separated from the other signals present in the diode output with straightforward band-pass filtering. When this is not the case, the low-level contributions from the second and third terms of equation (7.18) will introduce some distortion in the output.

This, then, is a SAW acousto-optic space-integrating convolver. It may be used to determine the correlation of two signals if one of the signals can be time-inverted. In Fig. 7.3, for example, time-inverting the signal $C(t) \cos \omega_a t$, which is nonzero only during the interval $0 \leqslant t \leqslant a$, yields $C(a - t) \cos \omega_a(a - t)$. The SAW generated by this signal can be described by

$$C(a - t) \cos \omega_a(a - t) \rightarrow C'\left(a - t + \frac{L}{2v} - \frac{z}{v}\right) \cos \omega_a \left(t - a \right.$$

$$\left. - \frac{L}{2v} + \frac{z}{v}\right) \tag{7.24}$$

where use has been made of the identity $\cos(-\omega) = \cos \omega$. Equation (7.22) would then become

$$I(t)_{2\omega_a} \sim 2E_0 A_2 \cos\left[2\omega_a\left(t - \frac{L}{2v} - \frac{a}{2}\right)\right] \int_{\tau = t - t_0}^{t} B'\left(t - \frac{L}{2v} - \frac{z}{v}\right)$$

$$\times C'\left(a - t + \frac{L}{2v} - \frac{z}{v}\right) dz \tag{7.25}$$

Again making the substitutions $\tau = t - z/v - L/2v$, $L/v = t_0$, and $d\tau = -dz/v$ yields

$$I(t)_{2\omega_a} \sim -2vE_0 A_2 \cos\left[\omega_a\left(2t - t_0 - \frac{a}{2}\right)\right] \int_{\tau = t - t_0}^{t} B'(\tau)$$

$$\times C'(\tau - 2t + t_0 + a) d\tau \tag{7.26}$$

Comparing equation (7.26) with equation (7.11) verifies that this is indeed the correlation of $B(t)$ and $C(t)$, although in a compressed time frame and after a time delay. The same real-time timing and signal-frequency conditions apply as for the convolver.

7.3 MAXIMIZING CONVOLVER PERFORMANCE

7.3.1 Maximum Useful Interaction Time

The usefulness of this SAW acousto-optic convolver as a signal processor is determined by two performance criteria: its time-bandwidth product and its dynamic range. The time-bandwidth product is determined by the maximum duration and bandwidth signal on which the device can properly operate. This very important performance index can be improved by increasing the acousto-optic interaction time and/ or by increasing the interaction bandwidth. The interaction time may be increased by increasing the length of the delay line, and 15-cm-long $LiNbO_3$ crystals with 40-μs delay apertures have been used. Further increases in physical length, although certainly possible, become less and less practical because of the difficulty of growing and finishing the $LiNbO_3$ crystals as well as the increasing size and tolerance requirements of the optical components.

Increasing delay-line length results in reduced acousto-optic interaction because of acoustic wave attenuation from propagation losses and diffraction losses. Acoustic propagation losses are approximately proportional to the square of the frequency (about 1.07 dB/μs at 1 GHz for y-z $LiNbO_3$), so very long delay lines are useful only at lower frequencies, limiting the attainable instantaneous bandwidth. Acoustic diffraction losses increase greatly in the far field; far-field distance D for isotropic propagation may be estimated as [3]

$$D = \frac{W^2}{2\Lambda}$$ (7.27)

The acousto-optic interaction is further reduced in the far field, because the acoustic waves are no longer planar. If y-z $LiNbO_3$ were isotropic for SAW propagation, the far-field distance D at 500 MHz would be about 10 cm (~29 μs). However, the acoustic anisotropy of the material extends the far-field distance [7] about a factor of 10, making acoustic propagation loss the limiting factor in determining usable interaction time. Using materials with slower acoustic propagation velocities, such as bismuth germanium oxide ($B_{12}GeO_{20}$), to obtain greater interaction time in a given physical length is not generally successful at increasing the attainable time-bandwidth product. Such materials tend to have greater acoustic attenuation per unit time delay; therefore, such materials are useful only at lower frequencies (and smaller bandwidths).

7.3.2 Maximum Bandwidth Techniques

Increasing the convolver time-bandwidth product by increasing the
acousto-optic interaction bandwidth involves solving several problems.
One is the previously mentioned bandwidth limit of efficient Bragg diffraction, and another is the bandwidth limit of efficient, nondispersive
delay-line transducers. Figure 7.4 shows a typical interdigitated
transducer of the type that has been used in many SAW acousto-optic
devices. Because it is nondispersive, time-frequency distortions are
not introduced in the processors by the transducer. The efficiency
of these transducers in converting electrical signals into SAW waves increases with the square of the number of finger pairs and directly
with the length of the fingers. Unfortunately, the bandwidth of the
transducers is inversely proportional to the number of finger pairs,
and increasing the finger length increases the width of the acoustic
phase front, which reduces the Bragg diffraction bandwidth.

   The conflicting requirements of bandwidth and efficiency, both for
the SAW delay line and the acousto-optic interaction, can be met by
using a tilted transducer array [8,9] as shown in Fig. 7.5. Each
transducer is designed for a different center frequency, with overlapping passbands. This allows each individual transducer to be of

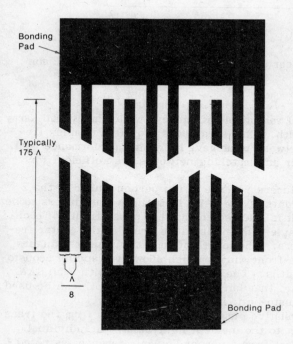

Figure 7.4 Typical SAW transducer pattern.

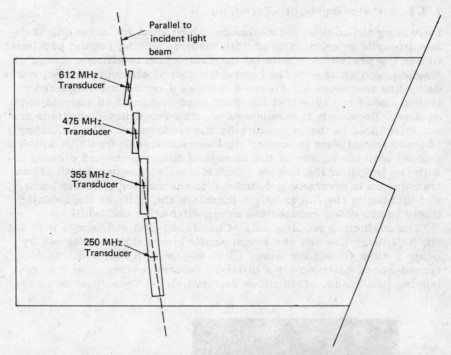

Figure 7.5 Multitransducer array for a wideband acousto-optic convolver.

moderate bandwidth (and reasonable efficiency) while the overall array
achieves a large bandwidth. This array does require a complex fre-
quency-selective feed network to achieve its design performance goal,
but straightforward filter and matching networks are sufficient for
this.

The tilt of the transducers relative to the perpendicular of the z
axis causes the phase fronts of the SAWs from these transducers to be
similarly tilted. This tilt is selected so that the phase fronts of each
SAW are at the Bragg angle with the incident light, at the center frequency of the transducers. The length of each transducer's fingers
is selected to give phase-front widths which allow overlapping acousto-
optic interaction bandwidths. The bandwidth needed with each SAW
is small enough, however, that fairly large acoustic depth can be used,
ensuring reasonable acousto-optic interaction efficiency.

To ensure constant relative phase between the SAWs from the transducer array with respect to the incident light beam, the individual
transducers must be offset from a perpendicular reference, as noted
in Fig. 7.5. The offset is simply the distance needed to ensure equal

propagation time from each transducer to a given propagation vector of the incident light.

A SAW acousto-optic convolver was made with a four-element tilted transducer array on a 15-cm-long y-cut, z-propagating LiNbO$_3$ crystal (the example used for Fig. 7.5) [10]. The center frequencies of the transducers were 250, 355, 475, and 612 MHz, yielding a combined passband from 174 to 718 MHz. The length of the transducer fingers was selected to give an acoustic phase-front width of slightly over 100 acoustic wavelengths at each transducer center frequency. With the 40-μs delay of the line, a time-bandwidth product exceeding 20,000 was achieved. However, the usable time-bandwidth product was only 10,000, as poor interaction efficiency with the SAWs from the 475- and 612-MHz transducers resulted in reduced dynamic range above 440 MHz.

This poor interaction efficiency was due to acoustic attenuation in the long line, combined with the small penetration depth of the acoustic waves at the higher frequencies ($\sim$ 6 μm at 600 MHz), with subsequent loss of illumination from the relatively thick ($\sim$ 60 μm) light sheet beam used. This thick beam resulted from using an f/40 cylindrical lens to achieve 4.8-mm depth of field at the back focal point, so that the full width of the delay line could be uniformly illuminated. Much improved high-frequency interaction efficiency can be obtained by using an optical waveguide in the surface of the delay line to confine the light to the SAW region. Using this technique [11], researchers in integrated-optic acousto-optic devices have reported interaction efficiencies exceeding 50% with more than 600-MHz bandwidth.

7.3.3 Dynamic Range Consideration

Several factors limit the attainable dynamic range of these acousto-optic convolvers and correlators. Acoustic attenuation, diffraction losses, and the difficulty of illuminating the very thin SAW region have been mentioned. Another factor, and a major one, is the photodetector that does the heterodyne detection. While PIN photodetector diodes have been found to give the best performance (in terms of noise and bandwidth) in these space-integrating signal processors, several operating considerations can markedly affect system dynamic range.

The Hewlett-Packard 5082-4207 PIN photodiode, operated at a bias potential of 20 V to maximize its frequency response, has been used extensively in space-integrating acousto-optic processors. The diode power dissipation limit of 100 mW restricts the incident light level (0.6328-μm light) to about 9 mW, which yields a diode current of $\sim$ 4.5 mA. In a typical double-diffraction convolver (Fig. 7.2), only about 1% of the incident light is initially diffracted by each acoustic wave. Approximately 2% of this light undergoes the second diffraction. When this doubly diffracted light is heterodyne-detected, a signal current is generated which yields a signal power in a 50-Ω load of about 4×10^{-7} W. The quantum noise from the local oscillator light (the undiffracted light of ~ 9-mW power) is about 1.4×10^{-11} W in a 200-MHz bandwidth. Thermal (Johnson) noise in this bandwidth is about 8×10^{-13} W, so the quantum noise is the limiting factor, and only about a 44-dB signal-to-noise ratio (and dynamic range) is attainable with this step.

A significant improvement in dynamic range can be obtained by heterodyne-detecting the two-first-order diffractions shown in Fig. 7.3 Recalling equation (7.14), which describes these two beams, it can be seen that they are collinear and differ in frequency by $2\omega_a$. By using a lens system with short focal length and low-F-number, the Fourier image of these diffractions [which has a spatial extent proportional to the bandwidth of the signals $B(t)$ and $C(t)$] can be reimaged onto the photodetector diode. The difference signal produced by the heterodyne detection is of the form

$$
D(t,z) \sim A_1^2 \cos\left[2\omega_a\left(t - \frac{L}{2v}\right)\right]\int_{z=-L/2}^{L/2} B'\left(t - \frac{L}{2v} - \frac{z}{v}\right)
$$

$$
\times \ C'\left(t - \frac{L}{2v} + \frac{z}{v}\right) \ dz \qquad\qquad (7.28)
$$

which is the convolution of $B(t)$ and $C(t)$ in a compressed time frame. The increase in dynamic range comes in part from the fact that much more illumination power can be used. With a 1% maximum diffraction from each acoustic wave, a 250-mW laser source gives a total diffracted light power of 5 mW incident on the detector diode. This yields a signal power of about 3.9×10^{-5} W and a quantum noise of 1×10^{-11} W. Thus a signal-to-noise ratio and convolution (or correlation) dynamic range of about 65 dB can be obtained for a 100-MHz bandwidth input signal. An example of this dynamic range improvement is the acousto-optic chirp-z transform discussed later in the chapter. With this device, changing from double-diffraction to two single-diffraction operations improved the dynamic range from about 45 to 65 dB. This improvement was attained, of course, at the expense of increased optical complexity in the processor and a significant increase in laser power.

7.4 CONVOLVER APPLICATIONS

7.4.1 Correlation and Matched Filter Detection

One use of a correlator is the detection of wideband signals buried in noise. As noted, a convolver may be used as a correlator if a time-reversed version of a signal can be generated for use as the reference input. In this application, the time-bandwidth produce is a direct measure of the maximum possible signal-to-noise ratio (SNR) enhancement that can be obtained. Figure 7.6 illustrates qualitatively the SNR

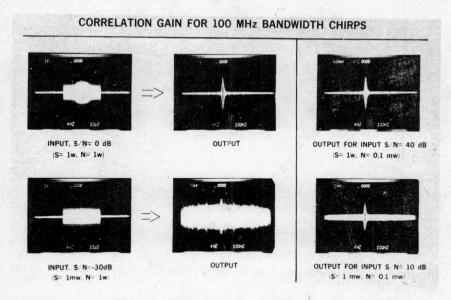

CORRELATION GAIN FOR 100 MHz BANDWIDTH CHIRPS

Figure 7.6 Signal detection with a SAW acousto-optic convolver.

improvement achieved in processing a 10-µs duration, 100-MHz bandwidth linear FM pulse (a chirp signal) [10]. Figure 7.7 shows that
an SNR increase of about 30 dB was obtained over the measurement
range, in good agreement with the chirp's time-bandwidth product
of 1000.

A matched filter is normally used as an optimum processor for signals in the presence of white stationary noise. Although a correlator
has identical SNR-enhancing properties, it has one distinct disadvantage. A correlator can only detect a signal when the reference
signal is present, while a matched filter can respond to a signal at any
time. Using the space-integrating SAW acousto-optic convolver as a
matched filter entails additional disadvantages. Maximum processing
gain is obtained only when the reference and the input signal occur
simultaneously and have duration equal to the full acousto-optic aperture of the device. Any mistiming between the input signal and the
reference, or the use of shorter duration signals, results in reduced
processing gain. A scheme which avoids this problem is one which
uses a system signal which has twice the duration of the convolver and
then uses a continuously repeated time-reversed version as the reference input to the device. An examination of the convolver output
versus relative delay between the reference and received signal shows
that correlation with the full processing gain of the convolver will
occur for any timing of the input signal. Thus 100% time coverage and

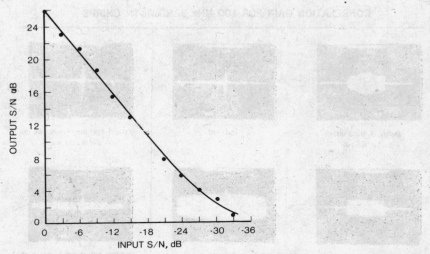

Figure 7.7 Signal-to-noise ratio improvement of a SAW acousto-optic convolver.

time-of-arrival information are obtained. Of course the processing gain is only half the time-bandwidth product of the signal, but this scheme obtains the advantage of the correlator's flexibility for this small sacrifice. This flexibility allows one to change the "matched" signal simply by changing the electronically generated reference signal, creating, in effect, a rapidly programmable matched filter.

7.4.2 Multichannel Operation

Figure 7.8 is a schematic drawing of a multichannel acousto-optic convolver, which was designed to independently process up to six signals simultaneously [12]. This device is made possible by the angle-frequency dependence of the Bragg acousto-optic interaction. Identical transducers for the six channels are tilted pairwise with respect to each other, as indicated in the figure. The SAWs generated by these interact with the six laser beams, where each beam is at the Bragg angle for one channel, and each beam is focused onto a separate photodetector diode. If the relative tilt between the transducers is properly selected, the adjacent channel acousto-optic interaction will be minimized, as indicated by the response curve in Fig. 7.9. Here it is seen that a relative tilt of about $1.6\theta_{Bn}$ achieves this minimization for the transducer aperture and center frequency used.

The six-channel convolver used a six-element array of transducers with a design center frequency and bandwidth of 300 and 30 MHz, respectively. The finger length of the transducers was 175 acoustic

MULTISIGNAL PROCESSOR USING
SIDE—BY—SIDE TRANSDUCER ARRAY

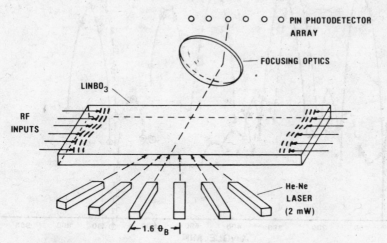

Figure 7.8 Multichannel SAW acousto-optic convolver.

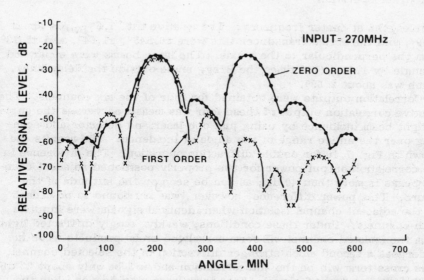

Figure 7.9 Acousto-optic interaction vs. angle of incidence in air.
Zero order refers to heterodyne detection of doubly diffracted light,
first order refers to heterodyne detection of first order diffractions
from two signals. Signal level at 65 min is −40 dB (zero order) to −60
dB (first order) relative to the peak signal at 200 min, corresponding
to ~1.6θ_B.

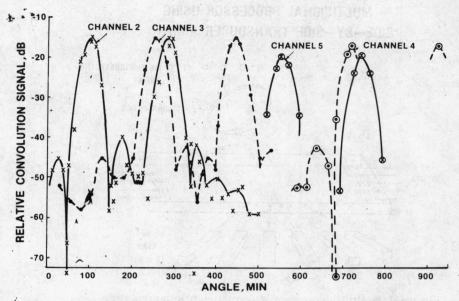

Figure 7.10 Multichannel convolver output vs. angle of incidence for zero order operation.

wavelengths at center frequency. The relative tilt, $1.6\Theta_{Bn}$, is about 1.09°, and the actual transducer tilts were ±0.545°, ±1.64°, and ±2.73° from the perpendicular to the z axis. The laser beams were separated in angle by $1.6\Theta_B$ (1.6 times the Bragg angle outside the delay line), which was about 2.39°.

Correlation outputs were obtained for four of the six channels. The relative correlation output of these four was measured versus the angle of light beam incidence by using just one laser and detector and scanning over the entire range of the angle of incidence. The results are shown in Fig. 7.10 for double-diffraction operation. The difference in the correlation output power for two properly positioned adjacent channel peaks is more than 40 dB, as can be seen on the left side of the figure. This power difference, however, was not found to be caused by the adjacent channel isolation when identical signals were input to both channels. Under these conditions, weakly, singly diffracted light from the isolated channel will form correlated cross products when it undergoes a second much stronger diffraction in the selected channel. This cross term will be the autocorrelation and will be only about 22 dB down from the desired signal. This term loses significance when the adjacent channel signals have small cross-correlation properties.

The obtainable channel isolation also depends on the bandwidth of each channel. The design bandwidth of 30 MHz corresponds to a diffraction angle deviation of about 19'. From Fig. 7.10, this angular extent, when centered at a diffraction minimum, results in a minimum isolation of about 22 dB.

At the maximum transducer tilt angle (2.73°) only about a 2.5-dB decrease in correlator output was observed. Theoretically, the power flow begins to deviate significantly from the z axis beyond a 2.5° tilt angle [7] (the anisotropic properties of y-cut, z-propagating $LiNbO_3$ contribute to this). This was verified qualitatively by measurements of the insertion loss of each channel of the delay line. Since this deviation did not affect the power flow (and acousto-optic interaction) greatly, it should be possible to increase the number of channels beyond six by adding transducers with increasing tilt from the normal to the z axis. The two channels that did not operate were those next to the edge of the delay line. The transducers did operate, but the power flow deviation from the z axis was great enough that the SAW generated by the transducer tilted toward the edge, struck the edge, and was lost. It is felt that even these channels would have worked if a wider slice of $LiNbO_3$ had been used for the delay line, allowing more clearance between the transducer and the edge.

7.5 FOURIER TRANSFORM PROCESSORS

7.5.1 Continuous Fourier Transform

The SAW acousto-optic convolver may be used to find, in real time, the continuous Fourier transform of a signal. This is done with an architecture which realizes the *chirp transform* algorithm. The Fourier transform X(f) of a function x(t) is defined as

$$X(f) = \int_{-\infty}^{\infty} x(t) \exp(-j2\pi ft) \, dt \qquad (7.29)$$

In the chirp transform algorithm, the identity

$$-2ft \equiv (f - t)^2 - f^2 - t^2 \qquad (7.30)$$

is substituted into equation (7.29). By rearranging the terms, one then obtains

$$X(f) = \exp(-j\pi f^2) \int_{-\infty}^{\infty} [x(t) \exp(-j\pi t^2)] \{\exp[j\pi (f - t)^2]\} \, dt \qquad (7.31)$$

The first bracketed term of the integral may be identified as the premultiplication of the function x(t) by a chirp (a linear FM signal). This product is then correlated with a chirp, and the result is post-multiplied by yet a third chirp. This equation is known as the mulitply-

CHIRP TRANSFORM IMPLEMENTATION

$X(f) = \int x(t)\ exp(-i2\pi ft)\ dt$: FOURIER INTEGRAL

LET: $-2\ ft = (f-t)^2 - f^2 - t^2$

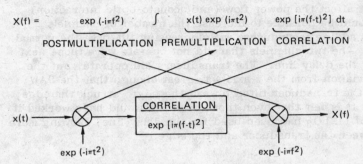

$$X(f) = \underbrace{exp\ (-i\pi f^2)}_{\text{POSTMULTIPLICATION}} \cdot \int \underbrace{x(t)\ exp\ (i\pi t^2)}_{\text{PREMULTIPLICATION}} \underbrace{exp\ [i\pi(f-t)^2]\ dt}_{\text{CORRELATION}}$$

Figure 7.11 Chirp-z transform algorithm.

convolve-multiply form of the chirp-z transform. Since the SAW
acousto-optic convolver can be used to determine the correlation of
two signals, it should be possible to use it as a structural block in
the realization of an architecture which performs the chirp-z transform.

Figure 7.11 is a block diagram of such an architecture. The signal
$x(t)$ is multiplied with a down chirp $C_1(t) = \cos[(\omega_1 - \alpha t)t]$ in a
double-balanced mixer. The desired sideband is selected with the
appropriate filter and is used as one input to an acousto-optic convolver. The other input is an up chirp $C_2(t) = \cos[(\omega_2 + \alpha t)t]$. Assuming that the signal timing, duration, and bandwidths have been
chosen to fall within the operating constraints of the convolver, the
output.(neglecting all constant terms) can be described by

$$S(t) = \int_{\tau=t-t_0}^{t} x(\tau)\ \cos[(\omega_1 - \omega_2 - 4\alpha t)\tau + (2\omega_2 + 4\alpha t)t]\ d\tau \qquad (7.32)$$

Using the identity $\cos(a + b) = \cos a \cos b - \sin a \sin b$ yields

$$S(t) = \cos(2\omega_2 + 4\alpha t)t \int_{\tau=t-t_0}^{t} x(\tau)\ \cos(\omega_1 - \omega_2 - 4\alpha t)\tau\ d\tau$$

$$-\sin(2\omega + 4\alpha t)t \int_{\tau=t-t_0}^{t} x(\tau)\ \sin(\omega_1 - \omega_2 - 4\alpha t)\tau\ d\tau \qquad (7.33)$$

If this output is postmultiplied with a chirp $\cos(\omega + 4\alpha t)t$ and the appropriate filter is used to select the difference frequency, the filter output can be described by

$$S(t) = \cos(2\omega_2 - \omega)t \int_{\tau=t-t_0}^{t} x(\tau) \cos(\omega_1 - \omega_2 - 4\alpha t)\tau \, d\tau$$

$$- \sin(2\omega_2 - \omega)t \int_{\tau=t-t_0}^{t} x(\tau) \sin(\omega_1 - \omega_2 - 4\alpha t)\tau \, d\tau \qquad (7.34)$$

If the Fourier transform of a real function $x(\tau)$ is written as

$$x(\Omega) = \int_{-\infty}^{\infty} x(\tau) \exp(-j\Omega\tau) \, d\tau \qquad (7.35)$$

with real and imaginary parts

$$Re[x(\Omega)] = \int_{-\infty}^{\infty} x(\tau) \cos(\Omega\tau) \, d\tau$$

and

$$Im[x(\Omega)] = \int_{-\infty}^{\infty} x(\tau) \sin(\Omega\tau) \, d\tau \qquad (7.36)$$

then equation (7.34) can be identified as

$$S = \cos(2\omega_2 - \omega)t \, Re[x(\Omega)] - \sin(2\omega_2 - \omega)t \, Im[x(\Omega)] \qquad (7.37)$$

where Ω is identified as $\Omega = \omega_1 - \omega_2 - 4\alpha t$.

Thus the output is seen to contain both the real and imaginary parts of the Fourier transform of $x(t)$ as quadrature components at frequency $2\omega_2 - \omega$.

Figures 7.12 to 7.16 summarize the results obtained using the convolver with the tilted transducer array shown in Fig. 7.5 to perform a partial chirp-z transform [13]. The postmultiply step was not performed, yielding a *microscan* type of output. The measured bandwidth of the transform was about 80 MHz, as shown in Fig. 7.12. Figure 7.13 demonstrates the linear dynamic range, which approached 70 dB. Figures 7.14 and 7.15 show that the structure of the sidelobes is strongly dependent on the spatial intensity distribution of the incident laser beam used in the SAW acousto-optic convolver. When a uniform intensity beam was used, a sinc function sidelobe pattern results when $x(\tau)$ is a constant (Fig. 7.14). The sidelobes are within 0.5 dB of the

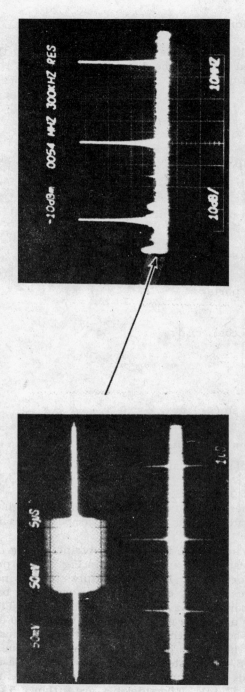

Figure 7.12 Output of a SAW acousto-optic chirp-z transform system. Top trace of left-hand photograph is input signal which consists of three CW tones covering almost 80 MHz as can be seen from spectrum analyzer output shown in right-hand photograph. Bottom trace of left-hand photograph, which is the output of the acousto-optic chirp-z-transform system similarly shows three CW tones. (From Ref. 13.)

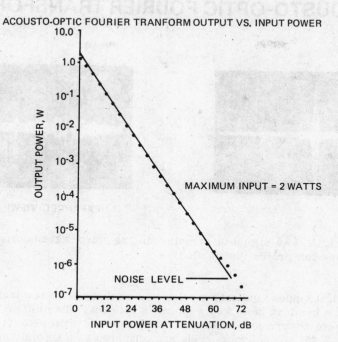

Figure 7.13 Measured dynamic range of a SAW chirp-z transform system. (From Ref. 13.)

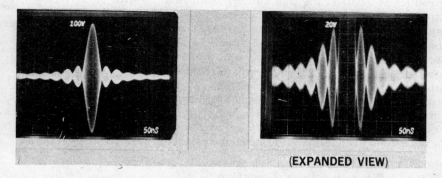

Figure 7.14 Chirp-z transform system output for uniform illumination.

ACOUSTO-OPTIC FOURIER TRANSFORM

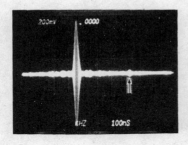 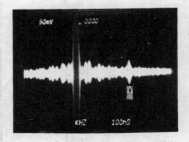

(EXPANDED VIEW)

Figure 7.15 Two-signal discrimation in the chirp-z transform system with gaussian profile illumination.

theoretical values, indicating relatively small error in the transform. When the incident beam had a gaussian intensity distribution, the side-lobes were suppressed to about 27 dB below the main peak (Fig. 7.15). In Fig. 7.15, the sidelobe levels are compared to a second, nearby signal with an amplitude 25 dB lower than the main signal.

A microscan system using a SAW acousto-optic chirp-z transform may be used to perform rapid spectrum analysis. Figure 7.16 shows the output of such a system when the input was the signals picked up by an antenna receiving the FM broadcast band in the Washington, D.C area. The chirp-z transform system (with a time-bandwidth product of 3200) scans this 20-MHz band in 2 μs with 30-kHz resolution. This is much faster than can be obtained with a conventional spectrum analyzer set for a comparable scan width and resolution and is also faster than a Bragg cell spectrum analyzer with present-day serial-readout detector arrays. The dynamic range of the SAW acousto-optic chirp-z transform is also somewhat greater than that obtained with Bragg cells. However, the SAW acousto-optic chirp-z transform operates with at most a 50% duty factor, because of the load-unload feature of the space-integrating acousto-optic convolver it uses. Two complete units used in "Ping-Pong" fashion would be required for a near 100% probability-of-intercept system, a decided disadvantage.

7.5.2 A Discrete Fourier Transform

A SAW acousto-optic processor which can determine the discrete Fourier transform of a sample set $\{g_n\}$ has also been developed. Speiser

ACOUSTO-OPTIC FOURIER TRANSFORM

FM RADIO

88.5	WAMU	97.1	WASH
89.3	WPFW	98.7	WMZQ
90.1	WGTB	99.5	WGAY
90.9	WETA	100.3	WOOK
91.9	WGTS	101.1	WWDC
93.9	WKYS	103.5	WGMS
94.7	WJMD	105.1	WAVA
95.5	WPGC	107.3	WRQX
96.3	WHUR		

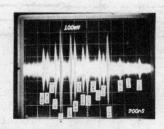

A-O FOURIER TRANSFORM OUTPUT

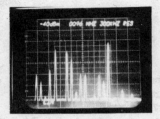

300 KHZ RESOLUTION

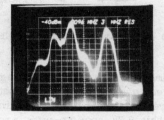

3 MHZ RESOLUTION

SPECTRUM ANALYZER

Figure 7.16 Spectrum analysis with the acousto-optic chirp-z transform system.

and Whitehouse [14] have manipulated the equation for the discrete Fourier transform G_k of a sample set $\{g_n\}$, where

$$G_k = \sum_{n=0}^{N-1} g_n \exp\left(\frac{-j2\pi nk}{N}\right) \tag{7.38}$$

By making the substitution $nk = (1/4)[(k+n)^2 - (k-n)^2]$, they obtained

$$G_k = \sum_{n=0}^{N-1} g_n \exp\left[\frac{-j\pi(k+n)^2}{2N}\right] \exp\left[\frac{j\pi(k-n)^2}{2N}\right] \tag{7.39}$$

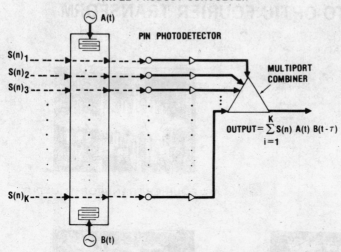

Figure 7.17 Acousto-optic triple-product convolver.

This architecture for performing the discrete Fourier transform is referred to as the triple-product convolver (TPC); a SAW acousto-optic realization of it is shown in Fig. 7.17.

In this SAW acousto-optic processor, the sheet beam of light used in the SAW acousto-optic convolver (Fig. 7.3) is replaced by a number of very narrow, parallel laser beams. Each beam is intensity-modulated (with an electro-optic modulator) by the data samples $\{g_n\}$, producing an incident light profile described by

$$D(z) = \sum_{n=0}^{N-1} g_n \, \delta \left(z - nd + \frac{L}{2} \right) \cos(\omega_\ell t) \qquad (7.40)$$

where d is the spacing between the beams, N is the number of beams, $L = (N - 1)d$ is the length of the interaction region, and $\delta(z)$ is the Dirac delta function.

For delay-line input signals $B(t) = \cos[(\omega_1 + \alpha t)t]$ and $C(t) = \cos\{[\omega_2 - (2\alpha L/v) - \alpha t]t\}$, the sum of the detected outputs in the frequency range of interest is (neglecting constant terms)

$$I(t) \sim \int_{z=-L/2}^{L/2} \sum_{n=0}^{N-1} g_n \, \delta\left(z - nd + \frac{L}{2}\right) \cos\left[(\omega_1 + \omega_2) \left(t - \frac{L}{2v} \right) \right.$$

$$\left. + (\omega_2 - \omega_1 - 4\alpha t) \frac{z}{v} - \frac{2\alpha t L}{v} + \frac{\alpha L^2}{v^2} \right] dz \qquad (7.41)$$

The integral picks up the delta function, yielding

$$I(t) \sim \sum_{n=0}^{N-1} g_n \cos\left[(\omega_1 + \omega_2)t - \left(\omega_2 + \frac{2\alpha L}{v}\right)\frac{L}{v} + (\omega_2 - \omega_1 - 4\alpha t)\frac{nd}{v}\right]$$

(7.42)

By again making use of the identity $\cos(a + b) = \cos a \cos b - \sin a \sin b$, one obtains

$$I(t) \sim \cos\left[(\omega_1 + \omega_2)t - \left(\omega_2 + \frac{2\alpha L}{v}\right)\frac{L}{v}\right] \sum_{n=0}^{N-1} g_n \cos\left[(\omega_2 - \omega_1 - 4\alpha t)\right.$$

$$\left. \times \frac{nd}{v}\right]$$

$$- \sin\left[(\omega_1 + \omega_2)t - \left(\omega_2 + \frac{2\alpha L}{v}\right)\frac{L}{v}\right] \sum_{n=0}^{N-1} g_n$$

$$\times \sin\left[(\omega_2 - \omega_1 - 4\alpha t)\frac{nd}{v}\right]$$

(7.43)

Equation (7.43) can be identified as

$$I(t) \sim \cos\left[(\omega_1 + \omega_2)t - \left(\omega_2 + \frac{2\alpha L}{v}\right)\frac{L}{v}\right] \text{Re DFT}$$

$$- \sin\left[(\omega_1 + \omega_2)t - \left(\omega_2 + \frac{2\alpha L}{v}\right)\frac{L}{v}\right] \text{Im DFT}$$

(7.44)

where DFT $= \sum_{n=0}^{N-1} g_n \exp(-j2\pi nK/N)$ and $(\omega_2 - \omega_1 - 4\alpha t)(Nd/2\pi v) = K$. Thus the summed output current contains the real and imaginary parts of the discrete Fourier transform as quadrature components at frequency $\omega_1 + \omega_2$. To obtain the G_K for each K, the chirp rate must be such that

$$\alpha = \frac{\pi v}{2Td}$$

(7.45)

where T is the design time duration of the output (which can be large with respect to L/v).

Figure 7.18 shows the output of a very simple SAW acousto-optic TPC for N = 8. The delay time $L/v = t_0 = 32$ μs, and the $\{g_n\}$ are all equal to unity. It should be noted that this device requires that the data samples by input in parallel, while the output is serial in time.

The discrete Fourier transform of a large sample set N, where $N = N_1 \cdot N_2$, can be manipulated by substituting $n = n_1 N_2 + n_2$ and $K = K_1 + K_2 N_1$ into equation (7.38), yielding

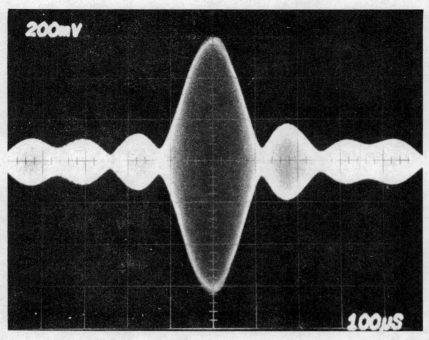

Figure 7.18 Output of a simple acousto-optic triple-product convolver.

$$G_{k_1 + k_2 N_1} = \sum_{n_2 = 0}^{N_2 - 1} \exp\left(\frac{-j2\pi k_2 n_2}{N_2}\right) \sum_{n_1 = 0}^{N_1 - 1} \left[(g_{n_1 N_2} + n_2) \exp\left(\frac{-j2\pi k_1 n_1}{N_1}\right) \right]$$ (7.46)

This indicates that a long one-dimensional transform can be achieved by first performing a partial DFT over N_1 and then multiplying by an appropriate phase factor and performing a second DFT over N_2 [14]. A system which could realize such an architecture is shown in Fig. 7.19. The N data samples have first been stored in N_2 buffer memories. The N_1 samples in each memory are then input into a serial-input, serial-output chirp-z transform module, such as can be constructed with charge-coupled device (CCD) transversal filters. The outputs of the N_2 chirp-z transform modules are then multiplied by the appropriate phase factors and fed into a parallel-input, serial-output DFT device like the TPC, which completes the transform.

LONG DISCRETE FOURIER TRANSFORM (DFT)

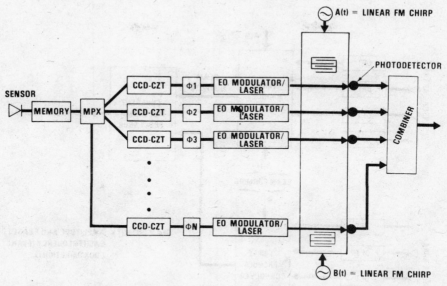

Figure 7.19 Using the triple-product convolver with CCD chirp-z transform modules to perform very long DFTs.

The system shown in Fig. 7.19 represents a way in which CCD signal processors and space-integrating acousto-optic signal processors might be advantageously combined. CCD signal processors have long interaction times ($\sim 10^{-2}$ to 10^{-1} sec) but small bandwidths, while space-integrating acousto-optic devices have large bandwidths (10^8 to 10^9 Hz) but small interaction times. Figure 7.20 shows a proposed combination processor for performing frequency-azimuth (ω-k) beam forming on the outputs of a very large sonar array. A Fourier transform is performed on the output of each hydrophone by CCD chirp-z transform modules. The frequency, amplitude, and phase information from these are input directly to an acousto-optic TPC. The convolver output can be shown to contain the frequency, amplitude, and direction-of-arrival information of the sound sensed by the array [15].

7.6 A TRUE SAW ACOUSTO-OPTIC CORRELATOR

Although a convolver can be used to find the correlation of two signals if a time-reversed version of one of the signals can be generated, this is not always convenient, especially if the cross correlation of two real-time signals is desired. Figure 7.21 shows a SAW acousto-optic

BEAM-FORMING ARCHITECTURE

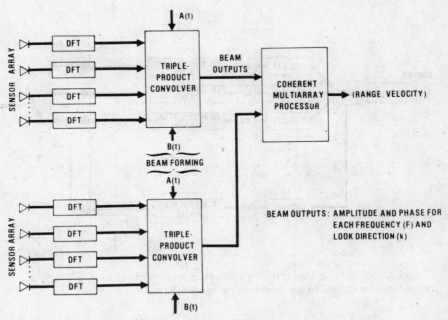

Figure 7.20 Beam forming with a triple-product convolver.

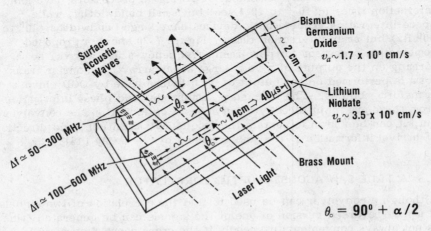

$$\theta_\circ = 90° + \alpha/2$$

Figure 7.21 Two-crystal real-time acousto-optic correlator.

architecture for finding the real-time correlation of two signals. It makes use of the different SAW propagation velocities of bismuth germanium oxide ($B_{12}GeO_{20}$ or BGO) and y-z $LiNbO_3$ delay lines and is referred to as a *two-crystal* correlator [16]. The SAW propagation velocity in 001-cut $B_{12}GeO_{20}$ is approximately half that of $LiNbO_3$. The SAW generated by the signal $B(t/2) \cos(\omega_a/2)t$ in the BGO can be described as

$$B\left(\frac{t}{2}\right) \cos\left(\frac{\omega_a}{2}\right)t \rightarrow B'\left(\frac{t}{2} - \frac{z}{v}\right) \cos \omega_a\left(\frac{t}{2} - \frac{z}{v}\right) \qquad (7.47)$$

where v is the SAW velocity in $LiNbO_3$, which is twice the SAW velocity in BGO. The point z = 0 is at the transducer, and the duration of $B(t/2) \leqslant L/v$. After a time $t_0 = L/v$, a signal $C[t - (L/v)] \cos \omega_a[t - (L/v)]$ is applied to the transducer on the $LiNbO_3$ delay line (also at z = 0) and generates a SAW:

$$C\left(t - \frac{L}{v}\right) \cos \omega_a\left(t - \frac{L}{v}\right) \rightarrow C'\left(t - \frac{z}{v} - \frac{L}{v}\right) \cos \omega_a\left(t - \frac{z}{v} - \frac{L}{v}\right)$$

$$(7.48)$$

The double diffracted light can be described (Bragg interaction) by

$$C'\left(t - \frac{z}{v} - \frac{L}{v}\right)B'\left(\frac{t}{2} - \frac{z}{v}\right) \cos\left[\left(\omega_\ell t + \omega_a\left(t - \frac{z}{v} - \frac{L}{v}\right)\right.\right.$$
$$\left.\left. - \omega_a\left(\frac{t}{2} - \frac{z}{v}\right)\right]\right. \qquad (7.49)$$

A lens is used to collect the undiffracted and doubly diffracted light and focus it onto a large-area photodiode, where heterodyne detection yields a term

$$I(t) = \int_0^L C'\left(t - \frac{L}{v} - \frac{z}{v}\right) B'\left(\frac{t}{2} - \frac{z}{v}\right) \cos\left[\left(\omega_a - \frac{\omega_a}{2}\right)t\right.$$
$$\left. - \frac{\omega_a z}{v} - \frac{\omega_a L}{v} + \frac{\omega_a z}{v}\right] dz \qquad (7.50)$$

or

$$I(t)_{\omega/2} = \int_0^L C'\left(t - \frac{L}{v} - \frac{z}{v}\right)B'\left(\frac{t}{2} - \frac{z}{v}\right) \cos\left[\omega_a\left(\frac{t}{2} - \frac{L}{v}\right)\right] dz$$

$$(7.51)$$

Substituting $\tau = t - L/v - z/v$, $t_0 = L/v$, and $d\tau = -dz/v$ yields

$$I(t)_{\omega/2} = -v \cos \omega_a\left(\frac{t}{2} - t_0\right) \int_{t-t_0}^t C'(\tau)B'\left(\tau - \frac{t}{2} + t_0\right) d\tau \qquad (7.52)$$

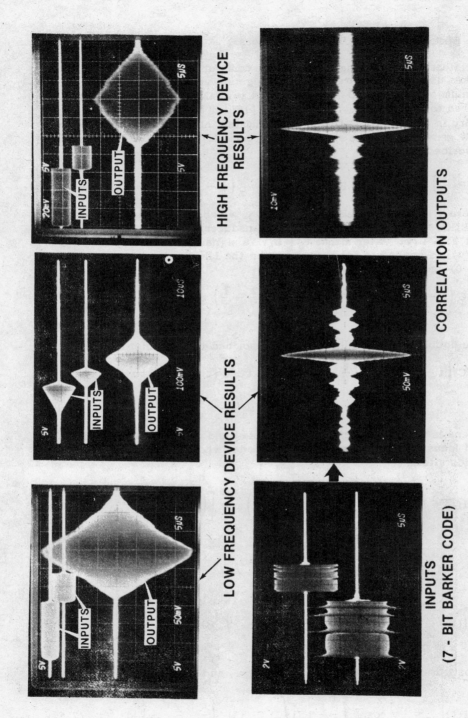

Figure 7.22 Two-crystal correlator outputs.

provided the duration of $C(t) \cos \omega_a t$ is $\leqslant t_0/2$. This is recognized
as the correlation of $B(t)$ and $C(t)$ in an expanded time frame, after
a delay t_0.

The difficulty with this scheme is generating $B(t/2) \cos \omega_a(t/2)$ from
the original $B(t) \cos \omega_a t$. The two-crystal setup shown in Fig. 7.21
may also be used to obtain this time-expanded signal. A delta function,
approximated as one cycle at $\omega_a/2$, is input to the BGO delay line, and
the signal $B(t) \cos \omega_a t$ is input to the $LiNbO_3$ delay line. The detector
output contains a term

$$I(t) = \int_{-L/2}^{L/2} \delta \left(t - \frac{2z}{v}\right) B'\left(t - \frac{z}{v}\right) \cos \left[\omega_a \left(t - \frac{z}{v}\right)\right.$$

$$\left. - \frac{\omega_a}{2}\left(t - \frac{2z}{v}\right)\right] \, dz \qquad\qquad (7.53)$$

If $B(t) \cos \omega_a t$ has duration $\leqslant L/v$, then

$$I(t) = B'\left(t - \frac{t}{2}\right) \cos \left[\omega_a \left(t - \frac{t}{2}\right)\right] \qquad\qquad (7.54)$$

which is the desired input signal. So a real-time space-integrating
SAW acousto-optic correlator can be realized by combining this two-
crystal time expander with the two-crystal correlator. Figure 7.22
shows the performance obtained with a two-crystal correlator which
used 15-cm-long $LiNbO_3$ and $B_{12}GeO_{20}$ crystals. A usable time-
bandwidth product of 5000, with a 30-dB dynamic range, was measured.

7.7   SUMMARY

Space-integrating surface-acoustic-wave acousto-optic devices can
perform a variety of useful signal-processing functions. Real-time
convolution and correlation of wideband moderate-duration signals
have been achieved. A scheme for realizing a programmable matched
filter has been described. A SAW acousto-optic realization of the
chirp-z transform algorithm for determining the Fourier transform of
a real-time signal has been detailed, and its use as a microscan analyzer has been described. An acousto-optic triple-product convolver
which may be used to determine the discrete Fourier transform of
a sample sequence has been described, and a scheme for combining this
acousto-optic device with charged-coupled-device chirp-z transform
modules to perform frequency-azimuth beam forming on sonar signals
has been proposed. Clearly, space-integrating SAW acousto-optic
processors have the flexibility and performance to warrant serious
consideration for complex signal-processing applications.

ACKNOWLEDGMENT

The authors wish to thank Dr. N. Karayianis of the Harry Diamond Laboratories for his help in developing the analyses of the acousto-optic processors described in this chapter.

REFERENCES

1. W. R. Klein and B. D. Cook, Unified approach to ultrasonic light diffraction, *IEEE Trans. Sonics Ultrason. SU-14*:123-134, July 1967.
2. C. F. Quate, C. D. W. Wilkenson, and D. K. Winslow, Interaction of light and microwave sound, *IEEE Trans. Sonics Ultrason. SU-14*:123-134, July 1967.
3. E. H. Young, Jr. and S. K. Yao, Design considerations for acousto-optic devices, *Proc. IEEE 69*:54, Jan. 1981.
4. T. M. Smith and A. Korpel, Measurement of light-sound interaction efficiencies in solids, *IEEE J. Quantum Electron. QE-1*:283-284, Sept. 1965.
5. E. G. H. Lean, J. M. White, and C. D. W. Wilkinson, Thin-film acousto-optic devices, *Proc. IEEE 64*:779-788, May 1976.
6. E. Salyman and D. Weisman, Optical detection of Rayleigh waves, *J. Appl. Phys. 40*:3408, 1969.
7. T. L. Szabo and A. J. Slobodnick, Jr., *Acoustic surface wave diffraction and beam steering, AFCRL-TR-73-0302*, May 1973.
8. J. Sapriel and R. Lacroin, *Rev. Phys. Appl. 7*:35, 1972.
9. C. S. Tsai, L. T. Nyugen, S. K. Yua, and M. A. Alhaidar, High-performance acousto-optic guided-light-beam device using two-tilting surface acoustic waves, *Appl. Phys. Lett. 26*:140-142, Feb. 1975.
10. N. J. Berg and B. J. Udelson, Large time bandwidth acousto-optic convolvers, *Proc. Ultrason. Symp.*, 183, 1976.
11. C. C. Lee, K. Y. Liao, C. L. Chang, and C. S. Tsai, Wideband guided-wave acousto-optic Bragg deflector using a tilted finger chirp transducer, *IEEE J. Quantum Electron. QE-15*:1166, 1979.
12. J. N. Lee, N. J. Berg, and M. W. Casseday, Multichannel signal processing using acousto-optic techniques, *IEEE J. Quantum Electron. QE-15*:1210-1214, Nov. 1979.
13. N. J. Berg, J. N. Lee, M. W. Casseday, and E. Katzen, Real-time Fourier transformation via acousto-optics, *Appl. Phys. Lett. 34*:15, Jan. 1979.
14. J. M. Speiser and H. J. Whitehouse, *NUC TN 1355R*, Naval Ocean Systems Center, San Diego, California, May 1974.
15. L. Armijo, K. W. Daniel, and W. M. Labuda, EASCON 1974, p. 381.
16. N. J. Berg, B. J. Udelson, J. N. Lee, and E. Katzen, An acousto-optic real-time "Two-crystal" correlator, *Appl. Phys. Lett. 32*:85-87, Jan. 1978.

8

Signal Processing Using an Acousto-Optic Memory Device

JOHN N. LEE / U.S. Naval Research Laboratory, Washington, D.C.

8.1 INTRODUCTION

The capability of real-time or near-real-time operation is one of the
major attractions of using acousto-optic devices for signal processing.
However, it is possible to greatly increase processing flexibility in
certain applications if signals corresponding to known quantities need
not be generated each time they are required but could be stored,
in analog form, in the acoustic delay-line medium itself. Generally,
it appears that space-integrating acousto-optic architectures (see
Chap. 7) would be most suited to utilizing a capability for storage
in an acoustic medium. The general building-block component would
be a space-integrating memory correlator. Such an acoustic-optic
memory correlator would operate in exactly the same manner as the
space-integrating convolver described in Chap. 7; however, instead
of two counterpropagating acoustic waves, there is one fixed signal
in the delay line and one propagating acoustic signal. We shall assume
the fixed signal has the appropriate properties for acousto-optic signal processing. A description of the memory correlator output can
then be derived as a simple extension of the photodetector output of
the real-time space-integrating convolver of Chap. 7, which was
given as

$$I(t) = A \int_{-L/2}^{+L/2} \left\{ B\left(t - \frac{L}{2v} - \frac{z}{v}\right) C\left(t - \frac{L}{2v} + \frac{z}{v}\right) \right. $$

$$\left. \cos\left[2\omega_a\left(t - \frac{L}{2v}\right)\right] \right\} \, dz \qquad (8.1)$$

where B and C are counterpropagating input signals, L is the length
of the acoustic delay line, v is the acoustic velocity, ω_a is the acoustic

carrier frequency carrier for B and C, and A is a constant. The origin $z = 0$ is chosen to be at the midpoint of the delay line to allow B and C to be easily described in a common coordinate system. By setting $\tau = t - (L/2v) - z/v$ and $t_0 = L/v$, one recognizes that equation (8.1) is a convolution integral for signals of duration less than L/v; i.e.,

$$I(t) = A' \cos[\omega_a (2t - t_0)] \int_{-\infty}^{\infty} B(\tau) C(2t - t_0 - \tau) \, d\tau \qquad (8.2)$$

but in a compressed time frame and on a carrier at frequency $2\omega_a$. Correlation is obtained by time-reversing either of the input signals. For a memory correlator, one of the signals, C, may be taken to be time invariant. Two important consequences follow. One is that the interaction of the light with the two signals results in a total shift in light frequency of only ω_a, since one signal is stationary. Hence, the output will be on a carrier at frequency ω_a. Second, one usually has the freedom to choose the sense (or direction) of the stationary signal. Hence, a correlator can be implemented without the need for time reversal of one input. With these points in mind, the modified form of equation (8.1) for the memory correlator is

$$I(t) = A \int_{-L/2}^{L/2} \left\{ B\left(t - \frac{L}{2v} - \frac{z}{v}\right) C\left(-\frac{z}{v} - \frac{L}{2v}\right) \cos\left[\omega_a\left(t - \frac{L}{2v}\right)\right] \right\} dz$$

$$(8.3)$$

Substituting with τ as given above results in

$$I(t) = A' \cos\left[\omega_a\left(t - \frac{t_0}{2}\right)\right] \int_{-L/2}^{L/2} B(\tau) C(\tau - t) \, d\tau \qquad (8.4)$$

Again, equation (8.4) represents a correlation if B and C are shorter than the acoustic line delay and length, respectively.

It is easy to envision the advantages of a memory correlator as described above. For example, by having such a memory capability in a space-integrating acousto-optic correlator which is used in a radar receiver, there would be no need to generate a reference signal for the correlator each time a radar signal is transmitted; this capability not only simplifies the system, but, more importantly, obviates the requirement to have some a priori knowledge of radar return times to at least within the time window of the correlator. Storage of several radar references would allow simultaneous processing for several different radar sources, as could be encountered with bistatic radars, or would allow for signal agility with a single radar at relatively low system complexity. A second application could involve storage of libraries of signals or data to be either recalled or correlated with large quantities of unknown signals.

Before proceeding to the details of specific memory correlators, it is worthwhile to examine the desired characteristics of such devices and to briefly discuss the relationship between any acousto-optic memory correlators and various analog signal-processing memory devices (both optical and nonoptical).

For the ideal memory correlator, several characteristics should be obtainable simultaneously. First, it is desired that information storage bandwidth be as wide as possible. Second, it is desirable that times to write and retrieve information be short. Third, there should be a rapid erase-rewrite capability. Finally, storage time should be long, provided the erase-rewrite capability does not suffer, since long-storage mechanisms together with erase-rewrite capability results in flexibility to handle situations calling for widely differing data storage times. Existing analog methods, including acousto-optic methods, can handle signals directly at RF frequencies, whereas digital memory is generally accessed at low speed compared to RF frequencies and is ultimately limited by the speed of components such as D/A (or A/D) converters. Of the various analog signal-processing memory devices not involving acousto-optics, the simplest is the fixed matched filter [1] such as a tapped delay line. It is not possible to change the memory signal of such a filter very easily, and therefore a series of filters is required to handle a variety of signals. Also, such filters generally have either limited bandwidth or limited speed compared to acousto-optic devices. A second nonoptical device still under development involves analog memory storage that is both adaptive and high speed. This high-speed storage has been achieved using surface-acoustic-wave (SAW) inputs to impress, via acoustoelectric interactions, signal waveforms onto either surface defect states or an array of Schottky barrier diodes on a silicon slab suspended above the SAW medium [2-4]. Subsequent introduction of SAW signals allows signal-processing functions such as correlation to be carried out using the resultant stored charge pattern as the second, nontraveling, input signal. Storage times of several hundred milliseconds are typical; hence, continual refreshing of the memory is required in many applications.

Two different optical correlators have some of the desired characteristics for an acousto-optic memory correlator. One proposed some time ago uses an acoustic delay line device for the live signal, and the memory signal is stored on photographic film [5,6]. A second type of correlator uses a fine-line photolithographic pattern of finger electrodes on a $LiNbO_3$ delay line which can be electrically programmed to induce a specific refractive index pattern immediately below the fingers [7]. The memory persists as long as the electrical signal is applied.

It has been found that adaptive storage of acoustic signals is possible in LiNbO$_3$, [8] such that an acousto-optic memory correlator
based on such storage could very well possess all of the four desired
characteristics for the ideal device. Several versions of such acousto-
optic memory correlators have been developed, and it is these devices
that will be discussed in detail in the following sections. First, the
various possible mechanisms for signal storage in LiNbO$_3$ will be discussed (Sec. 8.2), since it appears that at least two different mechanisms have been used in the developed devices. Next, the performance details of the various memory correlators are discussed (Sec. 8.3).
Finally, possible device applications are discussed (Sec. 8.4).

8.2 STORAGE MECHANISMS

Acousto-optic signal processing is based on light diffraction by changes
in refractive index (or dielectric constant) induced by an acoustic
wave, as explained in Chap. 1. Any storage effect that replicates these
refractive index changes can therefore be expected to produce memory
that may be accessed by the same light diffraction process involved in
the processing of "live" acoustic wave signals. It is well known that
many popular acoustic materials such as LiNbO$_3$ are strong electro-
optic materials; i.e., there is a relatively large refractive index change
with applied electric field. Thus, a useful memory would be obtained if
one could produce a permanent electric field distribution that results in
a refractive index pattern corresponding to an acoustic signal at a
given instant of time. It has been determined that exposure of y-z
LiNbO$_3$ to short-duration pulses of high-intensity laser light results in
semipermanent refractive index changes that can replicate those of any
SAW signal that may be present [8]. This effect has been called the
acoustophotorefractive effect.

Resultant index changes must arise from the transport of charge.
There are, however, several possibilities as to the nature of the
charge transport process; two major possibilities have been identified
as being most probably responsible for the acoustophotorefractive
effect. One possible process is the so-called nonlinear photorefractive
effect [9], where primarily internal photovoltages due to the laser light
illumination result in bulk transport of electrons in one direction along
the ferroelectric axis of LiNbO$_3$. The second possible process involves
modulated photoemission of electrons from the near-surface region of
the LiNbO$_3$.

8.2.1 Photorefractive Storage Processes

Electro-optic components such as laser beam modulators have often
been made of LiNbO$_3$ because of its large electro-optic coefficient. However, exposure of LiNbO$_3$ to even moderate laser light intensities

($\geq$ 10 W/cm^2) at green or shorter light wavelengths resulted in optical "damage" in the form of altered refractive index within the region of exposure [10]. A photovoltaic mechanism was determined to be the mechanism for charge transport in the LiNbO$_3$, and much subsequent research was done to determine the origin of the photovoltages. Also, this "photorefractive" effect was investigated as a potential means for writing permanent holograms [11]. Efforts to increase hologram-writing sensitivity led to investigation of writing with short laser puls-es, where nonlinear processes could result in larger index changes [9]. Nonlinear photorefractive storage is of primary interest for acoustic signal storage, since writing times must be short compared to the acoustic period.

For the purposes of acoustophotorefractive storage, it is necessary to determine whether the presence of an acoustic wave will result in nonlinear photorefractive storage with a component proportional to the amplitude of the acoustic wave. Possible means of obtaining storage of an acoustic signal include (1) modulation of the nonlinear photore-fractive effect itself by the acoustically induced pressure or density variations, (2) modulation of the nonlinear photorefractive effect by the acoustoelectric fields associated with acoustic signals in piezoelec-tric media, and (3) indirect storage whereby light diffracted by the acoustic signal produces nonlinear photorefractive storage. All three of these possibilities would be applicable to either bulk- or surface-acoustic-wave signal storage.

8.2.2 Photoemission and Surface Storage Processes

Storage processes at or near the surface of an acoustic material such as LiNbO$_3$ would be applicable to acoustophotorefractive storage of SAW signals. The electric field pattern due to a surface charge pat-tern would induce, via the electro-optic effect, corresponding refrac-tive index changes immediately below the surface. The effective depth of such index changes will be approximately equal to characteristic lengths in the surface pattern. For the case of acoustic signal storage, the characteristic length would correspond to one acoustic wavelength.

The required surface charge pattern could be obtained in a number of ways, both optical and nonoptical. One could "spray" electrons onto the surface of a LiNbO$_3$ SAW delay line in an appropriate pattern to simulate the effects of an acoustoelectric field. An electron beam gun would be programmed to write the pattern in a raster fashion. The ultimate limitation of this method would be the achievable resolution, which is limited by secondary electron emission. Alternatively, one can impinge a short electron beam pulse onto the surface of a LiNbO$_3$ delay line with a SAW signal in transit [12]. The implementation of this idea relies on redistribution of secondary electrons by the acoustoelectric field to produce mechanical stresses. Depending on primary electron beam energies and secondary electron yields, resultant surface charge patterns may represent either a net gain or loss of charge [13].

It is also possible to envision photorefractive processes involving
only the surfaces of materials. An advantage with optically induced
storage is the versatility and variety of light sources, especially high-
intensity, short-pulse lasers. If a photoemission process is possible,
the photoemitted electrons may be redistributed or the photoemission
current modulated by acoustoelectric fields to produce storage via
electron trapping at the surface. Photoemission has, in fact, been observed in $LiNbO_3$ [14].

In the following discussions, any optically induced storage of acoustic signals, whether originating from bulk or surface mechanisms, will
be referred to as acoustophotorefractive storage. Aside from effecting
storage of an acoustic signal, other important considerations for a memory device include memory duration and erase-rewrite capability. The
importance of such considerations can determine the type of storage
mechanism utilized. Storage times for photorefractive processes are on
the order of $\rho\varepsilon$, where ε is the dielectric constant and ρ the bulk or
surface resistivity of the material. For pure bulk $LiNbO_3$, values of
$\rho\varepsilon$ imply storage times of several weeks—much longer than the charge
storage times in Schottky barrier diodes (< 1 sec) [4] or the persistence
of electron-beam-induced stress patterns in $LiNbO_3$ (< 10 min). [12].

In the following section, the performance characteristics of acousto-
optic memory correlators using acoustophotorefractive storage will be
described. This description will include details of evidence for nonlinear photorefractive effects modulated by acoustoelectric fields and
for photoemission-based storage. Although the evidence for these
particular correlators is for these two mechanisms, the other storage
mechanisms need not be precluded as bases for memory correlators.

8.3 MEMORY-CORRELATOR DEVICE PARAMETERS

Two rather different write configurations were found to result in successful acoustophotorefractive storage in y-cut, z-propagating single-
crystal $LiNbO_3$ [8,15]. These are shown in Figs. 8.1 and 8.2. Experiments were performed on a y-z $LiNbO_3$ SAW delay line. In the case
of Fig. 8.1, the writing laser beam is shaped into a sheet with cylindrical lenses and passed through the near-surface region of the $LiNbO_3$
crystal where the acoustic energy of the SAW is concentrated. This
case will be termed the side-entry configuration. In the case of Fig.
8.2, the writing beam is introduced from above the $LiNbO_3$ crystal,
i.e., along the y axis for y-z-cut crystals. This case will be termed
the top-entry configuration. The readout is the same for both configurations, using a low-power He-Ne laser beam formed into a sheet
as in the real-time SAW acousto-optic processors described in Chap. 7.
For memory-correlator operation, the stored refractive index changes
(δn) and the δn produced by a live propagating acoustic wave both
modulate the low-power continuous-wave (CW) laser beam simultaneously.

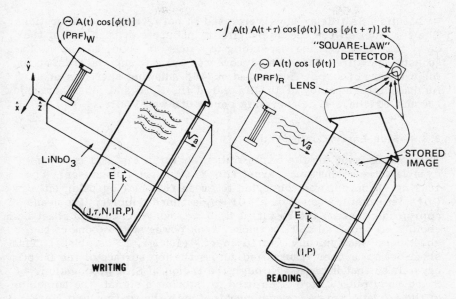

Figure 8.1 Acousto-optic memory correlator in side-entry configuration, showing both writing (left) and reading (right) modes. (From N. J. Berg, B. J. Udelson, and J. N. Lee, *IEEE Ultrason. Symp.*, 500, 1977.)

ACOUSTO-PHOTOREFRACTIVE EFFECT

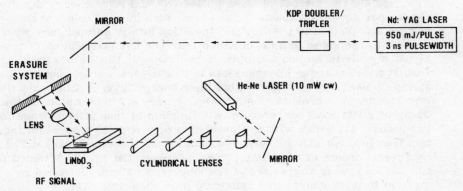

Figure 8.2 Acousto-optic memory correlator in top-entry configuration showing arrangement for writing, reading, and erasure. (From Ref. 4.)

Identical SAW delay lines were used in both writing configurations. The spacing between the interdigital transducers at each end of the delay line was 7 cm, corresponding to a delay of about 20 μsec. The acoustic aperture of the transducers was 1.5 cm, and the transducer fingers were of a split-finger design [16], allowing operation at a fundamental frequency of 10 MHz and at the third and ninth harmonics (30 and 90 MHz). The operating bandwidth was 1 MHz.

8.3.1 Side-Entry Configuration

The writing laser for the configuration shown in Fig. 8.1 is a neodymium yttrium aluminum garnet (Nd:YAG) short-pulse laser. The 1060-nm IR output was converted to green (530 nm) by using either a CD*A temperature-tuned or a KDP angle-tuned doubler. By means of appropriate lenses, the resultant light was converted into a sheet beam about 1 cm wide and 250 μm thick. Peak power at the focus of the sheet beam was typically 8 to 10 MW/cm^2 (100 mJ, 12-ns pulse). This sheet beam was then transmitted across the top surface of the LiNbO$_3$ crystal, so that it passed through the region of SAW propagation. Since many pulses were often used for storing a signal, the launching of the acoustic waves was synchronized with the writing (Nd:YAG) laser pulse to within 1 ns. The synchronization was done to ensure that the acoustic wave was in the same position during each laser pulse. The light beam used for both writing and reading were incident along the x axis, perpendicular to the z direction (optical c axis) of acoustic propagation.

The variation of correlation output power ($\sim \delta n^2$) at 10 MHz was measured as a function of number of laser pulses (N), incident laser energy density per pulse (joules, J), and RF input power during storage (P). These results have been summarized in the graph of Fig. 8.3. The axes are the number of laser pulses (N) and laser energy density (joules per square centimeter) per pulse, with lines of constant insertion loss plotted in the figure. Insertion loss is defined here with respect to the known output obtained from the live convolution of two 10-mW signals in an acousto-optic convolver. It can be observed from Fig. 8.3 that the insertion loss is $\sim$ 30 dB for a single laser storage pulse of 10^3 mJ/cm^2. This laser energy level is still below the physical damage threshold for LiNbO$_3$. Figure 8.4 shows plots of the decay of δn at room temperature as a function of time after storage for two cases: (1) green writing illumination only and (2) green illumination combined with IR. The time constants for these two cases differ by several orders of magnitude. The relatively flat regime obtained for the second case is suggestive of the long-term natural dielectric relaxation time for charge in a relatively pure dielectric [17].

The time constant data appear consistent with bulk photorefractive storage. However, there are some notable differences from reported

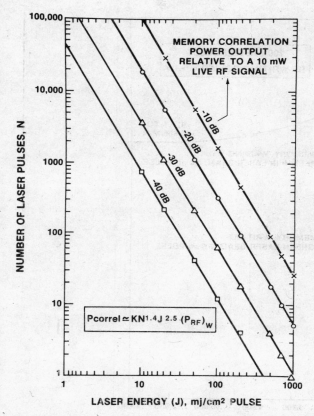

Figure 8.3 Curves of constant output power from memory correlator as function of number of laser pulses and of laser energy density. P_{RF} is the RF power level for the live signal. (From N. J. Berg, B. J. Udelson, and J. N. Lee, *IEEE Ultrason. Symp.*, 503, 1977.)

behavior of the nonlinear photorefractive effect. The acoustophotorefractive effect (δn) varies as $N^{0.7}$ and $J^{1.3}$, whereas the nonlinear photorefractive effect varies linearly with N and as J^2. Also, the long time constant data were obtained with a light beam consisting of green pulse IR (unconverted 1060-nm light), whereas nonlinear photorefractive effects generally are observable with green light alone. Some of these differences might be explained by the magnitude of the index change contributing to correlation signal (δn_{ac}) compared to the index change occurring regardless of the presence of an acoustic signal (δn_{dc}).

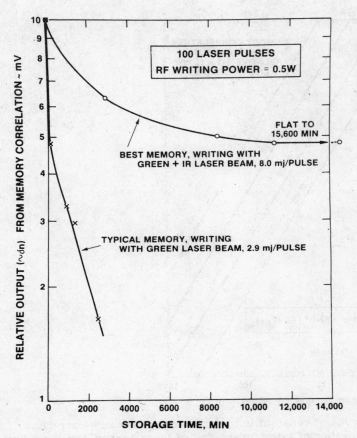

Figure 8.4 Relative correlator output power vs. storage time for two cases: green writing beam alone and writing beam combining green and IR. (From Ref. 8.)

The magnitude of δn_{ac} (normalized with respect to n) produced by the acoustophotorefractive effect can be estimated by comparison with the index of refraction change produced by the elasto-optic effect and was found to be $\sim 10^{-7}$. This is to be compared with a value of $\delta n_{dc} \sim 10^{-4}$ based on data for the nonlinear photorefractive effect [9]. If the acoustophotorefractive effect were merely a modulation of the nonlinear photorefractive effect produced by the acoustically induced strain (s), then (since $s \sim 10^{-6}$ [18]) a value of $\delta n_{ac} \sim 10^{-10}$ would be expected. This value is almost three orders of magnitude smaller than that observed. This result leads one to speculate that the electric field accompanying the acoustic wave in the piezoelectric material (rather than changes of δn due to density changes alone) may be responsible for the acoustophotorefractive effect. This model is further supported by experiments in which two strong photorefractive materials, bismuth germanium oxide and bismuth silicon oxide, were found to have no detectable acoustophotorefractive sensitivity. These two materials differ from LiNbO$_3$ in that their photocarrier lifetimes are long ($\sim$ 20 μs) [19, 20] compared to lifetimes in LiNbO$_3$ (< 1 ns) and to the acoustic signal period (100 ns), so that acoustoelectrically driven transport of conduction-band carriers will not result in storage. Finally, it is probable that the storage in this configuration is not entirely bulk storage in the LiNbO$_3$. Surface storage mechanisms discussed in Sec. 8.2.2 are not precluded in this configuration.

Erasure results on acoustophotorefractively stored signals are very similar to what has been observed for the photorefractive effect [21-23], indicating a similarity for charge-trapping mechanisms. Erasure has been accomplished using (1) exposure to ^{60}Co γ-radiation, (2) ultraviolet exposure such as from a mercury lamp, and (3) a temperature anneal at 250°C. The memory correlator using the side-entry configuration was successfully used for correlating live signals, consisting of relatively complex waveforms, with similar waveforms that had been stored for as long as several weeks. This is illustrated in Figs. 8.5 and 8.6. Figure 8.5 illustrates the output obtained by correlating a live 10-MHz, 10-μs-wide rectangular pulse having a linear FM chirp of 1 MHz with a similar previously stored signal. In Fig. 8.5A, the reading beam had a gaussian intensity distribution across the length of the stored image; the pictures in Fig. 8.5B were obtained for a uniform beam intensity. Comparison of the expanded output pulse with the computer simulations (shown at the right of Fig. 8.5) for both types of beam distribution demonstrates good agreement for both the null-to-null spacing and the peak-to-sidelobe ratio (R). Figure 8.6 shows long-term storage of a seven-bit Barker code. Memory-correlator outputs are in good agreement with theory when distortion of the input waveform due to limited transducer bandwidth is taken into account.

8.3.2 Top-Entry Configuration

The writing configuration shown in Fig. 8.2 has the advantage of permitting simultaneous reading and writing. The writing laser is again a Nd:YAG laser which produces a short-pulse (< 3 ns), high intensity circular beam (1-cm diameter) of 1060-nm light. By using this configuration, it was possible to store acoustic signals using the 1060-nm wavelength directly, as well as with the frequency-doubled 530-nm light. With the 3-ns laser pulse width it was possible to store signals at 10, 30, and 90 MHz.

The ability to store using 1060-nm light indicated a storage mechanism other than the nonlinear photorefractive effect, since no photorefractive holograms have been successfully written in pure, bulk

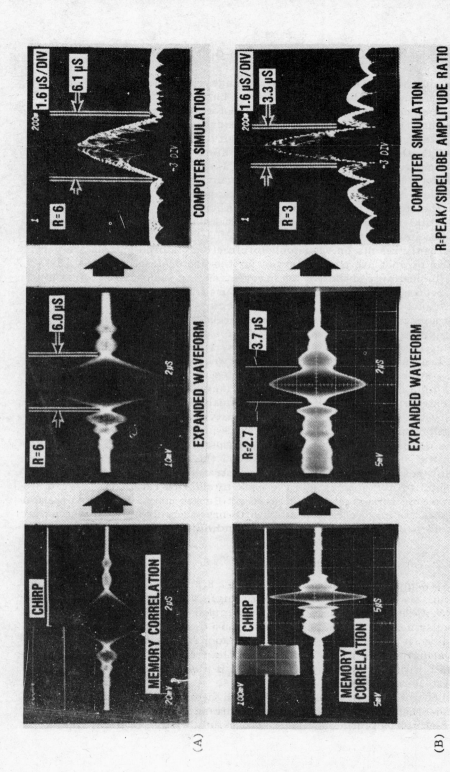

Figure 8.5 Output waveforms of memory correlator for linear FM chirp and comparison with computer simulation using (A) gaussian and (B) uniform reading beams. (From N. J. Berg, J. N. Lee, and M. W. Casseday, *Opt. Eng.* 18:427, July-Aug. 1979.)

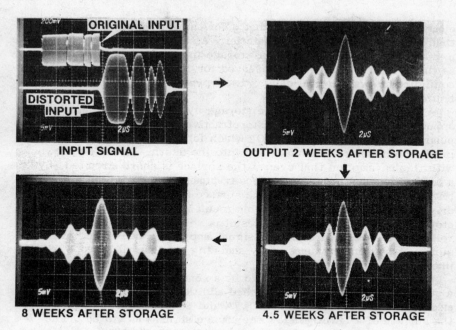

Figure 8.6 Changes with time of output waveform of memory correlator for seven-bit Barker code. (From N. J. Berg, B. J. Udelson, and J. N. Lee, *IEEE Ultrason. Symp.*, 504, 1977.)

LiNbO$_3$ at 1060 nm without special pretreatment of the material [10,24]. There is a large amount of data, both direct and indirect, indicating that this 1060-nm storage involves surface storage mechanisms only [25,26]. Experimentally, it was found that the stored signal could be removed by surface treatments alone. Erasure could be effected by wiping the surface of the LiNbO$_3$ with solvents such as acetone or by exposing the surface to a plasma discharge such as from a Tesla coil [25]. A second experimental test was to attempt storage at 1060 nm on a delay line with conducting surfaces [26]. Regions of a LiNbO$_3$ delay line were coated with a high-conductivity film of SnO$_2$ which would discharge any variations in surface charges only. The SnO$_2$ layers were sufficiently thin so as not to load the surface mechanically, nor shield the Nd:YAG radiation, nor introduce any significant change in SAW velocity. No storage whatsoever was observed in the coated areas, whereas the uncoated area behaved normally [26].

The observed lifetimes of stored signals also tend to support a surface-only mechanism. The lifetime would be approximately $\rho\epsilon$, as discussed in Sec. 8.2, but where ρ is the surface resistivity in this case. Since no special precautions were taken to maintain extremely clean surfaces, it is expected that ρ for these surfaces should be less than the value for pure bulk material. As mentioned in Sec. 8.3.1, the ρ value for bulk material implies storage times of several weeks, whereas the maximum storage time observed for 1060 nm using the top-entry configuration was several days, with typical storage times of several hours.

A further test of the surface storage hypothesis was to assume an opposite hypothesis—that a photorefractive storage results in a charge-polarization profile in the $LiNbO_3$ which follows the SAW electric field profile both along the surface and into the depth. It can be shown with this assumption that even if the surface is short-circuited (by a conductive coating or by surface treatment) a substantial net electric field component normal to the surface must exist: $\sim 15\%$ of the original normal field [25,27]. This result would apply to both live and stored signals. However, this result is not borne out either by correlation measurements of stored signal amplitudes before and after surface treatment erasures or by scanning electron microscope (SEM) photography of the surfaces.

SEM photography was found to be a sensitive method for observing a stored signal and was able to shed additional light on the storage mechanism at 1060 nm. Figures 8.7A and B show SEM photographs of the surface of a $LiNbO_3$ delay line after a signal was stored. The periodicity of the pattern was exactly that of the 10-MHz acoustic signal. By using an electrostatic probe, it was found that the dark regions in the photograph corresponded to positively charged regions. The SEM photographs in Figs. 8.7C and D illustrate a *fatiguing* effect whereby repeated cycles of writing immediately after surface treatment erasure resulted in successively lower storage amplitudes. This fatigue had also been observed with the correlation measurement technique. These observations may be explained by the presence of a dc or bias-level change in refractive index in addition to the ac change corresponding to the acoustic signal. Electrostatic probe measurements on $LiNbO_3$ samples exposed to the 1060-nm laser beam (without an acoustic signal present) indicate the probable origin of the dc change. For such samples both the top and bottom surfaces through which the laser beam had traversed became positively charged. Since both surfaces were charged to the same polarity, a photoemission process, rather than a photovoltaic process, appears to be the most likely origin.

Measurements of correlator output power versus writing pulse intensity J were obtained for 10- and 30-MHz signal storage with single and multiple synchronized laser pulses. Output was found to vary as J^n, where n ranged from 1.4 to 2. These power law dependences, although exhibiting a degree of variability, strongly suggested a multiphoton process. It was also found that n tended to decrease with number of writing pulses used, indicating saturation effects. With higher-frequency acoustic signals, a direct detection method was found to be more rapid and effective in determining power law dependences.

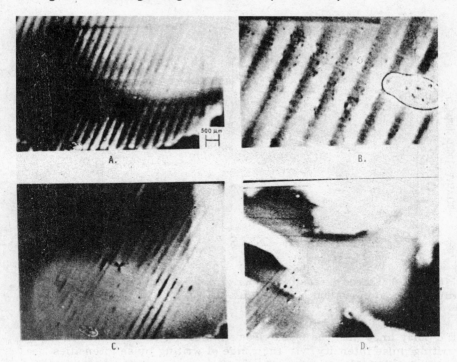

Figure 8.7 SEM photograph of LiNbO$_3$ surface with a stored 10-MHz signal (A) and expanded magnification view of the same surface (B). Photographs after one (C) and two (D) erase-rewrite cycles, using surface treatment erasure, illustrate reduced amplitudes for storage. (From Ref. 25.)

Storage at higher frequencies (30 and 90 MHz) allowed the stored signal to be sensed by other than cross-correlation techniques. Since the light diffraction angle is larger at the higher acoustic frequencies, the first-order beam from a stored signal is distinctly separated from the zero-order undiffracted beam, and its intensity can be directly measured with a photodetector [27]. Further, this direct detection method allowed measurement of storage amplitude immediately after writing. To increase dynamic range, a reference channel was obtained by beam-splitting the reading He-Ne beam and used to null out (before storage) the background undiffracted light that spilled over into the photodetector.

Direct detection measurements were taken of the relative stored signal amplitude at 90 MHz versus writing pulse intensity, and the results are shown in Fig. 8.8. The error bars in Fig. 8.8 show the measurements taken at the same position and at different positions along

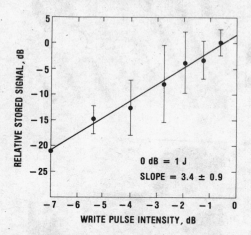

Figure 8.8 Stored intensity vs. write pulse intensity at 90 MHz, using direct detection method. (From Ref. 26.)

the delay line, with the black circles indicating the averages at each writing pulse intensity. In the range of writing pulse intensities measured, 0.2 to 1.0 J, the dependence of the stored SAW intensity I as a function of the writing intensity J is approximately $I \propto J^{3.4}$. These results again suggest a multiphoton storage mechanism. In particular, this power law dependence is very close to that expected for a multiphoton process using 1060-nm photons to bridge the fundamental band gap of pure $LiNbO_3$ (~ 3.5 eV) [28].

Using the direct detection method, decay time constants were measured immediately after one-shot storage. These measurements showed the presence of a rapidly decaying component to the storage amplitude, as well as the longer decay constants (approximately hours) mentioned earlier. These fast time constants, determined by measuring the slope of the stored signal decay, are plotted versus stored signal frequency in Fig. 8.9. The $F^{-1/2}$ line, where F is the relative frequency, is shown for reference only, since the data are insufficient to draw any conclusions regarding a fundamental dependence of this form. The fast time constants were observed to be independent of the storage pulse intensity and the acoustic power.

If storage at 1060 nm is indeed due to modulated photoemission, as is suggested by much of the data described above, a particularly effective method for erasure and rejuvenation using electron beams might be possible. Depending on the amount of charge lost from the surface, a pulse of electrons of the proper energy, current density, and dura-

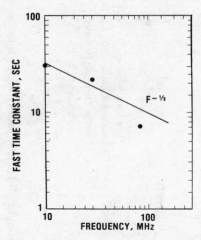

Figure 8.9 Frequency dependence of time constants, where F is the relative frequency. (From Ref. 26.)

tion could return the surface of the $LiNbO_3$ to its original, neutral state [13]. This method of erasure would remove both dc and ac refractive index changes, in contrast to surface treatment methods, so immediate rewriting would be possible. Pulsed electron guns and microchannel plates are possible electron beam sources. A microchannel plate source has, in fact, been used to both write information on and erase an $LiNbO_3$ spatial light modulator plate at 100-Hz rates [29]. Hence, even though all erasure mechanisms applicable in the side-entry configuration are also effective for the top-entry configuration, an electron beam method would be much faster.

In summary, with the top-entry configuration, it is possible to obtain SAW signal storage using a 1060-nm laser pulse. It can be inferred from the data that the storage mechanism is the trapping of surface charges, with the trapping time much shorter than 11 nsec (one period at 90 MHz, the maximum frequency stored so far). Further, there is strong evidence for a multiphoton photoemissive process as the origin of the surface charging.

8.4 APPLICATION AND FUTURE DIRECTIONS FOR ACOUSTO-PHOTOREFRACTIVE DEVICES

A major issue in the application of the acoustophotorefractive effect is the implementation into compact packages of the present laboratory arrangements for the correlators described in Sec. 8.3. This almost certainly requires a utilization of integrated-optics and miniature-optics

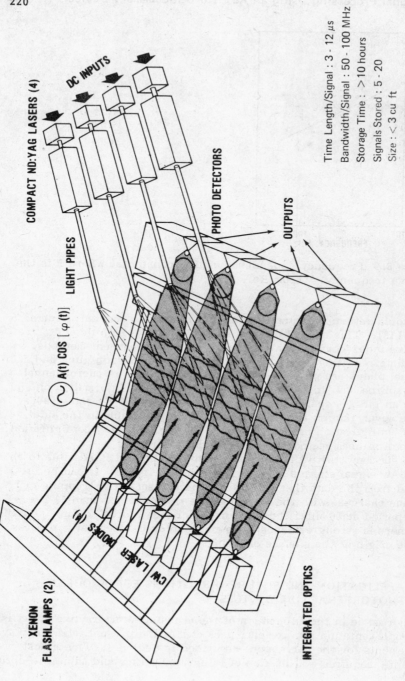

Figure 8.10 Memory correlator using integrated-optics readout and compact Nd:YAG lasers, with projected size, weight, and performance parameters.

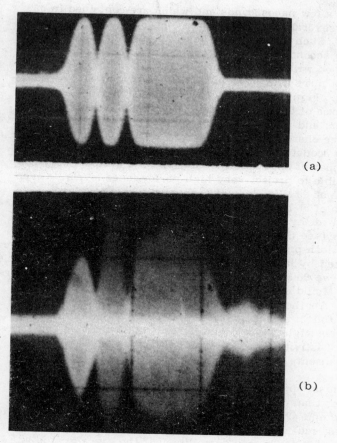

(a)

(b)

Figure 8.11 Retrieval of stored five-bit Barker code using impulse input to memory correlator. (a) Input acoustic signal; (b) output signal. (From N. J. Berg, J. N. Lee, and B. J. Udelson, *Acoust. Imaging 8*:382, 1980.)

technologies such as described in Chaps. 12 and 4, respectively. Integrated optics has obvious application for compacting the readout system. The writing systems may be limited in their use of guided optical waves, because the optical power densities could be above damage thresholds for optical waveguides. With the top-entry configuration there is no need for optical waveguides in the writing phase, but the writing-laser output requirements are increased by the need to have high energy density over a large surface area. However, laser output requirements could be met with a multiplicity of existing, compact Nd:YAG lasers which have an output of about 100 mJ in a pulse

with a duration of a few nanoseconds and which are contained in a
package weighing several kilograms with a volume of a few hundred
cubic centimeters. Such lasers can be feasibly operated from battery
power sources. A second approach to the laser output problem is to
use a raster-scanned writing mode whereby a long signal is written
in sections using a number of laser pulses synchronized with a repeating acoustic pulse. Figure 8.10 shows a conceptual memory-correlator
system utilizing some of the ideas outlined above and with some projected size, weight, and performance parameters.

The performance characteristics described in Sec. 8.3 and developments in real-time acousto-optic processors allow one to project performance in a number of application areas. For the basic memory correlator, it is possible to project very high performance levels. Given
successful storage at 90 MHz, it is entirely reasonable to expect a
storage bandwidth of at least 50 MHz. Together with the development
of y-z $LiNbO_3$ SAW delay lines with 40-μs delay times and large-bandwidth transducers (see Chap. 7), one can project a memory correlator
with a time-bandwidth product of at least 2000. Presently, the storage
bandwidth is limited by laser pulse width. Storage should be obtainable
at frequencies above 90 MHz using mode-locked or cavity-dumped lasers.
The ultimate limit would eventually be set by the retrapping time for
surface charges. Another potential attraction of future devices would
be the ability to control storage or memory time to match application
requirements. This might be achieved by control of material properties
such as surface resistivity, through ion implantation, ion etching, or
other surface treatments, to attain any storage time in the range from
seconds to weeks.

Possible additional application areas for acoustophotorefractive memory devices, other than correlation, include (1) high-speed, high-
density recording and (2) spatial light modulation for optical processing.
For data recording and retrieval, one recognizes that memory-correlator output is exactly the stored signal itself if the live signal is an
impulse function. Data retrieval was illustrated with the side-entry
device of Fig. 8.1, and the results are shown in Fig. 8.11. A five-
bit Barker code was stored and subsequently correlated with a live
"impulse" function. The output can be recognized as the original
Barker code but with rounding of the pulse shape due to the limited
input transducer bandwidth. From the data of Sec. 8.3, it is possible
to project devices capable of storing 50-MHz bandwidth signals in
microseconds. Adaptability of storage times would again be an advantage. A spatial light modulator for use as a Fourier plane filter in
a two-dimensional optical processor might be possible using raster
scanning of the writing laser beam onto a slab of $LiNbO_3$. This
utilization would be generically similar to a device using microchannel-
plate electron sources to write information onto a thin $LiNbO_3$ plate
[29].

REFERENCES

1. M. I. Skolnik, *Introduction to Radar Systems*, McGraw-Hill, New York, 1962.
2. G. S. Kino, *Proc. IEEE 64*:724, 1976.
3. A. Bers and J. H. Cafarella, *Appl. Phys. Lett. 25*:133, 1974.
4. J. H. Cafarella, *Proc. 1978 IEEE Ultrason. Symp.*, 78CH1344-1SU, 1978, p. 769.
5. E. B. Felstead, *Appl. Opt. 7*:105, 1968.
6. H. R. Carleton, W. T. Maloney, and G. Meltz, *Proc. IEEE 57*:769, 1969.
7. C. M. Verber, R. P. Kenan, and J. R. Busch, *Opt. Commun. 34*:32, 1980.
8. N. J. Berg, B. J. Udelson, and J. N. Lee, *Appl. Phys. Lett. 31*:555, 1977.
9. D. von der Linde, A. M. Glass, and K. F. Rodgers, *Appl. Phys. Lett. 25*:155, 1974.
10. F. S. Chen, *J. Appl. Phys. 40*:3389, 1969.
11. A. M. Glass, *Opt. Eng. 17*:470, 1978.
12. A. G. Bert, B. Epsztein, and G. Kantorowicz, *IEEE Trans. Sonics Ultrason. SU-20*:173, 1973.
13. B. Kazan and M. Knoll, *Electronic Image Storage*, Academic Press, New York, 1968.
14. G. Massey, M. Jones, and J. Johnson, *1980 Conference on Lasers and Electro-optic Systems, Digest of Papers*, 1980, p. 60.
15. N. J. Berg and J. N. Lee, *Proc. 1978 IEEE Ultrason. Symp.*, 78CH1344-1SU, 1978, p. 95.
16. T. W. Bristol, W. R. Jones, P. B. Snow, and W. R. Smith, *Proc. 1972 IEEE Ultrason. Symp.*, 1972, p. 343.
17. J. P. Huignard, F. Micheron, and E. Spitz, *Optical Systems for Photosensitive Materials for Information Storage*, North-Holland, Amsterdam, 1976, Chap. 16.
18. N. Uchida and N. Niizeki, *Proc. IEEE 61*:1073, 1973.
19. J. P. Huignard and F. Micheron, *Appl. Phys. Lett. 29*:591, 1976.
20. R. A. Sprague, *J. Appl. Phys. 46*:1673, 1975.
21. J. J. Amodei, W. Phillips, and D. L. Staebler, *Appl. Opt. 11*:390, 1972.
22. Y. Ohmori, M. Yamaguchi, K. Yoshino, and Y. Inuishi, *Jpn. J. Appl. Phys. 16*:181, 1977.
23. D. L. Staebler, W. J. Burke, W. Phillips, and J. J. Amodei, *Appl. Phys. Lett. 26*:182, 1975.
24. C. M. Verber, Batelle Columbus Laboratories, private communication, 1979.
25. J. N. Lee, N. J. Berg, and P. S. Brody, *Proc. 1979 IEEE Ultrason. Symp.*, 79CH1482-9, 1979, p. 81.

26. H. Dropkin, J. N. Lee, and N. J. Berg, *Proc. 1980 IEEE Ultrason. Symp.*, 1980, p. 1044.

27. R. P. Leavitt, *Appl. Phys. Lett.* 34:771, 1979.

28. K. Bärner, R. Braunstein, and H. A. Weakliem, *Phy. Stat. Sol.* 68:525, 1975.

29. C. Warde, A. D. Fisher, D. M. Cocco, and M. Y. Burmawi, *Opt. Lett.* 3:196, 1978.

9

Incoherent-Light Time-Integrating Processors

JONATHAN D. COHEN / Department of Defense, Fort Meade, Maryland

9.1 INTRODUCTION

The operation performed by an optical signal processor generally takes
the form of an integral transform. Optical processors are categorized
into one of two classes depending on how this integration is carried out.
Space-integrating processors, as the name implies, integrate across
one or two dimensions in space. Time-integrating processors, on the
other hand, generate an integral by accumulating the result in time.
The processors we shall deal with here use incoherent-light sources
to perform time integration. By *incoherent* light, we mean light whose
coherence length[†] is small compared to the dimensions of optical components used in the processor.

We are interested in processors which use incoherent light for two
reasons: the source and the light itself. Inexpensive compact incoherent sources are readily available. This is particularly true with
the maturing of light-emitting diodes, which have long life and are
rugged. Incoherent light does not generate *coherent artifacts*, which
are commonly seen in coherent-light systems. Also, polychromatic
light tends to average some nonuniformities which occur in optical
processors.

Time-integrating processors are built around the basic time-integrating correlator. Accordingly, a major portion of the discussion is
devoted to the presentation and analysis of correlator architectures,
of which there are many. With such a large number of architectures
available, the question naturally arises, "Which is best?" Our intent

---

[†]Consider the temporal autocorrelation of the light. If the half-power
width of the autocorrelation is τ, then the coherence length is $c\tau$,
where c is the speed of light.

is to provide the reader with data to assist in choosing an appropriate architecture.

We shall begin by determining which operations are achievable with time integration. We shall then describe and analyze various correlator architectures and follow this with a description of the associated postprocessing approaches. Next we shall determine output signal-to-noise ratio (SNR) as a function of input SNR for several architectures. Then we shall return to some of the more interesting operations achievable and examine them in greater detail. A summary of architecture characteristics concludes the discussion. An appendix of device characteristics is included for convenience.

9.1.1 The Operations

The heart of any strictly time-integrating optical processor is an optical correlator. Its function is to generate the cross correlation of two inputs (three inputs in the two-dimensional case). Mathematically, the (one-dimensional) correlator accepts time-varying inputs $g(t)$ and $h(t)$ and produces the output

$$R_{gh}(\tau) = \int_T g(t)h^*(t - \tau) \, dt \qquad (9.1)$$

where the integration takes place over some interval lasting T sec. This is an approximation of the full correlation

$$R_{gh}(\tau) = \int_{-\infty}^{\infty} g(t)h^*(t - \tau) \, dt \qquad (9.2)$$

Note that $R_{gh}(\tau)$ is calculated for many values of τ simultaneously. By including the complex conjugate (*) in (9.1), the implication is made that complex data may be processed. In fact, we shall find that the majority of correlator architectures do allow direct handling of complex data.

The fact that processing must be done via the correlation integral is not as restrictive as one might suppose. Assume that we wish to implement the (complex) integral

$$I(\tau) = \int_T \phi(\tau,t) \, dt \qquad (9.3)$$

Since the correlator may be followed by some postprocessor capable of weighting the outputs, we are able to generate any operation of the form

$$J(\tau) = w(\tau)R_{gh}(\tau)$$

$$= w(\tau) \int_T g(t)h*(t - \tau)\, dt \tag{9.4}$$

So to generate (9.3), we must be able to write $\phi(\tau,t)$ as

$$\phi(\tau,t) = w(\tau)g(t)h*(t - \tau) \tag{9.5}$$

Obviously, not every function decomposes in this manner. Hence, we seek the conditions under which $\phi(\tau,t)$ may be written as in (9.5). Whitehouse et al. [1] have shown that a sufficient condition for such decomposition is that

$$\left(\frac{\partial^3}{\partial\tau\,\partial^2 t} + \frac{\partial^3}{\partial\tau^2\,\partial t} \right) \log \phi(\tau,t) = 0 \tag{9.6}$$

More generally, a two-dimensional optical correlator may be constructed, implementing the function

$$R_{ghq}(\tau_1,\tau_2) = \int_T g(t)h*(t - \tau_1)q*(t - \tau_2)\, dt \tag{9.7}$$

We may also weight the output with a factor $w(\tau_1,\tau_2)$. Now if we desire to generate the integral

$$I(\tau_1,\tau_2) = \int_T \phi(\tau_1,\tau_2,t)\, dt \tag{9.8}$$

then it is sufficient that ϕ satisfies

$$\left(\frac{\partial^3}{\partial\tau_1\,\partial t^2} + \frac{\partial^3}{\partial\tau_1^2\,\partial t} \right) \log \phi(\tau_1,\tau_2,t) = 0 \tag{9.9a}$$

and

$$\left(\frac{\partial^3}{\partial\tau_2\,\partial t^2} + \frac{\partial^3}{\partial\tau_2^2\,\partial t} \right) \log \phi(\tau_1,\tau_2,t) = 0 \tag{9.9b}$$

As an example (of more than passing interest), consider the Fourier transform of a signal truncated to the period T:

$$\mathcal{F}_T\{x(t)\} = \int_T x(t)e^{-j2\pi ft}\, dt \tag{9.10}$$

We observe that

$$\left(\frac{\partial^3}{\partial f\,\partial t^2} + \frac{\partial^3}{\partial f^2\,\partial t}\right) \log[x(t)e^{-j2\pi ft}] = 0 \tag{9.11}$$

and conclude that we can implement the Fourier transform. Unfortunately, (9.6) offers no insight as to the method. To generate the Fourier kernel $e^{-j2\pi ft}$, we require a signal which connects time delay, as found in the correlation integral, with frequency. This suggests use of a signal often encountered in radar called a chirp [2]. A chirp, written as

$$c(t) = e^{j(\alpha/2)t^2} \tag{9.12}$$

consists of a single frequency which increases linearly with time. We refer to α as the angular acceleration. If we choose the correlator inputs

$$g(t) = x(t)c(t) \tag{9.13}$$

and

$$h(t) = c(t) \tag{9.14}$$

then

$$R_{gh}(\tau) = \int_T x(t)c(t)c^*(t-\tau)\,dt$$

$$= \int_T x(t)e^{j(\alpha/2)(2t\tau-\tau^2)}\,dt$$

$$= e^{-j(\alpha/2)\tau^2}\int_T x(t)e^{j\alpha\tau t}\,dt \tag{9.15}$$

We may set $w(\tau) = \exp[j(\alpha/2)\tau^2]$. Then the output becomes

$$J(\tau) = \int_T x(t)e^{j\alpha\tau t}\,dt \tag{9.16}$$

or

$$J\left(-\frac{2\pi f}{\alpha}\right) = \int_T x(t)e^{-j2\pi ft}\,dt \tag{9.17}$$

Thus, we have achieved the desired result. Since c(t) was used to generate the required Fourier kernel, we shall refer to it as the *kernel function* for a Fourier transform. We shall return to the Fourier transform in more detail later.

As another example, consider the Hilbert transform of x(t) defined as

$$\tilde{x}(\tau) = \int_T x(t) \, \frac{1}{\pi(\tau - t)} \, dt \tag{9.18}$$

(again we have truncated the integration interval to time T). The Hilbert transform is already decomposed in the proper form. The appropriate kernel function for Hilbert transformation is

$$h(t) = -\frac{1}{\pi t} \tag{9.19}$$

With g(t) = x(t),

$$R_{gh}(\tau) = \int_T x(t) \, \frac{1}{\pi(\tau - t)} \, dt \tag{9.20}$$

In selecting kernel functions, we must keep in mind that they are generated and processed by physical equipment. Certainly, this precludes unbounded functions like that of (9.19). Observe that if all frequency components in x(t) are less than B, then

$$\int_{\tau-\delta}^{\tau+\delta} x(t) \, \frac{1}{\pi(\tau - t)} \, dt \doteq x(\tau) \int_{\tau-\delta}^{\tau+\delta} \frac{1}{\pi(\tau - t)} \, dt = 0 \tag{9.21}$$

provided that, say, $\delta < 1/4B$. Hence, with little effect we may let

$$h(t) = \begin{cases} -\dfrac{1}{\pi t} & |t| > \dfrac{1}{4B} \\[2ex] 0 & \text{otherwise} \end{cases} \tag{9.22}$$

and thus render h(t) realizable.

A two-dimensional optical correlator may be used to generate two-dimensional operations. The cross-ambiguity function (a generalization of Woodward's autoambiguity function [3]) follows directly from our implementation of the Fourier transform. The cross ambiguity of x(t) and y(t) may be defined as

$$A_{xy}(\tau, f) = \int_{-\infty}^{\infty} x(t) y^*(t - \tau) e^{-j2\pi ft} \, dt \tag{9.23}$$

which we shall approximate by

$$A_{xy}(\tau,f) = \int_T x(t)y^*(t-\tau)e^{-j2\pi ft}\,dt \qquad\qquad (9.24)$$

Since the two-dimensional correlator generates

$$R_{ghq}(\tau_1,\tau_2) = \int_T g(t)h^*(t-\tau_1)q^*(t-\tau_2)\,dt \qquad\qquad (9.7)$$

we may use the same kernel function as for the Fourier transform and choose

$$g(t) = x(t)c(t) \qquad\qquad\qquad\qquad (9.25)$$

$$h(t) = y(t) \qquad\qquad\qquad\qquad (9.26)$$

$$q(t) = c(t) \qquad\qquad\qquad\qquad (9.27)$$

The result is

$$R_{ghq}(\tau_1,\tau_2) = e^{-j(\alpha/2)\tau_2^2}\int_T x(t)y^*(t-\tau_1)e^{j\alpha\tau_2 t}\,dt \qquad (9.28)$$

Upon weighting the output by $w(\tau_2) = \exp[j(\alpha/2)\tau_2^2]$, we produce the desired result with $\tau = \tau_1$ and $f = \alpha\tau_2/2\pi$.

Finally, let us mention an example that makes use of two kernel functions—one for each dimension. Often one wishes to produce a Fourier transform with a very large number of resolvable frequencies. The result of such a transform generally takes the form of a two-dimensional raster, as pictured in Fig. 9.1 [4]. Frequency increases

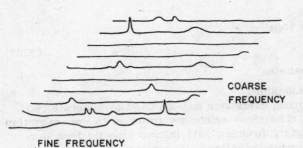

COARSE
FREQUENCY

FINE FREQUENCY

Figure 9.1 Result of a raster format transform. The frequency at the left end of a raster line is the same as at the right end of the line above.

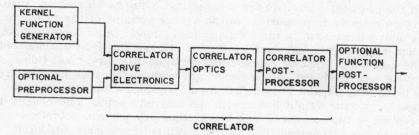

Figure 9.2 General time-integrating optical processor system architecture.

slowly in one direction and rises in large discrete steps in the other direction. The output may be viewed as a long frequency axis which has been partitioned into equal-length segments with the segments stacked in order to fill a rectangle. We may produce this transform by employing two repeating chirps—one of high angular acceleration to produce the coarse frequency axis and the other of low angular acceleration to produce the fine frequency axis. We shall consider this application in detail when we return to the implementation of the Fourier transform.

We have seen that a time-integrating optical processing system includes a correlator and a source for a kernel function. In general, we may picture a processing system as shown in Fig. 9.2. The correlator is composed of some drive electronics, the correlator optics, and the postprocessor. The drive electronics, peculiar to the correlator architecture used, serve as interface to the optical modulators and provide references needed by the optics. Correlator postprocessing is required both to strip away unwanted terms in the output of the optics and to extract the correlation. To perform a particular function, the correlator is preceded by a kernel function generator and is followed by the appropriate postprocessor. Weighting of the output may be done either in the postprocessor or in the correlator optics.

In the following sections we shall examine correlator architectures and their characteristics. We shall then return to implementation of some of the more interesting functions.

9.2 ARCHITECTURES

In this section we shall examine architectures of incoherent-light, time-integrating correlators. One aim will be to characterize each approach to assist a designer in choosing the most appropriate. Wherever possible, these characterizations will be numeric in the form of several figures of merit defined along the way.

In the physical world, we are blessed and cursed with the fact that detectors respond in proportion to the square modulus of the field amplitude, rather than to the field amplitude itself. As a consequence, we must design optical processors so that information to be accumulated on the detector is linearly represented by light intensity.* Yet this may pose some problems, since many light modulators cause field amplitude to be proportional to electrical input. Two methods are used to achieve a detector output linear with the desired result. These methods correspond to two classes of time-integrating processors: interferometric and noninterferometric. In the noninterferometric case, light intensity is made proportional to the desired output by using modulators that act directly on light intensity. Interferometric processors, on the other hand, illuminate the detector with light having an amplitude proportional to the sum of two terms. When the square (modulus) is taken by the detector, one of the resulting cross products bears the desired output term.

In the following pages a variety of correlators will be examined. We shall begin by describing two noninterferometric architectures: one which uses a modulated source and another which uses a fixed source. We shall then turn to interferometric correlators, again considering the cases of fixed and modulated sources. The fixed source architecture will then be modified by spatial filtering, leading to two additional interferometric implementations. Although it is not necessary to examine all architectures at first reading, it is recommended that they be studied in chronological order, as each description logically builds on the previous one.

9.2.1 Noninterferometric Architectures

The most straightforward correlator is the noninterferometric version shown in Fig. 9.3 where a light-emitting diode (LED) is the light source. The LED is biased by voltage a_0, making the light intensity become linear with drive $g(t)$ [5]. The radiation is collected and collimated† by lens L0. A cylindrical lens L1 compresses the light into a line in its focal plane where Bragg cell AO2 is located.

Cell AO2 modulates the intensity of the emerging light as follows. The intensity of diffracted light with sine-wave electrical drive is‡

$$I_d = c \sin^2 \phi \qquad\qquad (9.29)$$

where c is some constant and ϕ is proportional to the sine-wave amplitude [6]. Let us write

---

*By *intensity* we mean the square modulus of field amplitude.
†Made into a beam of parallel rays.
‡We assume operation at the Bragg angle.

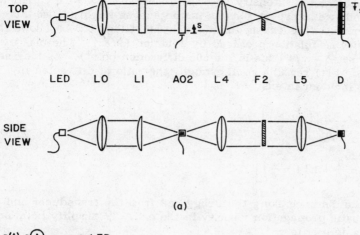

LED   LO   LI   AO2   L4   F2   L5   D

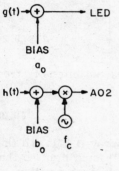

(b)

Figure 9.3 LED noninterferometric one-dimensional correlator: (a) optical system, (b) electrical drive. Spatial filter F2 blocks undiffracted light.

$$\phi = \frac{\pi}{4} (1 + \Delta)$$

(9.30)

Thus (9.29) may be expressed as

$$I_d = \frac{c}{2} \left(1 + \sin \frac{\pi\Delta}{2}\right)$$

(9.31)

If Δ is constrained to be small, then we may make the approximation

$$I_d \doteq \frac{c}{2} \left(1 + \frac{\pi\Delta}{2}\right)$$

(9.32)

That is, the diffracted intensity becomes linear with Δ. With equation (9.30) in mind, we interpret Δ as an instantaneous amplitude modulation of a carrier. Thus the modulation scheme of Fig. 9.3(b) allows the linear intensity modulation promised by equation (9.32). The bias b_0 is chosen to set $\phi = \pi/4$ (this is the 50% diffraction point). As long as the modulation h(t) remains small enough, the ratio of diffracted intensity I_2 to incident intensity I_1 is

$$\frac{I_2}{I_1} = \frac{1}{2}\left[1 + \frac{\pi}{2b_0}h\left(t - \frac{s}{v}\right)\right]$$

$$= \frac{\pi}{4b_0}\left[\frac{2b_0}{\pi} + h\left(t - \frac{s}{v}\right)\right] \tag{9.33}$$

where s is the distance along the Bragg cell from the transducer and v is the acoustic propagation velocity in the cell. To simplify notation, let $b = 2b_0/\pi$ and write

$$\frac{I_2}{I_1} \propto b + h\left(t - \frac{s}{v}\right) \tag{9.34}$$

Considering the LED modulation, we have the diffracted intensity from AO2 as

$$I_2 \propto [a + g(t)]\left[b + h\left(t - \frac{s}{v}\right)\right] \tag{9.35}$$

Lenses L4 and L5 image AO2 into the detector array D [7]. In the focal plane of L4, spatial filter F2 blocks the undiffracted light so that the intensity I_3 at the detector is the same as I_2. At each position[†] s, a detector element (*pixel*) integrates impinging light intensity for a period T. The resulting output is

$$C(\tau) = \int_T I_3(t,\tau)\, dt$$

$$= Tab + b\int_T g(t)\, dt + a\int_T h(t - \tau)\, dt$$

$$+ \int_T g(t)h(t - \tau)\, dt \tag{9.36}$$

[†]Note that s corresponds to unique positions on both the Bragg cell and the detector array.

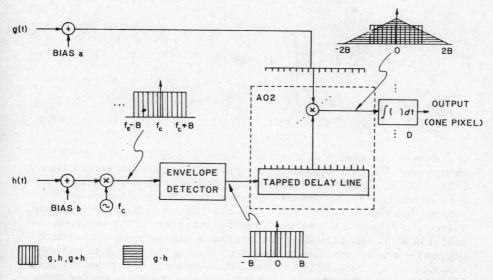

Figure 9.4 Electrical equivalent of LED noninterferometric correlator (with drive). Temporal frequency spectra are shown at several points. Although only one multiplication and integration are shown, many are done in parallel.

where $\tau = s/v$. The proportionality constant has been arbitrarily set to 1.

Figure 9.4 shows an electrical equivalent of the Fig. 9.3 correlator. The formation of the output at one of the many pixels is traced. Note that the Bragg cell is modeled as an envelope detector followed by a tapped delay line. Optical information here is carried by light intensity. At various stages, appropriate portions of the spectrum are shown. It is clear that the Bragg cell's bandwidth B_B must accommodate twice the signal bandwidth B. For the purpose of comparing architectures, we shall define a figure of merit ρ_B as the ratio of signal bandwidth to bandwidth required of the Bragg cell; that is,

$$\rho_B = \frac{B}{B_B} \tag{9.37}$$

For this architecture, $\rho_B = 1/2$.

It is convenient to rewrite (9.36) as

$$C(\tau) = u(\tau) + v(\tau) + R_{gh}(\tau) \tag{9.38}$$

where

$$u(\tau) = Tab \qquad (9.39)$$

$$v(\tau) = b \int_T g(t) \, dt + a \int_T h(t - \tau) \, dt \qquad (9.40)$$

$$R_{gh}(\tau) = \int_T g(t)h^*(t - \tau) \, dt \qquad (9.41)$$

is the cross correlation of g and h. Here, h is real, so that h = h*.
In this way, we have broken the output into signal-independent background $u(\tau)$, signal-dependent background $v(\tau)$, and the desired
correlation $R_{gh}(\tau)$. [For this implementation, $u(\tau)$ and $v(\tau)$ are
actually independent of τ, since τ is constrained to be much less than
T (see the Appendix). We shall find the retention of the argument
useful later.] Since the detector integrates intensity—a nonnegative
quantity—it is no surprise to find $u(\tau)$ biasing the output to ensure
that $C(\tau) \geqslant 0$. Because of the modulation constraints imposed by both
the LED and the Bragg cell, $v(\tau)$ will generally be much smaller than
$u(\tau)$ and may, in fact, be zero if g and h have no dc component. Even
so, $v(\tau)$ may not be ignored, as it contributes variance when input
noise is present and causes fluctuation of the background level.

Two parameters that best characterize a correlator are time span
Δ_τ (the range of τ) and time resolution δ_τ. Time resolution is easily
determined by examining the correlation integral. Since the input sig-
nals g(t) and h(t) are constrained to the bandwidth B, we may write
their transforms[†] as

$$G(f) = \mathcal{F}\{g(t)\} = G(f)p\left(\frac{f}{2B}\right) \qquad (9.42)$$

and

$$H^*(f) = \mathcal{F}\{h^*(-t)\} = H^*(f)p\left(\frac{f}{2B}\right) \qquad (9.43)$$

where

$$p(x) = \begin{cases} 1 & |x| < \frac{1}{2} \\ \\ 0 & \text{otherwise} \end{cases} \qquad (9.44)$$

[†]$\mathcal{F}\{g(t)\} \equiv \int_{-\infty}^{\infty} g(t)e^{-j2\pi ft} \, dt.$

Writing the correlation integral as a convolution, we see that

$$R_{gh}(\tau) = [g(t) * h^*(-t)](\tau)$$

$$= \mathcal{F}^{-1}\{G(f)H^*(f)\}$$

$$= \mathcal{F}^{-1}\left\{G(f)H^*(f)p\left(\frac{f}{2B}\right)\right\}$$

$$= \left[g(t) * h^*(-t) * \mathcal{F}^{-1}\left\{p\left(\frac{f}{2B}\right)\right\}\right](\tau)$$

$$= R_{gh}(\tau) * [2B \; \text{sinc}(2\pi B\tau)] \tag{9.45}$$

where

$$\text{sinc } x = \frac{\sin x}{x} \tag{9.46}$$

This result states that correlation resolution is limited by a sinc function of width related to B. We shall use the Rayleigh resolution criterion, which states that two adjacent sinc functions are just resolved when the peak of one is located at the first zero of the other. This occurs when $\tau = 1/2B$. We may say that the correlator has a resolution

$$\delta_\tau = \frac{1}{2B} = \frac{1}{2\rho_B B_B} \tag{9.47}$$

The range of τ is clearly determined by the Bragg cell aperture. Here again a figure of merit is appropriate: let ρ_τ be the ratio of achieved delay range Δ_τ to the time aperture τ_B of the Bragg cell used; that is,

$$\rho_\tau = \frac{\Delta_\tau}{\tau_B} \tag{9.48}$$

For this architecture, $\rho_\tau = 1$. The number of resolution elements obtainable at the output is simply

$$n = \frac{\Delta_\tau}{\delta_\tau} = 2B \; \Delta_\tau \tag{9.49}$$

It is useful to rewrite (9.49) using (9.37) and (9.48) to read

$$n = 2\rho_\tau \rho_B(\tau_B B_B) \tag{9.50}$$

The quantity $\tau_B B_B$ is known as the Bragg cell's time-bandwidth product and is typically 10^3. $\tau_B B_B$ may be viewed as the information capacity of the cell. Similarly, n is the information capacity of the correlator. It is no surprise that they are related by the quantity $2\rho_\tau \rho_B$, a measure of how well an architecture makes use of a Bragg cell's capacity. For this processor, $2\rho_\tau\rho_B = 1$, the maximum achievable with a single Bragg cell.

Finally, let us define one more figure of merit ρ_D, which is the inverse of the number of detector pixels required to cover one output resolution element. For this architecture, $\rho_D = 1$, although we shall find in general that this is not the case. The number of detector pixels required to cover all n resolution elements is

$$N_D = \frac{n}{\rho_D} \qquad (9.51)$$

To fully utilize the capacity of the Bragg cells in any architecture, the number of pixels required is

$$N_D = \frac{2\rho_\tau\rho_B}{\rho_D}\,\tau_B B_B \qquad (9.52)$$

The numbers ρ_B, ρ_τ, and ρ_D are of great interest because Bragg cells and detectors are physical devices. As such, there are practical (and sometimes prohibitive) limits on τ_B, B_B, $\tau_B B_B$, and N_D (see the Appendix). The parameters ρ_B, ρ_τ, and ρ_D represent efficiency of use of these limited resources for a particular architecture.

A more flexible[†] architecture results if the LED of Fig. 9.3 is replaced by a fixed-intensity source and Bragg cell AO2 is replaced by two Bragg cells as in Fig. 9.5. Cell AO1 is imaged onto AO2 by means of L2 and L3. (Note that the image of AO1 is inverted.) Spatial filter F1, located in the back focal plane of L2, blocks the undiffracted light from reaching AO2. Both cells are driven in the manner previously discussed, as shown. The light intensity I_1, diffracted by AO1, is

$$I_1 \propto a + g\left(t + \frac{s}{v}\right) \qquad (9.53)$$

provided that g(t) remains appropriately small, where $a = 2a_0/\pi$. Again the diffracted intensity I_2 from AO2 is

$$\frac{I_2}{I_1} \propto b + h\left(t - \frac{s}{v}\right) \qquad (9.54)$$

Since the image of AO1 onto AO2 is inverted, an increase in s advances g and delays h. Hence, the intensity seen by the detector is

$$I_3 \propto \left[a + g\left(t + \frac{s}{v}\right)\right]\left[b + h\left(t - \frac{s}{v}\right)\right] \qquad (9.55)$$

[†]To be demonstrated later.

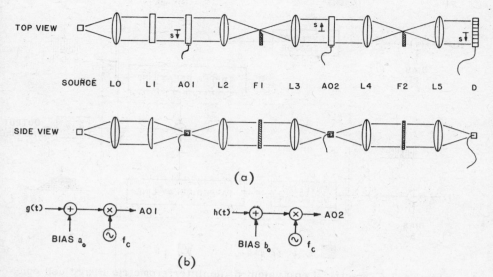

Figure 9.5 Bragg cell noninterferometric correlator: (a) optical system, (b) electrical drive. Spatial filters F1 and F2 block undiffracted light. Note that the light source has a constant intensity.

With an arbitrary choice of the proportionality constant, we may write the detector's output as

$$C'\left(\frac{s}{v}\right) = \int_{T} \left[a + g\left(t + \frac{s}{v}\right)\right]\left[b + h\left(t - \frac{s}{v}\right)\right]\ dt$$

$$\doteq \int_{T} [a + g(t)]\left[b + h\left(t - \frac{2s}{v}\right)\right]\ dt \qquad (9.56)$$

This approximation is valid since physical constraints dictate that $2s/v \ll T$. It is natural to make the substitution $\tau = 2s/v$ and to write the output as

$$C(\tau) = u(\tau) + v(\tau) + R_{gh}(\tau) \qquad (9.57)$$

where u, v, and R_{gh} are defined as before. Figure 9.6 shows an electrical equivalent of Fig. 9.5.

Comparing equations (9.57) and (9.38), one might conclude that the characteristics of both architectures are the same; however, since $\tau = 2s/v$, the range of τ is twice as large; that is, $\rho_\tau = 2$. As before, $\rho_B = 1/2$ so $n = 2(\tau_B B_B)$. This is hardly a surprise, since

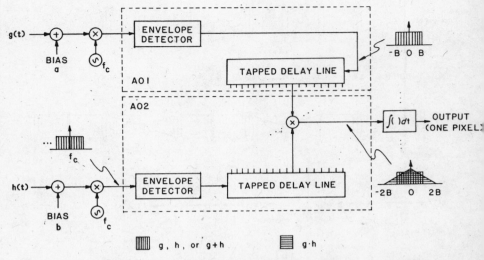

Figure 9.6 Electrical equivalent of noninterferometric Bragg cell correlator (with drive). One output is shown.

two Bragg cells are used instead of one. Again, $\rho_D = 1$, so that $N_D = 2(\tau_B B_B)$.

9.2.2 Unfiltered Interferometric Architectures

The interferometric processors make direct use of light amplitude to carry information. Let us suppose that the field amplitude of light striking the detector is $e(t)$. We wish to coherently integrate this information, that is, to form the integral $\int e(t)\, dt$. The detector, however, responds to the square modulus of the field amplitude and then integrates, forming $\int_T |e(t)|^2\, dt$. Processors making use of coherent light often illuminate the detector with two beams—one bearing the information with amplitude $e_1(t)$ and one a *reference* with amplitude e_0. The detector sees

$$I = |e_1(t) + e_0|^2 = |e_1(t)|^2 + |e_0|^2 + 2\,\mathrm{Re}\,e_0^* e_1(t) \qquad (9.58)$$

The intensity is the sum of the desired term proportional to $e_1(t)$, a constant background term, and an undesired term $|e_1(t)|^2$. This interaction of the two beams is called *interference*, and the processor is said to be *interferometric*. The approach taken with two beams suggests one with a single beam whose amplitude is $e_1(t) + e_0$. The result is identical except that there are no path length differences between the constituents, so that incoherent light may be used. The

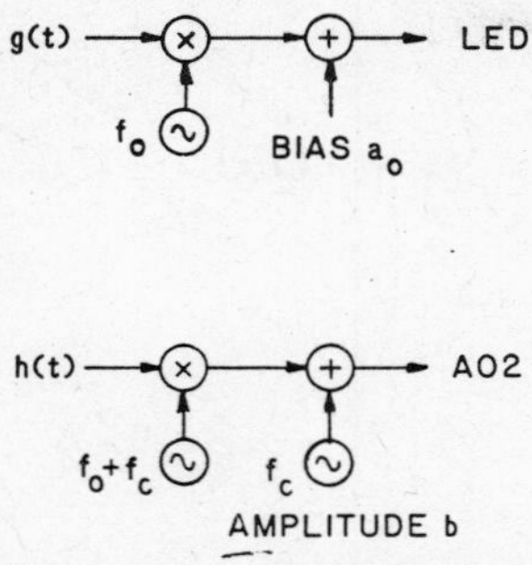

Figure 9.7 Electrical drive for interferometric LED correlator.

term *interferometric* is also applied in this case due to the similarity to the two-beam approach.

In the present section we shall deal with interferometric correlators that use a single path carrying both information and reference. The architectures will be identical in optical construction to the noninterferometric processors presented earlier. In the following section we shall study interferometric correlators which use transform plane filtering to remove some of the undesirable terms occurring in the output.

An interferometric correlator may be made using the optical arrangement of Fig. 9.3(a) in which the electrical drive of Fig. 9.7 replaces the one of Fig. 9.3(b). Signal g(t) now enters the LED on a carrier of offset frequency f_0. Bragg cell AO2 is operated without a bias so that diffracted light amplitude is proportional to electrical drive [6]. The signal is introduced on a carrier of $f_0 + f_c$ with a tone at f_c which will form the reference. The field amplitude E_1 illuminating AO2 is given by

$$|E_1|^2 = a + g(t) \cos 2\pi f_0 t \qquad (9.59)$$

The diffracted amplitude is[†]

―――――――――

[†]Consider the real signal f(t). We define the analytic signal $f_+(t)$ associated with f(t) by

$$f_+(t) = \frac{1}{2}[f(t) + j\tilde{f}(t)]$$

where $\tilde{f}(t)$ is the Hilbert transform of f(t). Thus, $f_+(t)$ is formed by removing the negative frequency components of f(t). Similarly, form the *antianalytic* signal $f_-(t)$ by removing the positive frequency components. Suppose that a Bragg cell is driven directly by f(t). By choosing positive or negative diffraction order, we select modulation by $f_+(t)$ or $f_-(t)$, respectively.

$$E_2 = E_1[b + e^{-j2\pi f_0(t-\tau)} h^*(t-\tau)]e^{-j2\pi f_c(t-\tau)} \tag{9.60}$$

where complex conjugation arises from the proper choice of diffraction order.

At the detector, the intensity is

$$I_3 = |E_2|^2$$

$$= ab^2 + a|h(t-\tau)|^2$$

$$+ b\, \text{Re}[g(t)h^*(t-\tau)e^{j2\pi f_0\tau}]$$

$$+ \{b\, \text{Re}[g(t)h^*(t-\tau)e^{-j2\pi f_0(2t-\tau)}]$$

$$+ b^2 g(t)\cos 2\pi f_0 t$$

$$+ 2ab\, \text{Re}[h^*(t-\tau)e^{-j2\pi f_0(t-\tau)}]$$

$$+ g(t)|h(t-\tau)|^2 \cos 2\pi f_0 t\} \tag{9.61}$$

Recalling that g and h are constrained to the frequency range $[-B,B]$, we see that the terms in braces in (9.61) have no frequencies in the neighborhood of zero if $f_0 > 3B$. Assuming this, we see that the terms in braces vanish[†] with detector integration, leaving

$$C(\tau) = \int_T I_3(\tau,t)\, dt$$

$$= u(\tau) + v(\tau) + b\, \text{Re}[e^{j2\pi f_0\tau} R_{gh}(\tau)] \tag{9.62}$$

where

$$u(\tau) = Tab^2 \tag{9.63}$$

and

$$v(\tau) = a\int_T |h(t-\tau)|^2\, dt \tag{9.64}$$

As before, we have a signal-independent bias $u(\tau)$ and a signal-dependent term $v(\tau)$; however, $v(\tau)$ here is always nonnegative. Fig-

[†]Approximately, since T is finite.

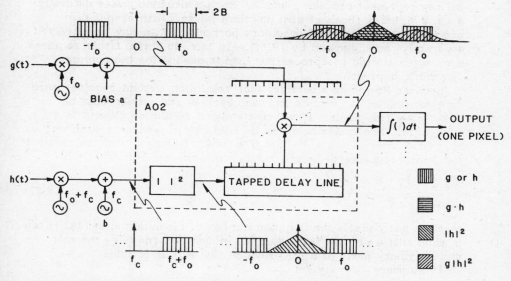

Figure 9.8 Electrical equivalent of interferometric LED correlator (with drive). Temporal spectra are shown for $f_0 = 3B$. Information is carried by light intensity—hence the square modulus in AO2.

ure 9.8 is an electrical equivalent of the correlator and shows the frequency extent of each intermediate and final term. It is clear from Fig. 9.8 that the choice of $f_0 > 3B$ is correct. Note that the Bragg cell must accommodate frequencies in the interval $[f_c, f_c + f_0 + B]$ so that

$$\rho_B = \left(1 + \frac{f_0}{B} \right)^{-1} \tag{9.65}$$

In particular, $\rho_B < 1/4$. The full aperture of one Bragg cell is used; hence $\rho_\tau = 1$.

A feature characteristic of interferometric correlators is illustrated here: The correlation appears at the output on a spatial (τ) carrier. This allows direct processing of complex (as opposed to merely real) inputs. We may write

$$\mathrm{Re}[e^{j2\pi f_0 \tau} R_{gh}(\tau)] = \cos(2\pi f_0 \tau)\, \mathrm{Re}\, R_{gh}(\tau)$$
$$- \sin(2\pi f_0 \tau)\, \mathrm{Im}\, R_{gh}(\tau) \tag{9.66}$$

Suppose that rather than (real) signals being processed at baseband, they are introduced on carriers whose phases may vary. In this way, we may represent complex g and h. Such a situation arises naturally when a signal is received with unknown phase. With proper post-processing[†], the real and imaginary portions of R_{gh} may be extracted separately, as suggested by (9.66). In fact, to obtain either requires more sophisticated postprocessing than is needed for the noninterferometric approach.

Because R_{gh} is on a carrier, each resolution element requires more detector pixels. At a minimum, each cycle of the carrier must be sampled by two pixels. Recall that a signal resolution element is $\delta_\tau = 1/2B$ wide. The spectrum of the desired output term (τ frequency) spans the interval $[f_0 - B, f_0 + B]$; thus, the output must be sampled for τ intervals each of length $1/2(f_0 + B)$. As a result, we need

$$\frac{1}{\rho_D} = \frac{f_0 + B}{B} = \frac{1}{\rho_B} > 4 \tag{9.67}$$

times as many pixels for the same number of resolution elements. Keep in mind that we obtain twice as much information (namely, the real and imaginary parts of R_{gh}) provided that R_{gh} is complex.

In summary, we may get

$$n = \frac{2B}{B + f_0} \tau_B B_B < \frac{1}{2} \tau_B B_B \tag{9.68}$$

resolution elements, requiring

$$N_D = \frac{B + f_0}{B} n = 2\tau_B B_B \tag{9.69}$$

detector pixels.

To process a baseband (real) signal, we may make better use of Bragg cell bandwidth by employing single-sideband (SSB) rather than double-sideband (DSB) modulation. Figure 9.9 shows SSB input circuitry used to remove one sideband from each input and shows the resulting spectra. Using $\tilde{g}(x)$ to represent the Hilbert transform of $g(x)$, we have

$$I_1(t) = a + g(t) \cos 2\pi f_0 t - \tilde{g}(t) \sin 2\pi f_0 t \tag{9.70}$$

and

$$E_2(t) = E_1(t)[b + h(t - \tau)e^{-j2\pi f_0(t-\tau)}$$

$$- j\tilde{h}(t - \tau)e^{-j2\pi f_0(t-\tau)}]e^{-j2\pi f_c(t-\tau)} \tag{9.71}$$

[†]See Sec. 9.3.

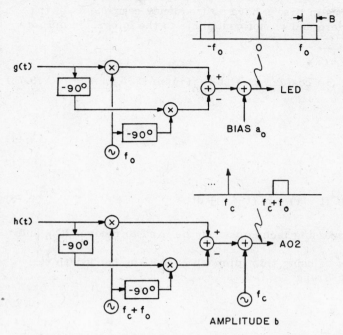

Figure 9.9 Single-sideband drive circuitry for interferometric LED correlator.

The intensity at the detector becomes

$$I_3(t) = ab^2 + a[h^2(t - \tau) + \tilde{h}^2(t - \tau)]$$

$$+ b \cos(2\pi f_0 \tau)[g(t)h(t - \tau) + \tilde{g}(t)\tilde{h}(t - \tau)]$$

$$- b \sin(2\pi f_0 \tau)[\tilde{g}(t)h(t - \tau) - g(t)\tilde{h}(t - \tau)]$$

$$+ \{b^2[g(t) \cos(2\pi f_0 t) - \tilde{g}(t) \sin(2\pi f_0 t)]$$

$$+ 2ab[h(t - \tau) \cos(2\pi f_0(t - \tau)) - \tilde{h}(t - \tau) \sin(2\pi f_0(t - \tau))]$$

$$+ b \cos[2\pi f_0(2t - \tau)][g(t)h(t - \tau) - \tilde{g}(t)\tilde{h}(t - \tau)]$$

$$- b \sin[2\pi f_0(2t - \tau)][\tilde{g}(t)h(t - \tau) + g(t)\tilde{h}(t - \tau)]$$

$$+ [g(t) \cos(2\pi f_0 t) - \tilde{g}(t) \sin(2\pi f_0 t)]$$

$$\times [h^2(t - \tau) + \tilde{h}^2(t - \tau)]\} \qquad (9.72)$$

If $f_0 > B$, the terms in braces have no frequency components in the neighborhood of zero and do not contribute to the integrated output. Hence,

$$C(\tau) = u(\tau) + v(\tau)$$
$$+ 2bR_{gh}(\tau) \cos(2\pi f_0 t) + 2bR_{g\tilde{h}}(\tau) \sin(2\pi f_0 t) \qquad (9.73)$$

where

$$u(\tau) = Tab^2 \qquad (9.74)$$

and

$$v(\tau) = a \int_T [h^2(t-\tau) + \tilde{h}^2(t-\tau)] \, dt \qquad (9.75)$$

The same postprocessing techniques may be used to recover R_{gh} and $R_{g\tilde{h}}$.

The advantage of using this approach is that the bandwidth requirement for the Bragg cell is less:

$$\rho_B = \frac{B}{B + f_0} < \frac{1}{2} \qquad (9.76)$$

This is not surprising, since we have removed a redundant sideband from a real signal, thereby making better use of the Bragg cell's information capacity. As a result,

$$n = 2\rho_B \rho_\tau \tau_B B_B < \tau_B B_B \qquad (9.77)$$

may be twice as large.

Another architecture, which is better viewed as a stepping stone to those of the next section rather than as an end in itself, results from use of the optical system pictured in Fig. 9.5(a). This (originally non-interferometric) processor may be made interferometric by driving the cells as shown in Fig. 9.10. Both are driven without bias so that dif-

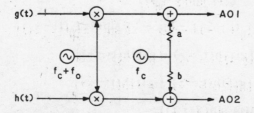

Figure 9.10 Drive circuitry for interferometric Bragg cell correlator.

fracted amplitude is proportional to input voltage. Tones which will provide a reference are added at a frequency offset of f_0. Figure 9.11 illustrates the resulting frequency spectra at intermediate points.

Light diffracted by AO1 has amplitude

$$E_1(t) = \left[a + g\left(t + \frac{s}{v}\right) e^{j2\pi f_0 [t+(s/v)]} \right] e^{j2\pi f_c [t+(s/v)]} \tag{9.78}$$

The doubly diffracted amplitude from AO2 is

$$E_2(t) = E_1(t) \left[b + h^*\left(t - \frac{s}{v}\right) e^{-j2\pi f_0 [t-(s/v)]} \right] e^{-j2\pi f_c [t-(s/v)]}$$

$$= \left[ab + ah^*\left(t - \frac{s}{v}\right) e^{-j2\pi f_0 [t-(s/v)]} \right.$$

$$+ bg\left(t + \frac{s}{v}\right) e^{j2\pi f_0 [t+(s/v)]}$$

$$+ g\left(t + \frac{s}{v}\right) h^*\left(t - \frac{s}{v}\right) e^{j4\pi f_0 (s/v)} \left] e^{j4\pi f_c (s/v)} \right. \tag{9.79}$$

We make the substitution $\tau = 2s/v$ and write the intensity at the detector as

$$I\left(t - \frac{s}{v}\right) = \left| E_2\left(t - \frac{s}{v}\right) \right|^2$$

$$= a^2 b^2 + a^2 |h(t - \tau)|^2 + b^2 |g(t)|^2$$

$$+ |g(t)|^2 |h(t - \tau)|^2$$

$$+ 2ab\, \mathrm{Re}[g(t)h^*(t - \tau)e^{j2\pi f_0 \tau}]$$

$$+ \{2a^2 b\, \mathrm{Re}[h(t - \tau)e^{j2\pi f_0 (t-\tau)}]$$

$$+ 2ab^2\, \mathrm{Re}[g(t)e^{j2\pi f_0 t}]$$

$$+ 2ab\, \mathrm{Re}[g(t)h(t - \tau)e^{j2\pi f_0 (2t-\tau)}]$$

$$+ 2a|h(t - \tau)|^2\, \mathrm{Re}[g(t)e^{j2\pi f_0 t}]$$

$$+ 2b|g(t)|^2\, \mathrm{Re}[h(t - \tau)e^{j2\pi f_0 (t-\tau)}]\} \tag{9.80}$$

Again, the choice $f_0 > 3B$ guarantees that the terms in braces have no frequencies in the neighborhood of zero. The correlator output becomes

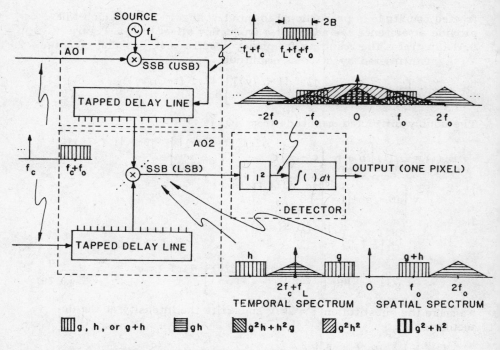

Figure 9.11 Electrical equivalent of interferometric Bragg cell correlator with no transform plane filtering (drive not shown). Information
is carried by light amplitude on a light carrier of frequency f_L. The
Bragg cells act as single sideband mixers. $f_0 = 3B$.

$$C(\tau) = u(\tau) + v(\tau) + 2ab\ \mathrm{Re}[R_{gh}(\tau)e^{j2\pi f_0 \tau}] \tag{9.81}$$

where

$$u(\tau) = Ta^2b^2 \tag{9.82}$$

and

$$v(\tau) = a^2 \int_T |h(t-\tau)|^2\ dt + b^2 \int_T |g(t)|^2\ dt$$

$$+ \int_T |g(t)|^2 |h(t-\tau)|^2\ dt \tag{9.83}$$

We have again made use of the fact that $\int_T I[t - (s/v)]\, dt \doteq \int_T I(t)\, dt$, since $T \gg s/v$.

As in the interferometric correlator previously described, the desired correlation is on a carrier and we have $\rho_D = \rho_R = B/(B + f_0^*)$. However, in this case two cells are used, giving $\rho_\tau = 2$. Thus, we have

$$n = \frac{4B}{B + f_0}(\tau_B B_B) < \tau_B B_B \tag{9.84}$$

resolution elements requiring

$$N_D = 4\tau_B B_B \tag{9.85}$$

detector pixels.

When the processor is operated with single-sideband modulations, the output becomes

$$C(\tau) = u(\tau) + v(\tau)$$

$$+ 4abR_{gh}(\tau) \cos(2\pi f_0 \tau)$$

$$+ 4abR_{\widetilde{gh}}(\tau) \sin(2\pi f_0 \tau) \tag{9.86}$$

where

$$u(\tau) = Ta^2 b^2 \tag{9.87}$$

and

$$v(\tau) = a^2 \int_T [h^2(t - \tau) + \tilde{h}^2(t - \tau)]\, dt$$

$$+ b^2 \int_T [g^2(t) + \tilde{g}^2(t)]\, dt$$

$$+ \int_T [g^2(t) + \tilde{g}^2(t)][h^2(t - \tau) + \tilde{h}^2(t - \tau)]\, dt \tag{9.88}$$

Here we have made the assumption that $f_0 > B$, allowing $\rho_R = 1/2$.

Before concluding our examination of this architecture, let us note a characteristic of interferometric correlators made with Bragg cells. Bragg cells typically respond to a range of frequencies covering an octave, for example, $[f, 2f]$. With interferometric correlators, input frequencies occur in the range $\{f_c\} \cup [f_c + f_0, f_c + f_0 + B]$. When matched to the Bragg cell, f_c is chosen to fit the octave, giving the range of frequencies $\{f_0 + B\} \cup [2f_0 + B, 2f_0 + 2B]$. We are "wasting" $1 - \rho_B \geqslant 1/2$ of the Bragg cell bandwidth by not having any information in the interval $(f_0 + B, 2f_0 + B)$. An alternative is the use $f_c = 0$, that is, to let the undiffracted light act as the reference tone. Now the input frequencies cover the interval $[f_0, f_0 + B]$ so that we utilize $2\rho_B$ of the bandwidth. The drawback of this approach is that the reference tone amplitudes (a and b) cannot be varied and are large (most light is not diffracted). As a result, $v(\tau)$ becomes much larger than the desired output term, causing a loss of dynamic range in the detector.

Before proceeding to the next section, we remark that the hardware of an interferometric processor may be used to generate an incoherent correlation

$$\int |g(t)|^2 |h(t - \tau)|^2 \, dt$$

which does have application. This integral arises very simply by removing the reference tones and allowing the signals to fill the input bandwidth.

9.2.3 Filtered Interferometric Architectures

The interferometric correlator just described suffers from several contributions to the signal-dependent bias $v(\tau)$. Not only does $v(\tau)$ increase the postprocessing difficulty and clutter the output, but it also contributes markedly to output variance when input noise is present and uses up detector dynamic range. We seek to modify the (interferometric) processor shown in Fig. 9.5(a) to remove certain contributions to $v(\tau)$. In the discussion which follows, we shall examine how optical filtering may be used to accomplish this purpose.

Recall that light diffracted by a Bragg cell leaves at an angle which is proportional to the electrical drive frequency [8]. The sign of the angle is determined by choice of diffraction order. In particular, for light wavelength λ_L and drive frequency f, the exit angle (measured as a deviation from the undiffracted path) is

$$\theta = \pm \frac{\lambda_L f}{v} \tag{9.89}$$

where v is again the acoustic propagation velocity. When two Bragg cells, driven at frequencies f_1 and f_2, respectively, are cascaded, the doubly diffracted light exits at an angle

$$\theta = \pm \frac{\lambda_L (f_1 \pm f_2)}{v} \tag{9.90}$$

assuming the same velocity for both cells. This mapping of frequency to angle allows spatial separation of frequency components. Refer to

Fig. 9.5(a). Filter F2, which blocks undiffracted light, is located in the focal plane of L4. Here, parallel rays leaving AO2 gather at a point. The modulation spectrum of the doubly diffracted light is seen spatially separated in this *transform* plane (see Fig. 9.11) but corrupted. The corruption results both from angular dispersion of the "collimated" source (the collimation is not perfect due to the source extent) and from the frequency dispersion of the source (since it is not monochromatic). To see the extent of this corruption, let us examine the range of diffraction angles when a Bragg cell is driven by frequencies in the interval $[f_1, f_2]$. Assume that the light wavelengths are in the range $[\lambda_1, \lambda_2]$ and that the input angles are in the interval $[\theta_1, \theta_2]$. From (9.90) the diffracted angles are then in the interval $[\theta_1 - (f_1 \lambda_1 / v), \theta_2 + (f_2 \lambda_2 / v)]$ when the positive diffraction order is used and in the interval $[\theta_1 - (f_2 \lambda_2 / v), \theta_2 + (f_1 \lambda_1 / v)]$ when the negative order is used. Suppose that the collimated source is dispersed over the range $[-\theta_s, \theta_s]$. Then the contributions to the doubly diffracted light amplitude seen in the plane of F2 will have angles as shown in Table 9.1. Note that because of image inversion, the sign of diffraction angle from AO1 appears reversed in the doubly diffracted light. We must create the product $g(t)h^*(t - \tau)$ at the detector. This product is already present in the fourth term of Table 9.1. If this term is combined with a reference (for example, the first entry of Table 9.1), the correlation will result. We seek then to block the second and third terms from proceeding while allowing the others to pass through F2 to the detector. Separation is possible if and only if the frequencies of the desired terms do not overlap with those of the undesired terms. From Table 9.1, this occurs when

$$f_0 > \frac{1}{2\lambda_1 - \lambda_2} [2v\theta_s + B(2\lambda_1 + \lambda_2) + 2f_c(\lambda_2 - \lambda_1)] \tag{9.91}$$

provided that $\lambda_2 < 2\lambda_1$. If the source wavelengths cover more than one octave, then separation is not possible. In the case of monochromatic light ($\lambda_2 = \lambda_1 = \lambda$) relation (9.91) reduces to

$$f_0 > 3B + \frac{2v\theta_s}{\lambda} \tag{9.92}$$

With the second and third terms removed, intensity at the detector becomes

$$I_3\left(t - \frac{s}{v}\right) = a^2 b^2 + |g(t)|^2 |h(t - \tau)|^2$$

$$+ 2ab \ \text{Re}[g(t)h^*(t - \tau)e^{j2\pi f_0 \tau}] \tag{9.93}$$

The detector output is

Table 9.1 Diffraction Angles of Each Term Found in Plane of F2 (Passive Reference)

Term	Range of angles
ab	$\left[-\theta_s + \dfrac{2f_c\lambda_1}{v},\ \theta_s + \dfrac{2f_c\lambda_2}{v}\right]$
$ah^*\!\left(t - \dfrac{s}{v}\right)e^{-j2\pi f_0(t-(s/v))}$	$\left[-\theta_s + \dfrac{(2f_c + f_0 - B)\lambda_1}{v},\ \theta_s + \dfrac{(2f_c + f_0 + B)\lambda_2}{v}\right]$
$bg\!\left(t + \dfrac{s}{v}\right)e^{j2\pi f_0(t+s/v)}$	$\left[-\theta_s + \dfrac{(2f_c + f_0 - B)\lambda_1}{v},\ \theta_s + \dfrac{(2f_c + f_0 + B)\lambda_2}{v}\right]$
$g\!\left(t + \dfrac{s}{v}\right)h^*\!\left(t - \dfrac{s}{v}\right)e^{j4\pi f_0(s/v)}$	$\left[-\theta_s + \dfrac{2(f_c + f_0 - B)\lambda_1}{v},\ \theta_s + \dfrac{2(f_c + f_0 + B)\lambda_2}{v}\right]$

$$C(\tau) = u(\tau) + v(\tau) + 2ab \, Re[e^{j2\pi f_0 \tau} R_{gh}(\tau)] \qquad (9.94)$$

where

$$u(\tau) = Ta^2b^2 \qquad (9.95)$$

and

$$v(\tau) = \int_T |g(t)|^2 |h(t - \tau)|^2 \, dt \qquad (9.96)$$

Comparison of this result with equations (9.81) through (9.83) shows that we have removed some of the contributions to $v(\tau)$. This has come at the expense of a tradeoff between source characteristics and efficient use of bandwidth:

$$\rho_B = \frac{B}{f_0 + B} < (2\lambda_1 - \lambda_2) \left[\frac{2v\theta_s}{B} + \frac{2f_c}{B}(\lambda_2 - \lambda_1) + 4\lambda_1 \right]^{-1} \qquad (9.97)$$

Figure 9.12 is an electrical model of the processor. Note that the spatial filter F2 has been modeled as a band-pass filter.

For this processor, we chose a reference (ab) which carried no time-varying information. Accordingly, we shall refer to this processor as one which uses a *passive reference*. We may construct another filtered processor which uses an *active reference*, that is, one that carries (time-varying) information. We observe that the second and third entries of Table 9.1 carry the terms whose product we desire. This suggests that if only these terms are allowed to pass F2 (rather than the other terms), we may achieve the desired correlation. It is necessary, however, that we have h rather than h*. This is accomplished by using the positive diffraction order for both Bragg cells with the result that

$$E_2(t) = \left[ab + ah\left(t - \frac{s}{v}\right) e^{j2\pi f_0[t-(s/v)]} \right.$$

$$+ bg\left(t - \frac{s}{v}\right) e^{j2\pi f_0[t+(s/v)]}$$

$$\left. + g\left(t + \frac{s}{v}\right) h\left(t - \frac{s}{v}\right) e^{j4\pi f_0 t} \right] e^{j4\pi f_c t} \qquad (9.98)$$

Again, we determine the range of angles for each term in (9.98) and find that the separability requirements are the same as for the passive case. With the first and fourth terms removed, the intensity at the detector becomes

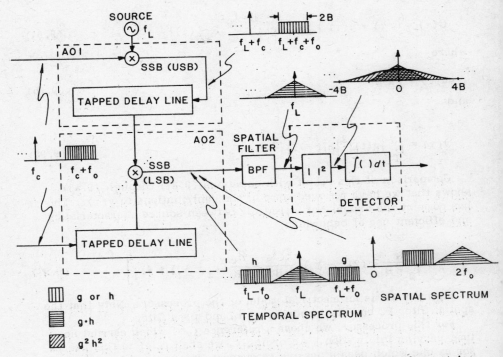

Figure 9.12 Electrical equivalent of passive reference interferometric correlator (less drive). Only one spatial filter (BPF) is needed to filter all outputs. $f_0 = 3B$.

$$I_3\left(t - \frac{s}{v}\right) = a^2 \left|h(t - \tau)\right|^2 + b^2 \left|g(t)\right|^2$$

$$+ 2ab \ Re[g(t)h^*(t - \tau)e^{j2\pi f_0 \tau} \tag{9.99}$$

Integration over T produces

$$C(\tau) = v(\tau) + 2ab \ Re[R_{gh}(\tau)e^{j2\pi f_0 \tau}] \tag{9.100}$$

where

$$v(\tau) = a^2 \int_T \left|h(t - \tau)\right|^2 dt + b^2 \int_T \left|g(t)\right|^2 dt \tag{9.101}$$

Note that there is no constant bias to the output. This property of having minimum bias will be mentioned later. An electrical equivalent of the active reference correlator is shown in Fig. 9.13.

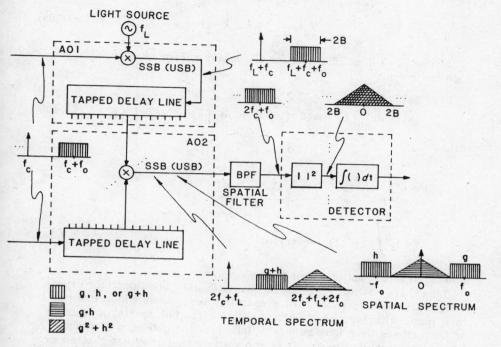

Figure 9.13 Electrical equivalent of active reference interferometric correlator (less drive). Note that both modulators choose the upper sideband. $f_0 = 3B$.

If strictly real signals are to be processed, the two architectures with transform plane filtering may use single-sideband modulations. In the case of a passive reference, the output is

$$C(\tau) = u(\tau) + v(\tau)$$
$$+ 4abR_{gh}(\tau) \cos(2\pi f_0 \tau) + 4abR_{g\tilde{h}}(\tau) \sin(2\pi f_0 \tau) \qquad (9.102)$$

where

$$u(\tau) = Ta^2 b^2 \qquad (9.103)$$

and

$$v(\tau) = \int_T [g^2(t) + \tilde{g}^2(t)][h^2(t - \tau) + \tilde{h}^2(t - \tau)] \, dt \qquad (9.104)$$

Separability requires that

$$f_0 > \frac{1}{2\lambda_1 - \lambda_2} [2v\theta_s + 2f_c(\lambda_2 - \lambda_1) + B\lambda_2] \qquad (9.105)$$

Similarly, SSB modulations for the active reference correlator produce the output

$$C(\tau) = v(\tau)$$
$$+ 4abR_{gh}(\tau) \cos(2\pi f_0 \tau) + 4abR_{g\tilde{h}}(\tau) \sin(2\pi f_0 \tau) \qquad (9.106)$$

with

$$v(\tau) = a^2 \int_T [h^2(t-\tau) + \tilde{h}^2(t-\tau)] \, dt$$

$$+ b^2 \int_T [g^2(t) + \tilde{g}^2(t)] \, dt \qquad (9.107)$$

The separability requirement is the same.

This discussion of correlators has ostensibly been limited to time-integrating architectures. In presenting approaches which use transform plane filtering, we stretched this a bit: The spatial separation of frequencies by a lens generally falls into the category of space-integrating architectures. It is appropriate that they are classed as time integrators, however, because the correlation integral still arises from detector time accumulation.

9.2.4 Two-Dimensional Architectures

The correlators which we have discussed may be extended to allow the implementation of a two-dimensional correlation. We have used two spatial dimensions in our optical systems: one which is followed by the optical path and another to hold an entire time window. Position in the latter dimension corresponds to variation in delay of one input. To implement a two-dimensional correlation of the form

$$R_{ghq}(\tau_1, \tau_2) = \int_T g(t)h(t-\tau_1)q(t-\tau_2) \, dt \qquad (9.108)$$

it is clear that use of another spatial dimension is in order. Suppose that the first dimension corresponds to the optical axis and the second to delay of h. Then position in the third dimension must represent delay in the input q. This suggests an architecture employing a Bragg cell (with acoustic propagation) in the, say, vertical direction and one in the horizontal direction such that light diffracted by any point in the first cell illuminates every point in the second. In this way, all products of the form $h(t - \tau_1)q(t - \tau_2)$ are generated for τ_1 and τ_2 in some interval. All that remains is to multiply by $g(t)$ and integrate.

A two-dimensional extension of the one-dimensional LED correlator is pictured in Fig. 9.14. We have used *crossed* Bragg cells with AO1 in the vertical direction and AO2 in the horizontal. The LED source is modulated by $g(t)$. L0 collimates the light, which is then focused to a vertical line in AO1 by L1. AO1 is driven by $h(t)$. Diffracted light from AO1 illuminates AO2, which is in the focal plane of L2. (Undiffracted light misses the aperture of AO2). Here, the light is modulated by $q(t)$. Light leaving AO2 passes through cylinder lens L4, spherical lens L5, and filter F2 and falls on a two-dimensional detector array. Light not diffracted by AO2 is blocked by F2. Hence, any light reaching the detector has been modulated by g, h, and q. Lenses L2 and L5 serve to image AO1 onto the detector in the vertical direction. (L4 has no power in this direction.) Hence, each x position on the detector corresponds to a point on AO1. Similarly, lenses L4 and L5 image AO2 onto the detector in the horizontal direction. Therefore, light at any point (x,y) on the detector passes through unique points on AO1 and AO2. Hence, the detector pixel at position (x,y) provides the output

$$R_{ghq}(\tau_1,\tau_2) = \int_T g(t)h(t - \tau_1)q(t - \tau_2) \, dt \qquad (9.109)$$

where $\tau_1 = x/v$, $\tau_2 = y/v$, v is the Bragg cell acoustic propagation velocity, and T is the detector integration period. This is the result sought.

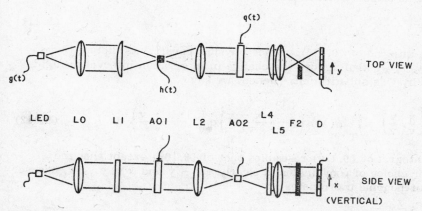

Figure 9.14 LED triple product processor optics. Undiffracted light (not shown) from AO1 misses the aperture of AO2. Undiffracted light from AO2 is blocked by F2.

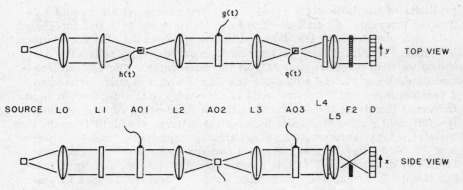

Figure 9.15 Bragg cell triple product processor.

In a similar manner, we may extend the unmodulated source architectures to two dimensions as pictured in Fig. 9.15. Here, three
Bragg cells are employed, two in the vertical direction and one in the
horizontal. Lenses L2 and L3 image AO1 onto AO3, so that AO1 appears
to be in coincidence with AO3 but inverted. Following AO2, the optical
system is the same as for the LED implementation. The term of interest in the output of a detector pixel at (x,y) is

$$C\left(\frac{x}{v}, \frac{y}{v}\right) = \int_T h\left(t + \frac{x}{v}\right) g\left(t - \frac{y}{v}\right) q\left(t - \frac{x}{v}\right) dt \qquad (9.110)$$

Let us make a variable change of

$$\lambda = t - \frac{y}{v} \qquad (9.111)$$

in the integral of (9.110). Since physical constraints dictate that
T >> y/v, we shall ignore the change in integration interval brought
about by this substitution. Hence, we say

$$C\left(\frac{x}{v}, \frac{y}{v}\right) = \int_T g(\lambda) h\left(\lambda - \frac{-x - y}{v}\right) q\left(\lambda - \frac{x - y}{v}\right) d\lambda \qquad (9.112)$$

The integral of (9.112) resembles that of (9.108) except that the
proper choice of coordinates is clearly −x − y and x − y. So, choose
(the orthogonal coordinates)

$$x' = -x - y$$
$$y' = x - y$$

We may then write the correlation as

$$
C'\left(\frac{x'}{v}, \frac{y'}{v}\right) = C\left(\frac{-x' + y'}{2v}, \frac{-x' - y'}{2v}\right)
$$

$$
= \int_{T} g(\lambda)h\left(\lambda - \frac{x'}{v}\right)q\left(\lambda - \frac{y'}{v}\right) d\lambda
$$

$$
= R_{ghq}\left(\frac{x'}{v}, \frac{y'}{v}\right) \qquad\qquad (9.113)
$$

We have made no mention of modulation schemes used for the two-dimensional architectures. As direct extensions of one-dimensional correlators, the two-dimensional processors inherit the same choice of approaches. In particular, both interferometric and noninterferometric implementations are possible [8,9]. We shall not repeat all of the possibilities here.

The major differences in characteristics of the one- and two-dimensional correlators (aside from the additional dimension) are the integration time and the number of pixels (see the Appendix). In general, a two- to three-order-of-magnitude increase in the number of outputs is achievable with two-dimensional correlators. The upper limit is usually determined by the number of available detector pixels and not by other devices. The readout rate of two-dimensional detectors is limited. Combined with the larger number of pixels, this results in an integration period which is several orders longer than that of the typical one-dimensional arrays.

The two-dimensional correlator described here, dubbed the *triple product processor* (TPP), is one of the most versatile of optical processors, owing to the range of achievable operations. Later we shall examine one of these applications more closely.

9.3 CORRELATOR POSTPROCESSING

Correlator postprocessing hardware, which is generally electronic, follows the correlator optics. It is responsible for taking the optics output $C(\tau)$ and presenting an approximation of the desired correlation $R_{gh}(\tau)$. This usually entails two operations: removal of unwanted terms in $C(\tau)$ and, in the case of interferometric implementations, extraction of R_{gh} from its carrier. Several postprocessing approaches will be presented. The appropriateness of each, taken by itself or in combination with others, will vary with the application. Note that this presentation is not exhaustive but suggests general techniques. Since the same postprocessing techniques are amenable to both one- and two-dimensional architectures, we shall consider the one-dimensional case only.

Before proceeding, we shall let the real world intrude into our simple formulation of the output. $C(\tau)$ is actually corrupted by both additive and multiplicative nonuniformities. Additive contributions come from the detector array in the form of pixel-to-pixel background variations characteristic of solid-state detectors. Multiplicative variations are the result of nonuniformities in the optical system itself. Sources include variation of illumination and Bragg cell acoustic beam nonuniformity. Given such effects, it is clear that we were justified in retaining the argument τ in $u(\tau)$. For the present, we shall not consider how the multiplicative nonuniformities affect R_{gh} but shall be content with removing unwanted terms under this corruption. We shall continue to use the earlier formulation of $C(\tau)$ but shall assume that $u(\tau)$ and $v(\tau)$ include variations from their stated values. In particular, the additive nonuniformities have been lumped into $u(\tau)$.

9.3.1 Rejection of Unwanted Terms

We shall first consider several methods to remove unwanted terms in the output. We shall find that the approach to extracting the correlation will strip off all undesired output contributions except the variations in $u(\tau)$. Thus, many of the following methods may be more powerful than necessary for interferometric correlators.

It is useful to express $C(\tau)$ in terms of its dependence on the sign of an input, say $g(t)$. Let us denote the term bearing $R_{gh}(\tau)$ by $d(\tau)$ and write

$$C(\tau) = u(\tau) + v^{(2)}(\tau) + v^{(1)}(\tau) + d(\tau) \qquad (9.114)$$

where $v(\tau)$ has been decomposed into $v^{(1)}(\tau)$ and $v^{(2)}(\tau)$, the terms of odd and even dependence on $g(t)$, respectively. Suppose that we invert (multiply by -1) $g(t)$. We shall denote the resulting output by $C_-(\tau)$ and write

$$C_-(\tau) = u(\tau) + v^{(2)}(\tau) - v^{(1)}(\tau) - d(\tau) \qquad (9.115)$$

since $R_{gh}(\tau)$ is linear with $g(t)$. Now we observe that the difference $D(\tau)$ of the outputs with and without inversion is

$$D(\tau) = C(\tau) - C_-(\tau) = 2v^{(1)}(\tau) + 2d(\tau) \qquad (9.116)$$

This suggests a method of removing many of the unwanted terms. Figure 9.16 shows an implementation of equation (9.116). During an even frame, $g(t)$ is not inverted, and $C(\tau)$ accumulates on the detector. At the end of an even frame, $g(t)$ is inverted, and $C_-(\tau)$ begins to accumulate, while $C(\tau)$ is read out of the detector and into a frame memory. The memory is capable of storing one value for each pixel and can be viewed as a delay one frame long. In general, dur-

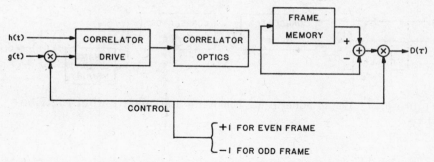

Figure 9.16 Simple method of removing terms of even parity in g(t).

ing an even frame, $C(\tau)$ is accumulating, and $C_-(\tau)$ is being written into memory and being subtracted from $C(\tau)$. During an odd frame, $C_-(\tau)$ accumulates, $C(\tau)$ passes from detector to memory, and $C_-(\tau)$ is subtracted from $C(\tau)$. In either case, the result is as in equation (9.120). Let us in general denote the output of the nth frame by $C_n(\tau)$. For this postprocessing scheme, the nth output is

$$D_n(\tau) = (-1)^n [C_n(\tau) - C_{n-1}(\tau)] \qquad (9.117)$$

For this method to work as stated, it is necessary that $v^{(2)}(\tau)$ and $d(\tau)$ remain essentially unchanged between successive frames.

This requirement may be relaxed somewhat by only taking differences of the form $C_n - C_{n-1}$, where n is odd. In other words, we need only require that $v^{(2)}(\tau)$ and $d(\tau)$ remain unchanged between frames n and n − 1 for n odd. This situation may be forced by placing one period's length of input data in a memory and playing it through the processor for two periods. Repeating this allows processing in real time with a sacrifice of half of the input data.[†] More elaborate schemes inverting different combinations of the inputs may be applied.

As another example, suppose that the nonzero portion of $R_{gh}(\tau)$ remains in the processor's time aperture for frames n − 1 and n. Consider the arrangement shown in Fig. 9.17. Every even frame (say n − 1), the switch is set to position (2) so that g(t) is delayed by $\rho_\tau \tau_B$, causing the correlation peak to move outside the correlator time window. During the following frame, the switch is in position (1), allowing g(t) to enter the correlator normally. The postprocessor output becomes

---

[†]This may be avoided by time compression. See the closing remarks.

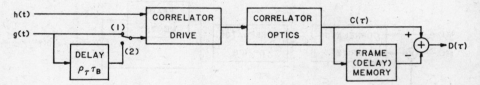

Figure 9.17 Simple scheme for removing stationary output contributions.

$$D_n(\tau) = C_n(\tau) - C_{n-1}(\tau)$$

$$= [v_n^{(2)}(\tau) - v_{n-1}^{(2)}(\tau)]$$

$$+ [v_n^{(1)}(\tau) - v_{n-1}^{(1)}(\tau)]$$

$$+ [d_n(\tau) - d_{n-1}(\tau)] \qquad (9.118)$$

By assumption, $d_{n-1}(\tau) = 0$. In many practical cases, $v_n^{(1)}(\tau) = v_{n-1}^{(1)}(\tau)$ and $v_n^{(2)}(\tau) = v_{n-1}^{(2)}(\tau)$. If this is true, then

$$D_n(\tau) \doteq d_n(\tau) \qquad (9.119)$$

In cases where none of the above approaches is appropriate, a simple but less powerful approach may be taken. Here we seek to remove $u(\tau)$ only. Since $u(\tau)$ does not change with time, it suffices to record $u(\tau)$ in memory once and subtract it from all outputs. The recording is done simply by setting the correlator inputs to zero and recording the result in memory. The inputs are then restored, and $u(\tau)$ is subtracted, leaving $D(\tau) = v(\tau) + d(\tau)$. Although this *background subtraction* is a simple operation, it is necessary at a minimum, since the additive nonuniformities must be removed.

When portions of $v(\tau)$ may not be removed by the above method, knowledge of the forms of $v(\tau)$ and $d(\tau)$ may allow separation. Suppose, for example, that $v(\tau)$ is independent of τ (within the correlator time window Δ_τ). For a given frame, let $v(\tau) = c$. Now if

$$\int_{\Delta_\tau} d(\tau) \doteq 0 \qquad (9.120)$$

we may estimate

$$\hat{c} = \frac{1}{\Delta_\tau} \int_{\Delta_\tau} D(\tau) \, d\tau \doteq c \qquad (9.121)$$

Hence, by averaging the outputs, an estimate of $v(\tau)$ is made, which may then be subtracted, leaving $d(\tau)$. This is called a *riding baseline* subtraction. More generally, if $v(\tau)$ varies more slowly than $d(\tau)$, a running average across the outputs may provide a good estimate of $v(\tau)$. Thus, we estimate $v(\tau_0)$ by averaging $D(\tau)$ in the neighborhood of τ_0. The chosen neighborhood is large enough to minimize the contribution of $d(\tau)$ and small enough that $v(\tau)$ remains nearly constant.

9.3.2 Extraction of Correlation

Interferometric architectures require additional postprocessing to detect $R_{gh}(\tau)$ on its carrier. Here, $d(\tau)$, the term bearing $R_{gh}(\tau)$, usually takes on the form

$$d(\tau) = a\,\mathrm{Re}[e^{j(2\pi f_0 \tau + \phi)} R_{gh}(\tau)] \qquad (9.122)$$

where a and ϕ are real constants. Recall that R_{gh} may be complex. We may write the input to our "correlation extractor" as

$$D(\tau) = a\,\mathrm{Re}[e^{j(2\pi f_0 \tau + \phi)} R_{gh}(\tau)] + v_r(\tau) \qquad (9.123)$$

where $v_r(\tau)$ is the residual $v(\tau)$ left by preceding postprocessing. Consider the product

$$A(\tau) = \cos(2\pi f_0 \tau + \phi)D(\tau)$$

$$= \frac{a}{2}\,\mathrm{Re}\,R_{gh}(\tau)$$

$$+ \frac{a}{2}\,\mathrm{Re}[R_{gh}(\tau)e^{j(4\pi f_0 \tau + 2\phi)}]$$

$$+ \cos(2\pi f_0 \tau + \phi)v_r(\tau) \qquad (9.124)$$

We have generated a term with the desired correlation stripped of its carrier, as well as terms of no interest. By our choice of f_0 made earlier we have forced the frequency components of the terms in (9.124) to be disjoint. In particular, $R_{gh}(\tau)$ has frequencies confined to the interval $[-B,B]$, while those of the other terms are outside this interval. This suggests that $D(\tau)$ (which is presented serially) need only be multiplied by $\cos(2\pi f_0 \tau + \phi)$ and low-pass-filtered to produce $\mathrm{Re}\,R_{gh}(\tau)$. The arrangement pictured in Fig. 9.18 may be used to extract both real and imaginary portions of R_{gh}. Note that any part of v not removed earlier is eliminated here. Also note that the additive nonuniformities lumped in with $u(\tau)$ have frequency components over the whole spectrum and are not eliminated by this filtering. Hence, for interferometric architectures it is necessary and sufficient to remove $u(\tau)$ before extracting R_{gh}.

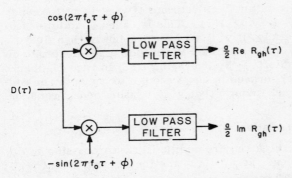

Figure 9.18 Extracting the real and imaginary portions of the correlation. Both filters have cutoff frequency B. $D(\tau)$ comes from subtraction circuitry.

Finally, the multiplicative effects on R_{gh} may be removed by storing a correction value for each pixel in a memory. The output from each pixel is multiplied by the corresponding correction value after other postprocessing steps.

9.4 OUTPUT NOISE

We have treated the correlator output as being deterministic. In fact, this is not the case: The output is corrupted by a variety of noise sources. Certainly, if the correlator input signals are accompanied by noise, this will give rise to random variations in the output. Moreover, the correlator itself contributes noise to its output. The primary source for this inherent noise is the discrete nature of light. Sources arising from the detector [7] will not be treated here.

In this section we shall examine correlator output variance, expressing our result as a signal-to-noise ratio (SNR). In particular, the output SNR will be a function of the input SNRs. Throughout the discussion, simplifying assumptions will be stated. These assumptions will be realistic and appropriate for the majority of applications. We shall treat the inputs as being real. The complex generalization follows similarly.

9.4.1 Variance Due to Input Noise

We begin by deriving the major result of this section: the contribution of input noise to output variance. We shall treat each input as the sum of a deterministic signal and a noise term. The noise terms are assumed to be independent, stationary, zero-mean, band-limited, white, gaussian processes. Specifically, this means that the noise is evenly distributed over the input frequency band $[-B,B]$. As a result, the autocorrelation of each noise source is of the form $\sigma^2 \operatorname{sinc}(2B\pi\tau)$, where σ^2 is the noise variance.

Let us write the correlator inputs as

$$g(t) = x(t) + w(t) \tag{9.125}$$

and

$$h(t) = y(t) + z(t) \tag{9.126}$$

where x and y are the desired deterministic signals and w and z are noise. Let σ_w^2 and σ_z^2 be the variance (power) of w and z, respectively. Then the autocorrelations of w and z are

$$R_w(\tau) = \sigma_w^2 R(\tau) \tag{9.127}$$

and

$$R_z(\tau) = \sigma_z^2 R(\tau) \tag{9.128}$$

where

$$R(\tau) = \operatorname{sinc}(2\pi B\tau) \tag{9.129}$$

Recall that the correlator output results from integration over a period T. The signals are characterized by their average powers

$$\sigma_x^2 = \frac{1}{T} \int_T x^2(t)\, dt \tag{9.130}$$

and

$$\sigma_y^2 = \frac{1}{T} \int_T y^2(t)\, dt \tag{9.131}$$

and their average values

$$m_x = \frac{1}{T} \int_T x(t)\, dt \tag{9.132}$$

and

$$m_y = \frac{1}{T} \int_T y(t)\, dt \tag{9.133}$$

Now the input signal-to-noise ratios may be written simply as

$$\Gamma_g = \frac{\sigma_x^2}{\sigma_w^2} \tag{9.134}$$

and

$$\Gamma_h = \frac{\sigma_y^2}{\sigma_z^2} \tag{9.135}$$

We shall treat the interferometric and noninterferometric cases simultaneously by writing the general output as

$$C = \int_T P(t)\, dt \tag{9.136}$$

where

$$P(t) = g(t)h(t) + ah(t) + bg(t) + c \tag{9.137}$$

The constants a, b, and c are determined by the architecture. Note that we have not included the delay τ in (9.137): To make the notation less cumbersome, we shall assume that h includes the appropriate delay. Substituting for g and h in (9.137), we obtain

$$P(t) = w(t)[b + y(t)] + z(t)[a + x(t)] + w(t)z(t)$$
$$+ [x(t)y(t) + ay(t) + bx(t) + c] \tag{9.138}$$

We shall find the above grouping by noise terms convenient. Indeed, for the present, let us use the following definitions for deterministic terms in (9.138):

$$\alpha(t) = b + y(t) \tag{9.139}$$

$$\beta(t) = a + x(t) \tag{9.140}$$

$$\gamma(t) = c + ay(t) + bx(t) + x(t)y(t) \tag{9.141}$$

Then we may write (9.138) as

$$P(t) = w(t)\alpha(t) + z(t)\beta(t) + w(t)z(t) + \gamma(t) \tag{9.142}$$

Using E{ } to denote *expectation of*, we find the output variance by the usual expression

$$\text{Var}\{C\} = E\{C^2\} - E^2\{C\} \tag{9.143}$$

Now

$$E\{C^2\} = E\left\{\int_T P(t_1)\,dt_1 \int_T P(t_2)\,dt_2\right\}$$

$$= \int_T \int_T E\{P(t_1)P(t_2)\}\,dt_1\,dt_2 \tag{9.144}$$

The product in (9.144) results in many terms whose expectation is zero since the noise terms have zero mean and are independent. With these removed, we have

$$E\{P(t_1)P(t_2)\} = E\{\alpha(t_1)\alpha(t_2)w(t_1)w(t_2)$$

$$+ \beta(t_1)\beta(t_2)z(t_1)z(t_2)$$

$$+ w(t_1)w(t_2)z(t_1)z(t_2)$$

$$+ \gamma(t_1)\gamma(t_2)\} \tag{9.145}$$

By definition,

$$R_w(t_2 - t_1) = E\{w(t_1)w(t_2)\} \tag{9.146}$$

and similarly for R_z. Thus, we find that

$$E\{C^2\} = \int_T \int_T [\sigma_w^2 \alpha(t_1)\alpha(t_2) + \sigma_z^2 \beta(t_1)\beta(t_2)]R(t_1 - t_2)\,dt_1\,dt_2$$

$$+ \sigma_w^2 \sigma_z^2 \int_T \int_T R^2(t_1 - t_2)\,dt_1\,dt_2$$

$$+ \int_T \int_T \gamma(t_1)\gamma(t_2)\,dt_1\,dt_2 \tag{9.147}$$

But

$$E^2\{C\} = \int_T \int_T \gamma(t_1)\gamma(t_2)\,dt_1\,dt_2 \tag{9.148}$$

and

$$\int_T \int_T R^2(t_1 - t_2) \, dt_1 \, dt_2 \doteq \frac{T}{2B} \qquad (9.149)$$

Hence, the variance of C may be expressed as

$$\text{Var}\{C\} = \int_T \int_T [\sigma_w^2 \alpha(t_1)\alpha(t_2) + \sigma_z^2 \beta(t_1)\beta(t_2)]R(t_1 - t_2) \, dt_1 \, dt_2$$

$$+ \sigma_w^2 \sigma_z^2 \frac{T}{2B} \qquad (9.150)$$

We observe that $R(t_1 - t_2)$ assumes large values only when t_1 and t_2 are close to each other. This suggests that it might be reasonable to approximate R by a delta function of equal area. In fact, if α and β vary slowly relative to R, then this would be a good approximation for purposes of (9.150). Let us quantify the goodness of this approximation by constants depending on the signals. Define

$$\Lambda_y = \frac{\int_T \int_T y(t_1)y(t_2)R(t_1 - t_2) \, dt_1 \, dt_2}{\int_T \int_T y(t_1)y(t_2)(1/2B)\delta(t_1 - t_2) \, dt_1 \, dt_2} \qquad (9.151)$$

Similarly, define Λ_x in terms of x. To put (9.150) in terms of Λ_x and Λ_y, we write

$$\int_T \int_T \alpha(t_1)\alpha(t_2)R(t_1 - t_2) \, dt_1 \, dt_2 = b^2 \frac{T}{2B} + b \frac{T}{B} m_y$$

$$+ \int_T \int_T y(t_1)y(t_2)R(t_1 - t_2) \, dt_1 \, dt_2 \qquad (9.152)$$

Also, we observe that

$$\int_T \int_T y(t_1)y(t_2) \frac{1}{2B} \delta(t_1 - t_2) \, dt_1 \, dt_2 = \frac{T}{2B} \sigma_y^2 \qquad (9.153)$$

so that

$$\Lambda_y = \frac{2B}{T\sigma_y^2} \int_T \int_T y(t_1)y(t_2)R(t_1 - t_2) \, dt_1 \, dt_2 \qquad (9.154)$$

A similar expression results for Λ_x. We may substitute (9.152) and (9.154) into (9.150) to obtain

$$\mathrm{Var}\{C\} = \frac{T\sigma_w^2\sigma_z^2}{2B}\left(1 + \frac{a^2 + 2am_x + \Lambda_x\sigma_x^2}{\sigma_w^2} + \frac{b^2 + 2bm_y + \Lambda_y\sigma_y^2}{\sigma_z^2}\right)$$

(9.155)

This may be expressed in terms of input SNRs as

$$\mathrm{Var}\{C\} = \frac{T\sigma_x^2\sigma_y^2}{2B\Gamma_g\Gamma_h}\left[1 + \Gamma_g\left(\Lambda_x + \frac{a^2 + 2am_x}{\sigma_x^2}\right)\right.$$

$$\left. + \Gamma_h\left(\Lambda_y + \frac{b^2 + 2bm_y}{\sigma_y^2}\right)\right]$$

(9.156)

Now that we have the variance, we may determine the output SNR for the case where other noise sources are not significant. The output *signal* power is the square of the correlation and may be written as $T^2\sigma_x^2\sigma_y^2 r^2$, where r is the correlation coefficient of x and y; that is,

$$r = \frac{1}{\sigma_x\sigma_y}\frac{1}{T}\int_T x(t)y(t)\,dt$$

(9.157)

The output SNR arising only from input noise is

$$\Gamma'_0 = \frac{T^2\sigma_x^2\sigma_y^2 r^2}{\mathrm{Var}\{C\}}$$

$$= 2BTr^2\Gamma_g\Gamma_h$$

$$\times\left[1 + \Gamma_g\left(\Lambda_x + \frac{a^2 + 2am_x}{\sigma_x^2}\right) + \Gamma_h\left(\Lambda_y + \frac{b^2 + 2bm_y}{\sigma_y^2}\right)\right]^{-1}$$

(9.158)

We may specialize (9.158) for the interferometric correlators by noting that postprocessing (specifically, correlation extraction) removes all but the correlation term. Thus, we may set a = b = 0. Equation (9.158) then simplifies to

$$\Gamma'_0 = \frac{2BTr^2\Gamma_g\Gamma_h}{1 + \Gamma_g\Lambda_x + \Gamma_h\Lambda_y} \tag{9.159}$$

In the case of a noninterferometric correlator, a and b are simply the input transducer bias levels a and b defined earlier. Linear operation of Bragg cells requires that a >> m_x, b >> m_y, a^2 >> σx^2, and b^2 >> σy^2 if both devices are Bragg cells. Since $\Lambda_x \approx 1$ and $\Lambda_y \approx 1$, we may approximate

$$\Gamma'_0 = \frac{2BTr^2\Gamma_g\Gamma_h}{1 + \Gamma_g a^2/\sigma_x^2 + \Gamma_h b^2/\sigma_y^2} \tag{9.60}$$

for the case when both input transducers are Bragg cells and

$$\Gamma'_0 = \frac{2BTr^2\Gamma_g\Gamma_h}{1 + \Gamma_g[\Lambda_x + (a^2 + 2am_x)/\sigma_x^2] + \Gamma_h(b^2/\sigma_y^2)} \tag{9.61}$$

when the first input device is an LED.

9.4.2 Total Noise

We shall now consider the variance contribution of photon shot noise. Information is represented discretely by photon-produced electrons, which are collected by the detector. The arrival of photons is probabilistic, as is the generation of an electron from a photon. The resulting probability distribution is Poisson. If a large number of electrons is collected; the electron distribution is well approximated by a normal distribution. In particular, if the mean number of electrons is n, then the standard deviation [10] is $\sqrt{n}$.

Let us suppose that our output C is currently expressed in *units*. We wish to determine output variance in electrons. Thus, let us define k to be the number of electrons per unit. Let n be a random variable equal to the number of electrons which accumulate in a detector pixel. The conditional expectations of n are

$$E\{n|C\} = kC \tag{9.162}$$

and

$$E\{n^2|C\} = var\{n|C\} + E^2\{n|C\}$$
$$= kC + (kC)^2 \tag{9.163}$$

Now

$$E\{n^2\} = E\{E\{n^2|C\}\}$$

$$= E\{kC + (kC)^2\}$$

$$= kE\{C\} + k^2[\text{Var}\{C\} + E^2\{C\}] \tag{9.164}$$

Since

$$E\{n\} = kE\{C\} \tag{9.165}$$

then

$$\text{Var}\{n\} = E\{n^2\} - E^2\{n\}$$

$$= kE\{C\} + k^2 \, \text{var}\{C\} \tag{9.166}$$

Now that we have output variance in electrons, we must express the correlation in electrons in order to form the SNR. The output signal power is

$$T^2\sigma_x^2\sigma_y^2 r^2 \text{ units}^2 = k^2 T^2 \sigma_x^2 \sigma_y^2 r^2 \text{ electrons}^2 \tag{9.167}$$

Hence, the output signal-to-noise ratio is

$$\Gamma_0 = \frac{k^2 T^2 \sigma_x^2 \sigma_y^2 r^2}{kE\{C\} + k^2 \, \text{var}\{C\}}$$

$$= \left(\frac{E\{C\}}{kT^2\sigma_x^2\sigma_y^2 r^2} + \frac{1}{\Gamma_0'} \right)^{-1} \tag{9.168}$$

It remains to determine k. We choose k to make the best use of detector dynamic range; that is, k is made as large as possible without saturating the detector. Let us suppose that we operate the processor so that the expected number of electrons is N_e. Then $kE\{C\} = N_e$. Recall that the correlation integral (our desired output) can assume a maximum value of $T\sigma_x\sigma_y$ units ($T\sigma_x\sigma_y k$ electrons). For each architecture, this value can be up to some fraction of the average output. Let ρ_s be the architecture-dependent ratio

$$\rho_s = \frac{T}{E\{C\}} \, \max\{\sigma_x\sigma_y\} \tag{9.169}$$

The maximum value will be determined by linearity requirements. The figure of merit ρ_s represents the architecture's use of available dynamic range. We shall suppose that σ_x and σ_y are operated at this maximum (and optimal, in the signal-to-noise sense) value. Then we find that

$$\frac{E\{C\}}{k^2 T^2 \sigma_x^2 \sigma_y^2 r^2} = \frac{1}{N_e \rho_s^2 r^2} \tag{9.170}$$

Hence,

$$\Gamma_0 = \left(\frac{1}{N_e \rho_s^2 r^2} + \frac{1}{\Gamma_0'}\right)^{-1} \tag{9.171}$$

As it stands, (9.171) applies only to the noninterferometric correlators. In the derivation above, we assumed that all variance due to
photon shot noise contributes to the output variance. The correlation extraction process admits only frequency components of interest,
rejecting much of the noise. In fact, we find that the proportion of
shot noise variance retained is approximately ρ_D. Thus,

$$\Gamma_0 = \left(\frac{\rho_D}{N_e \rho_s^2 r^2} + \frac{1}{\Gamma_0'}\right)^{-1} \tag{9.172}$$

Note that for noninterferometric architectures, $\rho_D = 1$, so that (9.176)
applies in general.
Since $r^2 \leqslant 1$, equation (9.172) dictates that

$$\Gamma_0 \leqslant \frac{N_e \rho_s^2}{\rho_D} \tag{9.173}$$

The shot noise, then, represents an upper bound on output SNR. For
$\Gamma_0' \ll N_e \rho_s^2 r^2$, $\Gamma_0 \doteq \Gamma_0'$.
Before concluding this section, we shall determine values of ρ_s for
two architectures. We shall find that ρ_s depends on the choice of the
average rms input values σ_x and σ_y relative to the respective bias
levels a and b. Since ρ_s is used to determine the upper bound of Γ_0,
we shall calculate ρ_s under the assumption that $\sigma_x^2 \gg \sigma_w^2$ and $\sigma_y^2 \gg \sigma_z^2$.
The first case we consider is a noninterferometric architecture.
Recall that

$$C(\tau) = Tab + b\int_T g(t)\,dt + a\int_T h(t-\tau)\,dt$$

$$+ \int_T g(t)h(t-\tau)\,dt \tag{9.174}$$

in this case. Now

$$\int_T g(t) \, dt \leq T\sigma_x \tag{9.175}$$

$$\int_T h(t - \tau) \, dt \leq T\sigma_y \tag{9.176}$$

$$\int_T g(t)h(t - \tau) \, dt \leq T\sigma_x \sigma_y \tag{9.177}$$

Hence, from (9.169) we see that

$$\rho_s^{-1} \geq \frac{ab}{\sigma_x \sigma_y} + \frac{b}{\sigma_y} + \frac{a}{\sigma_x} + 1 \tag{9.178}$$

For linearity, $b \gg \sigma_y$ and $a > \sigma_x$, so

$$\rho_s \doteq \frac{\sigma_x}{a} \frac{\sigma_y}{b} \tag{9.179}$$

From a signal-to-noise point of view, it is clearly optimal to operate the correlator with σ_x/a and σ_y/b as large as possible. On the other hand, σ_x/a and σ_y/b are chosen as small as possible for linearity. In general, for noninterferometric correlators, we can expect $\rho_s \ll 1$ so that $\Gamma_0 \ll N_e$.

Let us now examine an interferometric correlator. In particular, let us look at the active reference architecture. In this case, the output normalized to the correlation term is

$$C(\tau) = \frac{a^2}{2ab} \int_T |h(t - \tau)|^2 \, dt + \frac{b^2}{2ab} \int_T |g(t)|^2 \, dt$$
$$+ \frac{2ab}{2ab} \mathrm{Re}[R_{gh}(\tau)e^{j2\pi f_0 \tau}] \tag{9.180}$$

Recall that

$$\int_T |g(t)|^2 \, dt = T\sigma_x^2 \tag{9.181}$$

and

$$\int_T |h(t - \tau)|^2 \, dt = T\sigma_y^2 \tag{9.182}$$

For r = 1,

$$\rho_s = \frac{2abT\sigma_x\sigma_y}{a^2T\sigma_y^2 + b^2T\sigma_x^2 + 2abT\sigma_x\sigma_y}$$

$$= \left(\frac{1}{2}\frac{a}{\sigma_x}\frac{\sigma_y}{b} + \frac{1}{2}\frac{b}{\sigma_y}\frac{\sigma_x}{a} + 1\right)^{-1} \tag{9.183}$$

It is clear that ρ_s is maximized by setting $\sigma_x = a$ and $\sigma_y = b$. This done, we have $\rho_s = 1/2$.

An examination of all other interferometric correlators (see Table 9.2 in the Summary) shows that $\rho_s \leqslant 1/2$ and that ρ_s is maximized by choosing $\sigma_x = a$ and $\sigma_y = b$. Thus, the active reference architecture makes the best use of the detector dynamic range due to its having the minimum detector bias.

Finally, let us note what effect combining multiple frames during postprocessing has on SNR. In each such case, outputs are added or subtracted in order to enhance the correlation term. Specifically, if n frames are combined, the output signal power increases by n^2. Noise in each frame is independent. Thus, if each frame has the same variance, the combined frames will have n times the variance of one frame. The result is that output SNR increases by a factor of $n^2/n = n$.

9.5 IMPLEMENTATION OF THE FOURIER TRANSFORM

In this section we shall examine more closely the implementation of the one-and two-dimensional Fourier transforms. Recall that the appropriate kernal function is the chirp: a signal whose frequency increases linearly with time. As it stands, this frequency grows without bound, occupying an infinite bandwidth. A more physically reasonable choice of kernel function is a *repeating chirp*, which increases linearly in frequency for a period T_c, resets to the initial frequency, and again ramps up. This is depicted in Fig. 9.19. Suppose that a repeating chirp is used with a correlator having an integration period T which is longer than T_c. At some time during any integration period, the chirp will reset, causing a phase change of the generated Fourier kernel. This phase change depends on frequency. The result is that the correlation will be a nonuniform rendering of the desired spectrum. Hence, it is undesirable for the chirp to reset during integration, and T_c is chosen to be a multiple of T. To make best use of limited bandwidth, T_c should be the smallest possible multiple of T; however, to make use of postprocessing enhancements that involve n frames, the chirp must be continuous over those n frames. Thus, we choose $T_c = nT$.

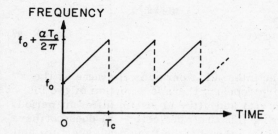

Figure 9.19 Repeating chirp with angular acceleration α and period T_c.

9.5.1 Implementing the Chirp Algorithm

Let us first look at implementing the one-dimensional Fourier transform with interferometric correlators, as they can accept complex inputs. We are then permitted to use the complex chirp whose ramp is

$$c(t) = e^{j[(\alpha/2)t^2 + 2\pi f_0 t]} \qquad\qquad t \; \varepsilon \; [t_0,\, t_0 + T_c) \qquad (9.184)$$

The chirp ranges between the frequencies f_0 and $f_0 + (\alpha/2\pi)T_c$. We choose the correlator inputs

$$g(t) = s(t)c(t) \qquad\qquad (9.185)$$

and

$$h(t) = c(t) \qquad\qquad (9.186)$$

where s is the signal to be processed. Integrating over the interval $[t_0,\, t_0 + T]$, the correlator produces

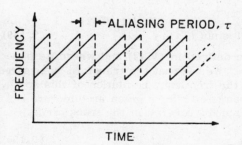

Figure 9.20 Repeating chirp and replica delayed by τ. An aliasing period of length τ occurs every period.

$$R(\tau,t_0) = \int_{t_0}^{t_0+T} s(t)c(t)c^*(t - \tau) \, dt \tag{9.187}$$

We shall assume here that the integration period is the same as the chirp period. Since the chirp repeats, there is a portion of the integration period during which $c(t)$ and $c(t - \tau)$ are on different periods, as shown in Fig. 9.20. During this time, $c(t)c^*(t - \tau)$ does not have the proper value. Since τ is bounded by the Bragg cell aperture and T determined by detector technology, it usually happens that T_c is many orders of magnitude larger than τ, and this period overlap has negligible effect. When T_c is not much greater than all values of τ, a more sophisticated approach is required. In his dissertation [9], Kellman suggests such an approach which uses multiple chirps to maintain the proper product at all times but is necessarily inefficient in bandwidth usage. We shall be content to ignore the effect. With this note in mind, the output of the correlator becomes

$$R(\tau,t_0) = e^{-j[(\alpha/2)\tau^2 - 2\pi f_0 \tau]} \int_{t_0}^{t_0+T} s(t)e^{j\alpha t \tau} \, dt \tag{9.188}$$

Denote the Fourier transform of $s(t)$ as $S(f)$. We may replace the integral of (9.188) over a finite interval by the Fourier transform of the product of $s(t)$ and a rectangle function. Hence,

$$\int_{t_0}^{t_0+T} s(t)e^{j\alpha t \tau} \, dt = \mathcal{F}\left\{ s(t)p\left(\frac{t - t_0 - T/2}{T}\right) \right\}$$

$$= \mathcal{F}\{s(t)\} * \mathcal{F}\left\{ p\left(\frac{t - t_0 - T/2}{T}\right) \right\}$$

$$= S(f) * [T \, \mathrm{sinc}(\pi T f)e^{-j2\pi f(t_0 + T/2)}] \tag{9.189}$$

where p is the rectangle function defined in (9.44) and where we have made the substitution $f = -\alpha\tau/2\pi$. We see that the transform is smeared by a sinc of width $1/T$. Hence, the frequency resolution of this approach is $1/T$. Recall that the range of τ for a given architecture is $\rho_\tau \tau_B$. Thus, the range of frequencies covered in the transform is

$$\Delta_f = \frac{\alpha}{2\pi} \rho_\tau \tau_B \tag{9.190}$$

Combining range and resolution, we see that $\rho_\tau \tau_B T \alpha/2\pi$ frequencies may be resolved. It would appear that the number of resolution ele-.

ments may be made arbitrarily large by increasing α. In fact, α is constrained in the following way: Recall that the correlator can accommodate a bandwidth of $2B = \rho_B B_B$ Hz. This must include both the excursion of the chirp and the bandwidth of the signal, since their product is one of the inputs. The chirp requires a bandwidth of $T_c \alpha / 2\pi$. If we choose the signal bandwidth to be equal to Δf, then

$$B_B \geqslant \Delta f \left(1 + \frac{T}{2\rho_\tau \tau_B} \right) \tag{9.191}$$

We find that the number of resolution elements is limited by

$$n \leqslant \rho_B \rho_\tau B_B \tau_B \left(\frac{T}{4\rho_\tau \tau_B} + \frac{1}{2} \right)^{-1} \tag{9.192}$$

Note that

$$n < 2\rho_B \rho_\tau B_B \tau_B \tag{9.193}$$

the information capacity of the correlator employed. Despite this constraint, it is an interesting characteristic of correlator Fourier transform implementations that the frequency range is electrically variable.

From equations (9.188) and (9.189), we see that the phase of the output is not the phase of $S(f)$ but has been modified by a function of f (that is, τ). If correct phase is required, this modification must be considered. Note, however, that Re R and Im R do represent quadrature components of S. Hence, the sum of their squares provides the power spectrum of s without concern for the phase modification.

9.5.2 The Raster Transform

We observed that frequency span is determined by the chirp's angular acceleration. This may suggest a method of generating a Fourier transform with a large number of resolution elements using a two-dimensional correlator. We shall use two chirps: a "slow" chirp $c_1(t)$ with low angular acceleration α and a "fast" chirp $c_2(t)$ of high angular acceleration β. The idea will be to use the fast chirp to produce a discrete coarse frequency axis and the slow chirp to generate a fine frequency axis which fills in the frequencies between adjacent coarse frequencies.

The coarse frequency axis becomes discrete in a natural way: The fast chirp completes many excursions during the period of the slow chirp, which is taken to be the integration period here. We have mentioned that repeating the chirp during the integration period causes the spectrum to become nonuniform. Indeed, many repetitions cause the spectrum to become discretely sampled, as we shall see shortly. Along the coarse frequency axis, then, we view the transform through a comb filter. The slow chirp serves to shift the spectrum of $s(t)$ as one moves along the fine frequency axis, causing the teeth of the comb to fall on frequencies missed by applying the comb directly to $S(f)$.

Let us apply the signals

$$g(t) = s(t)c_1(t)c_2(t) \qquad\qquad (9.194)$$

$$h(t) = c_1(t) \qquad\qquad (9.195)$$

$$q(t) = c_2(t) \qquad\qquad (9.196)$$

to the inputs of a two-dimensional correlator. The slow chirp c_1 has a period equal to the integration time T, which is a multiple of the fast chirp period T_c. For ease of computation, we shall take the integration interval to be $[-(T/2), T/2]$ and the integration period to be $2N + 1$ times the fast chirp period, for some integer N. For t confined to one integration period, we may write

$$c_1(t) = e^{j[(\alpha/2)t^2 + 2\pi f_0 t]} \qquad\qquad (9.197)$$

and

$$c_2(t) = \left[p\left(\frac{t}{T_c}\right) e^{j[(\beta/2)t^2 + 2\pi f_0 t]} \right] * \sum_{n=-N}^{N} \delta(t - nT_c) \qquad\qquad (9.198)$$

where p is the rectangle function defined earlier. Keeping in mind the same considerations as in the one-dimensional case, we write the output as

$$R(\tau_1, \tau_2) \doteq \int_{-T/2}^{T/2} g(t)h^*(t - \tau_1)q^*(t - \tau_2) \, dt$$

$$\doteq e^{j\phi(\tau_1, \tau_2)} \int_{-\infty}^{\infty} s(t)p\left(\frac{t}{T}\right)$$

$$\times \left\{ \left[e^{j\beta t \tau_2} p\left(\frac{t}{T_c}\right) \right] * \sum_{n=-N}^{N} \delta(t - nT_c) \right\} e^{j\alpha t \tau_1} \, dt$$

$$(9.199)$$

where

$$\phi(\tau_1, \tau_2) = -\left[\frac{\alpha}{2}\tau_1^2 + \frac{\beta}{2}\tau_2^2 - 2\pi f_0(\tau_1 + \tau_2)\right] \qquad (9.200)$$

The above integral is a Fourier transform with frequency argument

$$f_f = -\frac{\alpha\tau_1}{2\pi} \qquad (9.201)$$

Hence we may write

$$R(\tau_1, \tau_2)e^{-j\phi(\tau_1, \tau_2)} = \mathcal{F}\left\{s(t)p\left(\frac{t}{T}\right)\left\{\left[e^{-j\beta\tau_2 t}p\left(\frac{t}{T_c}\right)\right]\right.\right.$$

$$\left.\left. * \sum_{n=-N}^{N} \delta(t - nT_c)\right\}\right\}$$

$$= S(f_f) * \mathcal{F}\left\{p\left(\frac{t}{T}\right)\right\}$$

$$* \mathcal{F}\left\{\left[e^{-j\beta\tau_2 t}p\left(\frac{t}{T_c}\right)\right] * \sum_{n=-N}^{N} \delta(t - nT_c)\right\}$$

$$(9.202)$$

where the Fourier transforms are evaluated at f_f. But

$$\mathcal{F}\left\{p\left(\frac{t}{T}\right)\right\} = T \operatorname{sinc}(\pi f_f T) \qquad (9.203)$$

and

$$\mathcal{F}\left\{\left[e^{-j\beta\tau_2 t}p\left(\frac{t}{T_c}\right)\right] * \sum_{n=-N}^{N} \delta(t - nT_c)\right\}$$

$$= \mathcal{F}\left\{e^{-j\beta\tau_2 t}p\left(\frac{t}{T_c}\right)\right\}\mathcal{F}\left\{p\left(\frac{t}{T}\right)\sum_{n=-\infty}^{\infty} \delta(t - nT_c)\right\}$$

$$= T_c \operatorname{sinc}\left[\pi T_c\left(f_f - \frac{\beta\tau_2}{2\pi}\right)\right]$$

$$\times \left[T \operatorname{sinc}(\pi T f_f) * \frac{1}{T_c}\sum_{n=-\infty}^{\infty} \delta\left(f_f - \frac{n}{T_c}\right)\right] \qquad (9.204)$$

By substituting (9.203) and (9.204) into (9.202), we get

$$R(\tau_1, \tau_2)e^{-j\phi(\tau_1, \tau_2)} = T^2 S(f_f) * \mathrm{sinc}(\pi f_f T) * \left\{ \mathrm{sinc}[\pi T_c(f_f - f_c)] \right.$$

$$\left. \times \left[\mathrm{sinc}(\pi T f_f) * \sum_{n=-\infty}^{\infty} \delta\left(f_f - \frac{n}{T_c}\right) \right] \right\} \qquad (9.205)$$

where we have defined

$$f_c = \frac{\beta \tau_2}{2\pi} \qquad (9.206)$$

This formidable expression is easily understood in the following way. We have a convolution of three terms: the desired Fourier transform $S(f_f)$, a sinc function, and a term enclosed in braces which we shall call $K(f_f, f_c)$. The sinc function limits frequency resolution of $S(f_f)$ to $1/T$ and arises from having a finite observation time T. It would seem that these first two terms would be sufficient for the desired output and that K could only corrupt the result. This is not the case. Recall, by the definition of f_f, that our observation of the f_f axis is constrained to an interval $\alpha \rho_\tau \tau_B / 2\pi$ long, where $\rho_\tau \tau_B$ is the time delay available in the fine frequency dimension. Since α is chosen to be small, this provides a very limited view of $S(f_f)$. We would like some way of stepping this small interval across the whole of $S(f_f)$. In other words, in addition to the *fine frequency* f_f, we want a *coarse frequency* (f_c) axis which corresponds to placement of this interval. The function K provides this stepping.

Let us examine K. The expression

$$\mathrm{sinc}(\pi T f_f) * \sum_{n=-\infty}^{\infty} \delta\left(f_f - \frac{n}{T_c}\right)$$

is a comb of sincs separated by $1/T_c$, each having a width of $1/T$. The function

$$\mathrm{sinc}[\pi T_c(f_f - f_c)]$$

of width $1/T_c$ multiplies the comb and serves to select teeth of the comb. Since $T \gg T_c$, $\mathrm{sinc}(\pi T f_f)$ varies much more rapidly than $\mathrm{sinc}[\pi T_c(f_f - f_c)]$. If we restrict f_c to multiples of $1/T_c$, we find that one tooth is selected and that K may be approximated by

$$K(f_f, f_c) \doteq \mathrm{sinc}[\pi T(f_f - f_c)] \qquad (9.207)$$

The convolution of two sincs is a sinc with the wider of the two widths. Hence, we have

$$R'(f_1, f_2) = R\left(-\frac{2\pi f_f}{\alpha}, \frac{2\pi f_c}{\beta}\right)$$

$$= Te^{j\theta(f_1, f_2)} \left\{ S(f_f) * \mathrm{sinc}[\pi T(f_f - f_c)] \right\} \qquad (9.208)$$

for f_c a multiple of $1/T_c$, where

$$\theta(f_f, f_c) = -4\pi^2\left(\frac{f_f^2}{2\alpha} + \frac{f_c^2}{2\beta} + \frac{f_0 f_f}{\alpha} - \frac{f_0 f_c}{\beta}\right) \qquad (9.209)$$

We see that K serves as promised. For $f_c = k/T_c$, the observation window of frequencies is moved by k/T_c. To avoid redundancy in the output while not missing any frequencies, it is clear that the range of the fine frequency axis should be equal to $1/T_c$; that is, we should choose

$$\alpha = \frac{2\pi}{\rho_\tau \tau_B T_c} \qquad (9.210)$$

As observed earlier, the fine frequency resolution is $1/T$. Hence, the number of fine frequency elements is

$$n_f = \frac{T}{T_c} \qquad (9.211)$$

Steps in coarse frequency correspond to a change in frequency of $1/T_c$. With a time delay range of $\rho_\tau \tau_B$ available, the range of f_c is

$$\Delta_f = \frac{\beta \rho_\tau \tau_B}{2\pi} \qquad (9.212)$$

Thus, there are

$$n_c = \frac{\beta T_c \rho_\tau \tau_B}{2\pi} = T_c \Delta_f \qquad (9.213)$$

coarse frequency intervals and a total of

$$n = n_f n_c = T \Delta_f \qquad (9.214)$$

resolvable frequencies.

Physical limitations of the transducers restrict the choice of system parameters. The major concerns are the Bragg cell time-bandwidth product and detector resolution and integration time. In fact, detector technology generally determines T and offers few choices for the maximum values of n_f and n_c. Also, n_f and n_c are limited by the Bragg cell time-bandwidth product in the following way. The slow and fast chirps occupy bandwidths of $\alpha T/2\pi = n_f/\rho_\tau \tau_B$ and $\beta T_c/2\pi = n_c/\rho_\tau \tau_B$, respectively. Therefore, the Bragg cells which have only chirps as inputs require time-bandwidth products of

$$\tau_B B_B \geq \frac{n_f}{2\rho_\tau \rho_B} \qquad (9.215)$$

and

$$\tau_B B_B \geqslant \frac{n_c}{2\rho_\tau \rho_B} \qquad (9.216)$$

A more severe requirement is placed on the input transducer which carries the product of the chirps and the signal and must accommodate the sum of the respective bandwidths.

The Fourier transform implementations which have been presented use a complex chirp, which may be used only with an interferometric correlator. Noninterferometric correlators require real inputs. Hence, we shall employ *cosine chirps* of the form

$$c_R(t) = \cos\left(\frac{\alpha}{2} t^2 + 2\pi f_0 t\right) \qquad (9.217)$$

and *sine chirps* of the form

$$c_I(t) = \sin\left(\frac{\alpha}{2} t^2 + 2\pi f_0 t\right) \qquad (9.218)$$

These are the real and imaginary portions of the complex chirp.
Suppose that we choose

$$g(t) = s(t) c_R(t) \qquad (9.219)$$

and

$$h(t) = c_R(t) \qquad (9.220)$$

as inputs to a one-dimensional correlator. The resulting correlation is

$$R_{gh}(\tau) = \int_T s(t) c_R(t) c_R(t - \tau)\, dt$$

$$= \frac{1}{2} \int_T s(t) \cos\left[\frac{\alpha}{2} \tau^2 - 2\pi f_0 \tau - \alpha t \tau\right] dt$$

$$+ \frac{1}{2} \int_T s(t) \cos\left[\frac{\alpha}{2} (2t^2 - 2t\tau + \tau^2) + 2\pi f_0 (2t - \tau)\right] dt$$

$$\qquad (9.221)$$

Recall that the signal is constrained to the band $[-B, B]$. Hence, the second integral vanishes if we choose $f_0 > B$. This being done, we get

$$R_{gh}(\tau) = \frac{1}{2} \int_T s(t) \cos[\phi(\tau) - \alpha t \tau]\, dt \qquad (9.222)$$

where

$$\phi(\tau) = \frac{\alpha}{2}\tau^2 - 2\pi f_0 \tau \tag{9.223}$$

Similarly, if we choose

$$g(t) = s(t)c_R(t) \tag{9.224}$$

and

$$h(t) = c_I(t) \tag{9.225}$$

then

$$R_{gh}(\tau) = \frac{1}{2}\int_T s(t) \sin[\phi(\tau) - \alpha t\tau] \, dt \tag{9.226}$$

provided that $f_0 > B$. We recognize equations (9.222) and (9.226) as the cosine and sine transforms of $s(t)$ with a phase error of $\phi(\tau)$. Note that the phase error is the same for both, so that they remain in quadrature.

Since the sine and cosine transforms require different correlator inputs, generation of the complete transform either entails the use of two correlators or some sort of multiplexing.

9.6 SUMMARY

We shall finish by summarizing the characteristics of the various correlator architectures. In particular, we shall tabulate values for the figures of merit we have defined. The figures of merit represent an architecture's use of available resources: ρ_B and ρ_τ refer to the use of a Bragg cell's capabilities and ρ_D and ρ_S to those of a detector array. For an architecture which uses Bragg cells of bandwidth B_B and can accommodate input frequencies in the interval $[-B, B]$,

$$\rho_B = \frac{B}{B_B} \tag{9.40}$$

is a measure of how well the bandwidth is used. Similarly, we define

$$\rho_\tau = \frac{\Delta_\tau}{\tau_B} \tag{9.53}$$

where τ_B is the Bragg cell time aperture and Δ_τ is the range of time delays generated in the correlator. Recall that a correlator which requires N_D detector pixels to resolve n outputs has

Table 9.2 Figures of Merit for Double-Sideband Architectures [a]

	Non-interferometric, diode	Non-interferometric, Bragg cell	Interferometric, diode	Interferometric, Bragg cell, no filtering	Interferometric, Bragg cell, passive reference	Interferometric, Bragg cell, active reference
ρ_B	$\frac{1}{2}$	$\frac{1}{2}$	$< \frac{1}{4}$	$< \frac{1}{4}$	$< \frac{1}{4}$	$< \frac{1}{4}$
ρ_τ	1	2	1	2	2	2
ρ_D	1	1	$< \frac{1}{4}$	$< \frac{1}{4}$	$< \frac{1}{4}$	$< \frac{1}{4}$
ρ_S	$\ll 1$	$\ll 1$	$< \frac{1}{3}$ [1]	$\frac{1}{3}$ [2]	$\frac{1}{2}$ [2]	$\frac{1}{2}$ [3]

[a]*Notes:*   1. a/σ_x as small as possible, $b/\sigma_y = 1$.
              2. $a/\sigma_x = b/\sigma_y = 1$.
              3. $a/\sigma_x = b/\sigma_y$.

Table 9.3 Output Terms for Various Architectures. Coefficients Normalized to Correlation Term

	Noninterferometric, diode	Noninterferometric, Bragg cell	Interferometric, diode	Interferometric, Bragg cell, no filtering	Interferometric, Bragg cell, passive reference	Interferometric, Bragg cell, active reference
1	Tab	Tab	Tab	$\dfrac{T}{2}\,ab$	$\dfrac{T}{2}\,ab$	
$\int g(t)\,dt$	b	b				
$\int h(t-\tau)\,dt$	a	a				
$\int |g(t)|^2\,dt$			$\dfrac{a}{b}$	$\dfrac{b}{2a}$		$\dfrac{a}{2b}$
$\int |h(t-\tau)|^2\,dt$				$\dfrac{a}{2b}$		$\dfrac{b}{2a}$
$\int |g(t)|^2|h(t-\tau)|^2\,dt$				$\dfrac{1}{2ab}$	$\dfrac{1}{2ab}$	
$\mathrm{Re}[e^{j\pi f\tau}R_{gh}(\tau)]$			1	1	1	1
$R_{gh}(\tau)$	1	1				

$$\rho_D = \frac{n}{N_D} \qquad (9.56)$$

Finally, as a measure of an architecture's use of detector dynamic range, we define

$$\rho_s = \frac{T \sigma_x \sigma_y}{E\{C\}} \qquad (9.173)$$

where T is the integration time, σ_x and σ_y are the optimal rms inputs, and $E\{C\}$ is the normalized expectation of the output at the point where a full correlation of inputs is achieved. In each case, a larger figure of merit is an asset. Table 9.2 summarizes the achievable values of ρ_B, ρ_τ, ρ_D, and ρ_s for the double-sideband architectures.

For postprocessing considerations we are interested in output terms which accompany the desired correlation. Table 9.3 is a summary of the coefficients of each term, normalized to the correlation term. A blank entry indicates that the term does not occur.

Finally, we shall point out some features and drawbacks of various architectures. Noninterferometric correlators, while restricted to processing real signals directly, are the simplest and make the best use of detector pixels. Linearity generally requires that $\rho_s \ll 1$ so that the noninterferometric architectures cannot achieve output SNRs as high as interferometric implementations. Also, the Bragg cells must be operated about the 50% diffraction point, which cannot be reached at high bandwidths.

Architectures which make use of modulated LED sources are hampered by the difficulty of simultaneously achieving both high power and fast response. Since Bragg cell diffraction efficiency drops markedly at high frequencies, the use of a modulated LED here requires both large bandwidth and high power. Hence, LED processors may be unable to reach bandwidths achievable by implementations which use Bragg cells only. On the other hand, light-emitting diodes are inexpensive and compact.

Bragg cell architectures which use transform-plane filtering have fewer undesired terms in the output, simplifying postprocessing. This comes at the expense of restrictions on the source characteristics. In particular, the active reference architecture has no signal-dependent bias and achieves the minimum background level, allowing most efficient use of the detector dynamic range.

As a final note, we should observe that various preprocessing operations may be performed. The most powerful of these is time compression. By storing T sec of data of bandwidth B in a memory and then reading the data at N times the input rate, T/N sec of data is produced having bandwidth NB. In this way, the optical processor may be made to have widely different effective characteristics.

ACKNOWLEDGMENTS

The author wishes to thank Douglas Brown and Arthur Valliere III
for their patient editing and helpful suggestions. He is deeply in-
debted to Joanne Lantz for her careful preparation of the manu-
script.

APPENDIX

Many approximations which we have made relied upon the magnitude
of physical device characteristics. To justify these approximations
and to offer a feeling for physical constraints, this appendix has
been included for convenience. Table 9.A lists the approximate limits
of practical devices currently available.

Table 9.A Approximate Characteristic Limits for Practical Commercially
Available Devices

Device/parameter	Minimum	Maximum	Units
Bragg cells			
Bandwidth	10	10^3	MHz
Time aperture		50	μs
Time-bandwidth product		2×10^3	
Light-emitting diodes			
Bandwidth		30	MHz
1-D detector arrays			
Number of pixels		2×10^3	
Pixel saturation level		10^7	Electrons
Integration time	2		μs
2-D detector arrays			
Number of pixels		2×10^5	
Pixel saturation level		10^6	Electrons
Integration time	10^{-2}		s

REFERENCES

1. Whitehouse, Speiser, and Means, High speed serial access linear transform implementations, *NUC Internal Report TN1026*, Jan. 1973; reprinted in *ARPA Quarterly Technical Report QR1*, Image transmission via spread spectrum techniques.
2. Merrill I. Skolnik, ed., *Radar Handbook*, McGraw-Hill, New York, 1970.
3. P. M. Woodward, *Probability and Information Theory, with Applications to Radar*, McGraw-Hill, New York, 1953.
4. C. E. Thomas, Optical spectrum analysis of large space bandwidth signals, *Appl. Opt.* 5:1782-2790, 1966.
5. D. J. Channin, Emitters for fiberoptic communications, *Laser Focus*, Nov. 1982, p. 105.
6. Naoya Uchida and Nobukazu Niizeki, Acousto-optic deflection materials and techniques, *Proc. IEEE 61*(8):1073-1092, Aug. 1973.
7. David F. Barbe, Imaging devices using the charge coupled concept, *Proc. IEEE 63*:38-67, Jan. 1975.
8. Terry M. Turpin, Time integrating optical processing, in *Proc. SPIE Symp. on Real Time Signal Processing*, San Diego, CA, Vol. 154, Aug. 1978, pp. 196-203.
9. Peter Kellman, Time Integrating Optical Signal Processing, Dissertation, Stanford University, Stanford Calif., June 1979.
10. Athanasios Papoulis, *Probability, Random Variables, and Stochastic Processes*, McGraw-Hill, New York, 1965, p. 145.

10

Coherent Time-Integration Processors

IRWIN J. ABRAMOVITZ[*], NORMAN J. BERG, and MICHAEL W.
CASSEDAY / Department of the Army, Harry Diamond Laboratories,
Adelphi, Maryland

10.1 INTRODUCTION

The use of time-integrating processors has become increasingly popular
as a means of handling large-bandwidth signals which may be of long
duration. These signals, obtained from advanced modulation techniques such as spread spectrum, require a very large processing gain
(time-bandwidth product) not achievable with space-integrating architectures. Space-integrating processors perform integration over the
aperture of the acoustic delay line and are thus limited by practical
crystal lengths and optical component size. Furthermore, space-integrating correlators are basically convolvers with a time-inverted reference. This may not be feasible for long-duration signals or when
the reference is not known a priori. Since time and space in an acoustic delay line are related by the acoustic velocity, time integration
may perform similar processing functions to space integration; thus,
time integration is the natural alternative when space integration is
inappropriate.

Time-integrating acousto-optic processing takes advantage of photodiode array technology to provide efficient sensors. The application of
photodiode arrays to image processing and spectroscopy has resulted
in the development of arrays with large dynamic range. This dynamic
range exceeds that available with SAW (surface-acoustic-wave) acoustoelectric time-integrating correlators. Acousto-optic architectures permit two-dimensional processing using two one-dimensional devices, i.e.,
without the use of two-dimensional electro-optic modulators. Finally,
it provides large processing gains, performs analog signal processing
at bandwidths unobtainable with digital signal processing, and produces outputs at data rates readily manageable by digital processors.

---

[*]Current affiliation: Westinghouse Electric Corporation, Advanced
Technology Division, Baltimore, Maryland

For example, two 60-MHz-bandwidth signals may be correlated over an integration interval of 30 msec, producing a time-bandwidth product of 1.8×10^6. The result from a 1024-diode array may be output in 3 msec. This data rate of 3.4×10^5 samples/sec is well within the capability of current A/D converter and microprocessor technology. Processing gain and dynamic range may be extended by postdetection digital integration.

The limitation of time-integration processing with respect to space-integration processing when used for quasi-matched filtering is the restricted range of delay over which the correlation may be observed. In the space-integrating processor, delay may be observed over a range greater than the acoustic aperture; however, processing gain is based only on the bandwidth and acoustic aperture. In the time-integrating processor, only delay times less than or equal to the delay of the acoustic delay line may be observed. In some architectures, time compression can effectively double this range.

The simplest implementations are incoherent, not requiring a coherent light source (although one may be used) and producing intensity modulation of the light about a bias level. The detector array thus responds to light intensity variations without the need for heterodyne detection. Coherent implementations require coherent sources, amplitude modulation of the light by the acousto-optic interaction, and heterodyne detection at the detector array. The incoherent implementation by Sprague and Koliopoulos [1], shown in Fig. 10.1, adds signal $S_1(t)$ to a bias V_1 and intensity-modulates a light source with this sum. Signal $S_2(t)$ is added to bias V_2; the sum modulates an RF carrier which in turn drives an acoustic delay line illuminated by the modulated light source resulting in a second intensity modulation. The light diffracted by the acoustic wave is imaged onto a detector array producing an output voltage V which is proportional to the light intensity integrated over time:

$$V \propto V_1 V_2 T + \int_T S_1(t) S_2 \left(t + \frac{z}{v} \right) dt \qquad (10.1)$$

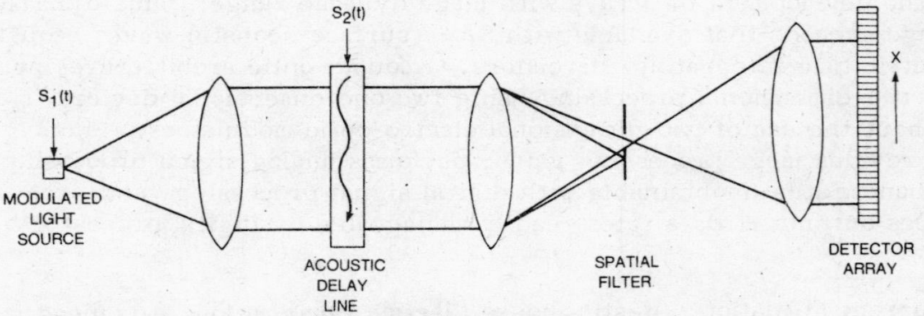

Figure 10.1 Incoherent time-integrating correlator.

where z is the distance along the delay line and v is the acoustic velocity. This output voltage is seen to be the correlation integral on a bias. Cross terms $V_1 S_1(t)$, $V_1 S_2(t)$, $V_2 S_1(t)$, and $V_2 S_2(t)$ integrate to zero.

Achievable processing gain is limited by the correlator dynamic range consisting of the detector dynamic range, which is based on the ratio of saturation to rms noise, and the signal-to-bias ratio, which is determined by the light intensity modulation depth. Modulation depth in the signal driving the acoustic delay line is generally kept small to achieve linear intensity modulation. Due to the small modulation depth, dynamic range may be limited.

Another incoherent implementation, described by Kellman [2], addresses the problem of limited dynamic range due to small modulation depth. The acoustic delay line input RF carrier frequency is offset by a reference oscillator. This reference oscillator is also used as a carrier for the light source modulation. The acoustic delay line is then used to amplitude-modulate the light. This is an incoherent, interferometric architecture with an electronic reference. In this way undesirable nonlinear terms arising from greater modulation depth are offset in frequency and may be removed. The correlation itself, however, is now multiplied by a spatial carrier. The detector array element density must therefore be increased to a density adequate for the bandwidth of the signal plus reference oscillator frequency. Incoherent processors are discussed in more detail in Chap. 9.

The remainder of this chapter will deal with coherent time-integrating structures. Section 10.2 discusses basic coherent architectures. These include multiplicative and additive schemes. A more sophisticated additive architecture, which uses a balanced two-beam approach, is presented in Sec. 10.3. Section 10.4 discusses system applications of the one-dimensional correlators. Two-dimensional coherent time-integrating correlator architectures and system applications are presented in Sec. 10.5 and 10.6.

10.2 BASIC COHERENT PROCESSOR ARCHITECTURES

Coherent time-integrating processors operate in a region of the acousto-optic interaction where the incoming light beam is amplitude-modulated by the acoustic wave as opposed to intensity- (power-) modulated. The modulation is linear for low diffraction efficiencies but is, however, adequate for even complex architectures. Since no bias is used, a larger linear region is available, resulting in larger dynamic range. Coherent processors take advantage of the frequency- and phase-shifting properties of the acousto-optic effect and thus require a reference beam for detection.

Since current modulating a laser diode results in intensity modulation, two acoustic delay lines, Bragg cells, are generally used to

provide amplitude modulation of the light. Two basic correlator architectures are possible, multiplicative [3] and additive [4]. In the multiplicative architecture a single light beam is subjected to two successive Bragg diffractions, first upshifting and then downshifting the light
frequency. A portion of the original light beam may then be used as
a reference beam for heterodyne detection on a detector array. In the
additive architecture, the light beam is split into two paths; each path
is modulated by a Bragg cell. Both light beams are either upshifted
or downshifted and then combined on a single detector array. In this
manner, one of the modulated beams serves as a reference.

The multiplicative architecture is shown in Fig. 10.2(a). Coher-
ent light of amplitude $L_0(t) = A_0 \cos \omega_\ell t$ illuminates the first Bragg

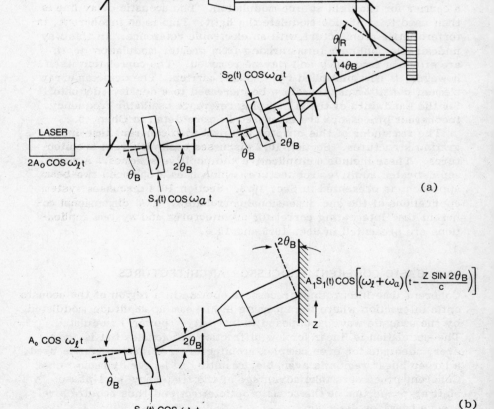

Figure 10.2 (a) Coherent multiplicative time-integrating correlator
and (b) detailed acousto-optic diffraction.

cell at the Bragg angle θ_B with respect to the perpendicular to the cell. This is accomplished by tilting the cell as shown in Fig. 10.2 to maximize the upshifted diffracted beam. Here, $\theta_B = \sin^{-1}(\lambda/2\Lambda)$, where λ = light wavelength and Λ = acoustic wavelength for frequency ω_a. The light is point-modulated by $S_1(t) \cos \omega_a t$, where ω_a is the acoustic wave center frequency, and the diffracted beam is spatially filtered from the zero-order beam. The amplitude of this first-order diffracted beam $L_1(t)$ is given by

$$L_1(t) = A_1 S_1(t) \cos(\omega_\ell + \omega_a)t \qquad (10.2)$$

where A_1 is a proportionality constant which includes the input light amplitude and the diffraction efficiency.

Since this diffracted light exists at an angle twice the Bragg angle with respect to the incoming light beam, upon beam expansion its amplitude along the z axis is given by

$$L_1(t) = A_1 S_1(t) \cos\left[(\omega_\ell + \omega_a)\left(t - \frac{z \sin 2\theta_B}{c}\right)\right] \qquad (10.3)$$

where ω_ℓ is the light source frequency and c is the velocity of light, as shown in Fig. 10.2(b). The expanded light beam now illuminates the second Bragg cell at the Bragg angle. Since, for the configuration shown, the acoustic wave in the second cell is traveling in the opposite direction from that of the first cell, the downshifted first-order diffraction is maximized. The expanded light beam is spatially modulated by $S_2(t + z/v) \cos \omega_a(t + z/v)$, resulting in a first-order diffracted beam which must be spatially filtered from the *straight-through* (zero-order) beam. This beam, $L_2(t)$, is described by

$$L_2(t) = A_1 A_2 S_1(t) S_2\left(t + \frac{z}{v}\right)\cos\left[(\omega_\ell + \omega_a)\left(t - \frac{z \sin 2\theta_B}{c}\right)\right.$$
$$\left. - \omega_a\left(t + \frac{z}{v}\right)\right] \qquad (10.4)$$

where A_2 is a proportionality constant which includes the diffraction efficiency for this interaction. Since, for frequencies of interest, θ_B is generally a few degrees at most, $\sin 2\theta_B \approx \omega_a c/\omega_\ell v$ and $\omega_a/\omega_\ell \ll 1$, this expression for $L_2(t)$ becomes

$$L_2(t) \approx A_1 A_2 S_1(t) S_2\left(t + \frac{z}{v}\right) \cos\left(\omega_\ell t - \frac{2\omega_a z}{v}\right) \qquad (10.5)$$

The effect of the device being tilted from the z axis by the small angle shown in Fig. 10.2(a) is on the order of ω_a/ω_ℓ and has been neglected. Both the doubly diffracted light beam $L_2(t)$ and reference beam $L_R(t)$ illuminate the detector array. The output voltage of the detector array V is proportional to the intensity (square of the amplitude) of the incident light integrated over a time interval T. Thus,

$$V \propto \int_T \left| L_2(t) + L_R(t) \right|^2 dt \tag{10.6}$$

$$V \propto \int_T \left[L_2^2(t) + L_R^2(t) + 2L_2(t)L_R(t) \right] dt \tag{10.7}$$

This expression may be divided into two terms, a bias term V_B and a cross-product term V_S, where

$$V_B = \int_T L_2^2(t) + L_R^2(t) = \int_T \left[A_1 A_2 S_1(t) S_2\left(t + \frac{z}{v}\right) \cos\left(\omega_\ell t - \frac{2\omega_a z}{v}\right) \right]^2$$

$$+ \left[A_0' \cos \omega_\ell\left(t - \frac{z \sin \theta_R}{c}\right) \right]^2 dt \tag{10.8}$$

and

$$V_S = \int_T 2L_2(t)L_R(t)\, dt = \int_T 2A_0' A_1 A_2 S_1(t) S_2\left(t + \frac{z}{v}\right)$$

$$\cos\left(\omega_\ell t - \frac{2\omega_a z}{v}\right)$$

$$\times \cos\left(\omega_\ell t - \frac{\omega_\ell z \sin \theta_R}{c}\right) dt \tag{10.9}$$

Here θ_R is the incident angle of the reference beam.

The bias term integrates to a fixed bias value for times T large with respect to the minimum frequency of $S_1(t)$ and $S_2(t)$. V_S may be trigonometrically manipulated into frequency sum and difference terms:

$$V_S = \int_T \left[A_0' A_1 A_2 S_1(t) S_2\left(t + \frac{z}{v}\right) \cos\left(2\omega_\ell t - \frac{2\omega_a z}{v} - \frac{\omega_\ell z \sin \theta_R}{c}\right) \right.$$

$$\left. + A_0' A_1 A_2 S_1(t) S_2\left(t + \frac{z}{v}\right) \cos\left(\frac{\omega_\ell z \sin \theta_R}{c} - \frac{2\omega_a z}{v}\right) \right] dt$$

$$\tag{10.10}$$

The frequency sum term integrates to zero, leaving

$$V_S \propto V_C = \cos\left(\frac{\omega_\ell z \sin \theta_R}{c} - \frac{2\omega_a z}{v}\right) \int_T S_1(t) S_2\left(t + \frac{z}{v}\right) dt \tag{10.11}$$

Thus, V_C is the correlation of $S_1(t)$ and $S_2(t)$ on a spatial carrier, which may be varied by adjustment of the incident angle of the reference beam.

Since linear amplitude interaction occurs only for low diffraction efficiencies, the multiplicative or doubly diffracted architecture may result in very low light levels. For this reason, the additive architecture is often used. The additive architecture combines two singly diffracted beams on the detector array as opposed to a doubly diffracted beam and a reference. As depicted in Fig. 10.3, the coherent light beam is split into two parallel paths. In the first path, the light is point-modulated by $S_1(t) \cos \omega_a t$. The Bragg cell is tilted so that the angle of the incoming light with respect to the perpendicular to the cell is chosen to be the Bragg angle θ_B as shown so that the diffracted light is upshifted in frequency, with amplitude given by

$$L_1(t) = A_1 S_1(t) \cos(\omega_\ell + \omega_a)t \tag{10.12}$$

The diffracted light is then expanded. Since it exits the Bragg cell at twice the Bragg angle with respect to the incoming light beam, the expanded beam may be described by

$$L_1(t) = A_1 S_1(t) \cos\left[(\omega_\ell + \omega_a)\left(t - \frac{z \sin 2\theta_B}{c}\right)\right] \tag{10.13}$$

Since $\sin 2\theta_B \simeq \omega_a c/\omega_\ell v$ and $\omega_a/\omega_\ell \ll 1$, this expression becomes

$$L_1(t) \simeq A_1 S_1(t) \cos\left[(\omega_\ell + \omega_a)t - \frac{\omega_a z}{v}\right] \tag{10.14}$$

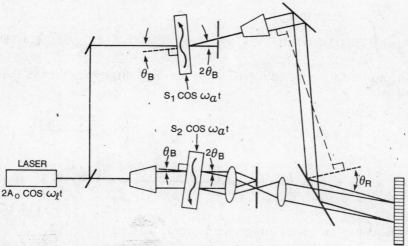

Figure 10.3 Coherent additive time-integrating correlator.

The light of the second path is expanded and illuminates another Bragg cell at the opposite Bragg angle. Since the acoustic wave is traveling in the opposite direction in this cell, the diffracted light is also up-shifted in frequency as a result of the spatial modulation. The light amplitude along this path is given by

$$L_2(t) = A_2 S_2\left(t + \frac{z}{v}\right) \cos\left[\omega_\ell t + \omega_a\left(t + \frac{z}{v}\right)\right] \tag{10.15}$$

which is

$$L_2(t) = A_2 S_2\left(t + \frac{z}{v}\right) \cos\left[(\omega_\ell + \omega_a)t + \omega_a \frac{z}{v}\right] \tag{10.16}$$

The effect of the device being tilted by the small angle shown in Fig. 10.3 is on the order of ω_a/ω_ℓ and has been neglected. The first light beam is changed in direction by an angle of θ_R so that both $L_1(t)$ and $L_2(t)$ illuminate the detector array. In this way, $L_1(t)$ becomes

$$L_1(t) \approx A_1 S_1(t) \cos\left[(\omega_\ell + \omega_a)\left(t + \frac{z \sin \theta_R}{c}\right) - \frac{\omega_a z}{v}\right] \tag{10.17}$$

and the output voltage of the detector array V is proportional to $[L_1(t) + L_2(t)]^2$ integrated over time interval T. In a manner similar to the multiplicative case, the output voltage may be divided into a bias term V_B and cross-product term V_S where

$$V_B = \int_T [L_1^2(t) + L_2^2(t)]\, dt \tag{10.18}$$

and

$$V_S = \int_T 2L_1(t) L_2(t)\, dt \tag{10.19}$$

Again, manipulating V_S into frequency sum and difference terms, the result is

$$V_S = \int_T \left\{ A_1 A_2 S_1(t) S_2\left(t + \frac{z}{v}\right) \cos\left[(\omega_\ell + \omega_a)\left(2t + \frac{z \sin \theta_R}{c}\right)\right] \right.$$
$$\left. + A_1 A_2 S_1(t) S_2\left(t + \frac{z}{v}\right) \cos\left[\frac{(\omega_\ell + \omega_a) z \sin \theta_R}{c} - \frac{2\omega_a z}{v}\right]\right\} dt \tag{10.20}$$

The frequency sum term integrates to zero, leaving

$$V_S \propto V_C = \cos\left[\frac{(\omega_\ell + \omega_a) z \sin \theta_R}{c} - \frac{2\omega_a z}{v}\right]\int_T S_1(t)S_2\left(t + \frac{z}{v}\right) dt$$

$$(10.21)$$

The output of the detector array is thus seen to be the correlation of $S_1(t)$ and $S_2(t)$ on a spatial carrier plus a fixed bias. The spatial carrier frequency depends on the angular change applied to the first light beam and the frequency of the acoustic wave.

10.3 TWO-BEAM SURFACE-ACOUSTIC-WAVE (SAW) TIME-INTEGRATING CORRELATOR

The coherent multiplicative and additive architectures described in the previous section may be implemented in either bulk acoustic wave or SAW delay lines. The use of SAW delay lines, particularly those fabricated from y-cut z-propagating lithium niobate ($LiNbO_3$), permits the development of unique architectures for time-integration correlation. Particularly in the case of the additive architecture, the use of y-z $LiNbO_3$ SAWs allows for much simpler and more compact optical systems. The need for acoustic absorber on the opposite end of a bulk-wave device from the transducer end precludes the generation of counterpropagating acoustic waves in a single bulk-wave device, and generally two separate bulk-wave devices are required, either as illustrated in Fig. 10.3 or with the diffracted output of the first cell imaged into the second cell [5]. However, in the case of SAWs, transducers may be deposited on the surface near opposite ends of the delay line with acoustic absorber placed between the transducer and the end of the crystal. Furthermore, due to the anisotropic nature of SAW propagation in y-z lithium niobate, a transducer may be tilted up to several degrees from the z axis, resulting in tilted wave fronts propagating along the z axis with negligible deviation from that axis [6,7]. The surface acoustic wave does not "walk off" the crystal. In this way, incoming light beam angles and device angles may be adjusted to allow novel architectures with interactions maximized by tilting transducers to maintain the appropriate Bragg angles. Additionally, the tilted transducer structure results in the almost complete reduction of reflections from the opposing transducer used in generating counterpropagating SAWs. (Another advantage of this anisotropy is that it allows a very long acousto-optic interaction region, because diffraction effects on the acoustic wave are minimized, and the SAW wave front remains relatively plane-wave for very long propagation distances, $\sim 10^4 \Lambda$ [6,7].) These properties allow coherent one-dimensional correlators to be implemented with only one SAW delay line and two-dimensional correlators with only two delay lines.

An additional advantage resulting from the use of counterpropagating SAWs is that *time compression* results from correlating signals of the

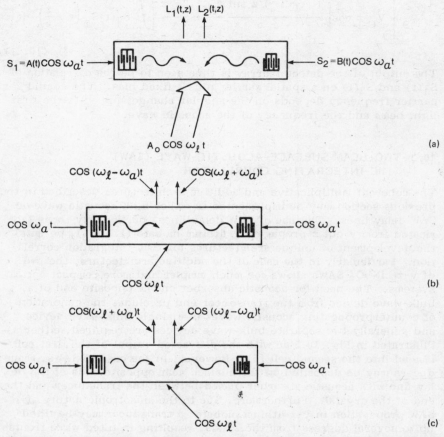

Figure 10.4 (a) Desirable coherent configuration, (b) first-order diffraction from light beam entering from left, and (c) from right.

form $S_1(t - z/v)$ and $S_2(t + z/v)$ as opposed to $S_1(t)$ and $S_2(t + z/v)$. The correlation aperture is effectively doubled, thus doubling the range of the observable correlation delay.

In examining the previous coherent correlator architectures, the difficult task of combining two light beams, either one modulated beam and one reference beam or two modulated beams, is apparent. Since SAW delay lines can accommodate two counterpropagating SAWs, a desirable additive correlator configuration should have two singly diffracted, spatially modulated beams which exit collinearly and at an angle different from the unmodulated or straight-through beam or beams, as shown in Fig. 10.4(a). Since in an interferometric architecture $L_1(t,z)$ and $L_2(t,z)$ must both be at the same light frequency $\omega_\ell - \omega_a$ or $\omega_\ell + \omega_a$, a light beam must enter from the left to interact with S_1, for example, and another light beam must enter from the right to interact with S_2, or vice versa, as shown in Figs. 4(b) and (c). For the remainder of this section only the former case, the left light beam interacting with S_1 and the right light beam interacting with S_2, resulting in diffracted light frequency $\omega_\ell - \omega_a$, will be considered. Since the angle between an incoming light beam and the first-order diffracted beam is $2\theta_B$, the incoming light beams must enter at opposing angles of $2\theta_B$ with respect to the perpendicular to the z axis ($4\theta_B$ between the incoming beams). Here θ_B is the Bragg angle in air at the design center frequency of the correlator (ω_0). To maximize interaction and minimize cross terms resulting from interaction of left-hand light beam with S_2 and right-hand light beam with S_1, the two transducers must each be tilted by opposing angles of $\theta_{Bn} = \sin^{-1}(\lambda/2n\Lambda)$, the Bragg angle in the delay line material at the correlator design center frequency. In this way, due to the strong angular dependence of the Bragg interaction, the right incoming beam interacts primarily with the SAW launched by the right transducer; likewise, the left incoming beam interacts primarily with the SAW generated by the left transducer. Cross terms are down by 40 dB [8].

The delay line must be fabricated from y-cut, z-propagating $LiNbO_3$ or another material at an orientation exhibiting the unique anisotropic nature for SAW propagation to permit tilted transducers to generate tilted wave fronts without substantially affecting the direction of SAW propagation.

The two-beam SAW acousto-optic correlator is depicted in Fig. 10.5. A coherent light beam is split and expanded into two beams. These beams converge on the device and are focused into sheet beams using cylindrical lenses with focus at the center of the device. The focal length of the cylindrical lenses must be compatible with the penetration depth of the SAW and the length of the acoustic aperture (transducer length), i.e., the region in which acousto-optic interaction occurs, for maximum efficiency. Usable focal lengths range from 20 to 100 cm. Compound lenses may be used to decrease this length. The minimum distance from laser to delay line is also dependent on the angle between the incoming beams $4\theta_B$ and the delay aperture (length along the z axis) desired. Since $4\theta_B$ is on the order of a few degrees at most, the converging, incoming beams must originate as separate beams at some significant distance in front of the delay line. This distance can be minimized using a modified Kosters prism [9] in the optical design, as shown in Fig. 10.6 (a view in the horizontal plane). Both beams should lie in the horizontal plane with no vertical deviation. The cylindrical lens used to focus the light into sheet beams may be placed either before or after the beam-splitting Kosters prism. The angle between the beams $4\theta_B$ may be adjusted by rotation of the prism.

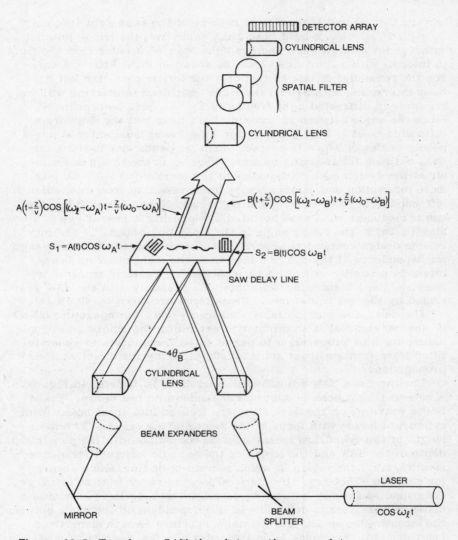

Figure 10.5 Two-beam SAW time-integrating correlator.

For equal sheet beams of uniform intensity the diffracted light may be described by

$$L_1(t,z) = A\left(t - \frac{z}{v}\right) \cos\left[\omega_\ell\left(t - \frac{z \sin 2\theta_B}{c}\right) - \omega_A\left(t - \frac{z}{v}\right)\right] \quad (10.22)$$

and

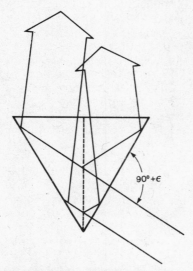

Figure 10.6 Modified Kosters prism.

$$L_2(t,z) = B\left(t + \frac{z}{v}\right)\cos\left[\omega_\ell\left(t + \frac{z\sin 2\theta_B}{c}\right) - \omega_B\left(t + \frac{z}{v}\right)\right] \quad (10.23)$$

Here, ω_ℓ is the light frequency, ω_A and ω_B are input signal carrier frequencies, t is time, z is the distance along the delay line and along the photodiode array (center is $z = 0$), v is the acoustic propagation velocity, and c is the free-space light velocity. The photodiode array output current, proportional to the square of the sum of $L_1(t,z)$ and $L_2(t,z)$, may be manipulated trigonometrically to generate frequency sum and difference terms. Upon time integration, only the difference term remains, yielding an output voltage proportional to

$$V(T,z) = \int_T A\left(t - \frac{z}{v}\right)B\left(t + \frac{z}{v}\right)\cos\left[\frac{2\omega_\ell z\sin 2\theta_B}{c}\right.$$

$$\left. + (\omega_A - \omega_B)t - (\omega_A + \omega_B)\frac{z}{v}\right]dt \quad (10.24)$$

where integration time $T \gg z/v$ and the acoustic signals exist on the SAW delay line during the entire integration period. Since $\sin 2\theta_B \simeq (\omega_0/v)/(\omega_\ell/c)$, for $\omega_A = \omega_B$ this output voltage becomes

$$V(T,z) = \cos\left[\frac{2z}{v}(\omega_0 - \omega_A)\right]\int_T A\left(t - \frac{z}{v}\right)B\left(t + \frac{z}{v}\right)dt \quad (10.25)$$

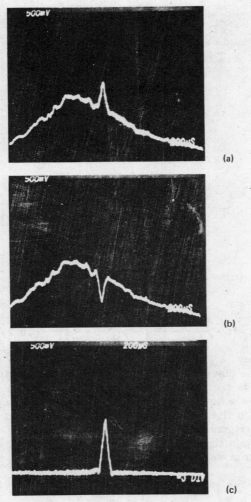

(a)

(b)

(c)

Figure 10.7 Correlator output for PN coded signal at ω_0 with (a) both inputs normal phase, (b) one input phase inverted, and (c) after bias subtraction, (a) − (b). [From M. W. Casseday, N. J. Berg, I. J. Abramovitz, and J. N. Lee, Wideband signal processing using the two-beam surface acoustic wave acoustooptic time integrating correlator, *IEEE Trans. Microwave Theory Tech. MTT-29*(5), May 1981.]

Thus, the output voltage provides the correlation of the input signals (modulation and carrier) about the correlator design center frequency.

When $\omega_A = \omega_0$, the correlator output voltage is

$$V(T,z) = \int_T A\left(t - \frac{z}{v}\right) B\left(t + \frac{z}{v}\right) dt \qquad (10.26)$$

This is the correlation of the modulation in a compressed time frame.
Figure 10.7(a) shows the correlation of a pseudonoise (PN), biphase-
coded (direct sequence spread spectrum) signal at a carrier frequency of ω_0 with a bandwidth of 4 MHz (code rate of two megabits
per second). The bias level, produced by the square terms proportional to the integral of $L_1(t,z)^2 + L_2(t,z)^2$, depicts the gaussian intensity profile of the sheet beams. When the incoming light beams are
made uniform in intensity, the bias level would be uniform with only
diode-to-diode fluctuations. This bias level may be easily removed by
high-pass filtering or by a subtraction of one output from a subsequent
output produced with one input phase inverted.

Figure 10.7(b) shows the correlation of the signals as in. Fig.
10.7(a) but with one input phase inverted. The difference between
the correlation outputs of Figs. 10.7(a) and (b) are shown in Fig.
10.7(c). This phase inversion and subtraction process may be performed automatically with postprocessing electronics, as depicted in
Fig. 10.8. Analog-to-digital conversion and digital memory elements
may be used here since data rates are relatively low, 3.4×10^5
samples/s.

When $\omega_A \neq \omega_0$, which is generally the case, the correlation is multiplied by a spatial frequency, $\cos[(2z/v)(\omega_0 - \omega_A)]$. This spatial
fringe pattern results when the light beams diffracted by the SAWs
are no longer parallel, as is true when $\omega_A = \omega_0$. By examining the
spacing and sense of the fringes, the input frequency relative to ω_0
can be determined. Figure 10.9 shows correlation outputs for one-
megabit-per-second PN, biphase-coded signals at frequencies offset
from ω_0.

The maximum frequency difference that can be determined is limited
by the spacing of the detector diodes in the array (which "samples"
the frings pattern). For z-propagating lithium niobate and a 2.54-cm
aperture, an array with 1024 diodes across the aperture has a fringe
resolution equivalent to ±34-MHz frequency deviation. Wider bandwidths may be obtained by using an array with more diodes per centimeter or by expanding the beam and examining only a portion at a
time.

The time difference of arrival (TDOA) or time delay between two
signals may be observed by a shift in correlation location. Examining
the correlator output for inputs $A(t) \cos \omega_A t$ and $A(t + t_0) \cos \omega_A(t + t_0)$, one obtains

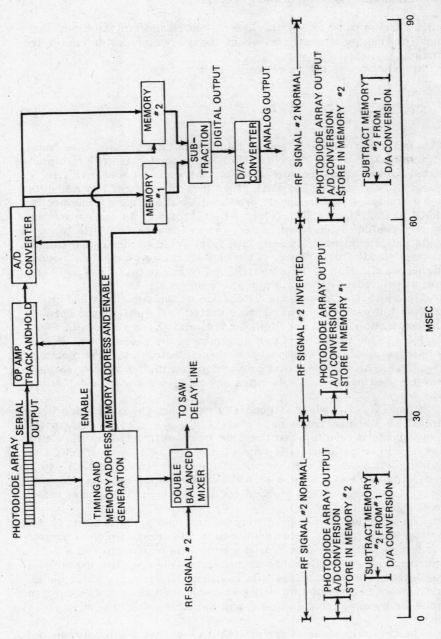

Figure 10.8 Time-integrating correlator postprocessing.

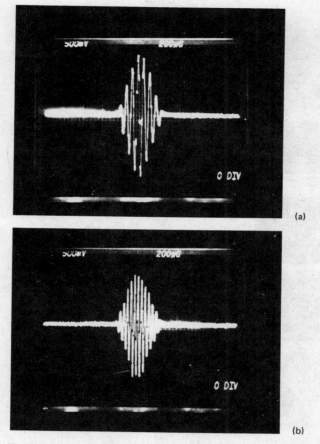

(a)

(b)

Figure 10.9 Correlator outputs for PN coded signals at (a) $\omega_0 + 4$ MHz and (b) $\omega_0 + 7$ MHz.

$$V(T,z) = \cos\left[\omega_A t_0 + \frac{2z}{v}(\omega_0 - \omega_A)\right] \int_T A\left(t + \frac{z}{v}\right) A\left(t + t_0 - \frac{z}{v}\right) dt$$

(10.27)

The correlation peak will now be centered about $z = t_0 v/2$. Figure 10.10 illustrates the TDOA feature for several delays.

For lithium niobate and a delay aperture of 2.54 cm, the limit on the TDOA measurement is ±7 μs, twice the time aperture of the delay line.

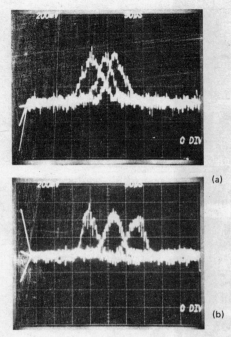

(a)

(b)

Figure 10.10 Time difference of arrival: (a) 0 and ±110 ns and (b) 0 and ±260ns. [From N. J. Berg, I. J. Abramovitz, J. N. Lee, and M. W. Casseday, A new surface wave acousto-optic time integrating correlator, *App. Phys. Lett. 36*(4), Feb. 15, 1980.]

The signal inputs used to illustrate the features of the two-beam SAW correlator have been pseudonoise, biphase-coded signals producing a triangular pulse as the correlation. However, any wideband signal having a prominant autocorrelation could have been used. Two wideband signals common in communications and radar today are the linear FM chirp and the frequency hopper. Consider chirp signals of the form

$$S_1(t) = S_2(t) = \cos(\omega_a + \alpha t)t \tag{10.28}$$

From equation (10.24), letting $\omega_A = \omega_B = \omega_a + \alpha t$ and $A(t) = B(t) = 1$, one obtains a correlator output

$$V(T,z) = \int_T \cos\left[\frac{2z}{v}(\omega_0 - \omega_a - \alpha t)\right] \, dt \tag{10.29}$$

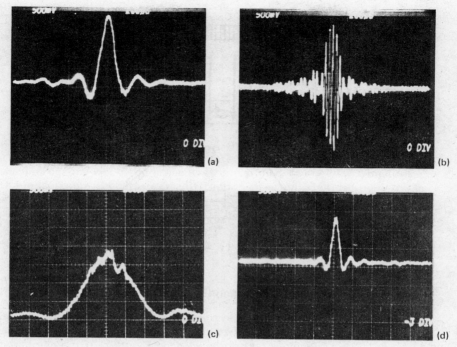

Figure 10.11 Correlator outputs for linear FM chirp inputs at chirp center frequency (a) equal ω_0, and (b) equal $\omega_0 + 7$ MHz and frequency hopped signals of 511 frequencies centered at ω_0 with bandwidth of (c) 500 kHz and (d) 8 MHz.

For ω_A equal to the chirp center frequency and T much greater than the delay aperture this becomes

$$V(T,z) \approx T \cos \frac{2z}{v}(\omega_0 - \omega_A) \ \frac{\sin(z\alpha T/v)}{z\alpha T/v} \tag{10.30}$$

Consider a frequency hopper of the form

$$S_1(t) = S_2(t) = \cos\left(\omega_A + n\,\frac{BW}{N}\right)t \tag{10.31}$$

where ω_A is the center frequency, BW is the bandwidth, N + 1 is the total number of discrete frequencies hopped during the integration periods, and n takes on the values $-(N/2)$, $-(N/2) + 1$, . . . , 0, 1, 2, . . . , N/2 in any order. The correlator output is

$$V(T,z) = \int_T \cos\left[\frac{2z}{v}\left(\omega_0 - \omega_A - n\,\frac{BW}{N}\right)\right]dt \tag{10.32}$$

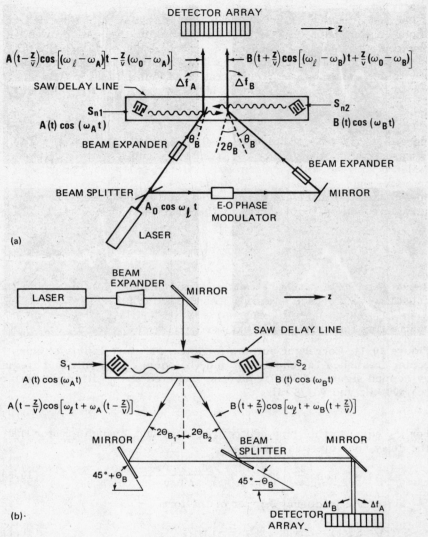

Figure 10.12 (a) Two-beam SAW correlator and (b) related single-input beam SAW correlator. (From Ref. 10.)

which can be manipulated to become

$$V(T, z) \simeq T \cos\left[\frac{2z}{v}(\omega_0 - \omega_A)\right] \frac{\sin[(z/v)BW]}{(N+1)\sin\left[\frac{z}{v}\frac{BW}{(N+1)}\right]} \qquad (10.33)$$

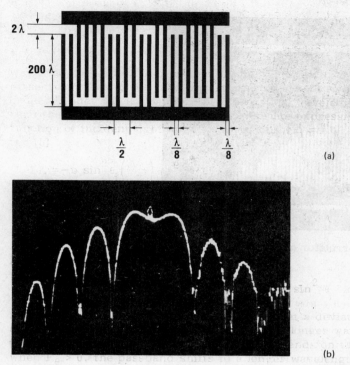

(a)

(b)

Figure 10.13 (a) Transducer array and (b) frequency response.

For very large N, this reduces to

$$V(T,z) \approx T \cos\left[\frac{2z}{v}(\omega_0 - \omega_A)\right] \frac{\sin[(z/v)BW]}{(z/v)BW} \qquad (10.34)$$

Outputs of the two-beam SAW correlator for both chirp and frequency hopped signals are shown in Fig. 10.11.

In examining the architecture of the two-beam SAW correlator depicted in Fig. 10.12(a) and described in previous discussion, one notes that the angle of an incoming light beam with respect to the wave-front transducer tilt of the SAW with which it interacts equals that for the diffracted beam. Thus, an inverse architecture using one input laser beam is possible, as shown in Fig. 10.12(b). The output voltage from the detector array can be shown to be identical to that for the two-beam correlator. Although intermodulation terms (the interaction of the SAW from the left transducer appearing at the right output diffracted beam and vice versa) are suppressed by less than the 40 dB achieved with the two-beam architecture, suppression is sufficient for most applications [10].

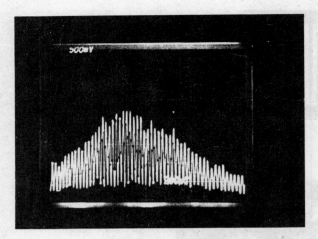

Figure 10.14 Correlator output for inputs of A cos ω_At.

The two-beam SAW correlator which has provided data for this
chapter used a delay line centered at 175 MHz with a bandwidth of 60
MHz. The bandwidth was achieved using a transducer designed with
three split finger pairs [11] and an inverted finger pair [12] on each
end, as pictured in Fig. 10.13(a). The frequency response of such
a transducer is approximated by

$$H(\omega) \propto \frac{3 \sin 3x}{3x} + \frac{4 \sin 4x}{4x} - \frac{5 \sin 5x}{5x} \qquad (10.35)$$

where $x = \pi(\omega - \omega_0)/\omega_0$ and ω_0 is the design center frequency. The
actual frequency response is shown in Fig. 10.13(b). The split finger
design reduces the effects of reflections in the transducer structure.
The use of an inverted finger pair at each end of the transducer extends the bandwidth at the expense of a small dip in the frequency
response at the center of the bandwidth. The coherent light source
was a 10-mW helium-neon laser. The beam expanders provided 2.54-cm
beams which were then focused into sheet beams by 100-cm focal length
cylindrical lenses. Following interaction in the SAW delay line, the
light beams were recollimated with a 20-cm focal length cylindrical
lens, and spatial filtering to eliminate the zero-order beams was performed using a pair of 55-mm, f/1.2 camera lenses. Another 20-cm
focal length cylindrical lens was used to focus the diffracted beams
onto a 2.54-in., 1024-element self-scanning photodiode array with
integration time of 30 ms. Bias subtraction was performed as previously described. Since the full 2.54-cm-diameter circular output
of the beam expanders was used, the light profile was gaussian in intensity. Figure 10.14 shows the output for equal intensity inputs of

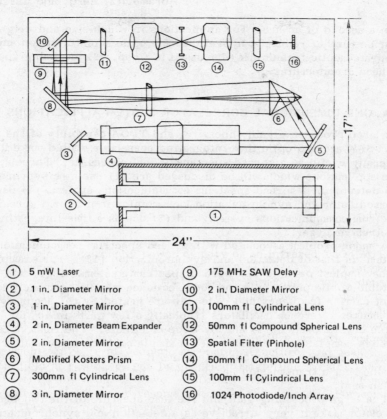

①	5 mW Laser	⑨	175 MHz SAW Delay
②	1 in. Diameter Mirror	⑩	2 in. Diameter Mirror
③	1 in. Diameter Mirror	⑪	100mm fl Cylindrical Lens
④	2 in. Diameter Beam Expander	⑫	50mm fl Compound Spherical Lens
⑤	2 in. Diameter Mirror	⑬	Spatial Filter (Pinhole)
⑥	Modified Kosters Prism	⑭	50mm fl Compound Spherical Lens
⑦	300mm fl Cylindrical Lens	⑮	100mm fl Cylindrical Lens
⑧	3 in. Diameter Mirror	⑯	1024 Photodiode/Inch Array

Figure 10.15 Compact two-beam SAW time-integrating correlator.

A cos $\omega_A t$, where A was held constant in time. Light scatter and non-equal diffraction, which would result in a larger dc bias (thus reducing the usable detector dynamic range), have little effect so that the sine-wave output from the photodiode array is near the maximum attainable.

A compact two-beam SAW correlator has been constructed occupying only 17 × 24 × 12 in. This correlator uses the central 2.54 cm of a 5.08-cm expanded beam to provide a more uniform intensity profile of the light beams. The platform was a 2-in.-thick aluminum plate isolated from vibration by air-cushion shock mounts. A drawing to scale of this compact correlator is shown in Fig. 10.15. The sensitivity of coherent interferometric optical processor to shock and vibration necessitates the use of special suspension systems. Tolerable relative displacements are fractions of a light wavelength (fractions of a micrometer), and platform bending or twisting must be kept to much less

than a second of an arc. For applications in which size and weight
must be further reduced, hybrid discrete optic miniaturization and
integrated optic techniques (discussed in Chap. 12) are being applied
to these architectures.

10.4 ONE-DIMENSIONAL CORRELATOR SYSTEM APPLICATIONS

The large processing gain, linearity, and TDOA capability of the two-
beam SAW acousto-optic time-integrating correlator should make it
generally useful as a spread spectrum signal processor. Three specific applications which will be discussed are (1) use as a synchronization detector in a spread spectrum communications system, (2) use as
a demodulator and synchronization lock monitor in a hybrid spread
spectrum communications system, and (3) use as a time-integrating
spectrum analyzer.

A major problem associated with spread spectrum communication
systems is that of detection and synchronization [13]. For example,
in the simplest *push-to-talk* spread spectrum systems, e.g., man-
portable mobile units, only the code sequence may be accurately known.
Exact carrier frequency and code rate are limited by the accuracy of
transmitter reference oscillators (typically a few parts in 10^6 for
simple crystal oscillators) and by Doppler effects. The relative code
phase is completely uncertain when a simple *cold start* transmitter is
used. With these system characteristics it can prove difficult to determine that a transmission has occurred, let alone decode the information sent.

The large processing gain and the time aperture of the two-beam
correlator make it very attractive as a detection and synchronization
processor. Many spread spectrum systems employ a short, information-
free code sequence (a preamble) at the start of a transmission. An
eight-megabit direct sequence system might, for example, employ a
1-ms word repeated 100 times before starting data transmission. A
two-beam correlator with one input consisting of this preamble as a
reference signal would have a processing gain of about 42 dB and
would search a relative code phase *window* equal to the time aperture
of the correlator. The reference code phase would be shifted by this
time aperture before each integration until a correlation peak occurs,
rather as a discrete version of the *sliding correlator*. The 14-μs time
window of the two-beam correlator would require an excessive number
of searches (1-ms integrations) to find the example signal. However,
SAW acousto-optic devices with 15-cm delay lines (80-μs apertures in
$LiNbO_3$) have been built [14] and could conceivably be used in a two-
beam time-integrating correlator. Such devices could search through
all relative phases of the example preamble in 13 integrations (each of
1-ms duration). This 13-ms acquisition time compares very favorably
with the 1.4 s required by a conventional sliding correlator having

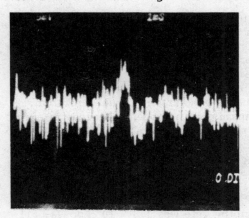

Figure 10.16 Two-beam correlator output for PN coded signals, one a noise-free reference and the other with signal-to-noise ratio of −56 dB Integration time was 30 ms.

similar processing gain [15]. The space-integrating AO (acousto-optic) correlator with a similar acoustic aperture would require only 1 ms but would have 11-dB less processing gain. The TDOA feature would allow code phase determination to within a fraction of a bit, thus allowing the receiver code reference to be synchronized for data recovery. An example of the achievable processing gain is shown in Fig. 10.16.

In more sophisticated spread spectrum communication systems where universal timing is employed, phase code uncertainties still exist because of clock errors (which can be made arbitrarily small) and range variation. In such systems the integrating correlator can be used as a high-gain processor for accurately determining the range between the transmitter and the receiver. However, system frequency errors and Doppler effects place definite limits on the processing gain which can be attained with the time-integrating correlator. The gain limit can be estimated by examining correlator response to two single-frequency CW (continuous-wave) signals, $\cos \omega_A t$ and $\cos \omega_B t$. From equation (10.24) one obtains

$$V(T,z) = 2T \cos\left[\frac{z}{v}(2\omega_0 - \omega_A - \omega_B) + \frac{(\omega_B - \omega_A)T}{2}\right]$$

$$\times \frac{\sin[(\omega_B - \omega_A)(T/2)]}{(\omega_B - \omega_A)(T/2)} \tag{10.36}$$

When the frequency difference $\omega_B - \omega_A$ is equal to $2\pi/T$, the output drops to zero because of the sine term. For a 1-ms integration time,

this corresponds to a total frequency difference of 1 kHz. This suggests that for modulated carrier systems (as opposed to special Dop-
ler-insensitive systems) there is a maximum frequency deviation which
cannot be exceeded if correlation detection with long integration times
(large processing gain) is to be used.

The time-integrating correlator may be used to demodulate biphase-
coded information while simultaneously monitoring synchronization.
Once synchronization with a transmission has been achieved, integration intervals may be locked to the information rate and information
obtained by noting the sense of the correlation peak. Synchronization may be monitored by noting the position of the peak. Figure
10.17 shows the output of the correlator, with bias subtracted, for
inputs consisting of a modulated, hybrid (direct sequence/frequency
hopped) spread spectrum signal and an unmodulated (information-
free) reference signal. The hopping rate was 1.6×10^4 hops/s, 511
channels, and 16-MHz bandwidth; the direct sequence bit rate was
1.3 megabits per second. The input signal-to-noise ratio for the
modulated input was -30 dB.

The large time-bandwidth product of the time-integrating correlator may be applied to spectrum analysis to achieve higher resolution
than with the space-integrating correlator-convolver. As in the case
of the space-integrating convolver, the chirp-z algorithm is used in
which the Fourier transform integral

$$S(f) = \int_{-\infty}^{\infty} s(t)e^{-j2\pi ft} \, dt \qquad (10.37)$$

is expressed as

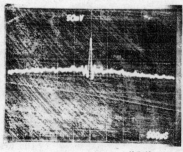 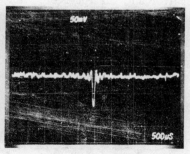

DIGITAL "1"   DIGITAL "0"

Figure 10.17 Time-integrating correlator as a demodulator for hybrid
spread spectrum communications system. (From Ref. 10.)

$$S(f) = e^{-j\pi f^2} \int_{-\infty}^{\infty} s(t) e^{-j\pi t^2} e^{j\pi (t-f)^2} \, dt \qquad (10.38)$$

by making use of the identity

$$2ft = f^2 + t^2 - (t - f)^2 \qquad (10.39)$$

The process of equation (10.38) can be performed using a time-integrating correlator so that resolution depends on integration time rather than delay line aperture. The number of resolvable spots remains fixed; however, the frequency range may be electronically controlled by varying chirp slopes so that greater resolution may be achieved over a smaller total frequency range.

10.5 TWO-DIMENSIONAL TIME-INTEGRATING CORRELATORS

One-dimensional time-integrating correlators have been developed with processing gains in excess of 10^6. In communications or radar systems where Doppler frequency shifts may occur, a limitation on usable processing gain results. As previously discussed, equation (10.36) suggests that the correlator output degrades significantly when the frequency difference between the reference signal and the received signal $\omega_B - \omega_A$ exceeds π divided by the integration time. A 10-GHz radar would experience Doppler shifts of about 9 kHz for radial target velocities of 500 km/h, and use of standard superheterodyne receiver techniques for IF conversion would give this same frequency shift at the correlator input. This would limit the correlator integration time to about 55 μs, yielding a time-bandwidth product (30-MHz processor bandwidth) of about 1.6×10^3. To make use of the increased processing gain available from the two-beam correlator would require using many correlators in parallel, each for a particular band of Doppler frequencies. Since 15 ms of integration time is required to obtain a 60-dB processing gain from the correlator at 30-MHz bandwidth, the Doppler bands would be 15 Hz wide, or 1200 correlators would be required to unambiguously process the return signals expected in the example system.

Two alternatives to such an unwieldy scheme which would still use only a one-dimensional correlator are (1) to use a spread spectrum signal which has a correlation unaffected by Doppler shift [16] or (2) to use an analog frequency divider instead of a superheterodyne downconverter for changing the signal frequency from 10 GHz to the processor frequency. A more elegant solution to the Doppler problem would be the use of a two-dimensional correlator. This would provide not only TDOA information but a measure of the actual Doppler shift as well.

Two-dimensional time-integrating correlators have been developed as three- or four-product processors [17]. Generally, these have been extensions of the basic one-dimensional correlators, both incoherent and coherent, with an additional Bragg cell placed perpendicular to the existing spatially modulating cell. An additional point modulator may be used, or two signals may be premultiplied before being applied to a single-point modulator. As in the case of one-dimensional correlators, SAW delay lines with two transducers per line may be used to minimize the number of delay lines required.

A unique two-dimensional, three- or four-product correlator using only two acoustic delay lines which features the interference between a spatially modulated doubly diffracted beam and another spatially modulated singly or doubly diffracted beam has been developed and demonstrated. As shown in Fig. 10.18, the initial source of the sheet beams is a single laser. Since the SAW devices are perpendicular, interaction in only one device is between light polarized perpendicular to the surface of travel of the SAWs in that device. This is the preferred polarization; for light polarized parallel to the surface of SAW propagation, the diffraction efficiency may be somewhat reduced, and a broadening of the Bragg angle dependence is experienced. Polarization rotators (half-wave plates) may be employed before and after one SAW device if desired to remedy this situation and obtain optimal performance.

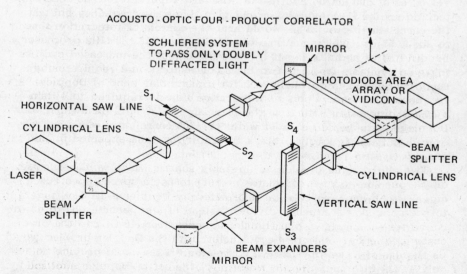

Figure 10.18 Two-dimensional SAW time-integrating correlator. (From Ref. 10.)

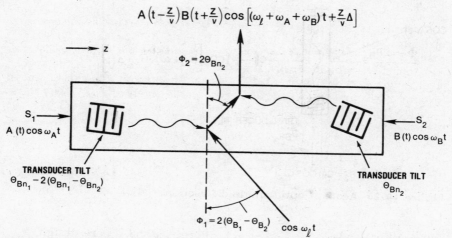

Figure 10.19 Acousto-optic diffractions producing a doubly diffracted beam. (From Ref. 10.)

The double-diffraction scheme is diagrammed in Fig. 10.19 for the horizontal SAW device. The light from the first diffraction is of the form

$$L_{H_1}(t,z) = A\left(t - \frac{z}{v}\right) \cos\left[\omega_\ell\left(t + \frac{z \sin \phi_1}{c}\right) + \omega_A\left(t - \frac{z}{v}\right)\right] \quad (10.40)$$

where the incoming light beam is $\cos \omega_\ell t$, the input signal is $A(t) \cos \omega_A t$, and the light beam enters at an angle ϕ_1 with respect to the perpendicular to the delay line. The doubly diffracted light is then of the form

$$L_{H_2}(t,z) = A\left(t - \frac{z}{v}\right) B\left(t + \frac{z}{v}\right) \cos\left[\omega_\ell\left(t + \frac{z \sin \phi_1}{c}\right)\right.$$

$$\left. + \omega_A\left(t - \frac{z}{v}\right) + \omega_B\left(t + \frac{z}{v}\right)\right] \quad (10.41)$$

for the second input signal $B(t) \cos \omega_B t$. Since $\phi_1 = 2(\theta_{B1} - \theta_{B2})$, $\sin \phi_1 \approx (\omega_1/v)/(\omega_\ell/c) - (\omega_2/v)/(\omega_\ell/c)$, and equation (10.41) reduces to

$$L_{H_2}(t,z) \approx A\left(t - \frac{z}{v}\right) B\left(t + \frac{z}{v}\right) \cos\left[(\omega_\ell + \omega_A + \omega_B)t + \frac{z}{v}\Delta_H\right]$$

$$(10.42)$$

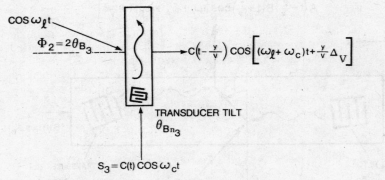

Figure 10.20 Acousto-optic single diffraction.

where $\Delta_H = \{\omega_1 - \omega_2\} - \{\omega_A - \omega_B\}$. Here, ω_1 and ω_2 are design center frequencies for which the Bragg angles are θ_{B_1} and θ_{B_2}, respectively. Frequencies ω_1 and ω_2 are selected to be different so that the doubly diffracted light may be separated from the undiffracted beam.

For a three-product correlator, the second light path requires a single diffraction from a vertical SAW device, as shown in Fig. 10.20. For an input signal $C(t) \cos \omega_C t$, the diffracted light is of the form

$$L_{V_1}(t,y) = C\left(t - \frac{y}{v}\right) \cos\left[\omega_\ell\left(t + \frac{y \sin \phi_2}{c}\right) + \omega_c\left(t - \frac{y}{v}\right)\right] \quad (10.43)$$

Since $\phi_2 = 2\theta_{B_3}$, where θ_{B_3} is the Bragg angle for ω_3, the design center frequency, $\sin \phi_2 = (\omega_3/v)/(\omega_\ell/c)$, and equation (10.43) becomes

$$L_{V_1}(t,y) = C\left(t - \frac{y}{v}\right) \cos\left[(\omega_\ell + \omega_c)t + \frac{y}{v}\Delta_V\right] \quad (10.44)$$

Here $\Delta_V = \omega_3 - \omega_C$. The two diffracted beams L_{H_2} and L_{V_1} are imaged onto an area detector array (photodiode array or vidicon) that integrates the output current which is proportional to the square of the sum of these beams. As in the one-dimensional two-beam SAW correlator, the correlation results from the frequency difference term derived from the cross product, which is proportional to $L_{H_2}(t,z)L_{V_1}(t,y)$.

The output voltage developed by this integration of photodetector current is

$$V(T,z,y) = \int_T A\left(t - \frac{z}{v}\right) B\left(t + \frac{z}{v}\right) C\left(t - \frac{y}{v}\right) \cos\left[(\omega_A + \omega_B - \omega_C)t\right.$$

$$+ \frac{z}{v} \Delta_H - \frac{y}{v} \Delta_V \bigg] \, dt \qquad (10.45)$$

If $\omega_C = \omega_A + \omega_B$, equation (10.45) becomes

$$V(T,z,y) = \cos\left(\frac{z}{v} \Delta_H - \frac{y}{v} \Delta_V\right) \int_T A\left(t - \frac{z}{v}\right) B\left(t + \frac{z}{v}\right) C\left(t - \frac{y}{v}\right) \, dt$$

$$(10.46)$$

Although useful, this device provides time compression in only one dimension, along the z axis, and may be used for only a limited class of processing. Since another signal may be added in the vertical dimension without adding another delay line, a four-product correlator can be easily developed. If the vertical device follows the design of the horizontal device as depicted in Fig. 10.19, the doubly diffracted light could similarly be described by

$$L_{V_2}(t,y) = C\left(t - \frac{y}{v}\right) D\left(t + \frac{y}{v}\right) \cos\left[(\omega_\ell + \omega_C + \omega_D)t + \frac{y}{v} \Delta_V\right]$$

$$(10.47)$$

where now $\Delta_V = \{\omega_3 - \omega_4\} - \{\omega_C - \omega_D\}$ for vertical inputs $C(t)$ $\cos \omega_C t$ and $D(t) \cos \omega_D t$ and vertical design center frequencies ω_3 and ω_4. If L_{H_2} and L_{V_2} are imaged onto a detector array, the relevant output voltage would be given by

$$V(T,z,y) = \int_T A\left(t - \frac{z}{v}\right) B\left(t - \frac{z}{v}\right) C\left(t - \frac{y}{v}\right) D\left(t + \frac{y}{v}\right)$$

$$\times \cos\left[(\omega_A + \omega_B - \omega_C - \omega_D)t + \frac{z}{v} \Delta_H - \frac{y}{v} \Delta_V\right] \, dt$$

$$(10.48)$$

If $\omega_A + \omega_B = \omega_C + \omega_D$, equation (10.48) reduces to

$$V(T,z,y) = \cos\left(\frac{z}{v} \Delta_H - \frac{y}{v} \Delta_V\right) \int_T A\left(t - \frac{z}{v}\right)$$

$$\times B\left(t + \frac{z}{v}\right) C\left(t - \frac{y}{v}\right) D\left(t + \frac{y}{v}\right) \, dt \qquad (10.49)$$

For $\omega_1 - \omega_2 = \omega_A - \omega_B$ and $\omega_3 - \omega_4 = \omega_C - \omega_D$, this further reduces to

$$V(T,z,y) = \int_T A\left(t - \frac{z}{v}\right) B\left(t + \frac{z}{v}\right) C\left(t - \frac{y}{v}\right) D\left(t + \frac{y}{v}\right) dt \qquad (10.50)$$

Thus, this device provides a two-dimensional, four-product correlation. It has the additional ability to measure some degree of deviation from design frequencies.

A four-product SAW correlator was constructed as shown in Fig. 10.18 using two identical delay lines. Transducers were designed for center frequencies of 75 and 115 MHz and bandwidths of 25 and 35 MHz, respectively, similar to those described for the one-dimensional, two-beam correlator. The transducers were tilted as shown in Fig. 10.19. Results are shown in the applications section which follows.

10.6 TWO-DIMENSIONAL CORRELATOR SYSTEM APPLICATIONS

The usefulness of the two-dimensional SAW correlator for processing signals containing Doppler shifts in frequency can be shown by replacing the generalized input signals to the vertical SAW delay line, $C(t)$ $\cos \omega_C t$ and $D(t) \cos \omega_D t$, by linear FM chirps, $\cos(\omega_C + \alpha t)t$ and $\cos(\omega_D - \alpha t)t$. Equation (10.47) becomes

$$L_{V_2}(t,y) = \cos\left[(\omega_\ell + \omega_C + \omega_D)t + \frac{y}{v}\Delta_H - 4\alpha\left(\frac{y}{v}\right)t\right] \qquad (10.51)$$

The output voltage then becomes

$$V(T,z,y) = \int_T A\left(t - \frac{z}{v}\right) B\left(t + \frac{z}{v}\right) \cos\left[(\omega_A + \omega_B - \omega_C - \omega_D)t \right.$$
$$\left. + \frac{z}{v}\Delta_H - \frac{y}{v}\Delta_V + 4\alpha\left(\frac{y}{v}\right)t\right] dt \qquad (10.52)$$

If $\omega_B = \omega_B' + \omega_{DP}$, where ω_B' is a known carrier frequency, ω_{DP} is an unknown Doppler shift, and $\omega_A + \omega_B' = \omega_C + \omega_D$, then equation (10.52) reduces to

$$V(T,z,y) = \int_T A\left(t - \frac{z}{v}\right) B\left(t + \frac{z}{v}\right)$$
$$\times \cos\left[\left(\omega_{DP} + 4\alpha\frac{y}{v}\right)t + \frac{z}{v}\Delta_H - \frac{y}{v}\Delta_V\right] dt \qquad (10.53)$$

It can be seen that there is a y position for which $\omega_{DP} = -4\alpha(y/v)$, and the Doppler shift is compensated. Figure 10.21 illustrates a direct sequence (PN) spread spectrum radar system using this four-product correlator. Correlation of the direct sequence code in the horizontal

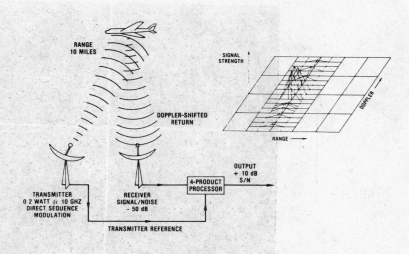

Figure 10.21 Spread spectrum LPI radar using the four-product correlator. (From Ref. 10.)

dimension provides range information, and Doppler compensation in the vertical dimension provides velocity data. The output from the four-product correlator is shown in Fig. 10.22, where Δ_H and Δ_V are nonzero. The correlation spot has been moved from the center of the vidicon output by TDOA (simulated range) and carrier frequency shift (simulated Doppler). Bias subtraction has been performed using a video image processor. The large processing gain of the AO correlator permits low transmit power to be used, thus providing low probability of interception (LPI) protection.

This input signal configuration using two linear FM chirps as vertical inputs may be classified as an ambiguity function processor, generally defined by

$$X(\omega, \tau) = \int_0^T f(t) g(t - \tau) e^{j\omega t} \, dt \qquad (10.54)$$

and is further discussed in Chap. 9.

Another application discussed in detail in Chap. 9 for which this SAW correlator may be used is two-dimensional spectrum analysis. By using a signal multiplied by an up-chirp which repeats many times during the integration period and a similar unmultiplied down-chirp as horizontal inputs, a comb filter is developed. Nonrepeating chirps of lower bandwidth are used as vertical inputs. The result is a spec-

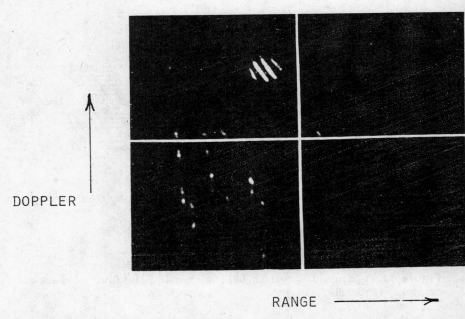

DOPPLER

RANGE ──────────────→

Figure 10.22 Output of the four-product correlator after bias subtraction. (From Ref. 10.)

trum analyzer with coarse and fine resolution along the z and y axes, respectively.

10.7 SUMMARY

Operational one- and two-dimensional coherent interferometric time-integrating acousto-optic correlators have been developed and discussed. These offer large processing gains for application to wideband spread spectrum signal-processing systems. Potential uses for synchronization, demodulation, and radar processing have been discussed. Such devices are no longer laboratory curiosities but are being integrated into fieldable systems. For applications in which size and weight must be kept small, miniaturized hybrid discrete optic and integrated optic implementations of these architectures are under development.

REFERENCES

1. Robert A. Sprague and Chris L. Koliopulos, Time integrating acousto-optic correlator, *Appl. Opt.* 15(1):89-92. Jan. 1976.

2. P. Kellman, Time integration optical signal processing, in
    *Proc. SPIE Symp. on Acousto-Optic Bulk Wave Devices,
    Monterey, CA.*, Vol. 214, Nov. 1979, pp. 63-73.
3. Terry M. Turpin, Spectrum analysis using optical processing,
    Proc. IEEE 69(1):79-92, Jan. 1980. N.Y.
4. P. Kellman, Time Integrating Optical Signal Processing, Ph.D.
    dissertation, Stanford University, Stanford, Calif., June 1979.
5. P. S. Guilfoyle, D. L. Hecht, and D. L. Steinmetz, Joint
    transform time-integrating acousto-optic correlator for chirp
    spectrum analysis, in *Proc. SPIE 23rd Annu. Tech. Symp.,
    Active Optical Devices, San Diego, CA.*, Vol. 202, Aug. 1979,
    pp. 154-162.
6. Thomas L. Szabo and Andrew J. Slobodnik, Jr., The effect of
    diffraction on the design of acoustic surface wave devices,
    IEEE Trans. Sonics Ultrason. SV-20(3):240-251, July 1973.
7. Thomas L. Szabo and Andrew J. Slobodnik, Jr., Acoustic wave
    diffraction and beam steering, *Report No. AFCL-TR-73-0302*,
    Air Force Cambridge Research Laboratories, Bedford, Mass.,
    May 1973.
8. John. N. Lee, Norman J. Berg, and Michael W. Casseday,
    Multichannel signal processing using acousto-optic-techniques,
    IEEE J. Quantum Electron. QE-15(11):1210-1215, Nov. 1979.
9. John Strong, *Concepts of Classical Optics*, W. H. Freeman,
    San Francisco, 1958, pp. 393-399.
10. I. J. Abramovitz, N. J. Berg, and M. W. Casseday, Inter-
    ferometric surface-wave acousto-optic time integrating correla-
    tors, in *Proc. 1980 IEEE Ultrason. Symp. Boston, MA.*,
    Nov. 1980, pp. 483-486.
11. T. W. Bristol, W. R. Jones, P. B. Snow, and W. R. Smith,
    Applications of double electrodes in acoustic surface wave device
    design, in *Proc. 1972 IEEE Ultrason. Symp. Boston, MA.*,
    Oct. 1972, pp. 343-345.
12. T. W. Bristol, Synthesis of periodic unapodized surface wave
    transducers in *Proc. 1972 IEEE Ultrason. Symp. Boston, MA.*,
    Oct. 1972, pp. 343-345.
13. R. C. Dixon, *Spread Spectrum Systems*, Wiley, New York, 1976,
    Chap. 6, pp. 177-215.
14. Norman J. Berg and Burton J. Udelson, Large time-bandwidth
    aocusto-optic convolver, *Proc. 1976 IEEE Ultrason. Symp.
    Annapolis, MD.*, Oct.-Nov. 1976, pp. 183-188.
15. R. C. Dixon, *Spread Spectrum Systems*, Wiley, New York, 1976.
    p. 183.
16. R. C. Thor, A large time-bandwidth product pulse-compres-
    sive technique, *IRE Trans. Military Electron. MIL-6*(1):169-
    173, Jan. 1962.
17. Terry M. Turpin, Time integrating optical processors, in
    *Proc. SPIE 22nd Annu. Tech. Symp. Real-Time Signal Proc-
    essing, San Diego, CA.*, Aug. 1978, pp. 196-203.

11

Optical Information-Processing Applications of Acousto-Optics

DAVID CASASENT / Carnegie-Mellon University, Pittsburgh, Pennsylvania

11.1 INTRODUCTION

In previous chapters, many acousto-optic (AO) signal-processing architectures that realize different one-dimensional (1-D) and two-dimensional (2-D) operations have been described. The operations possible with AO transducers that have been described thus far include spectrum analysis (1-D and folded spectrum 2-D), adaptive filtering, tunable filters, correlators (space integrating and time integrating), and ambiguity function computation. In this chapter, we shall consider various optical information-processing applications of these and other AO systems.

The basic signal-processing requirements are briefly reviewed in Sec. 11.2. This section includes a discussion of passive electronic warfare systems as well as ranging and communications. Use of the Fourier transform operation is emphasized in the former area, whereas the correlation operation is given major attention in the latter applications. Synchronization and the importance of the signal time-bandwidth product are then discussed. Complex-valued signal processing is then described, with attention to why such processing arises and a case study of how to realize it on an AO processor. One of the most computationally demanding signal-processing operations is calculation of the ambiguity function. A development of how this function arises is also included in Sec. 11.2. In the remaining subsections, various examples of these diverse applications are included.

Wideband signal spectrum analysis using the folded spectrum display is the subject of Sec. 11.3. Realization of this operation using the chirp-z algorithm (Chaps. 7 and 10) in a triple-product processor (Chap. 9) was noted earlier. We shall thus consider a space-integrating (SI) realization of this signal spectrum display and its use. The relationships among the different system parameters are developed, and several numerical examples are presented to provide a better understanding of this system and its many uses. A description of a newly fabricated folded spectrum system using snapshot AO addressing of a 2-D spatial light modulator concludes this section.

In Sec. 11.4, we continue with a description of other uses of the Fourier transform (FT) operation in information processing. Bragg receivers are the most familiar AO FT systems. Since these basic systems and their performance and use were described earlier (Chap. 3 and 4), more advanced multichannel AO FT systems are considered here. Two systems to provide 2-D frequency and direction-of-arrival signal displays are described together with a multichannel FT system using the chirp-z algorithm. A brief discussion of the use of the latter system for advanced Fourier spectroscopy is provided.

Several ambiguity function processors are then described in Sec. 11.5 for active radar and passive sonar signal processing. Simultaneous computation of the range and Doppler of multiple targets is one of the most demanding signal-processing functions and one for which AO processing techniques appear quite attractive. Thus, considerable attention is given to this application. The passive sonar ambiguity function computation included shows how 2-D (range and Doppler) output data displays can be obtained using only 1-D devices and detectors. This application is quite important since several AO systems to solve this problem are being fabricated, interfaced, and tested as this chapter goes to press. The radar ambiguity function processor described in this section represents a fully real-time optical signal-processing system that demonstrates what can be fabricated with presently available components. It thus represents an excellent case study in optical system engineering and in the fabrication of a hybrid optical-digital signal processor.

In Sec. 11.6, we conclude with several AO spread spectrum signal processors. The basic space- and time-integrating AO processors are directly useful for such applications. However, since these systems have been discussed earlier (Chaps. 7 and 10), attention is given instead to two advanced AO signal-processing techniques. These involve space-variant AO processors and a hybrid time- and space-integrating AO correlator. The first system provides increased flexibility in the operations achievable on an AO processor and offers a new unconventional technique for signal processing and communications. In the second system, time- and space-integrating processors are combined into a hybrid system with the best features of each processor. An example of one such system is provided to demonstrate the advantages such advanced AO architectures offer.

11.2 SIGNAL-PROCESSING REQUIREMENTS

The high-bandwidth and linear processing features of AO systems make them attractive front-end processors for use in dense electro-

magnetic signal environments. Electronic warfare is an obvious application for which much AO research has been directed. A brief review of the signal processing needs [1,2] of this application area is
presented in Sec. 11.2.1. Several multichannel AO processors for this
application are included in Sec. 11.4. The folded spectrum wideband
signal processor of Sec. 11.3 is also of use for such applications.

Different signal-processing applications require different operations
to be performed and different output data displays to be relaized. In
the last five parts of this section, we shall describe various applications for which the correlation operation is of use and then discuss the
role of several of the different AO processors described in prior chapters. Ranging, message decoding, and synchronization are considered
first, and then the issues of complex correlations and ambiguity functions are addressed.

11.2.1 Electronic Warfare

Passive electronic warfare systems are used to monitor the electromagnetic spectrum to provide the amplitude, frequency, direction, and time
of arrival, plus the pulse width, of all signals from single-pulse measurements (100% intercept probability). These operations require the
isolation, identification, and location of all intercepted emitters. Such
information is necessary for radar warning (self-defense) receivers,
SIGINT (signal intelligence), ELINT (electronic intelligence), and
management of jammer control systems. The wideband and linear features of AO systems make them especially attractive for such applications, as we shall discuss.

The magnitude of the search problem is complicated when direction-
of-arrival (DOA) information is necessary. This often requires a directional antenna to provide the necessary antenna gain. Consider the
simple case of covering the 2 to 3 GHz frequency band in 1-MHz steps
(i.e., 1000 frequency steps). For an average antenna beam width of
5°, 72 angular steps are necessary. The entire frequency-DOA coverage thus requires analysis of 72,000 frequency-angle resolution cells.
If the dwell time per cell is 10 ms, then in the above example we can
only interrogate each cell once every 720 s or once every 12 min. This
is clearly an intolerable situation. With a wideband receiver that can
simultaneously cover the necessary 1-GHz bandwidth, a revisit time of
720 ms is possible. In one channelized receiver system to be described,
continuous coverage in frequency and DOA is possible with 100% intercept probability from single-pulse measurements.

Instantaneous frequency-monitoring systems provide frequency
discrimination when used with crystal video direction-finding systems.
However, they cannot handle the simultaneous processing of multiple
signals and are thus not attractive for high-density signal environments. Conversely, the high bandwidth of AO cells enables high probability of signal intercept and allows the signals to be sorted on a

single-pulse basis. Moreover, the linearity of the AO system enables simultaneous overlapping signals to be extracted. These are essential features in dense signal environments and with present broadband radars. The sensitivity and number of signal frequencies required vary depending on the application. Although 150 frequencies may be adequate for a radar warning receiver, 1000 can be required for SIGINT applications (larger numbers can result in specific cases and as the communication and radar waveforms used increase in complexity). Conversely, in general, less sensitivity is necessary in warning receivers compared to SIGINT applications. However, the former requires accurate time-of-arrival (TOA) information, often to within 0.5 μsec; thus radar warning applications usually employ fast detectors and parallel outputs, whereas SIGINT systems will often use long integration times to extract weak signals.

Several advanced AO processors for such applications are described in Secs. 11.3 and 11.4.

11.2.2 Ranging

When a transmitted signal $f_T(t) = f(t)$ reflects from a target, the received signal (in the simplest case) will be a time-delayed version $f_R(t) = f(t - \tau_D)$ of the reference signal, where $\tau_D = 2R/c$ is proportional to the range R of the target. Thus, to measure range, the TOA or delay τ_D in the received signal must be determined. When noise is present, as is generally the case, f_R cannot be measured accurately by simple threshold detection, and correlation techniques are used since they are optimum for white gaussian noise. In such a system, the location of the correlation peak is proportional to the desired τ_D signal information.

Many issues affect the choice of the reference signal. Because the attenuation of electromagnetic waves varies as the second power of R, a large signal energy is necessary to enhance detection. This is especially important when large target ranges are to be searched and when the cross section of the target is small. When the range of interest is known and restricted, the receiver can be range-gated (i.e., the receiver is open only between some minimum and maximum delay times). This will reduce the magnitude of the problem but will not overcome it. This technique is especially necessary in weather radars to remove clutter or the strong reflected returns from nearby objects. Often the target object is present in a background. If the object is moving (whereas the background is not), moving-target-indication techniques can be used. We shall consider velocity information later in our ambiguity function discussion (Secs. 11.2.6 and 11.5) and for now ignore this effect except to note that different reference waveforms and analysis criteria are used when both range and velocity information are desired or necessary.

Let us return to the remark that large signal energies are necessary and note that the simplest way to achieve this is by use of signals

of long durations T. However, the width of the correlation function
for a pulse of duration T will be T, or the reciprocal of the bandwidth
of the signal, and its shape will be triangular. Thus, when a long
pulse is used to increase the energy of the signal to overcome the
range problem, the bandwidth B of the signal decreases, the width of
the correlation peak increases, and accurate measurement of τ_D is difficult. To simultaneously achieve large T and large B, sophisticated
coded waveforms with large BT products are necessary. We thus speak
of the time-bandwidth product (TBWP) = BT of the signal and processor in describing optical signal-processing (OSP) systems. The goal
is to achieve a narrow correlation peak and low sidelobe levels at all
other τ shifts. Pseudo-random-noise (PRN) codes and others have
been developed for different applications with the above criteria in
mind.

11.2.3 Communications

Communications [3] represents another signal-processing application
with somewhat different requirements and problems than in radar and
ranging [4]. In these cases, a signal is transmitted between two locations, and upon reception it must be demodulated or decoded to extract the message information. Here, different waveforms are used to
represent 1 and 0 bits in the message stream, and thus each correlation output denotes one bit of the message. Correlation provides a
useful demodulation technique, and as before large TBWP codes will
provide improved system performance and noise immunity. Frequency
hopped, direct sequence, and PRN codes are most useful for such
applications.

   Several problems that can arise in communication signal processing
are now noted. In some cases, the interference can be closer in range
to the receiver than the transmitter, thereby having a large range advantage in available energy. However, range gating (as used in radar) cannot always reduce this interference problem because the time
of transmission is not always known in many communication applications. If the interference is continuous or narrowband, its effective-
ness can be reduced by use of a large encoding bandwidth for the
message. This is commonly achieved by PRN coding either through
frequency hopping or phase modulating the RF carrier and results in
a spread spectrum communication system with the coded message
bandwidth B much larger than the information bandwidth B_I of the
message [5]. The ratio B/B_I determines the processing gain of the
spread spectrum system and allows transmission below the noise level
of the system. This is useful in secure communications when detection of the presence of a transmission and the code being used must be
avoided. Many communication systems also employ multiple users.
Such performance is usually accomplished by assigning different orthogonal codes to each user. In this case, attention must be given to the

good auto- and poor cross-correlation properties of the codes as well
as to their resistance to noise and interference.

For the above reasons, large TBWP codes are thus employed, and
correlation processing is used. To achieve the full advantage of a
large TBWP code, the correlation must be performed over the entire
code. However, when the time of arrival of the message is not known,
this can pose quite severe problems since the correlation must be done
for all possible arrival times or range delays. This process of time-
aligning the received signal and the reference or determining the time
of arrival of the signal is referred to as synchronization. This problem is much more severe in communications than in radar.

11.2.4 TBWP And Synchronization

To see how this issue affects the selection of the correlator receiver,
let us briefly review the space-integrating (SI) and time-integrating
(TI) AO correlators (Chaps. 7, 9, and 10) with these issues in mind.
In the simplified SI correlator system of Fig. 11.1, the reference signal $h(x)$ is stored as a transparency on a mask at plane P_{1b}, and the
received signal $g(t)$ is fed to an AO cell at P_{1a}. The transmittance
of the AO cell is a function of time t and space x and can be described
by

$$t(x,t) = g\left(t - \frac{x}{v}\right) \tag{11.1a}$$

or

$$t(x,t) = g(x - vt) \tag{11.1b}$$

where v is the velocity of sound in the cell. The representation in
(11.1a) will be of most use in describing TI systems, whereas the form
in (11.1b) is more useful for SI system descriptions. Both are compatible and can be obtained by variable substitution in the appropriate
correlation equations.

For the system of Fig. 11.1, we thus describe the transmittance of
plane P_{1a} by (11.1b). It is imaged onto plane P_{1b} [we shall discuss the

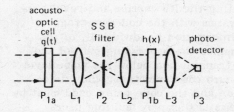

Figure 11.1 Simplified schematic diagram of a space-integrating AO
correlator.

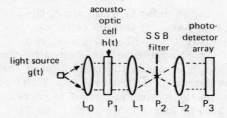

Figure 11.2 Simplified schematic diagram of a time-integrating AO correlator.

single-sideband (SSB) filtering at P_2 later], and the light distribution leaving P_{1b} is thus $g(x - v_t)h(x)$. Lens L_3 now Fourier-transforms this pattern, and the FT is evaluated by a detector on axis at P_3. This results in an output

$$u_3(x = 0, t) = \int h(x)g(x - vt)dx = h \circledast g \qquad (11.2)$$

that is the desired correlation of h and g.

In the simplified TI AO correlator (Fig. 11.2), the received signal g(t) is used to time-sequentially modulate the light source, and an active reference h(t) is fed to the AO cell at P_1. Plane P_1 is then imaged onto P_3 (with SSB filtering at P_2), where time integration occurs directly on the detector. The P_3 output pattern is thus

$$u_3(x) = \int_0^T g(t)h\left(t - \frac{x}{v}\right) dt = g \circledast h \qquad (11.3)$$

where we used (11.1a) to describe the transmittance of the AO cell. In obtaining (11.3), we have assumed zero average-value signals (preprocessing and SSB filtering can achieve this, and it is valid for codes with approximately an equal number of 1's and 0's) and that the integration of the carrier-modulated signals approaches 0 (this is valid for proper values of the carrier, signal bandwidth, and integration time T).

These correlators were described in detail earlier (Chaps. 7, 9, and 10). For now, our concern is with the TBWP, range delay measurement, and synchronization features of these basic systems. The SI system is self-synchronizing over essentially an infinite range delay. The fixed mask and moving window input provide this feature directly, since no output occurs until the reference signal is present in the AO cell. Conversely, the TI system requires that the received signal be present while the reference is within the AO cell's aperture. Thus, this system is only of use when the range delay is quite short (less than the aperture time T_a, perhaps 50 μsec, of the AO cell).

Let us next consider the signal TBWP that both correlators can accommodate. The signal TBWP of the SI system will be limited by the TBWP of the AO cell, the resolution of the mask, the resolution of the lenses, or the time response of the detector. In general, the TBWP of the AO cell is the limitation, and thus the system is limited to correlations of signal TBWPs of perhaps 2000 or less. Conversely, the TI system can provide integration times T that are limited only by the noise and dynamic range of the detector array. If $T = mT_a$, the system can accommodate signal durations m times longer than the aperture time of the AO cell. It is possible to extend the integration time to much longer values without the noise and dynamic range restraints of the detector (at the expense of added postprocessing complexity) by reading out the detector and digitally storing its contents after successive integration times T_1 and summing these respective partial output correlations digitally.

From this brief discussion, we see that the different AO correlators are of use in different applications and that none possess both large range delay search and large TBWP plus the self-synchronization features. Hybrid time- and space-integrating (TSI) AO processors have thus been developed for Fourier transform [6-9] and correlator [7, 10] applications to achieve the advantages of both systems and improved performance in different applications. Where the detailed numerical values of a given application require better performance than the SI or the TI system can provide, such hybrid TSI techniques are necessary. In Sec. 11.6, an example of such a processor is included.

11.2.5 Complex-Valued Signal Processing

In (Chap. 9) attention was given to optical and electronic detection techniques and to the operation of various systems to realize complex correlations. In this section, we shall discuss the reasons that such processing requirements arise and provide the details of how to implement them on a given SI AO correlator. Their use in two specific applications is included in Sec. 11.5.

Any physical quantity such as a signal is of course real and not complex. However, for transmission reasons, the signal information is encoded as a low-frequency envelope modulation on a high-frequency carrier (e.g., $f_c = \omega_c/2\pi = 10$ GHz). Since the processor cannot handle these high carrier frequencies, the received signal is heterodyned to lower frequencies upon reception. This causes the need for complex-valued data handling and gives rise to the use of analytic signals as in Chap. 9. To describe this, we represent the received signal by

$$z(t) = a(t) \cos[\omega_c t + \phi(t)]$$

(11.4)

where a and ϕ describe the amplitude and phase modulation. By trig-onometric identities, we can rewrite (11.4) as

$$z(t) = z_1(t) \cos \omega_c t - z_2(t) \sin \omega_c t \qquad (11.5)$$

Equation (11.5) is of importance because it shows that we can write z as two signals z_1 and z_2 in quadrature and that the low-frequency in-formation (a and ϕ) present on z can be recovered from both z_1 and z_2 (but not from only one of them) as

$$a(t) = [z_1^2(t) + z_2^2(t)]^{1/2} \qquad (11.6a)$$

$$\phi(t) = -\tan^{-1}\left[\frac{z_2(t)}{z_1(t)}\right] \qquad (11.6b)$$

In practice, we obtain z_1 and z_2 by quadrature heterodyne detec-tion and low-pass filtering (LPF) as

$$z_1(t) = z(t) \cos \omega_c t \big|_{LPF} \qquad (11.7a)$$

$$z_2(t) = -z(t) \sin \omega_c t \big|_{LPF} \qquad (11.7b)$$

From (11.5), we see that a complex notation with z_1 and z_2 as the real and imaginary orthogonal components of the signal is a valid represen-tation of the data. Let us now formulate the complex correlation prob-lem and three ways to realize it. We represent the complex signal by

$$s''(t) = s_R'(t) + js_I'(t) \qquad (11.8)$$

where double-prime superscripts denote complex functions, single-prime subscripts denote bipolar functions, and unipolar quantities have no prime on them. Subscripts R and I denote the real and imaginary parts of the complex signal, and subscripts 1 and 2 will denote dif-ferent signals.

We shall consider the correlation $s_1'' \circledast s_2''$ of two such complex sig-nals. If a complex correlator existed, this operation could be directly performed. In practice, only bipolar or unipolar correlators exist, and thus a complex correlation must be achieved by four real bipolar cor-relations or (depending on the representation used) by as few as nine unipolar correlations. As an example, we shall realize $s_1'' \circledast s_2''$ in a real and positive unipolar correlator, such as an optical system. The received signal z is first heterodyne-detected to yield the real and imaginary signal components z_1 and z_2. When this is done for two signals s_1 and s_2, we obtain the four components s_{1R}', s_{1I}' and s_{2R}', s_{2I}' on which we operate.

The first problem is how such bipolar functions can be properly processed for input to a real and unipolar correlator. We usually choose to quadrature-modulate these signals and add a bias B to the sum to produce the real and positive input signals.

$$s_1(x) = s'_{1R}(x) \cos \omega_c x + s'_{1I}(x) \sin \omega_c x + B \qquad (11.9a)$$

$$s_2(x) = s'_{2R}(x) \cos \omega_c x + s'_{2I}(x) \sin \omega_c x + B \qquad (11.9b)$$

where x or t can be the variable used. This preprocessing is simply the reverse of the operations performed in (11.7) upon detection. It is referred to as quadrature modulation and insertion of the bias level. The functions in (11.9) can now be fed to a correlator.

To demonstrate production of the complex correlation

$$s''_1 \circledast s''^*_2 = (s'_{1R} + js'_{1I}) \circledast (s'_{2R} - js'_{1I}) \qquad (11.10)$$

we consider the system of Fig. 11.1 in detail. The signal $s_1(x)$ in (11.9a) is recorded on the mask at plane P_{1b}, and $s_2(t)$ in (11.9b) is fed to the AO cell at plane P_{1a}. The FT of $s_2(x - vt)$ is formed at plane P_2 where we find

$$\mathcal{F}[s_2(x - vt)] = \mathcal{F}_x[B] \qquad \text{at } f = 0$$

$$+ \mathcal{F}_x[s''_2(x - vt)] \qquad \text{at } f = -f_c$$

$$+ \mathcal{F}_x[s''^*_2(x - vt)] \qquad \text{at } f = +f_c \qquad (11.11)$$

One can obtain (11.11) by writing (11.9b) using Euler's identity and substituting into $s_2(x - vt)$. The FT in x then yields (11.11). A slit is placed at $f = +f_c$ in P_2 that allows only the third term in (11.11) to pass plane P_2. The inverse FT is then formed by lens L_2 and $s''^*_2(x - vt) \exp(-j2\pi f_c x)$ is incident on plane P_{1b}. From the above analysis, we can see how quadrature modulation and SSB filtering allow the conjugate of the complex signal s''_2 to be produced with only real and positive input signals.

We now return to the rest of the system in Fig. 11.1. Leaving P_{1b}, we find $s''^*_2(x - vt)s_1(x) \exp(-j2\pi f_c x)$. Substitution of (11.9a) for $s_1(x)$ allows us to rewrite this product as

$$u_2(x,t) = (s'_{2R} - js'_{2I})(s'_{1R} - js'_{1I}) \exp(0)$$

$$+ (s'_{2R} - js'_{2I})(s'_{1R} + js'_{1I}) \exp(-j2\pi 2f_c x)$$

$$+ (s'_{2R} - js'_{2I})B \exp(-j2\pi f_c x) \qquad (11.12)$$

Lens L_3 forms the FT of (11.12) at P_3. From the form in (11.12), we see that this FT operation on the appropriately preprocessed input data produces three terms at three different locations in P_3. If we restrict attention to the $f = 2f_c$ location in P_3, we obtain the integration of the second term in (11.12) and thus the desired complex correlation

$$u_3(t, f = 2f_c) = \int [s'_{1R}(x) + js'_{1I}(x)][s'_{2R}(x - vt) - js'_{2I}(x - vt)] \, dx$$

$$= s''_1 \; \circledast \; s''^*_2 \tag{11.13}$$

Other techniques such as use of two successive system cycles, hetero-dyne detection at P_3, electronic postprocessing, etc., can also be used to realize a complex correlation. Time and space do not allow such a complete description of each technique for each AO processing system; thus the above system was chosen as one example to be fully detailed.

11.2.6 Ambiguity Function

In Chaps 9 and 10 several triple-product processor (TPP) systems to realize the ambiguity function were described. We shall now discuss how the need for such an operation arises. In this case, we shall describe the received signal by $s_R(t) = s_T[t - 2R(t)/c]$, where $s_T(t)$ is the transmitted signal and the time dependence of the range delay is $R(t) = R_0 + \dot{R}t + \cdots$, where only the first two terms are retained in the expansion. We thus write

$$s_R(t) = s_T(t - \tau_D - \nu_D t) \tag{11.14}$$

where $\tau_D = 2R_0/c$ is the range delay and $\nu_D = 2\dot{R}/c$ describes the signal's Doppler frequency shift $\omega_c \nu_D = 2v_r \omega_c/c$ due to a target with radial velocity v_r. When the transmitted signal is

$$s_T(t) = u(t) \exp(-j\omega_c t) \tag{11.15}$$

the received signal is

$$s_R(t) = u(t - \tau_D) \exp[-j\omega_c(1 - \nu_D)t] \tag{11.16}$$

Analytic signal descriptions are thus used as noted in Sec. 11.2.5. The amplitude and phase terms in (11.4) have been included in $u(t)$ to simplify the notation, and in (11.16) the conventional narrow band signal assumption was used. Comparing (11.15) and (11.16), we see that the target's range information is present in the envelope delay, where-as the target's velocity information is contained in the carrier phase and frequency.

To determine the target's range and velocity, we form the correlation and obtain

$$s_T \; \circledast \; s_R = \int u(t)u^*(t - \tau_D - \tau) \exp(-j\omega_c t \nu_D) \, dt \tag{11.17}$$

where constant phase terms have been suppressed for simplicity. This correlation is found to satisfy

$$s_T \circledast s_R = \chi_u(\tau - \tau_D, f_c \nu_D) \qquad (11.18)$$

where

$$\chi_u(\tau, f) = \int u(t)u*(t - \tau)e^{-j2\pi ft} \, dt \qquad (11.19)$$

is the ambiguity function [11] for the signal u(t). The peak of the ambiguity function occurs at the origin ($\tau = 0$, $f = 0$), whereas the correlation peak in (11.18) is located at coordinates proportional to τ_D and ν_D and hence proportional to the target's range R and Doppler velocity ν. Producing (11.17) for two input signals is one of the most complex signal-processing operations required. Thus, considerable attention was given to the triple-product processor system in Chaps. 9 and 10. In Sec. 11.5, we shall describe several other ambiguity function OSP systems.

11.3 FOLDED SPECTRUM PROCESSORS

We next consider the application of advanced AO techniques to wideband spectrum analysis. To achieve the FT of a long-duration and large-bandwidth signal, the full two dimensions of an optical processor must be utilized. A 2-D data representation of a 1-D input signal is most easily realized by raster-recording the input signal. Thomas [12] has shown that the 2-D FT of a raster-recorded 1-D signal yields a folded spectrum with coarse and fine frequency axes.' The input raster recording technique provides a convenient method by which to introduce a 1-D signal with a large time bandwidth product (TBWP) into a 2-D optical system. The folded spectrum output represents a compact 2-D display with coarse and fine frequency separation that makes wideband signal spectrum analysis possible with high resolution and large processing gain. Following a derivation of the input and output parameter relationships, a real-time system is described.

The signal s(t) of length $T = VT_h$ is divided into V parts each of duration T_h and raster-recorded on V lines on a 2-D device with spatial separation b between lines and with each line of physical length a. When this data plane is placed in front of a spherical lens of focal length f_L and illuminated with coherent light of wavelength λ, the 2-D optical FT of the input pattern appears in the back focal plane of the lens. This FT pattern (Fig. 11.3) contains a horizontal coarse frequency axis with input signal frequencies in increments of $f_h = 1/T_h$ separated by distances $\lambda f_L/a$. If H cycles of data are recorded along each line in the input, the maximum input frequency $f_m = H/T_h = Hf_h$, and H coarse frequency loci appear in the output at increments f_h. The vertical spacing b between input lines causes the frequency pattern to

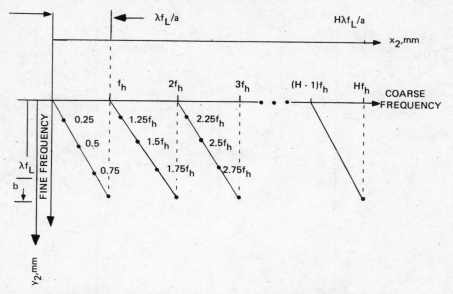

Figure 11.3 General description of a folded spectrum output plane pattern.

repeat vertically in the FT plane at distances $\lambda f_L/b$. The ratio b/a determines the slope of each coarse frequency line. Since $a \gg b$, the coarse frequency loci are nearly vertical and are exaggerated in Fig. 11.3 for clarity of notation.

A qualitative analysis of the input-output parameter relationships in the SI folded spectrum system is thus easily defined. With V input lines of data and H points per line recorded at a line scan rate f_h or in a line scan time $T_h = 1/f_h$, the input space-bandwidth product (SBWP) is VH, the maximum input spatial frequency if Hf_h, and the signal duration is $T = VT_h$. Since SBWP is conserved by the FT operation, the SBWP in the FT plane is also VH with H coarse frequency loci and V resolvable frequencies per coarse frequency locus. Each coarse frequency locus contains a bandwidth of f_h Hz in frequency, and thus the fine frequency resolution of the system is $f_h/V = 1/T_h V = 1/T$, as predicted by basic information and communication theory. The folded spectrum processor thus represents the equivalent of a VH point FFT on a signal of duration T with a fine frequency resolution $1/T$ and a bandwidth Hf_h with full processing gain possible over this range of data specifications. Several numerical examples are the best way to rapidly convey the extent of the processing performance possible with such a system. These are included in Table 11.1, where high- and low-frequency examples are given.

Table 11.1 Folded Spectrum Numerical Examples

Parameter	Symbol	High-frequency case	Low-frequency case
Input bandwidth	BW	100 MHz	2 kHz
Signal time duration	T	30 ms	10 s
Horizontal line rate	f_h	40 kHz	10 Hz
Horizontal line time	T_h	25 μs	0.1 s
Horizontal resolution	H	2500 cycles/line	200
Vertical resolution	V	1200 lines	100
Input space bandwidth	SBW	3×10^6	2×10^4
Output space bandwidth	SBW	3×10^6	2×10^4
Coarse frequency resolution	f_c	40 kHz	10 Hz
Fine frequency resolution	f_f	33.3 Hz	0.1 Hz
Number of coarse frequency loci	H	2500	400
Number of fine frequencies per coarse frequency locus	V	1200	250
Frequency resolution	R	1 part in 3×10^6	1 part in 2×10^4

The high-frequency case corresponds to a wideband radar and RF
signal-processing application in which a 3 million point FFT on 100-
MHz bandwidth data with a frequency resolution of 40 Hz is considered.
These data are of use when the PRF (pulse repetition frequency) of a
given transmission lying somewhere in a large-bandwidth space is desired. It is also of use when the frequency of a given transmission
varies with time. In this case, the time history of such an output display provides information on the frequency hopping code used and on
the presence of weak signals of short duration in the spectrum. The
time-history output at given FT plane locations contains information on
the transmissions made on different frequency carriers. Various spatial filtering techniques have been demonstrated to decode AM, FM,
and FSK modulation signals [13,14] on different carriers in such an
RF spectrum display.

The low-frequency example given is of use in biomedical data processing, nondestructive testing of engines, and other applications. In
one case, fetal EEG data has been analyzed [15] by such techniques
before and after application of a paracervical block. By folded spectrum techniques, one could detect noticeable changes in the frequency
content of the data at different times in the experiment. The use of
folded spectrum techniques to analyze the performance of aircraft and
automobile engines by nondestructive testing from analysis of time-
history data from accelerometers or other transducers on the engine
has also been demonstrated [16]. Much of this work is summarized
in Ref. 17. Many systems using this SI folded spectrum technique have
been fabricated using film [13] and real-time transducers such as the
GE light valve [18]. AO folded spectrum systems using the triple-
product processor and time integration have also been fabricated and
were described earlier (Chap. 9). We thus consider a new system recently fabricated by Ampex Corporation [19] that uses AO transducers
and a 2-D spatial light modulator (SLM) to achieve a folded spectrum
output display by space integration rather than time integration.

This processor is shown schematically in Fig. 11.4. In this system,
the RF antenna data are fed to an AO cell (bottom left of the figure),
and the pulsed output from a laser (top of the figure) is used to image
to the pattern in the AO cell onto a spatial light modulator, specifically
a liquid crystal light valve (LCLV) [20], shown at the bottom of the
figure. If the time aperture of the AO cell is T_h, then each T_h seconds
of data are recorded on separate lines on the LCLV by stepping a
vertical AO deflector at a slow rate $1/T_h$. A raster-scanned version
of the signal from the antenna is thus recorded on the LCLV. The
beam from a continuous laser (top of the figure) is then collimated to
uniformly illuminate the LCLV from the right-hand side through the
beam splitter (BS) shown. The light distribution leaving the LCLV is
reflected upward by the BS, its dc level is suppressed by the zero
stop shown, and its 2-D FT (or the desired folded spectrum output pattern) is produced on the vidicon shown in the center right of the
schematic.

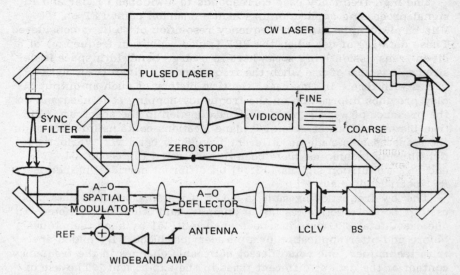

Figure 11.4 Schematic diagram of a snapshot AO-addressed folded spectrum space-integration processor. (From Ref. 19.)

This snapshot addressing technique by which an entire line of 750 points of data (a 5-μs signal time history) is recorded on one line in parallel represents a major new use and application of AO transducers. Rather than using AO cells as scanning deflectors, the contents of the cell are imaged in parallel. The present system allows 750 data points to be written in 5 μs or the equivalent of 1 point every 6.6 ns. This is significantly faster than conventional AO deflectors, and moreover the fidelity and registration accuracy of the recorded pattern in this system are far superior to what one can achieve by other methods. Thus, the snapshot addressing technique provides much larger signal bandwidth and more accurate data recording than do other methods and with a less complex optical system. The major limitation is now the laser pulse width T_a and its repetition rate. The maximum frequency f_m that can be recorded is [19]

$$f_m = \frac{0.265}{T_a}$$

(11.20)

For the present system, $T_a = 300$ ps, and a system with a bandwidth of 880 MHz is possible. In one version of Fig. 11.4 that was assembled, the 150-MHz bandwidth of the AO cell used was the limiting factor in the system bandwidth. AO cells with far larger bandwidths are available, and thus the bandwidth of the present system can be extended greatly with increased electronic complexity.

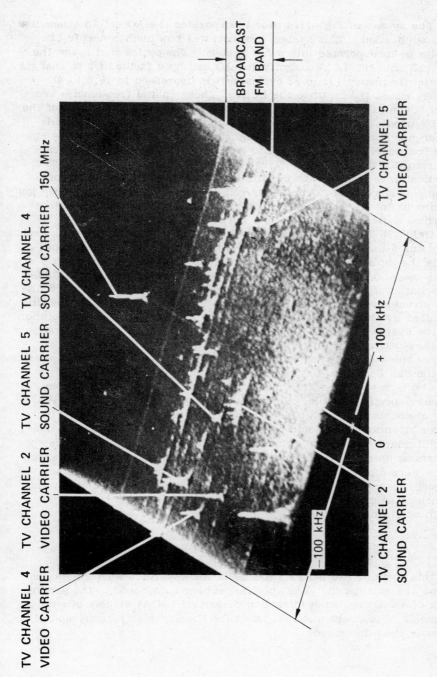

Figure 11.5 Real-time 150-MHz 192,000-time-bandwidth product folded spectrum output from the system of Fig. 11.4. (From Ref. 19.)

The system of Fig. 11.4 thus incorporates the AO cell in a new use and application. This system demonstrates how such concepts can easily be incorporated into a full system. The optics that image the AO cell onto the LCLV magnify the AO cell by a factor of 2 so that its spatial frequency (41 to 82 cycles/mm) is decreased to 20.5 to 41 cycles/mm at the input to the LCLV. These spatial frequencies are still beyond the 20-cycle/mm 3-dB spatial frequency bandwidth of the LCLV used. Thus, an interference technique (summing a 150-MHz reference signal with the input signal) is used to heterodyne the spatial frequencies of the AO cell to lower spatial frequencies that can be recorded on the LCLV. The vertical deflector can provide 400 vertical lines of data with 50-MHz bandwidth and an 8-μs aperture time. This vertical AO deflector cell is fed with a linear FM sweep generator to ensure a vertical scan linearity of 0.1% to ensure constant vertical deflection and a uniform horizontal line spacing.

Only 256 lines of data are recorded in the system assembled. Each contains 5 μs of data with a 150-MHz bandwidth or 750 cycles/line; thus the input data record corresponds to a signal time duration T.= 1.28 ms, and the LCLV data can be updated every 0.1 s. The folded spectrum output thus contains 750 coarse frequency loci with 256 fine frequencies per locus. A maximum system bandwidth is thus 150 MHz (limited by the horizontal AO cell used), and the frequency resolution of the system is 780 Hz for a system TBWP = 192,000. A vivid example of the isometric output from this system is shown in Fig. 11.5. It shows the 2-D 150-MHz bandwidth folded spectrum of the RF signals in the San Francisco Bay area produced in real time. When such a system is assembled with more advanced components, much better performance is possible. Bandwidths above 500 MHz and a TBWP of 10^6 are achievable with presently available components. Thus, the major attention in this and other AO systems to be described is their architecture and optical engineering rather than the performance specifications obtained at the time and with the avaiable funds with which they were fabricated. Presently available AO components and new algorithms (such as the triple-product processor) and architectures (such as snapshot addressing) make real-time signal processing at high bandwidths a reality.

11.4 MULTICHANNEL PROCESSORS

In this section, two AO FT processors for electronic warfare applications are considered. The specific problem considered is the production of a 2-D frequency/direction-of-arrival (DOA) display of multiple signals. A multichannel FT system for Fourier spectroscopy and other uses is then described.

11.4.1 Frequency-DOA Processors

The Bragg cell spectrum analyzer (Chap. 4) is the basic element used in many systems. Several such systems can be combined to provide direction finding, as we shall now describe. In an amplitude-ratio direction-finding system, two or more Bragg cell spectrum analyzers are used. The received signals from two or more identical antennas (whose main lobes are oriented in different directions) are fed to two AO cells, and the FT of each signal is formed on separate linear detector arrays. A two-channel system of this type is shown in simplified form in Fig. 11.6. For a signal at a given frequency, each FT output will contain a peak on a given detector element corresponding to the frequency of concern. For antennas with different look directions, a peak will occur in the same frequency detector channel, but its amplitude on each detector array will differ depending on the azimuth angle location of the source with respect to the boresight direction of the antenna. Thus, with two antennas steered to two different directions, the amplitude of the FT peaks on the same frequency channels on the two detectors can be compared to determine the azimuth angle or DOA of the signals at each frequency f_n. A two-channel version of this system fabricated by Itek Corp. exhibits an 0.5-GHz bandwidth centered at 1 GHz with 250 resolvable frequency channels and a 25-dB isolation between channels. Nearly equal (within 0.25 dB) amplitude response in each channel over the passband has been obtained by gain equalization circuits.

The system of Fig. 11.6 is quite simple in concept but cannot provide the fine angular resolution of less than 1° necessary in many higher-performance systems. A simultaneous display of the instantaneous frequency and DOA data on simultaneous signals with fine angular resolution can be achieved with the phase interferometric sys-

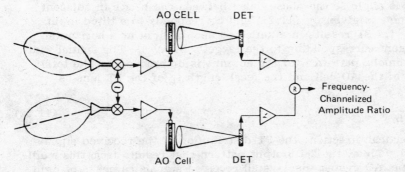

Figure 11.6 Simplified schematic diagram of an amplitude-ratio dual-channel Bragg cell system for target frequency and DOA determination. (From Ref. 1.)

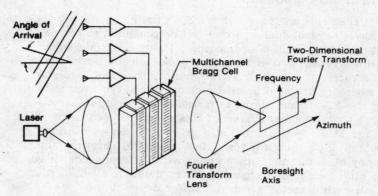

Figure 11.7 Simplified schematic diagram of a phase interferometric four-channel Bragg cell system for target frequency and DOA determination. (From Ref. 1.)

tem of Fig. 11.7. In this system, the received signals from N non-equally spaced antenna elements are fed to N transducers on an AO cell, and the 2-D FT of the acoustic pattern is formed. This system (and the one of Fig. 11.6) used the fact that the phase delay ϕ between adjacent antenna elements separated by a distance d is related to the DOA θ of the signal by

$$\phi = \frac{2\pi d}{\lambda} \sin \theta \qquad (11.21)$$

If the target is at boresight (0°), the acoustic waves in all channels are identical and aligned, and the FT produced by the lens yields diffracted spots on the vertical output axis. If the signal originates from an off-axis angle θ, the phase delay between the beams in adjacent AO channels is given by (11.21) and corresponds to a tilted input grating. Its FT results in a deflected spot of light at a horizontal displacement corresponding to the target's DOA, θ. The spatial width of the mainlobe pattern w of the antenna is determined by the total length L of the AO cell and the focal length f_L of the FT lens as

$$w = \frac{\lambda f_L}{L} \qquad (11.22)$$

In the vertical direction, the FT distribution of the received signals is formed. Thus, the 2-D output pattern that results from this multidimensional AO system displays all received signals as peaks of light whose locations correspond to the frequency and DOA of the corresponding signals with the amplitude of each peak of light proportional to the amplitude of each signal.

In the fabricated system, the AO cell channels were unevenly spaced. With proper optimization, a resolution of 0.7° resulted with the sidelobe levels of the antenna determined by the transducer element density. Several versions of this system have been fabricated by GTE Sylvania [21]. For the case of an AO cell with five active channels (corresponding to a five-element antenna), the element spacings in units of wavelengths at 12 GHz with respect to the first element were 4.5, 6, 8, and 12.5, respectively. This resulted in the above antenna pattern parameters. The general performance achieved in the present system is an 0.7° azimuth resolution and a 5-MHz frequency resolution over a 500-MHz bandwidth (100 frequency channels). Apodization control of the AO cell illumination is possible and is used in all the above systems to optimize their performance.

The key features in the use of such AO systems is their multi-dimensional outputs, together with the wide bandwidth and linearity of the system. The wide bandwidth greatly decreases the required computation time, whereas the linearity of the system allows processing of simultaneous signals. Such systems can thus provide 100% signal intercept probability from single-pulse measurements. The two AO signal processors described thus far require multiple AO cells or cells with multiple transducers. Although present technology permits limited extrapolation of this technique, alternate methods to realize 2-D OSP operations with 1-D AO devices exist.

11.4.2 Multichannel Fourier Transform

We shall now consider one such multidimensional AO processor. To provide numerical data on the system, we shall consider its use for advanced Fourier spectroscopy [22] signal-processing applications. We shall first consider the basic time-integrating (TI) AO correlator with an LED source at plane P_1 fed with a signal $f(t)$ whose output is imaged onto an AO cell at plane P_2 fed with the signal $g(t)$. As described earlier, the system output on a TI linear detector array at P_3 is

$$u_3(x_3) = \int f(t)g(t - x) \, dt \qquad\qquad (11.23)$$

or the correlation of f and g. For our present application, we shall first consider the use of this T. correlator to realize the FT rather than the correlation operation. To describe how this is achieved, we first recall the FT of a function $f(t)$ is

$$F(\omega) = \int f(t) \exp(-j\omega t) \, dt \qquad\qquad (11.24$$

Using the identity

$$(\omega - t)^2 = (t - \omega)^2 = \omega^2 + t^2 - 2\omega t \qquad (11.25)$$

we substitute ωt from (11.25) into (11.24) and obtain

$$F(\omega) = \exp\left(\frac{-j\omega^2}{2}\right) f(x) \exp\left(\frac{-jx^2}{2}\right) \circledast \exp\left(\frac{+jx^2}{2}\right) \qquad (11.26a)$$

or

$$F(\omega) = \exp\left(\frac{-j\omega^2}{2}\right) f(t) \exp\left(\frac{-jt^2}{2}\right) \circledast \exp\left(\frac{+jt^2}{2}\right) \qquad (11.26b)$$

where in (11.26a) an integration in space is implied and in (11.26b) a time integration is implied. We note that a correlator can thus be used to realize the FT by the chirp-z alogrithm. This simply requires that the signal $f(t)$ to be Fourier-transformed be premultiplied by a chirp signal $\exp(-jt^2/2)$ and correlated with a chirp $\exp(+jt^2/2)$.

We next recall that a vector-matrix multiplication can be optically obtained [23] with a linear input LED array whose outputs are imaged vertically and expanded horizontally to illuminate a mask. The output light is then integrated vertically to yield the desired vector-matrix product. Combining these two techniques, the system of Fig. 11.8 results [24] in which the output from each LED in the input array at P_1 is imaged vertically and expanded horizontally to uniformly illuminate the single AO cell at P_2. The output from the AO cell is then imaged onto the output plane P_3 where time integration is performed on the detector. The Schlieren filtering necessary between P_2 and P_3 is omitted for simplicity. This system thus realizes a multichannel correlation. When the input signals f_n are premultiplied by the same chirp signals and when the signal fed to the AO cell is another chirp, the output pattern at P_3 contains the multichannel Fourier transforms $F_1, \ldots, F_N$ of the N input signals $f_1, \ldots, f_n$ fed to the LEDs. Such a system has yet to be fabricated, but it demonstrates yet another technique by which multidimensional data processing is possible with single AO cell devices.

The system of Fig. 11.8 is of considerable interest since it allows multichannel operations to be achieved without the need for a multi-channel device. This multiple LED feature together with the chirp-z algorithm and the TI correlator concept can thus achieve a multidimensional AO processor with presently available components. Up to 1000 multichannel inputs can easily be obtained with present technology. This system is thus of use in frequency-DOA displays and in phased array radar processing. To describe yet another application area, we shall now consider its use for advanced Fourier spectroscopy signal processing.

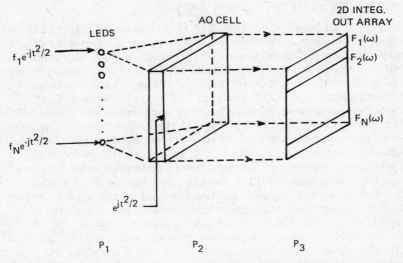

Figure 11.8 Schematic diagram of a multichannel AO FT system using the chirp-z algorithm. (From Ref. 24.)

Fourier spectroscopy systems [22] already have 16 detector elements using 0.1-sec integration times and an operational bandwidth of 250 Hz. Other single-detector systems use 10-s integration times and a 2400-Hz bandwidth. Advanced systems will use imaging spectrometers with 1000 or more separate imaging detector areas, integration times in excess of 10 s, and larger bandwidths above 2 kHz. These advanced systems and recent advances in AO signal processing have made optical techniques of interest in this application. As a numerical example for which to detail analysis of Fig. 11.8, we shall consider a Fourier spectroscopy system with 100 detector areas, 2.5-s sweep times or signal durations, and a 2-kHz signal bandwidth. For this case, we use a 100-element linear source array of LEDs and a 100-MHz-bandwidth AO cell with a 50-μs aperture time. Both devices are presently available and were thus chosen. Since the bandwidth of the AO cell is 5×10^4 times larger than that of the input signal, we can achieve an integration time 5×10^4 times the aperture time or 2.5 s as desired. The resultant system will then have a frequency resolution of 0.4 Hz and can satisfy the requirements of the assumed Fourier spectroscopy system. Quite modest component specifications were assumed in the above example, with much more impressive performance possible using more advanced components. Such data-processing performance is necessary for advanced Fourier spectroscopy applications.

11.5 AMBIGUITY-FUNCTION COMPUTATION

Simultaneous determination of the range and Doppler of a target is one
of the most demanding operations since it requires computation of the
ambiguity function. A development of the need for this operation was
provided in Sec. 11.2. The TPP system of Chap. 9 has already been
shown to produce such an output display. Thus, in this section,
rather than repeating the TPP analysis of Chap. 9, we shall first
describe a new passive ambiguity-function application and a new AO
processor for it. A different type of real-time AO ambiguity-function
processor that was recently fabricated will then be described in detail
as an optical engineering case study. It is worthwhile to recall that
optical ambiguity-function processors have existed for over 20 years;
however, the initial systems [25] required 2-D spatial light modulators on which different Doppler-shifted versions of the signal were recorded on different lines. Although considerable progress has been
made in 2-D spatial light modulators [26], these devices do not yet
have the bandwidth, resolution, optical quality, and ready commercial
availability enjoyed by AO transducers. For these reasons, AO signal
processors are of considerable current interest. A radar ambiguity-
function processor to be described combines both AO and 2-D light
modulator technology in an architecture that is quite practical with
present components. It thus merits attention and description because
of these features and because a well-engineered and fully real-time
version of the system has been fabricated.

11.5.1 Passive Ambiguity-Function Computation

In applications such as advanced sonar signal processing, use of active
signals is not attractive because it permits location of the sources being
used. Thus, to obtain accurate range and Doppler information on the
many potential signal sources (and to perform classification of them),
passive signal detection techniques are employed [27]. For such a
problem, passive detectors are used to receive signals at widely separated locations from all emissions in the search area of interest. As
a simplified scenario, we shall consider two detectors that receive
signals from the same source with range delays R_1 and R_2. Upon reception, the bulk range delays are removed, and basebanded complex
time-history data of each received signal in different frequency threat
bands of interest are produced by FFT techniques. To determine the
origin of each emission and additional information on interesting potential targets, the ambiguity functions for all pairs of signals in different frequency regions must be computed and subsequently analyzed.
Following a development directly analogous to that of Sec. 11.2.6, we
find that the location of the peaks in the resultant ambiguity surface
for this scenario will correspond to the differential range and Doppler
of the targets. Extensive postprocessing is still necessary to de-

termine the vector location of the different sources and to identify
them. For the present, we shall concentrate only on the optical system
to realize the necessary passive ambiguity surface outputs.

An image plane correlator [28] was fabricated to demonstrate the
use of optical processing in this application, and the quality of the
results obtained [29] was found to be quite good. This initial system
used film transparencies of the signal time-history records to demonstrate the concepts. A real-time image plane correlator system using
a photo-DKDP spatial light modulator was then fabricated [30] and
demonstrated together with a crossed-input ambiguity-function processor [31] using the same DKDP light valve [29,30]. The size and
shape of the resultant ambiguity-function surface were compared to
theory and to the results obtained using film, and again quite good
agreement was obtained. A modified real-time joint transform correlator system [32] using AO snapshot addressing (Sec. 11.3) is presently being fabricated for this application, together with a space-
integrating system using AO cells and astigmatic optics [33] and a TPP
system (Chap. 9). Since details on the design and performance of
these three systems are just becoming available, we shall describe the
use of a version of the SI system of Fig. 11.1 for this application.
This will allow discussion of the problems of Doppler generation and
operation on complex-valued basebanded data in this application together with quantitative data on the accuracy of an AO system and
demonstration of its performance with range-delayed and Doppler-
shifted signals.

Because of the digital FFT preprocessor, the input data for the
amgibuity function processor consist of baseband complex-valued time
histories of the real and imaginary parts of each signal in each frequency band of interest as described above. The quadrature modulation and bias insertion preprocessing of equation (11.9) are thus applied to these data as described in Sec. 11.2.5 to provide the necessary real and positive input signals for the optical processor. With
reference to the system of Fig. 11.1, the signal $s_1(x)$ in (11.9a) is
recorded at P_{1b}, and the signal $s_2(t)$ in (11.9b) is fed to the AO cell
at P_{1a}. The same SSB filtering at P_2 described in Sec. 11.2 is used to
realize the complex correlation. In this application, a complex correlation is desired because of the additional 3 dB of output correlation
plane SNR it provides over the simpler real correlation.

We shall now consider how the system of Fig. 11.1 can provide the
desired ambiguity function output pattern with differential range
$\tau_1 - \tau_2$ and Doppler $\nu_1 - \nu_2$ coordinate axes. The only modification necessary is the use of a parallel readout linear detector array at the P_3
output plane in place of the single photodetector previously used.
For this present application, we shall consider the two narrowband
received signals to be centered at a frquency f_0. Using the conventional narrowband approximation, we ignore the effect of Doppler
on the complex envelope modulation and include it only as a shift in the

carrier frequency f_0 as done in Sec. 11.2. We then describe the two baseband signals after heterodyning to dc, by multiplication by $\exp(-j2\pi f_0 t)$, as

$$s_1''(t) = u(t - \tau_1) \exp[-j2\pi f_0(1 - \nu_1)t] \exp(-j2\pi f_0 \alpha_1 \tau_1) \qquad (11.27a)$$

$$s_2''(t) = u(t - \tau_2) \exp[-j2\pi f_0(1 - \nu_2)t] \exp(-j2\pi f_0 \alpha_2 \tau_2) \qquad (11.27b)$$

where τ_1 and τ_2 denote the range delays and ν_1 and ν_2 are the Doppler factors of the two signals with respect to each receiver. By substitution of these signals for s_T and s_R in the general ambiguity-function derivation of Sec. 11.2, we obtain an output plane pattern at P_3 of Fig. 11.1 that varies with time t and distance x as

$$u_3(t,x) = u_3(\tau,f) = \int_{-\infty}^{\infty} u(x')u^*(x' - \tau') \exp[j2\pi x'(f - f_0\nu')] \, dx'$$

$$(11.28)$$

where $x' = x - \tau_1$, $\tau' = \tau_1 - \tau_2 - \tau$, and $\nu' = \nu_1 - \nu_2$. Compared to the conventional narrowband ambiguity function in (11.19), we find

$$u_3(\tau,f) = \chi(\tau_1 - \tau_2 - \tau, \; f - f_0\nu_1 + f_0\nu_2) \qquad (11.29)$$

From (11.29) we see that the time of occurrence $t = \tau$ of the output correlation peak at P_3 of Fig. 11.1 equals the desired differential range delay $\tau_1 - \tau_2$, and the spatial location of the output peak $x = f$ (along a linear detector array at P_3) is proportional to the differential Doppler $\nu_1 - \nu_2$ of the target with the proportionality factor f_0. It should be noted that the Doppler of these data is obtained by multiplying two signals at different frequencies proportional to $\nu_1 f_0$ and $\nu_2 f_0$ at P_{1b}. This generates signals at the sum and difference of these frequencies, and placing the detector array in the proper location in P_3 (as described in Sec. 11.2) selects the difference frequency component and removes the sum frequency component to provide an output proportional to the desired differential target Doppler.

This system was assembled and its performance tested with various input signals [29]. We shall consider the case of linear FM (LFM) signals, because the resultant ambiguity function is well known to be [34]

$$\chi(\tau,\nu) = \left(1 - \frac{|\tau|}{T}\right) \frac{\sin[(b\tau - \pi\nu)(T - |\tau|)]}{(b\tau - \pi\nu)(T - |\tau|)} \qquad (11.30)$$

for $|\tau| \leqslant T$ and 0 for $|\tau| \geqslant T$, where b is the chirp rate, T is the duration, and 2bT is the bandwidth of the LFM signal. For the P_{1b} mask, an LFM sweep from 4.5 to 8.6 cycles/mm was used. The sound velocity was v = 620 m/s for the AO cell used, and the starting frequency of the LFM signal fed to the cell was 32 MHz, and the chirp rate was

$b = 0.0794 \, \text{MHz}/\mu s$. Along the $b\tau = \pi\nu$ direction in the output τ, ν plane, (11.30) describes a ridge of width 2T with a slope of 0.1588 MHz/μs for the signals used.

In Fig. 11.9, we show the time-history outputs from different detector element locations in P_3 of Fig. 11.1 for the LFM test signal described above. Note that as the Doppler shift between the signals increases from the zero Doppler case (center trace in Fig. 11.9) the location of the correlation peak shifts in range τ and decreases in amplitude as predicted by (11.30). The expected width of the ambiguity peak is 2/2.45 MHz or 816 ns. The measured 825-ns value was within 1% of the theoretical value. The amplitude of the peaks of the ambiguity surface was also measured and compared to theory, and

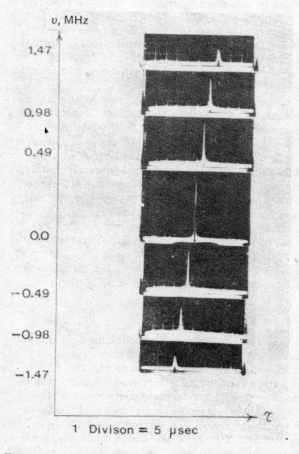

Figure 11.9 Real-time AO ambiguity-function output data from a modified version of the system of Fig. 11.1. (From Ref. 29; © 1979 IEEE.)

again better than 1% accuracy was obtained. The measured slope of
the ambiguity-function ridge was 2.94 MHz/19 μs = 0.1547 MHz/μs or
within 2.6% of the theoretical value.

Doppler shifts were also introduced between the two signals by
changing the starting frequency of the signal generator drive in the
AO cell. For a 200-kHz Doppler shift, the peak of the $\chi(0,\nu)$ function
should shift by a theoretical distance of 0.39 mm (for an optical system
with λ = 633 nm, f_L = 381 mm, and an output magnification factor of
5). Experimentally, translations of 0.37 mm were measured, with the
obtained accuracy limited by the nonflat field of the optical system at
the diffraction angles used. Range delays were also directly introduced
by varying the starting time of the signal. The measured τ delays in
the $\chi(\tau,0)$ output peaks were in excellent agreement with the theoretical
values.

The optical quality of the AO cell used in these data tests was not
optimized, nor were any extensive efforts made to optimize the optical
system itself. With these considerations, the system performance
obtained was quite good, and much better results can be expected with
a sufficient optical engineering effort.

This is an appropriate place at which to note that one of the major
component problems in present AO systems is the optical detector.
The parallel readout high-speed detector required in the modified
version of Fig. 11.1 is a case in point. For such 1-D outputs, several
candidate solutions exist. Litton Industries [35] has employed a detector system using 294 separate photodetectors for a spectrum analyzer application. Interconnection from the optical system to this photodiode array is achieved with fiber optics. Their most recent system
has achieved 5-μs response times and a 50-dB dynamic range. A
second detector technique that will be demonstrated late in 1982 by
Westinghouse [36] uses hybrid integration techniques to realize an
integrated detector array with various logic on the same chip. Extension of these techniques to 2-D arrays is not easy, but in general
optical systems with 2-D outputs employ time-integrating detectors.

11.5.2 Radar Ambiguity-Function Processor

An optical ambiguity function system for radar processing and analysis
[37,38] will now be discussed in some detail to provide a case-study
description of an alternative ambiguity-function system to the TPP of
Chap. 9. This system was the result of an effort whose intent was to
show what one could assemble (circa 1977, before the advent of the
TPP system architecture and the associated algorithms) with state-of-
the-art optical components without associated device development. The
resultant system combines AO and 2-D light modulator technology for
ambiguity function generation in a quite practical and realistic system
architecture.

Table 11.2 Design Specifications for the Real-Time Optical Ambiguity Function Processor

Parameter	Specification
TBWP	270,000
Bandwidth	150 MHz
Time resolution	7 ns
Time elements	900
Doppler resolution	530 Hz
Doppler elements	300
Reference change rate	30/s

The system specifics are summarized in Table 11.2. Most are self-explanatory. The waveform used is a pulse burst in which coded waveforms (such as a LFM) are sequentially transmitted in bursts. The TBWP of each burst is 900 (corresponding to a period of 6 μs and a signal bandwidth of 150 MHz). This yields the 900 range or time delay elements and the 6 μs/900 ≃ 7-ns time or range delay resolution noted. When a sequence of 300 such bursts is transmitted, a pulse burst waveform with the TBWP of the specified 900 × 300 = 270,000 results. Since Doppler information is obtained by integrating over the 300 successive bursts, 300 Doppler frequency channels and a Doppler resolution of $(300 \times 6 \ \mu s)^{-1} \simeq 530$ Hz results as specified in the table. The system was required to be fully real-time with no film used and with the ability to change the reference waveform at a rate of 30 frames/s under computer control.

A schematic diagram of the system (Fig. 11.10) shows that it consists of two parts [37]. The pulse compressor [Fig. 11.10(a)] is the SI AO correlator of Fig. 11.1 modified to include a real-time reference mask (an LCLV) and output optical heterodyne detection (not shown for simplicity). The second stage (Doppler processor) of Fig. 11.10(b) forms the 1-D vertical FT across the 300 output correlations of the 300 pulses in the pulse burst, as obtained from the time-history output from the first-stage photodetector. Let us now discuss each stage of the system in more detail.

We shall first consider the pulse compressor. This is a modified version of the SI AO correlator of Fig. 11.1 in which the contents of the input AO cell are imaged (with SSB filtering) onto the reference waveform (recorded on a liquid crystal). By denoting the input signals to the AO cell by g(t) and its transmittance by g(x − vt), the light distribution reflected from the LCLV is g(x − vt)h(x), where

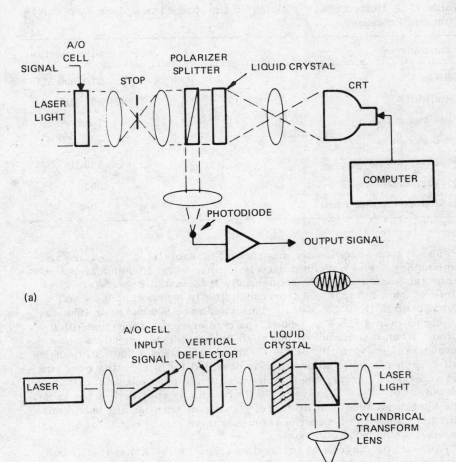

(a)

(b)

Figure 11.10 Schematic diagram of an optical radar ambiguity-function processor: (a) pulse compressor, (b) Doppler processor. (From Ref. 39.)

h(x) is the reference signal recorded on the liquid crystal. This signal product is integrated, and the correlation of g and h appears as the time-history output from the photodiode (as described in Sec. 11.2). Optical heterodyne detection on the output photodiode provides a complex-valued output with both the amplitude and phase of the correlation retained. When the received pulse burst radar signal is fed to the AO cell, the time output from the photodiode will be the correlation of the 300 pulses in the burst waveform with the reference signal, or a sequence of 300 correlation peaks. These correlation peaks will be separated in time by the reciprocal of the PRF of the signal (6 μs) and will be delayed in time (from the zero reference point) by the range delay τ_D of the target. To provide an adaptive reference waveform, the reference pattern h(x) written on the LCLV is obtained by continuously imaging a CRT (cathode-ray-tube) monitor display onto the reading (right-hand) side of the liquid crystal. The CRT is under computer control, thus allowing the reference waveform to be changed at the 30-frame/s rate of the CRT and LCLV.

We shall next consider the Doppler processor portion [Fig. 11.10(b)] of the system. To extract the Doppler information, recall that a target moving at constant velocity will result in a linear progression in the phase of the correlations of the 300 sequential pulses in the pulse burst. Thus, if the 1-D FT across these 300 complex correlations can be formed, the output light will be deflected by an amount proprotional to the linear phase progression and hence proportional to the target's Doppler velocity. The necessary 2-D signal formatting is achieved in the system of Fig. 11.10(b) by a combination of the snapshot AO addressing technique (Sec. 11.3) and a conventional AO deflector as follows.

The time-history output from the photodiode in Fig. 11.10(a) (corresponding to the complex correlations of the 300 sequential waveforms and the pulse burst) is fed directly to the AO cell in Fig. 11.10(b). The output of the laser in Fig. 11.10(b) is pulsed at a rep rate of 1/(6μs) (the reciprocal of the length of one pulse burst), with the duration of each output laser pulse satisfying (11.20). The snapshot AO recording technique in conjunction with a vertical AO deflector (operating at a deflection of one line every 6 μs in synchronization with the pulsed laser) thus allows an image of the correlation of the first pulse in the pulse burst to be recorded on the first line of a second liquid crystal, the correlation of the second pulse on the second line, etc. Thus, on the liquid crystal in Fig. 11.10(b), the 300 correlations from the pulse compressor of Fig. 11.10(a) are recorded on 300 different vertical lines. This liquid crystal pattern is then read out in reflection from the right-hand side in laser light as shown, and the 1-D vertical FT of the liquid crystal pattern is produced on the output display.

As noted earlier, the horizontal location of each of the correlation peaks corresponds to the target's range, and the vertical location of the FT across these correlation peaks corresponds to the target's

Doppler velocity. Thus, a $\chi(\tau, \nu)$ ambiguity-function output display results. When multiple targets are present, multiple peaks occur in the output with the (x,y) coordinates of each corresponding to the range and Doppler of the individual targets. A conventional 2-D vidicon output display, a pseudoisometric 3-D display, A-scope cross-sectional scans in range or Doppler, a real-time 2-D digitized output (from a 128 × 128 element solid-state detector), and a more exact (but slower read out) digitized output obtained by sequentially scanning a single photodiode with computer controlled x-y positioners are available in this system.

The choice of system architecture merits consideration from a practical viewpoint. The SI correlator system consists of imaging optics and an FT lens and thus does not require the interferometric stability of a conventional optical matched spatial filter correlator. The Doppler processor similarly consists of imaging optics, a vertical deflector with modest requirements, and a 1D-FT optical system. Thus, all system parts are quite stable, the resolution requirements and phase requirements on the 2-D SLMs are greatly reduced, and a most practical optical engineering ambiguity-function design results. This system was fabricated and demonstrated in full real-time operation by Ampex Corporation with most attractive performance [39].

The optical engineering of this system represents an excellent example of what can be assembled with off-the-shelf state-of-the-art optical components (circa 1977). Present technology, algorithm advances such as the chirp-z transform, and architectural advances such as the TPP system enable even higher-performance ambiguity-function processors to be fabricated today, with still more advanced performance possible in the near future.

The accuracy of this and any optical processor greatly resides with the digital control and interface systems used. To demonstrate this issue and to provide further details on the fabrication of this radar processor, we shall now discuss the minicomputer control system [38] associated with this processor with emphasis on the scan correction and timing features of the system. Other aspects of the digital support system are briefly noted for completeness.

Let us first consider the pulse compressor described by the more general hybrid optical-digital diagram of Fig. 11.11. To enable the system to be tested under well-controlled conditions, a radar signal generator was included. This consisted of a SAW device which produced an LFM output chirp in response to an input pulse. The number of chirps and their duration, center frequency, bandwidth, and repetition rate were controlled by the digital support system. Reference mask generation was also under computer and hardware control. In this part of the system, the desired reference radar waveform was computed and stored in a reference mask memory which then drove the CRT display through a video D/A converter under computer control. Pulse compression optimization was achieved by adjusting the reference

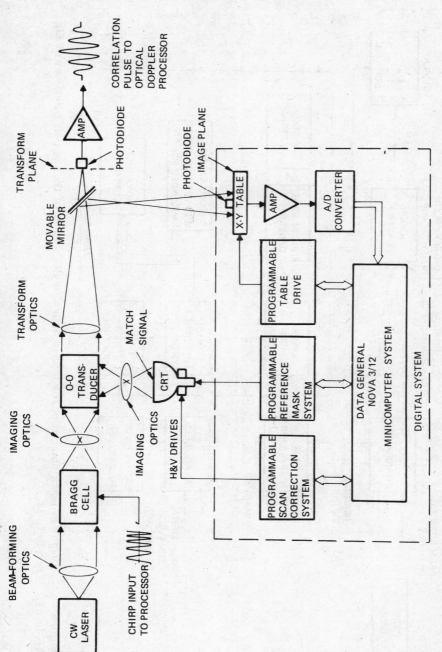

Figure 11.11 Simplified block diagram of the hybrid optical-digital aspect of the pulse compressor of Fig. 11.10(a). (From Ref. 38.)

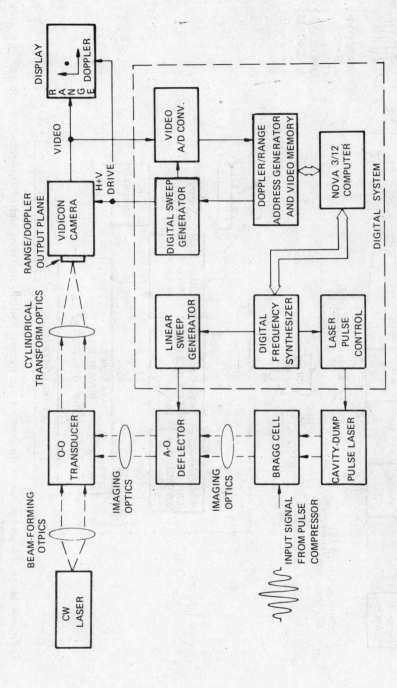

Figure 11.12 Simplified block diagram of the hybrid optical-digital aspect of the Doppler processor of Fig. 11.10(b). (From Ref. 38.)

mask parameters to optimize the correlation output for LFM test waveforms. These digital system control features are noted in the block
diagram of Fig. 11.11.

Let us now consider the CRT scan correction feature of this hybrid
processor. This is necessary to linearize the spatial response of the
optical pulse compressor. This is achieved by writing a set of reference marks from a reference mask memory on the CRT and imaging
the resultant pattern onto the x-y table shown in Fig. 11.11. This
table controls a single photodetector which scans the image plane to
provide an accurate map (after A/D conversion) of the resultant liquid
crystal image and hence the necessary information to allow system
linearity correction. This scan correction information is computed from
the image of the reference marks and transferred to a scan correction
memory, which is used to control the horizontal and vertical sweep
waveforms to the CRT. The above procedure is cyclically repeated
until system linearity is achieved. The associated system blocks are
shown in Fig. 11.11. The reference correction mask pattern is then
replaced by the desired radar waveform and the system can operate in
real time.

A simplified diagram of the hybrid optical-digital version of the
Doppler processor is shown in Fig. 11.12. The output ambiguity plane
data collection system includes a high-speed video A/D converter and
associated digitally controlled peripherals to allow a 2-D or pseudo-3-D
display of the output ambiguity surface or an operator-controlled
portion of it. The output detector system also allows an accurate digital
record of the selected ambiguity surface region to be recorded and
stored as a permanent or hard copy record. The timing associated
with the cavity-dumped laser source used in the Doppler processor
merits some expansion. This laser source must be pumped at its mode
locking frequency f_m and subsequently dumped by a short pulse modulated by a carrier at a frequency $f_c = f_m$. These signals control the
laser and snapshot AO cell. The digital system requires a frequency
of $0.1 f_c$, and the AO deflector requires frequencies of $0.75 f_m$.

The frequency f_c was thus chosen as the fundamental timing unit
because of environmental factors, and a digital frequency synthesizer
was used to provide this and other necessary signals. The digital
synthesizer uses a given frequency control number and clock source
to compute digital samples of the desired signal that are then fed to a
D/A converter and low-pass filter to provide the desired waveform.
The waveform to be synthesized is best viewed as a plot of amplitude
versus phase as a function of time. The amplitude of each discrete
phase point is determined from a lookup memory. It is then converted
to an analog value by the output D/A converter and fed through a low-
pass filter to the optical system. A phase accumulator provides the
key element in this waveform synthesis and timing control by accumulating the phase value at a rate related to the size of the digital control
word. When this phase value exceeds the capacity of the register, a

cycle is completed, and the rate of this overflow is used to obtain the synthesized frequency. A 200-MHz crystal oscillator was used as the absolute timing reference, and other necessary signals were produced by frequency division and appropriate SSB mixing of this signal.

This brief highlight summary of the digital support and control system for this optical processor provides one of the few available in-depth discussions associated with the fabrication of a fully automated, computer-controlled and corrected real-time optical processor.

11.6 SPREAD SPECTRUM COMMUNICATIONS

The basic SI and TI AO correlators described in previous chapters can be used for many of the ranging and message decoding applications noted in Sec. 11.2. They yield output correlations of good quality and accuracy, with the location of the correlation peak shifting proportional to the time of occurrence of reception of the signal and with the shape of the output correlation surface in good agreement with that predicted by theory. Because of the large computational burden associated with simultaneous determination of the range and Doppler of multiple targets, most AO correlator work has addressed incorporation of these transducers into larger systems for ambiguity-function generation. In Sec. 11.5, several of these AO ambiguity-function processors were discussed. The above remarks on the performance of the systems will be expanded in this later section.

In the present section, we shall describe two other types of AO correlators that demonstrate other system architectures and other operations that are achievable with such real-time transducers. These examples are included to show the growing flexibility of the operations achievable in real time on AO systems and to advance directions for future research. In the first example, a space-variant optical signal processor system, rather than the conventional space-invariant processor, is described. This system includes demonstration of the realization of an on-line coordinate transformation using an AO processor and its use in a nonlinear spread spectrum communication system. The second example describes a hybrid TSI AO correlator and its use in self-synchronization of long frequency-hopped coded waveforms for spread spectrum communications.

11.6.1 Space-Variant Processor

Linear system theory is used to describe most optical processors, and hence the operations achievable on these systems are restricted to linear shift-invariant functions. Considerable research has been devoted to extending the repertoire of operations achievable on optical systems [40]. Realization of space-variant optical systems is one method by which this increased flexibility can be achieved. Use of coordinate transformation preprocessing is one attractive technique by which space-variant optical systems can be realized [41-43]. Since such systems have direct use in optical signal processing and are realizable with AO technology, we shall restrict attention to this class of system in this section.

The basic philosophy in this type of space-variant processor is to correlate coordinate transformed versions of two signals rather than the original signals. Depending on the choice of the coordinate transformation used, the resultant correlation will be invariant to a selected type of signal deformation. A most attractive choice is an exponential coordinate transformation from $f(t)$ to $f_1(x) = f(\exp x)$. Consider two signals that differ in Doppler or scale. For simplicity, we describe them by $f(t)$ and $f'(t) = f(at)$. Applying the exp transformation we obtain $f_1(x)$ and $f'_1(x) = f(a \exp x)$. The correlation of these two coordinate transformed signals then yields [41]

$$R(\hat{x}) = f'_1(x) \circledast f_1(x) = f(\exp x) \circledast f(\exp x) \circledast \delta(\hat{x} - \ln a) \quad (11.31)$$

where x and $\hat{x}$ denote input and output coordinates. From equation (11.31), we see that the amplitude of the correlation remains constant even though a scale change is present between the original two functions. We also note that the correlation peak is located at coordinates proportional to the scale difference a. The FT of a logarithmic transformed function produces the Mellin transform of the original function and thus provides the above scale-invariant feature. The use of such a space-variant processor has been demonstrated for Doppler signal processing [41]. In such an application, a 1-D correlation allows one to automatically determine the target's velocity from the location of the correlation peak without the need for a multiple Doppler filter bank.

We shall now consider the system shown in block diagram form in Fig. 11.13 [42]. In this system, a conventional coded waveform $f(x)$ is coordinate-transformed prior to transmission. Upon reception, an inverse coordinate transformation is performed, and the resultant signal is then correlated with the original reference waveform. We first note that if $f(x) = \cos[\omega_0 x + \phi(x)]$, then the transmitted signal is

$$f_T(t) = \cos\{\omega_0 \ln(t + t_0) + \phi[\ln(t + t_0)]\} \quad (11.32)$$

where $t_0 > 0$ is a constant offset in the time reference that avoids the difficulty associated with implementing the log of zero. Inspection of equation (11.32) shows that the original carrier ω_0 has been nonlinearly spread by the log operation. This results in a nonlinear coded spread spectrum waveform with no carrier, thereby precluding its detection by spectrum analysis. Upon reception, the inverse transformation $t = \exp x - \hat{t}$ is applied to the received signal $f_R(t)$, where $\hat{t}$ is a delay variable that denotes that the transformation must be applied for all possible starting locations of the received signal. When this new $f_1(\hat{t},x) = f_T(\exp x - \hat{t})$ signal is correlated with $f(x)$ in a

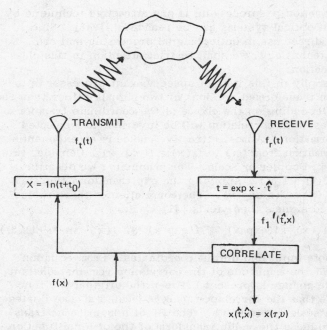

Figure 11.13 Block diagram of a space-variant signal processor.
(From Ref. 42.)

moving-window correlator, the time of occurrence $\hat{t}$ of the output correlation determines the target's range (or the synchronization time of the
signal in a communications application), and the spatial location x of
the correlation provides the target velocity information (or the Doppler
platform correction necessary in a communications application [42]
due to the Mellin transform operation performed).

An AO system to achieve the necessary receiver processing is shown
schematically in Fig. 11.14. The $P_1 - P_3$ portion of this system yields
the correlation of the input signal $f_R(t)$ and the reference function
h(x), whose FT is recorded on the mask at P_2. Let us for the moment
ignore the time-varying moving-window transducer at P_1 and assume
that a fixed signal $f_R(t) = f_R(x)$ is present at P_1. The 1-D FT lens
system $L_1 - L_2$ results in a multichannel correlation at P_3 given by
Σ_n f(x) ⊛ $h_n(x)$, where n denotes the channel and where the reference
function h at P_2 varies vertically in y as x = exp(y). When this pattern is evaluated along a vertical slit at P_3, we obtain the coordinate-
transformed output signal g(y) = f_R(exp y). When we now consider
the time-varying nature of the input AO transducer, we see that the
desired transformation is applied for each new $\hat{t}$ starting location of

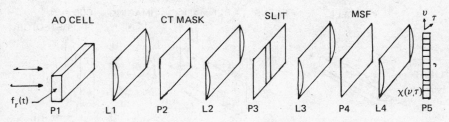

Figure 11.14 Schematic diagram of a space-variant AO spread spectrum signal processor.

the received signal [43]. This represents a quite unique use of AO transducers.

The remaining $P_3 - P_5$ portion of the system of Fig. 11.14 is a conventional matched spatial filter correlator, with the correlation pattern displayed along a linear vertical output detector array. The time-history output from such a detector array provides the desired 2-D space $\hat{x}$ and time $\hat{t}$ output from which the velocity and range of targets can be obtained. In spread spectrum systems in which platform motion and relative Doppler is not a problem, the time-history output from a single detector provides the necessary demodulation and hence the message information. This system was included to show how space-variant AO processors can be realized and how nonlinear data transformations can be achieved with existing AO components. The nonlinear spread spectrum communication system it produces offers improved processing gain, automatic Doppler correction, and improved immunity to detection of the existence of a transmission and determination of the code being used. These are all desirable features in secure communications and C^3I applications.

11.6.2 Hybrid TSI Processor

In Sec. 11.2, the need to synchronize long coded waveforms to obtain the full processing gain possible from the code being used was noted. Hybrid TSI AO systems that combine the advantages of the TI and SI architectures are of considerable use in such applications. We shall now describe one such system and its use in self-synchronization of a long frequency-hopped coded spread spectrum signal [10]. The TSI correlator is shown schematically in Fig. 11.15. It consists of an input AO cell whose contents are Fourier-transformed horizontally and expanded vertically to illuminate a fixed N-channel mask at P_2. The mask output is then imaged vertically and compressed horizontally onto a linear output shift register detector array.

We assume a chip duration T_c for each frequency in the frequency-hopped code and choose the aperture T_a of the AO cell to satisfy

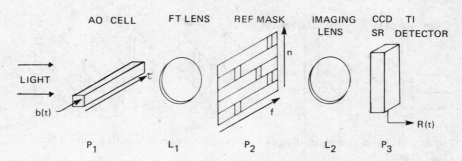

Figure 11.15 Schematic diagram of a hybrid time- and space-integrating AO processor for spread spectrum communications. (From Ref. 10.)

$T_a = T_c$ and the clock frequency f_c of the output shift register such that $f_c = 1/T_c$. A mask is placed at P_2 that contains one aperture on each horizontal channel n. The horizontal location of each aperture corresponds to the frequency f_n of the nth chip in the code. The output from the receiver is continuously fed to the AO cell, and the output shift register is continuously clocked at a rate f_c.

No output appears from the shift register detector until the transmitted signal enters the AO cell. Thus an infinite range delay search is possible as in the SI correlator. When the first chip at frequency f_1 enters the AO cell, its FT is incident on P_2. This FT will consist of a vertical line of light at a horizontal location corresponding to the frequency f_1. This pattern will pass through the aperture on the top row of the P_2 mask and illuminate the top detector element. When the second chip at frequency f_2 enters the AO cell, the aperture on the second row of the mask will pass light, which is then imaged onto the second output detector element. However, since the contents of the detector have now been shifted down at a rate f_c, the contents of the first and second detector elements will be added. This process continues for the N frequencies present in the code. At this time, a pulse appears at the output of the shift register detector that is the integrated sum of the contributions from all N chips in the code.

This combination of spatial integration by the lenses and temporal integration on the shift register detector thus provides a hybrid TSI correlator that self-synchronizes over very large range delays and demodulates transmitted messages of large time-bandwidth product. As a simple demonstration of the use of such a system a five-channel frequency-hopped code was chosen, and the associated mask was fabricated. In Fig. 11.16, the top trace shows the repetitive signal into the voltage controlled oscillator (VCO) driving the AO cell, and the lower trace shows the output from the shift register detector [10]. As shown, an output pulse occurs each time the five frequencies in the code are completed. Other tests on this system showed its ability

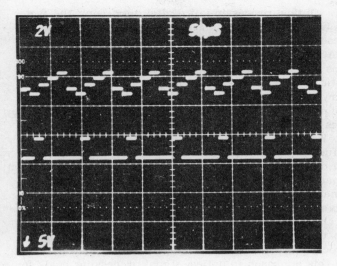

Figure 11.16 Real-time data from the system of Fig. 11.15: (a) VCO input, (b) shift register detector output correlations. (From Ref. 10.)

to discriminate against different codes and verified its performance against discrete frequency jammers.

11.7 SUMMARY AND CONCLUSION

In this chapter, a discussion of the necessary operations in electronic warfare, communications, ranging and simultaneous range, and Doppler signal processing was advanced and unified. Tutorial developments of the ambiguity function, the need for handling complex-valued data, and the methods by which such operations can be achieved were also advanced.

Several multidimensional AO systems that produce simultaneous frequency and DOA output displays with 100% intercept probability from single-pulse measurements were described together with a multi-channel FT system for Fourier spectroscopy that can be realized with one 1-D transducer. The parameter relationships for a folded spectrum processor and a new SI version of such a system using AO snapshot addressing were also included. These AO systems typify the advanced Bragg cell receiver systems and other system architectures that one can shortly expect to mature.

Two quite advanced AO correlator concepts demonstrating a space-variant AO signal processor and a hybrid TSI system were described as typical of what present research efforts might provide in future AO

signal processors. Optical processing of digital data using the fact
that the multiplication of two digital numbers is equivalent to the correlation of their coefficients [44], control of the wavelength of the
input light to an AO system as an added independent adjunct parameter in AO systems [45], and optical matrix-vector systolic systems
represent futuristic AO system processing concepts that deserve
mention in summary.

A passive ambiguity-function case study was then advanced to show
how AO techniques can be, have been, and are being applied to one
specific problem. We then concluded with a detailed description of a
radar ambiguity-function processor that combined AO snapshot addressing, 1-D AO deflectors, and 2-D light modulators into a practical,
fully automated and well-engineered real-time optical system with
digital control, analysis, and calibration.

This brief survey of some of the optical information-processing applications of new algorithms, architectures, devices, and AO systems
has clearly shown the advanced degree of sophistication and performance such processors have achieved, together with demonstrating
the bright future this approach to optical signal processing holds for
many practical problems and applications.

REFERENCES

1. C. Hoffman and A. Baron, *Microwave J.*, 24, Sept. 1980.
2. B. Elson, *Aviat. Week Space Technol.*, 101, Dec. 15, 1980.
3. W. Miceli, ed., Optical signal processing for C^3I, *Soc. Photo-Opt. Instrum. Eng. 209*, 1979.
4. B. Vatz, ed., Effective utilization of optics in radar, *Soc. Photo-Opt. Instrum. Eng. 185*, 1979.
5. R. C. Dixon, *Spread Spectrum Systems*, Wiley, New York, 1976.
6. T. Bader, *Appl. Opt. 18*:1668, 1979.
7. T. Bader, *Soc. Photo-Opt. Instrum. Eng. 185*:140, 1979.
8. T. Bader, *Soc. Photo-Opt. Instrum. Eng. 232*:82, 1980.
9. D. Psaltis and D. Casasent, *Appl. Opt. 18*:163, 1979.
10. D. Psaltis and D. Casasent, *Appl. Opt. 19*:1546, 1980.
11. A. Rihaczek, *Principles of High Resolution Radar*, McGraw-Hill, New York, 1969.
12. C. Thomas, *Appl. Opt. 5*:1782, 1966.
13. B. Markevich, *Third Annu. Wide Band Recording Symp.*, RADC, April 1969.
14. D. Casasent and R. Kessler, *Opt. Commun. 15*:242, 1976.
15. P. Peltzman, P. Goldstein, and R. Battagin, *Am. J. Obstet. Gynecol. 115*:1117, 1973.
16. K. Preston, *Coherent Optical Computers*, McGraw-Hill, New York, 1972.

17.   D. Casasent, in *Optical Data Processing: Applications* (D. Casasent, ed.), Springer, Berlin, 1978, Chap. 8.
18.   M. Noble, *International Optical Computing Conference*, 1978, p. 5 (IEEE Catalog Number 78CH1305-2C).
19.   J. Anderson, H. Brown, and B. Markevich, *Soc. Photo-opt. Instrum. Eng. 180*:128, 1979.
20.   W. Bleha et al., *Opt. Eng. 17*:371, 1978.
21.   R. Coppock and R. Croce, *Soc. Photo-Opt. Instrum. Eng. 214*:124, 1979.
22.   G. A. Vanesse, ed., Multiplex and/or high-throughput Fourier spectroscopy, *Soc. Photo-Opt. Instrum. Eng. 191*, 1979.
23.   J. Goodman, A. Dias, and L. Woody, *Opt. Lett. 2*:1, 1978.
24.   D. Casasent and D. Psaltis, *Appl. Opt. 19*:2034, 1980.
25.   L. Cutrona, E. Leith, C. Palermo, and L. Porcello, *IRE IT-6*:386, 1960.
26.   D. Casasent, *Proc. IEEE 65*:143, 1977.
27.   *EASCON 1979 Conference Record*, 1979, (IEEE Catalog Number 79CH1476).
28.   D. Casasent and B. Kumar, *Appl. Opt. 18*:1673, 1979.
29.   D. Casasent and B. Kumar, *EASCON 1979 Conference Record*, 1979, p. 595 (IEEE Catalog Number 79CH1476).
30.   D. Casasent and T. Luu, *Appl. Opt. 18*:3307, 1979.
31.   R. Said and D. Cooper, *Proc. IEE 120*:423, 1973.
32.   J. Rao, *J. Opt. Soc. Am. 57*:798, 1967.
33.   P. Tamura, J. Rebholz, and T. C. Lee, *Opt. Lett. 5*:401, 1980.
34.   C. Cook and M. Bernfeld, *Radar Signals*, Academic Press, New York, 1967.
35.   J. Zablotney and M. Price, *Soc. Photo-Opt. Instrum. Eng. 185*:163, 1979.
36.   G. Borsuk, *Proc. IEEE 69*:100, 1981.
37.   H. Brown and B. Markevich, *Soc. Photo-Opt. Instrum. Eng. 128*:204, 1977.
38.   S. Nobel, T. Marsh, W. Pearson, S. Smader, J. Anderson, H. Brown, and B. Vatz, *Soc. Photo-Opt. Instrum. Eng. 148*:8, 1978.
39.   *Aviation Week and Space Technology* (cover), May 22, 1978.
40.   J. Goodman, *Proc. IEEE 65*:29, 1977.
41.   D. Casasent and D. Psaltis, in *Progress in Optics*, Vol. XVI (E. Wolf, ed.), North-Holland, Amsterdam, 1978, pp. 291-356.
42.   D. Psaltis and D. Casasent, *Appl. Opt. 18*:1869, 1979.
43.   P. Kellman and J. Goodman, *Appl. Opt. 16*:2609, 1977.
44.   J. Trimble et al., *Soc. Photo-Opt. Instrum. Eng. 241*, 1980.
45.   W. Rhodes, ed., 1980 International Optical Computing Conference, *Soc. Photo-Opt. Instrum, Eng. 231, 232*, 1980.

IV
INTEGRATED OPTICS

Preface

A determining factor in the widespread utilization of acousto-optic
signal-processing devices will be the compactness and ruggedness of
the total device structure. Advances in obtaining coherent CW (continuous-wave) laser sources, e.g., gallium aluminum arsenide laser
diodes, coupled with advances in detector postprocessing technology
have resulted in decreased size; however, miniaturization in the optical
circuit itself must also be achieved. An approach using bulk optics,
referred to as the *minibench* approach, was discussed in Chap. 4. A
much more radical technique exists which is referred to as *integrated
optics*. In this approach optical waveguides are formed in the surface region of SAW (surface-acoustic-wave) devices, which together
with lenses ground into (or deposited onto) the surface, comprise entire acousto-optical circuits. These circuits together with laser diodes
and detector arrays can implement powerful acousto-optic signal-processing algorithms. The final part discusses the new technology of
integrated optics as it is applied to acousto-optical signal processing.
A theoretical discussion of guided optical waves is given together with
current experimental results. Various different acousto-optical devices
are discussed with special emphasis on the integrated-optic spectrum
analyzer, an ultraminiaturized Bragg cell.

12
Integrated Optics

D. MERGERIAN and E. C. MALARKEY / Westinghouse Electric
Corporation, Advanced Technology Division, Baltimore, Maryland

12.1 INTRODUCTION

The term *integrated optics* (IO) was coined in 1969 and refers to the
use of guided wave optics in thin-film optical waveguides to process
and handle information signals [1]. Analogous to the more commonly
known term *integrated circuits* (IC) which is applied to miniaturized
versions of electronic circuits, IO implies miniaturization relative to
conventional bulk optical systems which utilize classical optical components such as lenses, mirrors, and prisms and generally use the
atmosphere as the transmission medium. In IO, the transmission
medium is a thin-film optical waveguide which acts through the principle of total internal reflection to confine the optical carrier into
either a plane or a narrow strip. This confined carrier beam can be
operated upon using waveguide components which perform the role of
conventional lenses, prisms, mirrors, or electro-optic or acousto-
optic elements to achieve complex signal-processing functions such as
Fourier transformation, modulation, switching, and logic operations.

This chapter, being the final one in a text on acousto-optical signal processing, will be devoted to conveying the concepts involved in
using optical guided wave technology to perform many of the same operations treated using conventional optics in the previous chapters.
This technology surfaced during the late 1960s and early 1970s primarily in relation to fiber optic systems being developed for use in
optical communication lines. As a result, much of the early work in
this field was performed at the Bell Telephone Laboratories addressing
applications such as repeaters, switches, and multiplexers [2-4].

More recent efforts have been concentrated on the performance of
operations such as convolution, correlation, spectrum analysis, and
beam deflection, which are of considerable interest for military systems
applications. With this added impetus, rapid progress has been made

over the past five years and has led to the recent successful demonstration of the first complex hybrid IO circuit, an RF spectrum analyzer
[5]. Devices of this nature offer significant advantages over both
digital signal-processing devices and bulk optical processors. These
advantages center about the ability to handle very large amounts of
data in very complex signal environments in near real time with devices
which are small, rugged, lightweight, reliable, and less expensive, and
which consume little power.

Present IO device technology is based primarily on the development
of hybrid structures in which separate optical sources and detectors
are coupled to the waveguide using either butt, end-fire, or prism
coupling techniques. IO devices may eventually be realized in a truly
integrated format with the further development of such materials as
GaAs in which monolithic laser sources and detector elements may be
coupled to the waveguide on the same chip [6-7]. This chapter will
concern itself primarily with the hybrid-type structures which are
considered to be significantly further along in the development cycle
than are their monolithic counterparts.

This treatment has been prepared primarily for the systems engineer
who is not a specialist in the field of optics. It, therefore, begins with
a review of optical principles of importance in optical waveguide technology, including total internal reflection, evanescent wave effects,
dielectric waveguides, optical waveguide modes, and electro-optic and
acousto-optic interactions. Following this is a discussion of IO components which includes waveguides, lenses, mirrors, prisms, beam
splitters, sources, detectors,and surface-acoustic-wave transducers.
The final portion of this chapter is then devoted to a discussion of IO
devices and device concepts and features a detailed treatment of the
RF spectrum analyzer, including its design rationale, its performance
characteristics, and its ultimate limitations.

12.2 DIELECTRIC WAVEGUIDES

12.2.1 Total Internal Reflection

The physical principle on which integrated optics is based is the concept of total internal reflection of an optical beam incident upon the
interface between two dielectric media of differing refractive indices
from the direction of the denser medium, as shown in Fig. 12.1. Snell's
law of refraction states that

$$n_1 \sin \theta_1 = n_2 \sin \theta_2 \tag{12.1}$$

where θ_1 and θ_2, the angles of incidence and refraction, respectively,
lie in the plane of incidence and are measured from the normal to the
interface between the two media. If $n_1 < n_2$, every value of θ_1 will
produce a corresponding refracted beam in the denser medium which

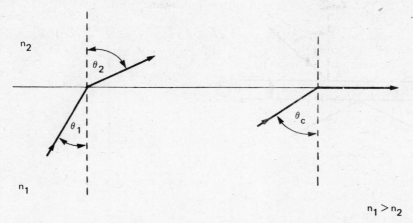

$n_1 > n_2$

Figure 12.1 Refraction of a light ray in passing from a high-index medium n_1 to a lower-index medium n_2 at (a) an angle less than the critical angle θ_c and (b) at the critical angle.

makes an angle θ_2 with respect to the normal. When $n_1 > n_2$, there exists a value of θ_1 for which sin θ_2 equals unity. This value of θ_1, given by

$$\theta_c = \sin^{-1} \frac{n_2}{n_1} \qquad\qquad (12.2)$$

is referred to as the critical angle, and it represents the case where the refracted beam travels at a grazing angle to the interface. At all angles of incidence $\theta_1 > \theta_c$ there is no resultant refracted beam since sin θ_2 cannot exceed unity, and all the energy incident upon the interface must be reflected back into the high-index medium, with a change in phase which is dependent on the angle of incidence. Integrated optics, as does fiber optics, makes use of this phenomenon to confine an optical beam in a high-index medium bounded by lower-index media. Such a structure is referred to as an optical waveguide.

The energy in the totally reflected wave is exactly equal to that in the incident wave, and there is no average flow of energy into the less dense medium. The electric field intensity in the rarer medium, however, is not zero because there is instantaneous energy flow through the surface even though the time-averaged value is zero. The electric field decreases exponentially with increasing distance from the interface while remaining constant (propagating unattenuated) along the interface. The exponentially decreasing field normal to the interface is referred to as an evanescent wave. A detailed treatment of the origin and characteristic behavior of evanescent waves can be found

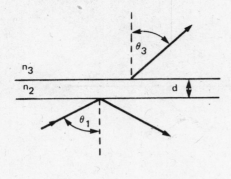

$$n_1 \text{ AND } n_3 > n_2$$
$$\theta_1 > \theta_c$$
$$\text{AND } d \sim \lambda$$

Figure 12.2 Excitation of a transmitted wave in a medium of index n_3 by an evanescent wave which exists in the lower-index medium n_2 upon total internal reflection of a beam incident at an angle θ_1 on the n_1, n_2 interface.

in textbooks on physical optics [8] and optical waveguides [9-11]. For the purposes of this treatment we need only point out that the amplitude of an evanescent wave propagating along the z axis, which will be set parallel to the interface, can be written as

$$A = A_0 \exp(-ik_2 x) \exp i(\omega t - \beta z) \qquad (12.3)$$

where x is the coordinate perpendicular to the interface, $k_2 = 2\pi n_2/\lambda$ is the wave vector, ω is the angular frequency, and $\beta = k_2 \sin \theta$. If, as shown in Fig. 12.2, a material with index $n_3 > n_2$ is brought into close proximity to the interface, the evanescent wave can excite a transmitted wave traveling at θ_3, again given by Snell's law, in the medium of index n_3. The energy in the evanescent field will couple into the higher-index medium with a net decrease being observed in the intensity of the reflected beam. The intensity in the new medium is strongly dependent on the thickness of the low-index medium which separates the two high-index media and on the refractive indices involved. The properties of evanescent waves are of considerable importance in prism coupling of an optical beam into a waveguide.

12.2.2 Waveguides for Integrated Optics

Waveguides for use in integrated optics can be classified as belonging
to either of two general categories. So-called planar waveguides confine the guided radiation in only one direction [Fig. 12.3(a)]. Those
in the second category, referred to as channel waveguides, confine
guided radiation in two directions, as shown in Fig. 12.3(b). In
Sec. 12.2.2.1 we shall concentrate on the planar type of waveguide
and shall discuss different types of planar guides as well as the
general properties of waveguide modes. In Sec. 12.2.2.2 we shall discuss various types of channel waveguides and techniques employed in
their fabrication.

12.2.2.1 Planar Waveguides

Planar waveguides consist of a high-index medium sandwiched between
two lower-index media, with the transverse dimensions of the waveguide considered as being infinitely greater than its thickness. In

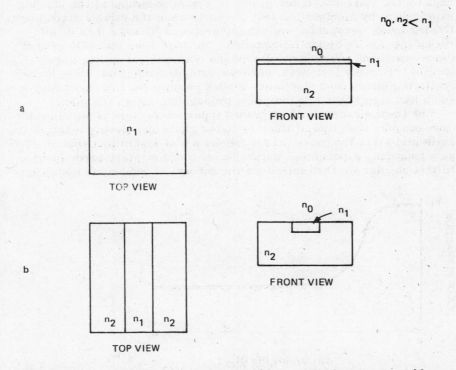

Figure 12.3 Integrated optical waveguides: (a) planar waveguides,
(b) channel waveguides.

general, the transverse dimensions in such a waveguide are determined by the macroscopic dimensions of the substrate material. If the two low-index materials n_0 and n_2 of Fig. 12.3(a) are of equal refractive index, the waveguide is referred to as symmetric, and if these indices are not equal, the waveguide is asymmetric. Most of the waveguides employed in integrated optics are of this latter variety with $n_1 > n_2 > n_0$.

One additional criterion which can be used in classifying optical waveguides is the refractive index profile within the guiding layer. If the waveguide is formed by two or three different media such that $n_1 > n_0$, n_2, it is called a *step index* guide since there are relatively distinct *step* boundaries between the different media. Waveguides can also be formed by techniques which result in gradual change in index, as depicted in Fig. 12.4. These are called *graded index* guides since there exists a high-index region from which the index decreases, usually in monotonic fashion, in either one or both directions until it assumes the index of the substrate or superstrate medium. The path followed by an optical ray in a graded index waveguide is gradually bent by the refractive index profile in a manner similar to the bending experienced by sunlight incident obliquely upon the earth's atmosphere. Graded index waveguides are usually prepared by some form of diffusion process or by ion implantation, and they have smoothly graded index variations which generally extend over several optical wavelengths. In many instances, such waveguides exhibit markedly lower scattering losses than step index guides because the interfaces play a much less significant role in optical propagation within the guide.

The theoretical analysis of graded index waveguides is significantly more complex than that of the step index guide and usually involves the assumption that the index profile follows a well-known distribution such as a gaussian, exponential, parabolic, or complementary error function. In this chapter we shall introduce the concept of waveguide modes in

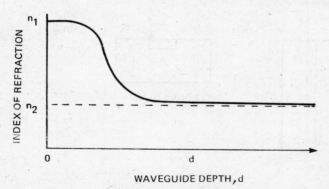

Figure 12.4 Refractive index profile as a function of waveguide depth in a graded index waveguide.

the simplest possible manner, namely, in idealized planar, step index, guides.

Several advanced treatments dealing with the properties of guided modes in graded index waveguides have been published, and the reader desiring a more thorough understanding of the theoretical detail of such guides is referred to these [12-15].

If a waveguide is irradiated with incoherent, polychromatic light, the guide will propagate this radiation over a continuum of reflection angles extending from the critical angle for the shortest wavelength constituent of the beam to $\theta_{inc} = 90°$ where the beam travels parallel to the plane of the waveguide. Such a beam would show no interference effects at the output end of the guide because all the waves making up the beam would have random phases and amplitudes. If, on the other hand, the incident beam is coherent, it will be possible to observe such interference effects, but it will no longer be sufficient to describe the behavior of the light in the guide by employing a geometrical or ray optical analysis. Instead, it is necessary to utilize a physical optics approach which consists of a superposition of a set of waves which propagate within the guide. The simplest solutions of Maxwell's equations are uniform plane waves such as those observed when light is radiated from a distant source and propagates without encountering any scattering sources or boundaries. Since it is possible to represent any source-free solution of Maxwell's equations as a superposition of uniform plane waves, these waves become very useful tools in describing wave phenomena in optical waveguides.

If an optical waveguide is illuminated by a coherent source, the light will propagate through the waveguide only at certain angles of incidence on the boundaries of the guide. Every such *allowed* angle of incidence which is propagated by the guide corresponds to a guided mode for that specific waveguide with its characteristic refractive indices and dimensions.

To indicate the manner in which waveguide modes are determined, it is convenient to consider a waveguide consisting of two parallel conducting metal planes of infinite conductivity which are separated by a uniform dielectric of index n and thickness d. We shall adopt the convention that the electromagnetic wave propagates along the z direction with the x direction corresponding to the thickness of the waveguiding layer and the y direction corresponding to the traverse direction in the plane of the waveguide. For a planar waveguide, y can be assumed to be infinite in comparison to the waveguide thickness. A polarized uniform plane wave which is incident on the waveguide boundary at an angle θ to the normal with its electric vector perpendicular to the plane of incidence (Fig. 12.5) will have a total electric field which is the superposition of two plane waves, one incident upon and the other reflected from one of the conducting planes. This total electric field will be given by

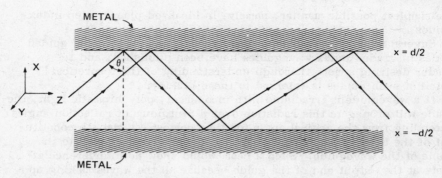

Figure 12.5 Optical waveguide formed by two plane parallel metallic plates.

$$E_z = E_x = 0$$

$$E_y = E_0 \sin (hx) \exp(i\omega t - i\beta z)$$

(12.4)

where E_0 is a complex-valued constant, ω is the angular frequency, and h and β are the transverse and longitudinal propagation constants given by $h = k \cos \theta$ and $\beta = k \sin \theta$. Since the electric field must vanish at the two conducting planes which define the waveguide, we see that once k $(=2\pi n/\lambda)$ and d have been specified, only certain values of θ such that the term $\sin (hx)$ in equation (12.4) will vanish at the boundaries $x = \pm d/2$, will be permitted. Any other value of θ will violate the boundary condition. If the waveguide thickness is allowed to increase, we see that an increasing number of guided modes of differing θ will be permitted such that

$$\frac{h_N d}{2} = \frac{\pi nd}{\lambda} \cos \theta = N\pi$$

(12.5)

where N is an integer. The modes are said to be symmetric if N is odd and antisymmetric where N is even. The first two symmetric and antisymmetric mode field profiles are shown in Fig. 12.6. Equation (12.5) is a simple relation between the waveguide thickness and the allowed angles for propagation, and we observe that each time the guide thickness d increases by a half wavelength, another mode will be propagated by the waveguide.

The modes described in this case had their electric vector polarized perpendicular to the plane of incidence, and they are referred to as transverse electric (TE) modes. They are also called H waves since they have a nonvanishing component of the magnetic field in the direction of propagation along the axis of the guide. A transverse magnetic (TM) mode or E wave is polarized such that the magnetic

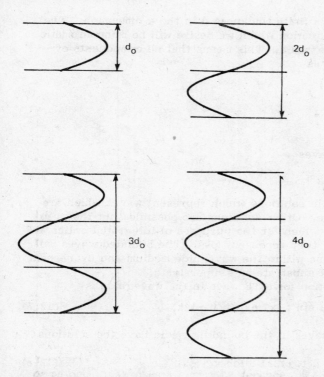

Figure 12.6 First two symmetric and antisymmetric waveforms for the metallic waveguide depicted in Fig. 12.5.

vector is perpendicular to the plane of incidence and the electric field has a component along the axis of the waveguide. The TM modes satisfy the same relations as the TE modes so that modes are degenerate and propagate in the guide with the same phase velocity.

Next we shall consider a more realistic integrated optical waveguide where the two conducting planes used to form the guide discussed above are replaced by low-index dielectric media. In this case the light will propagate by virtue of total internal reflection, as discussed earlier in Sec. 12.2.1.

We now seek solutions of the general wave equation

$$\nabla^2 \overline{E} = -\mu \, \varepsilon \left(i - \frac{i\sigma}{\omega \, \varepsilon} \right) \frac{\partial^2 \overline{E}}{\partial t^2} = 0 \tag{12.6}$$

where ε is the dielectric constant of the material, σ its conductivity, and μ its magnetic permeability. To simplify the example we shall treat a case where the lower-index media on both sides are identical and the waveguide has a finite thickness d in the x dimension. The solutions to the wave equation which we desire will be monochromatic plane waves in all three media. This means that all components of both E and H will vary as

$$E, H \propto \exp(i\omega t - i\beta z)$$

For TE waves

$$E_x = E_z = H_y = 0$$

and similarly for TM waves

$$H_x = H_z = E_y = 0$$

We are interested only in solutions which represent waves which are bound to the waveguide. Other solutions are possible, but they represent radiating modes which for the purposes of integrated optics are of interest only in that they represent loss. The bounded waves will have oscillating solutions within the waveguide medium and evanescent tails in the lower-index substrate and superstrate.

Such a general solution for a TE wave in the waveguide is

$$E_y = (A \cos h_1 x + B \sin h_1 x) \exp(i\omega t - i\beta z) \tag{12.7}$$

while the evanescent waves in the bounding media have the solutions

$$E_y = C \exp(-h_2 x + i\omega t - i\beta z) \quad \text{for } x > \frac{d}{2} \tag{12.8}$$

and

$$E_y = D \exp(ih_2 x + i\omega t - i\beta z) \quad \text{for } x < \frac{d}{2} \tag{12.9}$$

where h_1 and h_2 represent the transverse propagation constants in the guide and bounding media, respectively.

The magnetic fields H_z and H_x can be obtained from Maxwell's equation:

$$\overline{\nabla} \times \overline{E} = -\mu_0 \frac{\partial \overline{H}}{\partial t} \tag{12.10}$$

We find that

$$H_x = \frac{1}{i\omega\mu_0} \frac{\partial E_y}{\partial z} \tag{12.11}$$

and

$$H_z = -\frac{1}{i\omega\mu_0} \frac{\partial E_y}{\partial x} \tag{12.12}$$

The constants A, B, C, and D can be determined from the boundary conditions which require that both E_y and H_z be continuous at $x = \pm d/2$.

The symmetric TE modes inside the waveguide can be shown to have the form

$$
\left.
\begin{aligned}
E_y &= A \cos(h_1 x) \exp(i\omega t - i\beta z) \\[2mm]
H_x &= -\frac{\beta}{\omega \mu_0} E_y \\[2mm]
H_z &= -\frac{ih_1}{\omega \mu_0} E_y \tan(h_1 x)
\end{aligned}
\right\} \quad \text{for } |x| \leqslant \frac{d}{2}
\qquad (12.13)
$$

and in the lower-index media

$$
\left.
\begin{aligned}
E_y &= A \exp \left| \pm \frac{ih_2 d}{2} \right| \cos \frac{h_1 d}{2} \\[1mm]
&\quad \times \exp(\mp ih_2 x + i\omega t - i\beta z) \\[2mm]
H_x &= \frac{\beta}{\omega \mu_0} E_y \\[2mm]
H_z &= \pm \frac{h_2}{\omega \mu_0} E_y
\end{aligned}
\right\} \quad \text{for } |x| \geqslant \frac{d}{2}
\qquad (12.14)
$$

where the upper sign applies for $x > d/2$ and the lower for $x < -d/2$. Similarly, the antisymmetric TE modes are given by

$$
\left.
\begin{aligned}
E_y &= A \sin(h_1 x) \exp(i\omega t - i\beta z) \\[2mm]
H_x &= -\frac{\beta}{\omega \mu_0} E_y \\[2mm]
H_z &= \frac{ih_1}{\omega \mu_0} E_y \cot(h_1 x)
\end{aligned}
\right\} \quad \text{for } |x| \leqslant \frac{d}{2}
\qquad (12.15)
$$

and

$$
\left.
\begin{aligned}
E_y &= \pm A \exp \left| \pm i \frac{h_2 d}{2} \right| \sin \frac{h_1 d}{2} \\[1mm]
&\quad \times \exp(\mp ih_2 x + i\omega t - i\beta z) \\[2mm]
H_x &= -\frac{\beta}{\omega \mu_0} E_y \\[2mm]
H_z &= -\frac{h_2}{\omega \mu_0} E_y
\end{aligned}
\right\} \quad \text{for } |x| \geqslant \frac{d}{2}
\qquad (12.16)
$$

Mergerian and Malarkey

For additional details with regard to these expressions for the guided modes as well as for a discussion of the lossy modes of the guide the reader is referred to the text by Kapany and Burke [9].

Although a full understanding of the modes of a dielectric waveguide requires this type of physical optics treatment, considerable insight into the modal properties can be garnered from a ray optics formalism [2,10,11]. To this end we can consider a guide such as that depicted in Fig. 12.5 but with the metallic bounding media replaced by dielectrics of indices n_0 and n_2. A ray traveling so that it strikes the boundaries at an angle $\theta > \theta_c$ to the normal has a horizontal propagation constant given by $\beta = k_1 \sin \theta$. In addition it will undergo a phase shift upon each total internal reflection of $-2\phi_{1,0}$ or $-2\phi_{1,2}$ where ϕ is given for TE polarization by

$$\phi_{1,m} = \tan^{-1} \frac{(n_1^2 \sin^2 \theta - n_m^2)^{1/2}}{n_1 \cos \theta} \qquad m = 0,2 \qquad (12.17)$$

The corresponding expression for TM polarization has an additional factor of n_1^2/n_m^2 in the argument of the arctangent. A stable propagating mode of the system must have its phase reproduced after each complete zigzag traversal of the guide, and, since the phase shift in a one-way passage across the guide is $k_1 d \cos \theta$, this leads to a condition for a stable mode of order ℓ,

$$2k_1 d \cos \theta_\ell - 2\phi_{1,0} - 2\phi_{1,2} = 2\ell\pi \qquad (12.18)$$

where θ_ℓ is the propagation angle of the mode of order ℓ and d is the guide thickness. Given appropriate values of the indices of refraction and the waveguide thickness, equations (12.17) and (12.18) can be used to specify exactly the propagation angles of each of the possible modes of a slab waveguide system; conversely, measurement of each of the propagation angles of a multimode waveguide by means of prism or grating coupling into these modes allows the guide thickness and the relevant refractive indices to be calculated to a high degree of accuracy.

It can be shown, moreover [10], that the range of allowable horizontal propagation constants is bounded by

$$k_2 < \beta < k_1 \qquad (12.19)$$

and it is customary to define an effective index of refraction for each guided mode as

$$n_\ell^{eff} = \frac{\beta_\ell}{k} = n_1 \sin \theta_\ell \qquad (12.20)$$

where $k = 2\pi/\lambda$. Graphical or numerical solution of (12.18) for a symmetric slab waveguide ($n_0 = n_2$) shows that there is always at least one solution; thus, a symmetric waveguide will support at least the fundamental mode even as the thickness becomes extremely small. An asymmetric guide, on the other hand, exhibits a definite cutoff frequency for each thickness (or a definite cutoff thickness for each frequency). Following Kogelnik [11], we can define a normalized frequency and film thickness V for the case $n_2 > n_0$ by

$$V = kd(n_1^2 - n_2^2)^{1/2} \tag{12.21}$$

and a measure of the waveguide asymmetry by

$$a = \frac{n_2^2 - n_0^2}{n_1^2 - n_2^2} \tag{12.22}$$

Then, by using (12.17) and (12.18) for TE modes, the cutoff frequency of the fundamental mode ($\ell = 0$) becomes

$$V_0 = \tan^{-1} \sqrt{a} \tag{12.23}$$

or

$$\left(\frac{d}{\lambda}\right)_0 = \frac{1}{2\pi} (n_1^2 - n_2^2)^{-1/2} \tan^{-1} \sqrt{a} \tag{12.24}$$

The cutoff frequencies of higher-order modes are given by

$$V_\ell = V_0 + \ell \pi \qquad \ell = 1, 2, \ldots \tag{12.25}$$

The number of modes which can be supported by a waveguide is given approximately by

$$m = \frac{2d}{\lambda} (n_1^2 - n_2^2)^{1/2} \tag{12.26}$$

12.2.2.2 Channel Waveguides

The planar waveguides discussed above do not confine the light in the plane of the waveguide. For certain applications, such as high-speed switches and integrated optical interferometry, it is desirable to achieve such confinement. This can be realized by a variety of techniques which lead to guides in which the high-index material is surrounded on all four sides by lower-index material. Several different types of channel waveguides are sketched in Fig. 12.7. Figure 12.7(a) shows an embossed or rib guide which is formed by depositing the high-index material in the form of a planar waveguide, usually by sputtering, and subsequently removing the material from the two sides by etching or

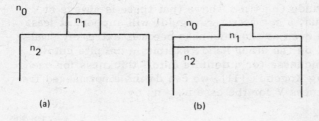

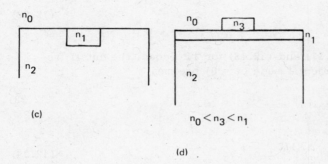

$$n_0 < n_3 < n_1$$

(d)

Figure 12.7 Four types of integrated optical channel waveguides.

reverse sputtering. If all the material is not removed, as depicted in
Fig. 12.7(b), a ridge waveguide is formed. Ridge guides have less
stringent tolerances on the waveguide edge quality than the embossed
guide. The remaining material at the two sides of the guide is generally of sufficient thickness to support at least one waveguide mode.

Figure 12.7(c) shows an embedded strip waveguide which can be
formed by diffusion of a narrow strip of material or by ion implantation
through a photolithographic mask to form a higher-index strip in the
lower-index substrate. These techniques produce a graded index
profile which can be very effective in providing a low-scattering, efficient channel waveguide.

The stripline guide shown in Fig. 12.7(d) is formed by applying a
low-index strip over a planar waveguide. Since the strip of index n_3
provides a region in which the index difference $n_1 - n_3 < n_1 - n_0$,
more of the energy in the guided mode will be transmitted in the lower-
index medium. This can result in improving the transmission of the
guide as well as in confining the guided light in the transverse direction. The use of a stripline guide again relaxes the tolerances placed
on the smoothness of the sides of the waveguide.

Theoretical analysis of channel waveguides is considerably more complex than that of planar guides and is not covered in most texts dealing with integrated optics. Exact solutions for the modes in two-dimensional guides have not been derived; however, an early treatment by Goell [16] using a circular harmonic computer analysis produced results which provide the propagation constants and mode patterns in these guides. Marcatili [17] developed an approximate analysis of homogeneous rectangular channels which yields accurate results if the modes are sufficiently far from cutoff that the fields are strongly confined to the high-index core region and there is minimal propagation in the evanescent tails. In a subsequent publication [18], he treated the case of a stripline guide, again obtaining approximate solutions, and more recently Yeh et al. [19] described the use of a finite-element technique to solve the same problem. They compared their results to those of Goell and Marcatili as well as to those of Furuta et al. [20], who used an effective index technique to obtain dispersion curves for these guides, and Ohtaka et al. [21], who used a vector variational method. Excellent agreement was seen with all but Marcatili's results where differences occur especially as the low-frequency cutoff is approached. The effective-index method, first introduced by Knox and Toulios [22], has also been used by Ramaswamy [23], Hocker [24], and Hocker and Burns [25] to modify Marcatili's results near cutoff and to analyze the behavior of both stripline and diffused channel waveguides. If these analytical methods are applied at frequencies well above cutoff, they all provide useful results which describe the field distributions of the modes, the propagation constants, and the dispersion curves.

Analyses of propagation in two-dimensional optical waveguides have been extended to include radiation losses from the guide as a function of bending radius in cases where the channel changes direction. Original work in this area was performed by Marcatili [26], with numerous theoretical modifications to his analysis having been made by Kuester and Chang [27], Marcuse [28,29], Taylor [30,31], and others. Experimental results for Ti-diffused $LiNbO_3$ channels reported by Hutcheson et al. [32] show that losses exceed 5 dB for two corner bend angles of about 1° and approach 40 dB/cm in short S bends having radii of curvature of 1 cm. More recently, however, Johnson and Leonberger [33] have employed the concept of coherent coupling, originally proposed by Taylor [30,31], to effect great reductions in bending losses in similar waveguides. They report having achieved a loss of only 6 dB in propagation through a 1.1-cm length of channel guide consisting of 60 abrupt 1° bends, each separated by 180 µm to form a structure with an effective radius of curvature of 1 cm. They also experimented with multisectioned coupled bends of the type shown in Fig. 12.8(a) and observed the results shown in Fig. 12.8(b) for two through six such bends.

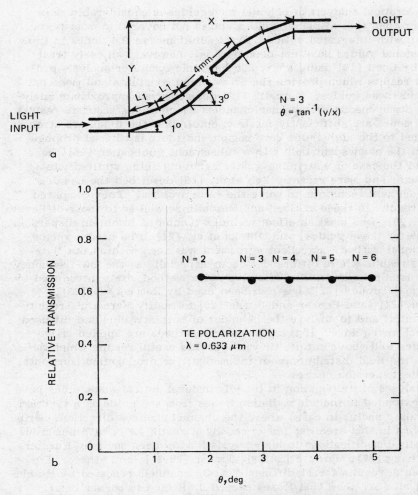

Figure 12.8 (a) Schematic of two coherently coupled multisection bends and (b) measured relative transmission at 632.8 nm for N = 2 through N = 6 abrupt 1° bends with 180-µm separations. (From Ref. 33.)

12.2.3 Coupling to Optical Waveguides

In an early review paper Tien [2] described three techniques which are still utilized in coupling light into an integrated optical waveguide. These include the prism coupler, the grating coupler, and the tapered film coupler. In addition direct end-fire or butt coupling of radiation into or out of a prepared edge of the waveguide constitutes a method of coupling that is employed both in integrated optical laboratory experiments and in demonstration devices fabricated to date. We shall describe each of these techniques briefly below.

12.2.3.1 Prism Coupler

The prism coupler is based on evanescent wave penetration through an air gap between a prism of high refractive index and a waveguide film upon which it is placed, as shown in Fig. 12.9. The incoming beam in a prism of index n_3 will have a wave vector of magnitude k_3, the horizontal component of which is $k_3 \sin \theta_3$, and it will in general be totally reflected at the prism-air interface. Since the fields above and below the prism base must have the same horizontal components, the evanescent field must vary as $\exp|ik_3 z \sin \theta_3|$. When the prism is placed on a thin-film waveguide, with a thin air gap between the faces, the evanescent field penetrates into the film and excites a light wave having the same horizontal component of wave motion in the film. If the horizontal component of the wave vector for any mode of the waveguide equals $k_3 \sin \theta_3$, the light in the prism will be coupled exclusively into this mode. It is therefore possible to excite any mode in the waveguide by varying the angle θ_3 for the incoming beam in the prism. For best coupling the air gap thickness should be in the $\lambda/4$ to $\lambda/8$ range.

A right-angle prism such as that shown in Fig. 12.9 is best used with the input beam extending right up to the coupling edge. This optimizes the coupling by preventing light from being evanescently coupled back out of the guide into the prism as would occur if the prism extended past the region illuminated by the input beam.

The maximum coupling efficiency which can theoretically be achieved with this type of coupling is 81% for a uniform input beam. By varying the input light distribution along the coupling gap or by varying the coupling efficiency along the gap, it is possible to increase this figure to 100%. In the case of output coupling by means of a prism, the coupling efficiency can be 100% regardless of the beam profile.

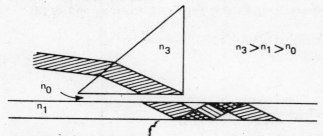

Figure 12.9 Prism light-wave coupler based on evanescent wave penetration through the air gap n_0.

A prism coupler can also be used to determine the refractive index and thickness of a waveguide. This is accomplished by measuring the angles of the synchronous directions and substituting these into the equation for the waveguide modes. This technique was first described by Tien et al. [34], who demonstrated that it is capable of yielding accuracies of 0.001 in measuring the index and of 1% in determining the thickness.

12.2.3.2 Grating Coupler

Light can be coupled into an optical waveguide through the use of a grating whose lines run more or less perpendicular to the direction of propagation in the waveguide, as shown schematically in Fig. 12.10. Gratings can be fabricated in a variety of ways, with holographic exposure and ion milling to produce a periodic variation in the effective refractive index of the guide being one of the most often used methods. The grating introduces a phase variation in an incident wave which is dependent on the depth and spacing of the grating. As a result the wave reaching the waveguide contains many Fourier components of the form

$$\exp\left[\frac{2\pi i}{\lambda}\left(\sin\theta + \frac{2\pi m}{d}\right)z\right]$$

where m is an integer and θ is the angle of incidence. If one of these components matches the waveguide mode of the film, the beam will be coupled exclusively into this mode. Grating coupling efficiencies can be comparable to those of prism couplers.

12.2.3.3 Tapered Film Coupler

The tapered film coupler shown in Fig. 12.11 utilizes the cutoff property of an asymmetric guide to couple energy into or out of a waveguide. It is especially useful for coupling into high-index films where higher-index materials for prism coupling are not available.

The tapered film is usually made by varying the thickness of the waveguide material itself, and it operates on the principle that as the film thickness decreases in the taper region between z_a and z_b, it

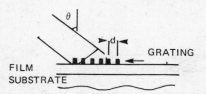

Figure 12.10 Grating light-wave coupler. (From Ref. 2.)

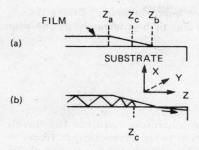

Figure 12.11 Tapered film light-wave coupler. As the wave enters into the tapered region, the angle it makes with the z axis becomes smaller and smaller until at x_c it is less than the critical angle of the film-substrate interface. The wave is the refracted into the substrate, and the film serves as an output coupler. (From Ref. 2.)

reaches a point, $z = z_c$, where the angle between the ray and the x axis is less than the critical angle for the film-substrate interface. The beam is then refracted out of the guide into the substrate, and the taper becomes an output coupler.

If we focus a light beam onto the taper through the substrate, the taper can also be used as an input coupler.

The taper is generally of the order of 10 to 100 wavelengths in length.

12.2.3.4 End-Fire or Butt Coupling

The coupling method which holds the greatest promise for actual integrated optical systems applications involves accurate preparation of the waveguide edge in order to permit the input beam either to be focused on the edge or, preferably, to be coupled into the guide through placement of the source in virtual contact with the edge. This approach offers the advantage that it is more consistent with the intended planar nature of integrated optical structures in that it does not employ fixtures or source emplacements which lie outside the waveguide plane, which is the case with each of the three previously discussed techniques. Edge preparation, on the other hand, is a tedious and time-consuming operation because the end of the waveguide must be polished square and chip-free over the area to be used in coupling into or out of the guide. Efficient coupling requires, moreover, that submicrometer tolerances be met and maintained in the alignment fixtures.

Rapid progress in these areas has been made in recent years. Polishing techniques to produce edges of adequate quality over widths of several millimeters have been developed, and precision alignment fixtures which allow butt coupling of diode lasers and photodetector

arrays to the ends of the waveguide have been devised. These fixtures can be made to be relatively small and to lie primarily in the plane
of the waveguide.

12.3 GUIDED LIGHT INTERACTIONS

12.3.1 Types of Interactions

Exploitation of IO in signal-processing applications requires the development of methods of imparting information to or extracting it from
guided optical waves. While many mechanisms may be suggested for
this purpose, only acousto-optic (AO), electro-optic (EO), and
magneto-optic (MO) interactions have received any serious consideration. Little of significance has yet been demonstrated in the application of MO to integrated optical processing, and attention will thus
be confined to AO and EO effects.

As is the case in bulk optical systems, AO interactions find their
greatest utility in applications involving frequency modulation and/or
rapid deflection to or scanning over a multiplicity of output ports.
Electro-optics is most useful in switching, beam splitting, and high-
speed amplitude or phase modulation. If advantage is to be taken of
the tight confinement of the optical beam in at least one dimension,
then the acoustic or electric fields should also be confined in that
dimension. To this end, the application of acousto-optics to IO has
been greatly accelerated by the availability of the extensive surface-
acoustic-wave (SAW) technology which has been developed independently in recent years in response to other electronic signal-processing
requirements. While no comparable surface EO capabilities had previously been developed, the fringing fields which penetrate to depths
of only a few micrometers below surfaces on which potentials are applied between closely spaced thin-film electrodes yield highly concentrated EO interactions, and these can be further concentrated by the
use of channel waveguides.

Bragg AO diffraction by SAWs is employed in the IO spectrum
analyzer and in several other devices, such as convolver-correla-
tors, time-integrating correlators, and digital deflectors, now under-
going exploratory development. Consequently, guided wave acousto-
optics has been the focus of considerable attention in recent years,
and this interest can be expected to remain heavy for several years
to come. Electro-optics is under investigation for application in IO
logic elements, A/D converters, modulators, interchannel switches,
and many other devices. The principles underlying integrated acousto-
optics are treated in Sec. 12.3.2 and those of integrated electro-
optics in Sec. 12.3.3. Only the basic concepts are covered here, with
discussion of specific components and devices deferred to later sections of this chapter. Considerably greater emphasis is placed on AO
interactions.

12.3.2 Integrated Acousto-optic Interactions

The fundamentals of acousto-optics and the principal areas of application of AO to bulk optical processing systems have been treated in earlier chapters. Our purpose here will be to build on those foundations, adding only what is necessary to identify basic differences between bulk and integrated AO interaction regimes and to outline the theory which explains those differences.

As in bulk optics, AO interaction in integrated optics can operate in either the Raman-Nath or the Bragg mode, and the criterion which serves to distinguish the two is the same. Only Bragg diffraction has received any appreciable attention in IO, and no further consideration of Raman-Nath interaction will be given. Three different forms of Bragg diffraction in IO have been demonstrated. The first is the diffraction of a guided wave into another guided wave by means of interaction with a SAW, as first observed by Kuhn et al. [35] in 1970 and since expanded upon by hosts of other researchers. The second, proposed by Chang [36] in 1971 and demonstrated by Giallorenzi [37] a short time later, uses the SAW to deflect from a guided mode out of the waveguide into a radiation mode of the substrate. The third has been described by Shah [38] and by Brandt et al. [39], and it employs bulk acoustic waves to interact with guided optical waves and produce guided-guided diffraction. Only the first has been pursued to any great extent, but the others have characteristic features which may someday be exploited to considerable advantage. Thus, for example, coupling into radiation modes of the substrate or superstrate may soon allow the development of a two-dimensional signal-processing capability in IO, while the interaction between bulk acoustic waves and guided optical waves has some potential in ultra-high-speed amplitude and phase modulation and in multiport deflection.

Within the guided-guided types of Bragg diffraction, it is necessary to distinguish between normal, or isotropic, and anisotropic classes of interaction, which either maintain or rotate the plane of polarization of the incident light, and to subdivide the normal class further according to whether the mode order is or is not maintained. These classes of diffraction are depicted schematically in the phase-matching or momentum conservation diagrams of Fig. 12.12, and they are described by the general forms of the Bragg diffraction conditions derived by Dixon [40]:

$$\sin \theta_i = \frac{\lambda}{2n_i \Lambda} \left[1 + \frac{\Lambda^2}{\lambda^2} (n_i^2 - n_d^2) \right]$$

$$\sin \theta_d = \frac{\lambda}{2n_d \Lambda} \left[1 - \frac{\Lambda^2}{\lambda^2} (n_i^2 - n_d^2) \right] \tag{12.27}$$

where the subscripts i and d refer to incident and diffracted waves, θ's are relevant angles, n's are relevant refractive indices, λ is the

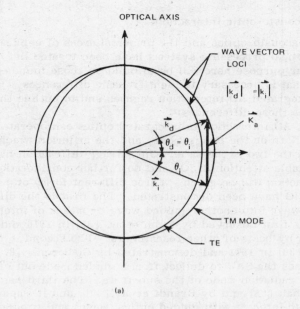

(a)

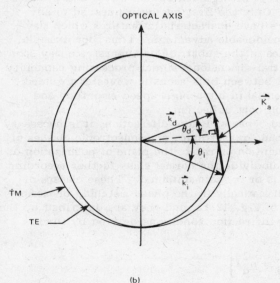

(b)

Figure 12.12 Momentum conservation diagrams for Bragg acousto-optic interaction in (a) normal diffraction in which mode order and polarization are maintained and (b) anisotropic diffraction in which polarization is rotated through $\pi/2$ radians.

free-space optical wavelength, and Λ is the acoustic wavelength. In the case of polarization-maintaining diffraction within the same mode order, these expressions reduce to the well-known isotropic bulk Bragg condition where, with $n_i = n_d = n$ and $\theta_i = \theta_d = \theta_B$,

$$\sin \theta_B = \frac{\lambda}{2n\Lambda} \qquad\qquad (12.28)$$

Diffraction with change of mode order has no bulk AO counterpart. It has not yet been found to be of any significance in optical signal processing, owing to the inherently low intermode coupling strength which arises in the orthogonality of modes, but it could prove to be useful in coupling among modes of like symmetry (even or odd), especially in coupling into and out of channel waveguide structures; Kuhn et al. [41] were the first to report observation of this form of mode conversion. Anisotropic diffraction has not yet been explored extensively even though it has been recognized for several years that anisotropy in IO should be far more amenable to application than is bulk anisotropy. This form of diffraction will be considered in more detail later in this section.

As already mentioned, SAW technology had undergone extensive development before the advent of IO. It was well known, for example, that surface acoustic waves, which are Rayleigh waves having both compression and shear components, propagate with exponentially decaying amplitudes below the surface. Like evanescent optical waves, they experience very weak interaction with the underlying medium because their decay is essentially complete within a wavelength of the surface, but they can interact quite strongly with disturbances which approach within the range of their decay tail. For most solid materials, SAW velocities range between 2 and 5×10^5 cm/s so that, for frequencies between 100 MHz and 2 GHz, acoustic wavelengths are in the range between ~40 and < 1 μm. Optical waveguide thicknesses, on the other hand, are typically between 1 and, at most, 10 μm. Thus, there is a good, though not perfect, match between the two.

The interaction between guided optical waves and surface acoustic waves is considerably more complex than is bulk AO interaction because of its dependence on the overlap between the two waves and because of the nonuniform profiles of both the guided optical mode in its waveguide and the tail of the SAW penetrating into the region of the waveguide. In addition, the propagating SAW causes particle displacements which create moving corrugations along both the air-waveguide and waveguide-substrate interfaces, and these corrugations constitute additional traveling gratings which contribute to the Bragg diffraction process. Schmidt has shown [42] that, especially in the case of coupling between modes of like polarization but different order, the effect of the corrugations can be significant. If the waveguide material is piezoelectric, moreover, particle displacements also generate local electric fields which, via the electro-optic effect, induce further changes

in the index of refraction, and these may add to or subtract from the
changes induced by the photoelastic effect. In most piezoelectric sub-
stances the photoelastic effect far outweighs the EO effect, but in
LiNbO$_3$ and some other ferroelectric materials the opposite is true,
and the EO contribution can dominate by as much as a factor of 10
or more [43].

The theory of integrated acousto-optics has been developed over a
period of several years, with significant contributions having been
made by, among others, Ohmachi [44], Kushibiki et al. [45], Giallorenzi and co-workers [37,46], Schmidt [42], Chang et al. [36,47],
and Tsai and his many coauthors [48]. Useful summaries of the theory
have been presented from somewhat different points of view, and with
some minor discrepancies between them, by Schmidt [42] and Tsai
[49]. For normal Bragg diffraction between modes of the same order,
the AO diffraction efficiency varies in a manner similar to that of bulk
AO but with an additional dependence on the overlap integral or coupling coefficient between the two types of waves. When the Bragg
condition is satisfied so that $\theta_i = \theta_d$ and $n_i = n_d = n$, Tsai's expression
for the diffraction efficiency reduces to

$$\zeta(f) = \sin^2 g(f) \tag{12.29}$$

where

$$g^2(f) = \left(\frac{\pi^2}{2\lambda^2}\right) \left(\frac{n^6 p^2}{\rho v^3}\right) C_{id}^2(f) \frac{L}{\cos^2 \theta} P_a \tag{12.30}$$

which is very similar to the corresponding expression for bulk AO diffraction efficiency but which contains the added coupling factor $C_{id}^2(f)$,
a normalized integral of the triple overlap product of the incident
light, diffracted light, and acoustic fields:

$$C_{id}^2(f) = \frac{[\int_0^\infty U_i(y)U_d(y)U_a(y)\,dy]^2}{\int_{-\infty}^\infty U_i^2(y)dy \int_{-\infty}^\infty U_d^2(y)\,dy \int_0^\infty U_a^2(y)\,dy} \tag{12.31}$$

The second term in the expression for $g^2(f)$ is the well-known bulk AO
figure of merit M_2, which, in its more general IO form, is written by
Tsai as

$$M_{2id} = \frac{n_i^3 n_d^3 p^2}{\rho v^3} \tag{12.32}$$

where p is the relevant photoelastic constant, ρ is the density, and v
is the SAW velocity. As is the case for weak diffraction efficiencies
in bulk AO, the IO acousto-optic diffraction efficiency can be seen to
vary linearly with L, the length of the acousto-optic interaction region.

For the special case where the contribution of the EO effect is either small or proportional to the photoelastic change in index and where the acoustic signal is uniform over the penetration depth of the optical beam, Tsai shows that the diffraction efficiency is given approximately by

$$\zeta(f_0) \simeq g^2(f_0) = \left(\frac{\pi^2}{2\lambda^2}\right) M_{2id} \left(\frac{f_0 L}{v \cos \theta_i \cos \theta_d}\right) P_a \qquad (12.33)$$

where f_0 is the center frequency of operation. Thus, in this case which can be approximated by thin, nonpiezoelectric waveguides at low to moderate acoustic frequencies, the diffraction efficiency becomes linearly proportional to the frequency as well as to the length.

The situation is much more complex in $LiNbO_3$ because of the strong EO effect, and it becomes necessary to use computer modeling to analyze the interactions. Such numerical analyses have been performed by, among others, Tsai et al. [48a] and White et al. [50]. Representative plots of the relative contributions of the electro-optic and photoelastic effects to the change in index of refraction at 632.8 nm for y-cut $LiNbO_3$ with acoustic propagation along the z axis (y cut, z propagating) are given in Fig. 12.13. The calculated frequency response of the Bragg efficiency $C_{id}^2(f)$ for this material, with optical penetration depth as a parameter, is shown in Fig. 12.14 [49], where it can be seen that the acousto-optic coupling for thin waveguides such as those which result from Ti indiffusion should be excellent in the frequency range from about 500 MHz to well above 1 GHz. In practice, however, increased SAW attenuation due to surface imperfections and other frequency-dependent losses, coupled with increased fabrication difficulties, has to date served to limit integrated acousto-optic device operation to frequencies of 1 GHz and below. Some progress toward AO operation at frequencies of up to 1.6 GHz has recently been reported [51].

It can also be deduced from Fig. 12.14 that, again especially in the case of waveguides yielding shallow optical penetration, y-cut, z-propagating $LiNbO_3$ is inherently capable of relatively uniform AO coupling efficiencies over broad frequency bandwidths. Achievements of such bandwidths requires that the SAW transducers operate with sufficient uniformity and that means be incorporated to allow the Bragg angular condition to be met throughout the band of interest. It will be shown in a later section that these requirements can be met and that useful integrated AO bandwidths approaching 1 GHz are being achieved.

Transducers for SAW generation on piezoelectric materials usually consist of a pattern of interdigitated metallic electrodes deposited directly onto the surface, as depicted in Fig. 12.15(a). For nonpiezoelectric substrates it is necessary to provide a film of piezoelectric material, either upon or below the electrode finger pattern, from which

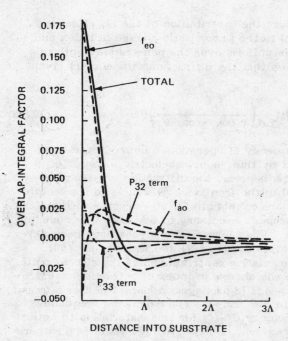

Figure 12.13 Change in index of refraction of y-cut $LiNbO_3$ caused by a surface acoustic wave propagating along the z direction. Electro-optic and acousto-optic contributions are designated as f_{eo} and f_{ao}, respectively; the photoelastic terms P_{32} and P_{33} contribute to f_{ao}. (From Ref. 50.)

the SAW can be launched onto the waveguide-bearing surface. Some possible electrode-film configurations are shown in Fig. 12.15(b) [52].

The theory of interdigital surface wave transducers was rather well developed prior to 1970 and is reviewed along with a summary of transducer design criteria by Smith et al. [53]. They show that the behavior of transducers on the most frequently used cuts of $LiNbO_3$ is best described by the *crossed-field* model which predicts that the radiation conductance at the center frequency of operation of the transducer and the electromechanical coupling efficiency vary as N^2, where N is the number of full-wave interelectrode periods. They show, further, that the fractional bandwidth of the transducer varies as $1/N$ and that there is an optimal fractional bandwidth for each material which is dictated by the effective electromechanical constant k^2,

$$N_{opt}^2 \simeq \frac{\pi}{4k^2}$$

(12.34)

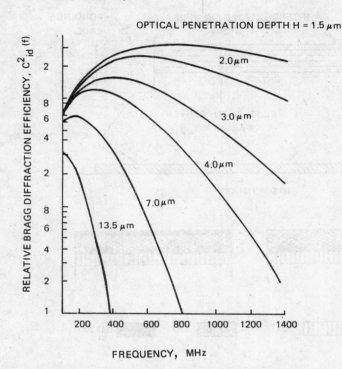

Figure 12.14 Calculated relative Bragg diffraction efficiency vs. frequency for y-cut, z-propagating LiNbO$_3$ for various optical penetration depths. (From Ref. 49.)

For acoustic propagation along z on y- or x-cut LiNbO$_3$ the optimal value of N is approximately 4, and the optimal fractional bandwidth is approximately 25%. This is the largest optimal fractional bandwidth among those tabulated for seven frequently used SAW substrate materials.

These considerations deal with the electromechanical and electrical performance of SAW transducers. To achieve broadband AO interaction, it is necessary to set the transducer aperture such that acoustic diffraction allows the Bragg condition to be met over the full fractional bandwidth of the transducer. A useful expression given by Tsai [49] allows the aperture L to be determined from the −3-dB fractional bandwidth according to

$$\frac{\Delta f_{-3dB, Bragg}}{f_0} = \frac{1.8 n v \cos \theta_0}{\lambda f_0} \frac{\Lambda_0}{L} \tag{12.35}$$

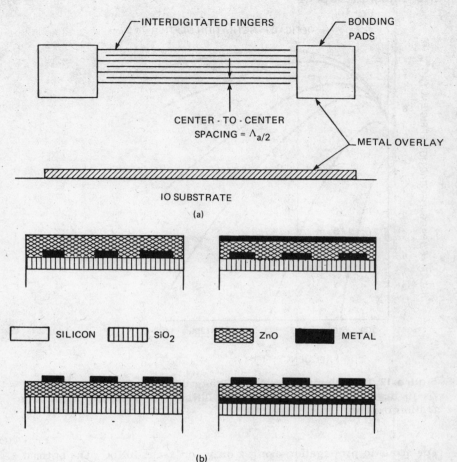

Figure 12.15 Schematic representations of transducers for SAW generation on (a) piezoelectric and (b) nonpiezoelectric substrates. (From Ref. 52.)

where θ_0 is the Bragg angle at the center frequency f_0 and Λ_0 is the acoustic wavelength at that frequency.

It is evident from the foregoing that in order to achieve very broad operational bandwidths with useful efficiencies it is necessary to use multiple transducers, each of rather limited fractional bandwidth. Tseng [54] has shown that interdigital SAW transducers produce only odd harmonics of the fundamental frequency so that it should be possible, in principle, to operate SAW devices over nearly two full octaves. In broadband acousto-optic signal-processing devices where

more than one strong signal may be present at any given time, however, the potential generation of spurious responses at sum and difference frequencies of these strong signals necessitates that operational bandwidths be limited to one octave or less. The achievement of a
1-GHz bandwidth in an integrated AO device, therefore, will require
that the center frequency be $\geqslant$ 1.5 GHz.

Time-bandwidth product or, equivalently, the number of resolvable
spots is another important parameter of spectrum analyzers and other
signal-processing devices. A bandwidth of 1 GHz has already been
noted to be within reach in the near future. Useful optical apertures
of IO devices are limited by lens manufacturing and crystal growth
technologies, but apertures of at least 1 cm and, perhaps, as much as
2 cm should be achievable within current limits. At the SAW velocity
of 3.48×10^5 cm/s for z propagation on x- or y-cut $LiNbO_3$ these
apertures yield acoustic transit times of 2.9 to 5.8 μs and time-bandwidth products (or numbers of resolvable spots) of 2900 to 5800. It is
worth noting that bulk-wave velocities in $LiNbO_3$ are approximately
twice the SAW velocity so that an equivalent bulk time-bandwidth
product requires a twofold increase in bandwidth or aperture.

Turning, finally to anisotropic diffraction, we note that, even in
isotropic media, TE and TM waveguide modes of the same order see
different effective indices of refraction. Thus, birefringence is a
general property of integrated optics, and, unlike the case in uniaxial bulk crystals, it is possible to exercise some degree of control
over the magnitude of the birefringence. Dixon's treatment of anisotropic AO diffraction showed that there is a specific angle of incidence
given by

$$\sin \theta_i = \frac{\lambda f_{opt}}{n_i v} \qquad\qquad (12.36)$$

where

$$f_{opt} = \frac{v}{\lambda} \left| n_i^2 - n_d^2 \right|^{1/2} \qquad\qquad (12.37)$$

for which the diffraction angle is zero and that, moreover, there is a
broad range of frequencies about f_{opt} wherein a large angular sweep
in θ_d occurs for virtually no change in θ_i, as illustrated in Fig. 12.16.
This makes it possible to match the Bragg angle over a large frequency
bandwidth while maintaining a relatively well-collimated acoustic beam.

In most birefringent bulk AO materials the magnitude of the birefringence is such as to place f_{opt} in the range of several gigahertz; as a
result, the use of anisotropic diffraction in bulk materials has largely
been confined to TeO_2, which exhibits an anomalously slow shear wave
but which is also a difficult crystal to grow and process. Tsai and
several of his students have reported [55], on the other hand, a measured bandwidth of 222 MHz at a center frequency of 400 MHz on y-cut,

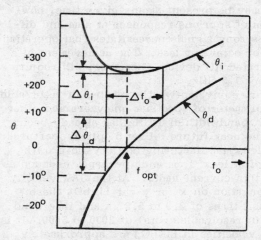

Figure 12.16 Variation of angles of incidence and diffraction with frequency for anisotropic Bragg diffraction. f_{opt} is the frequency at which the diffraction angle is zero and about which a large diffraction bandwidth is possible with only slight variation of the angle of incidence. (From Ref. 40.)

Ti-indiffused $LiNbO_3$ using SAWs of 7-mm aperture, an aperture which, in normal diffraction, allowed only 1/7 of that bandwidth. The RF drive power requirements were 5 times higher for the anisotropic case, but the increased bandwidth unmistakably demonstrates the attractiveness of this approach.

12.3.3 Integrated Electro-optic Interactions

The basis of most of the EO investigations that have led to useful results in IO is the linear electro-optic or Pockels effect which yields a linear change in the index of refraction of a crystalline solid under the application of an electric field. For a material to have a nonvanishing linear EO coefficient, it must lack a center of inversion symmetry, and this means that there is no Pockels effect in glass or other isotropic waveguide materials. Higher-order dependences of the index on the applied field as well as other electro-optic effects are known and could conceivably find application to integrated optics. One such interaction which will be given brief mention is the quadratic EO effect which has been investigated to some extent for an EO analog of RF Bragg diffraction.

The Pockels effect has been employed to great advantage in laser Q switches and high-speed modulators since soon after the development of the laser, and useful summaries of EO materials and their applications can be found in reference handbooks [56,57]. Detailed treatment of early applications of EO in integrated optics is given by Hammer [58] who also presents valuable discussions of modulation in both bulk and integrated optics and of the variation of EO properties with crystalline direction in $LiNbO_3$.

To take advantage of the confinement of the optical beam to within a few wavelengths of the surface, it is necessary to reduce the EO interaction to essentially a planar geometry by means of electrodes deposited on the surface; otherwise the applied fields have to traverse the entire thickness of the substrate, and the efficiency is reduced in the ratio of the waveguide thickness to the substrate thickness. Planar geometry can be accomplished by employing fringing fields which penetrate a short distance into the substrate, as depicted in Fig. 12.17. Either the vertical or the horizontal component of the field can give rise to a controlled variation in the index of refraction if the corresponding component of the EO tensor is nonzero. The change in index is given by

$$\Delta n_\alpha = -\frac{n_\alpha^3 r_{\alpha\beta} E_\beta}{2} \tag{12.38}$$

where n_α is the index of refraction for light polarized in the α direction, E_β is the component of the applied field in the β direction, and $r_{\alpha\beta}$ is the reduced electro-optic coefficient which couples these directions in the material of interest. Crystalline directions for which $r_{\alpha\beta} \neq 0$ are summarized by Kaminow and Turner [59] who also present extensive tables of known values of these coefficients.

One of the earliest applications of EO to integrated optics used an interdigital electrode structure and an applied field to form an EO Bragg diffraction grating modulator [60]. The condition for Bragg

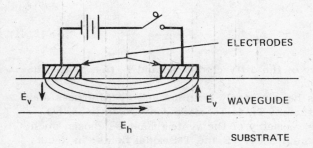

Figure 12.17 Schematic representation of fringing field penetration into a waveguide upon application of voltage between electrodes on the surface.

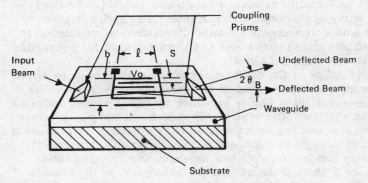

Figure 12.18 Electro-optic Bragg diffraction grating modulator for integrated optics using interdigitated electrodes to form the grating and prism input and output coupling. (From Ref. 60.)

diffraction in such a device, which is sketched in Fig. 12.18, is essentially the same as it is for AO interactions, namely,

$$\sin \theta_B = \frac{\lambda}{2n'S} \tag{12.39}$$

where n' is the total index of refraction in the presence of the applied field and S = 2s is twice the electrode period. Which component of the applied field is employed depends on the material, the crystalline direction being used, and the polarization of the guided light. The maximum phase shift imparted by the applied field is

$$\Delta \phi = \frac{2\pi \ell \, \Delta n}{\lambda} \tag{12.40}$$

where ℓ is the length of the electrode structure. The modulation produced is given by

$$\frac{I}{I_0} = \sin^2 \frac{\Delta \phi}{2} \tag{12.41}$$

where I is the intensity of the diffracted beam and I_0 that of the incident beam.

The same principles have recently been applied by Alferness and Buhl to demonstrate efficient TE to TM mode conversion in LiNbO$_3$ waveguides [61]. The geometry of the system must be chosen such that the applied field couples the TE and TM modal fields; in x-cut, y-propagating (optical) LiNbO$_3$ this is accomplished by way of interaction between the vertical component of the field and the guided light field through the r_{51} electro-optic coefficient. The coupling coefficient is given by

$$\kappa = \frac{\pi}{\lambda} n_s^2 \alpha r_{51} \frac{V}{d}$$ (12.42)

where V is the applied voltage, d is the interelectrode gap, n_s is the substrate index, and α is a parameter between 0 and 1 which measures the overlap between the applied electric field and the coupled light fields [similar to the $C_{id}^2(f)$ parameter discussed in the previous section]. Because the interaction is again based on Bragg diffraction, it can be employed as a high-resolution filter as well as a mode converter.

IO logic elements and A/D converters [62,63] make use of phase retardation in one leg of interferometers which, in their simplest form, consist of channel waveguides which are first separated and then rejoined, as shown in Fig. 12.19. Electrode structures placed on the sides of the branched channels are used to induce changes in the index of refraction to advance or retard the phase in a given channel by an amount given by equation (12.40).

The use of EO index modulation for directional coupling between channel waveguides was first proposed by Marcatili in 1969 [17] and has since undergone extensive development at Bell Laboratories and elsewhere. Marcatili's basic concept involves separating channel waveguide sections on a substrate by an amount just sufficient to prevent measurable coupling between channels under normal conditions and then using EO modulation of the index of the intervening material to induce switching. Recently Cross and Schmidt [64] described the operation of a one-gigabit/s directional coupler which requires only 5 V drive and which has yielded extinction ratios of 25 dB.

Electro-optic diffraction of light employing the quadratic EO effect at microwave frequencies was first described by Cohen and Gordon [65], who used the very high microwave dielectric constant of potassium tantaloniobate (KTN) to achieve appreciable modulation efficiencies in bulk samples at moderate input powers. Their analysis showed that modulation bandwidths of 10 GHz or more at center frequencies of 50 GHz should be realizable, and initial experiments supported these predictions. Utilization of EO diffraction has been impeded by material problems, by difficulty associated with achieving efficient microwave coupling, and by a lack of need for such high-speed deflection capabilities. Several approaches to achieving efficient microwave-optical interaction in an integrated optical format, based on meander lines or other slow wave structures, are under investigation in several laboratories, but no results have yet been published.

12.4 INTEGRATED OPTICAL DEVICE COMPONENTS

12.4.1 Waveguides

Integrated optical waveguides have been fabricated from a large variety of transparent dielectric materials including glasses, photoresist, poly-

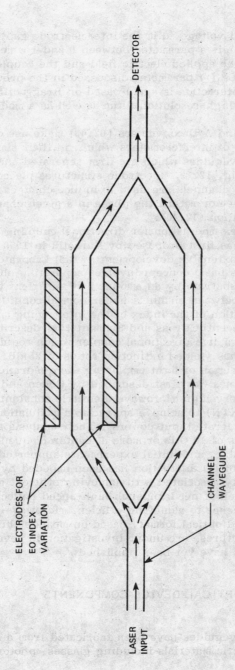

Figure 12.19 Simple integrated optical interferometer using channel waveguides and the electro-optic effect to control phase retardation in one of the channels.

LASER INPUT

CHANNEL WAVEGUIDE

ELECTRODES FOR EO INDEX VARIATION

DETECTOR

urethane, sputtered Nb_2O_5 and Ta_2O_5, and such single-crystal materials as $LiNbO_3$, ZnO, CdS, ZnSe, and GaAs. A great deal of experimental work has been reported on many of these waveguides, but at present only a few of these materials are being considered seriously for use in the development of integrated optical devices for signal processing. Those materials of most interest for such applications include Ti-indiffused $LiNbO_3$, sputtered Corning 7059 glass on SiO_2, and GaAs.

GaAs is receiving considerable attention as a waveguide material because it offers the possibility for development of monolithic integrated optical circuits which include the laser diode source and the detector or detector array on the same substrate with the waveguide. A considerable amount of work has been reported in the literature dealing with waveguides in this material [6,7], and still further work is currently in progress to improve upon its loss characteristics, which are of the order of 1.5 to 2 dB/cm as compared to 0.5 dB/cm or less for Ti:$LiNbO_3$ or sputtered glass waveguides. This material may be looked upon as the long-range answer to integrated optical systems if monolithic circuits do prove to be advantageous. This will not become apparent until improvements are realized in semiconductor yield rates so that economical tradeoff between monolithic and hybrid integrated optical circuits can be made during the design of specific devices.

At the present time the two main contenders for use in integrated optics are $LiNbO_3$ and glass. These two waveguide materials were very seriously considered for utilization in the development of the RF spectrum analyzer. The selection of $LiNbO_3$ was made on the basis of both optical and acoustic considerations, as will be discussed in Sec. 12.5 which deals with specific integrated optical devices.

Indiffused waveguides are formed in $LiNbO_3$ by depositing a film of Ti to a thickness of between 100 and 600 Å on a carefully polished surface and heating the coated substrate to a temperature of 960° to 1170°C for 1 to several hours. The actual diffusion time is a function of the Ti film thickness and the desired waveguide depth, but in general the minimum diffusion time sufficient to drive all the Ti into the substrate and leave the surface transparent is selected. If the diffusion time is insufficient, a cloudy film, which is thought to be TiO_2 and which adversely affects the waveguide properties, remains on the surface. Attempts to reheat the material to continue diffusion once the substrate has cooled to room temperature have not always been successful. The diffusion is generally carried out in an argon, nitrogen, or oxygen atmosphere. If argon or nitrogen is employed during diffusion, the substrate is cooled in an oxygen atmosphere in order to reoxidize the $LiNbO_3$ [66,67].

During the indiffusion process Li_2O is simultaneously outdiffused from the substrate [14,68]. This affects the extraordinary index of refraction n_e and forms a deeper lying outdiffused waveguide in addition to the Ti-indiffused guide. Several techniques have been de-

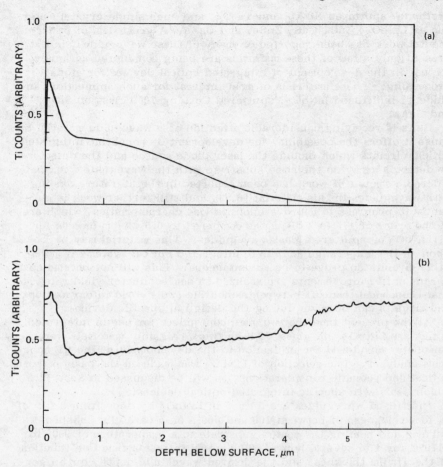

Figure 12.20 SIMS concentration profiles for (a) titanium and (b) lithium as a function of depth in a Ti-indiffused LiNbO$_3$ waveguide. (From Ref. 74.)

veloped to compensate for this outdiffusion process in order to eliminate the outdiffused modes [69-73].

A detailed study of Ti-diffused waveguides has recently been conducted by Burns et al. [74] to determine the anisotropic diffusion coefficients, the surface index changes, and the lateral diffusion rates from channel waveguides. Figure 12.20 shows the Ti concentration profile versus depth below the LiNbO$_3$ surface as measured using secondary ion mass spectrometry techniques. The high concentration of Ti$^+$ just below the surface and a similar peak in the Li$^+$ concentration at approximately the same depth are suggested to be the result of an Li-Ti-O compound which acts as a source for Ti indiffusion and a barrier to Li outdiffusion.

12.4.2 Waveguide Lenses

Many integrated optical devices require one or more lenses on the waveguide substrate to act as beam spreaders, collimators, or focusing elements in the optical system. In applications such as the integrated optical RF spectrum analyzer it is essential that these waveguide lenses be capable of delivering near-diffraction-limited image quality in order to ensure sufficient system resolution and dynamic range. Early efforts to fabricate waveguide lenses involved the formation of a thicker section of the waveguide in the shape of a lens [75,76], but the optical image quality of these lenses was not adequate. Three different classes of waveguide lenses with promising optical characteristics have more recently been studied, fabricated, and tested; these include the geodesic lens, the Luneburg lens, and the grating or Fresnel lens. In the following three sections we shall describe each of these components and discuss their reported performance characteristics.

12.4.2.1 Luneburg Lens

The concept of an integrated optical Luneburg lens was first suggested by Zernike [77]. It is a circular mode-index lens in which the mode index is a maximum at its center and decreases concentrically until it equals the mode index of the waveguide. The true Luneberg lens, which has an index profile that varies as $n(r) = \sqrt{2 - r^2}$, produces an image of an incident plane wave on the output rim of the lens, as shown in Fig. 12.21(a). Modified Luneburg lenses can be designed and fabricated to focus at any given distance from this output rim, as shown in Fig. 12.21(b). These lenses are fabricated by sputtering material through a properly shaped mask onto the waveguide surface. To achieve a reasonably short focal length, it is necessary to utilize a material whose refractive index is significantly greater than that of the waveguide. This has proven to be a problem to date in working with high-index waveguide materials such as $LiNbO_3$.

Yao and Anderson [78] used a numerically controlled lathe to produce a shadow mask through which a Ta_2O_5 thin-film lens was sputtered onto a glass waveguide. The resultant lens yielded near-diffraction-limited performance at F/5.

It has been shown that the tolerances on the lens thickness and thickness profile are extremely tight if diffraction-limited Luneburg lenses are to be realized [79]. Nevertheless, this technology may eventually be developed to the point where it will permit waveguide lens fabrication to be reduced to a single sputtering operation.

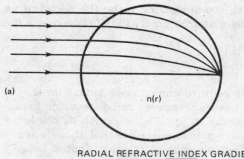

RADIAL REFRACTIVE INDEX GRADIENT

$$n(r) = \sqrt{2 - r^2}$$

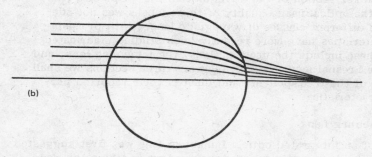

Figure 12.21 Integrated optical Luneburg lenses: (a) true Luneburg lens with specified index profile; (b) modified Luneburg lens designed to form a focus at a given distance from the rim of the lens.

12.4.2.2 Grating or Fresnel Lens

Fresnel lenses in thin-film optical waveguides rely upon Fresnel diffraction from a series of half-period zones to obtain the focusing effect [80]. Waveguide Fresnel lenses must be much longer in the direction of propagation than those in bulk form in order to achieve the necessary phase shift; they still have, however, much shorter propagation paths than Luneburg or geodesic lenses.

These lenses are formed by phase-shift or absorption pads which are either deposited on or embedded into the surface. To form a lens with a focal length f, it is necessary to introduce an appropriate amount of phase shift Δ in the optical path between any point on a plane wave front incident on the lens and the focal point, where Δ is given by [80]

$$\Delta = (s^2 + f^2)^{1/2} - f \tag{12.43}$$

and s is the transverse distance from the point on the wavefront to
the optical axis. If the plane wave front is divided into strip zones so
that at the distance s_m from the axis the value of Δ is

$$\Delta = \frac{m\lambda}{2} \qquad\qquad (12.44)$$

then an absorption Fresnel lens can be produced by absorbing the
optical power in all the odd zones where m = 1, 3, 5, ... Similarly,
in a phase-shift lens a constant phase shift $\phi = \pi$ must be introduced
in all the odd zones. The edge positions of the absorption or phase-
shift pads will be given by

$$s_m = (m\lambda f)^{1/2} \qquad\qquad (12.45)$$

for $\lambda \ll f$.

Ashley and Chang [80] constructed a Fresnel lens with a focal
length of 4 mm by depositing 1000 Å of CeO over a zone pattern on a
1-μm-thick single-mode BaO waveguide on glass, as shown in Fig.
12.22. The zone pattern was exposed in polymethylmethacrylate by
means of electron beam lithography, and it consisted of 105 zone pads
50 μm in length. The total width of the pattern was 0.8 mm, and the
lens thus operated at F/5. The lens has been shown to operate with
near-diffraction-limited performance, but Fresnel lenses have several
disadvantages relative to Luneburg or geodesic lenses. They are not
axially symmetric and therefore have a limited field of view, their
measured efficiency is only about 25%, and their scattering levels cause
the intensity in the sidebands to be significantly greater than should

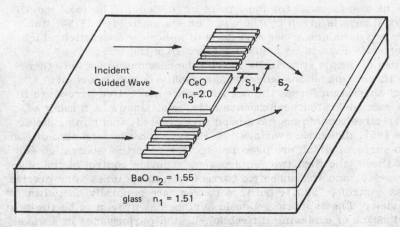

Figure 12.22 Integrated optical Fresnel lens formed by depositing
CeO onto a BaO waveguide on a glass substrate. (From Ref. 80.)

be the case for a diffraction-limited lens operating on a gaussian input beam.

Chang and co-workers at the University of California, San Diego, are currently investigating chirped Fresnel lenses in an effort to reduce scattering, improve efficiency, and increase the field of view [81]. Curved chirped gratings are expected to yield up to 90% efficiency, but a very small field of view, while linear chirped gratings should yield 40 to 50% efficiency over fields of view of up to 0.1 rad. If these experiments prove successful, Fresnel lenses will have considerable value in some integrated optical applications because of their ease of fabrication.

12.4.2.3 Geodesic Lenses

The idea of a geodesic lens as a physical path length counterpart of a Luneburg lens was introduced by Rinehart [82] in 1948, and the theory was developed extensively by Kunz [83] in 1954. Righini et al. [84] first demonstrated the applicability of geodesic waveguide lenses to integrated optics in 1972, and considerable development work has been conducted since that time [85-96]. A geodesic lens consists of a depression or a protrusion formed on the substrate before the waveguide is formed. This may be accomplished by a standard grinding and polishing operation to achieve a spherical depression followed by formation of the waveguide over the surface of the substrate, including the area of the depression. If we now consider a plane wave incident on such a lens (see Fig. 12.23), the central portion of the wavefront will be retarded relative to the peripheral portions by virtue of having traveled a greater physical path length in traversing the lens. As a result, the wave front emerging from the lens will be concave and will be brought to a focus at the focal point of the lens. The focal length for paraxial rays is given by the equation shown in Fig. 12.23, but geodesic lenses exhibit a negative form of spherical aberration which causes off-axis rays to be focused farther from the lens.

The use of simple spherically shaped depressions is limited, therefore, to those applications where image quality is not important. Spherical aberration forces the need for some corrective procedure if near-diffraction-limited performance is to be attained. A number of such corrective techniques have been investigated, including metallic overlays [85], dielectric overlays [79,86,87], and the formation of aspheric surfaces which are precorrected for spherical aberration [88-92]. Of these, the first two require very accurate control of the shape of the overlay, and the dielectric correction also requires very precise thickness control ($\sim$ 50 Å); both, moreover, are generally limited in field of view. The aspheric geodesic surface has proven to be the most practical means of achieving diffraction-limited performance in a waveguide lens [93-96]. These aspheric surfaces have been produced either by a recently developed diamond-turning technique [93,96] or by ultrasonic grinding [94,95].

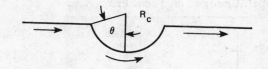

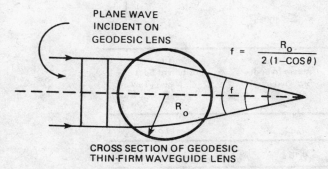

$$f = \frac{R_o}{2(1-\cos\theta)}$$

CROSS SECTION OF GEODESIC
THIN-FIRM WAVEGUIDE LENS

Figure 12.23 Focusing action of a geodesic waveguide lens caused by the central portion of an incident plane wave traveling over a longer physical path length than peripheral portions of the same waveform.

The tolerances on the surface contours of aspheric geodesic lenses have been analyzed by Betts et al. [88], and the results are shown in Tables 12.1 and 12.2. These results indicate that small errors in lens contour cause significant shifts (of up to 19 times the error) in the location of the lens focal plane. For the parameters of the output lens on the IO spectrum analyzer, a lens of 2.74-cm focal length operating at F/14, an error of 100 μm in locating the focal plane will produce a 50% increase in image spot size. Since such errors at the input and output ends of the device are cumulative, it is essential that the surface contour be held to tolerances of 1 to 2 μm.

Of the two geodesic lens fabrication methods, the ultrasonic technique suffers from the fact that the lens depth cannot be accurately controlled [94]. This requires that a waveguide be formed over the depression and a measurement be made to determine the lens focal length. If a source or detector is to be butt-coupled to the focal plane of the lens, the waveguide edge must then be ground and polished to coincide with said plane [95].

The diamond-turning technique has been shown to provide contour accuracies of better than a micrometer, and the lens focal plane can be

Table 12.1 Effect of Depth Changes on Focal Properties

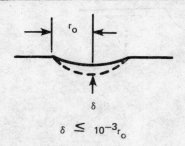

$$\delta \leq 10^{-3} r_0$$

Focal Length	Aperture	Increase In Spot Size Radius	Shift In Position of Spot ("−" Means Toward Lens)
$3r_0$	r_0	0.4δ	-14δ
$3r_0$	$3r_0/5$	0.15δ	-19δ

Source: Ref. 88.

Table 12.2 Effect of Edge Changes on Focal Properties of the Aspheric Lens

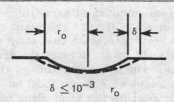

$$\delta \leq 10^{-3} \ r_0$$

Focal Length	Aperture	Increase In Spot Size radius	Shift In Position of Spot
$3r_0$	r_0	0.12δ	7.4δ
$3r_0$	$3r_0/5$	0.012δ	9.4δ
$6.2r_0$	r_0	0.039δ	15δ
$6.2r_0$	$3r_0/5$	0.010δ	19δ

Source: Ref. 88.

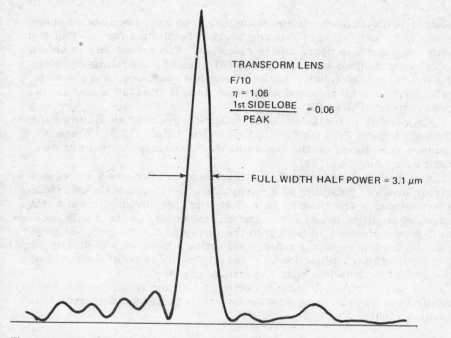

Figure 12.24 Far-field pattern produced by a geodesic waveguide lens in LiNbO$_3$ with a 2.74-cm focal length under uniform illumination of F/10.

accurately located with regard to a prepolished edge [96]. Figure 12.24 shows the diffraction pattern obtained from a diamond-turned aspheric geodesic lens operating at F/10. The central peak width is 1.06 times diffraction-limited, and the intensity of the first sidelobe is observed to be 6% of the peak intensity, whereas the ideal value is 4.8%.

While future developments in Fresnel or Luneburg lens technology may someday displace diamond-turning as a means for producing lenses, the latter technique has been shown to be capable of producing lenses of sufficient quality to meet practical device requirements.

12.4.3 Waveguide Mirrors

Mirrors can be formed in optical waveguides by utilizing a periodic grating array which is referred to as a distributed Bragg reflector (DBR) [97]. The grating is formed either on the surface of the wave-guide (SGR) or on the substrate surface before the waveguide is de-

posited (CGR). Such mirrors with 1200 lines have been shown theoretically to be capable of yielding 99.7% reflectivities for the TE_0 mode
with the major loss being due to radiation. The reflectivity is shown
to be dependent on both the number of lines in the grating and the
depth of the lines relative to the waveguide thickness, and the same
reflectivity can be obtained with fewer lines if the CGR structure is
used instead of the SGR.

Flanders et al. [98] developed reflection gratings exhibiting reflectivities of up to 75% with bandwidths of the order of 2 Å. These reflectors were based on the theory of thick holographic gratings developed by Kogelnik [99].

A second technique which has been used to fabricate a waveguide
mirror involves polishing of a waveguide edge to achieve a chip-free,
sharp corner. The beam to be reflected is then directed toward this
edge, at an angle greater than the critical angle, where it will undergo
total internal reflection back into the waveguide. The polished edge
can also be coated with a metallic reflecting film or with dielectric films
to permit efficient reflection in cases where the angle of incidence of
the optical beam is less than the critical angle.

The use of geodesic surfaces acting as corner reflectors has recently been suggested as another approach to waveguide mirror fabrication [100].

12.4.4 Beam Splitters

A guided optical beam can be split into two beams of approximately
equal intensities through control of the voltage applied to an interdigitated electro-optic Bragg modulator of the type previously discussed [60]. Tangonan et al. [101] fabricated an electro-optic modulator on Ti-diffused $LiTaO_3$ using some 130 pairs of interdigitated
fingers of 4.6-μm width on 9.2-μm centers. The modulator was shown
to produce extinction ratios in excess of 250:1 in either the deflected
or the undeflected beam. The drive voltage necessary for 50% deflection at the He-Ne laser wavelength was approximately 12 V. In the
case of a TE_0 mode in $LiNbO_3$ a 3-dB beam splitter can be realized
at $\lambda = 0.83$ μm at a potential of less than 10 V.

In working with waveguides in which accurate grooves can be
formed, it is possible to fabricate a beam splitter by other means [102].
One such technique involves anisotropic etching of V grooves in a
silicon substrate prior to waveguide deposition. By controlling the
groove depth it is possible to control the beam-splitting ratio, where
a portion of the beam is transmitted in its original direction, while the
remainder is reflected off the groove, as shown in Fig. 12.25.

12.4.5 Acousto-optic Transducers

The interaction between a guided optical beam and a surface acoustic
wave has been treated in Sec. 12.3. In this section we shall examine

OPTICAL BEAM

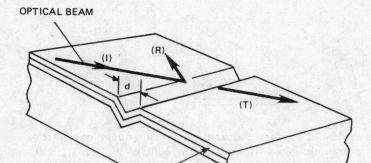

Figure 12.25 Integrated optical beam splitter formed by etching a V groove into the substrate material before waveguide formation.

several different types of surface acoustic wave transducers which are capable of launching a broadband acoustic wave into the region of the optical waveguide. We shall confine our attention to acousto-optically active waveguide materials such as $LiNbO_3$, $LiTaO_3$, ZnO, and GaAs where the transducer design is simpler than it is for a nonpiezoelectric material such as glass. In the latter case it is necessary to utilize an overlay of piezoelectric material in forming the transducer and then launch the generated surface acoustic wave from the piezoelectric layer onto the nonpiezoelectric, waveguiding layer [52,103-106]. In the case of the piezoelectric waveguide an interdigital (ID) electrode array can be deposited directly on the guide [53].

The Bragg deflector constitutes a very important component in such optical signal-processing devices as spectrum analyzers, convolvers, and correlators. In general it is desirable to fabricate optical processors with the largest possible bandwidth, and several techniques have been developed for realizing wideband transducers for these applications [49]. These approaches are outlined below.

12.4.5.1 Stepped-Frequency, Tilted Transducer Array

One method of achieving uniform transducer response over a broad bandwidth utilizes several separate transducers, each operating at a different center frequency [48a]. The transducer frequencies and number of fingers are selected so that each has approximately the same fractional bandwidth, and each transducer is tilted at the appropriate angle to satisfy the Bragg condition at its center frequency. Such a structure is depicted in Fig. 12.26. The aperture or finger length for

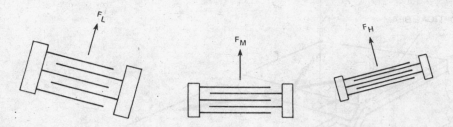

Figure 12.26 Broadband surface acoustic wave transducer consisting
of three separate transducers with center frequencies of f_L, f_M, and
f_H which are tilted with respect to the optical beam such that the Bragg
condition is satisfied at each center frequency.

each of the transducers in the array is selected to provide efficient
diffraction and Bragg bandwidth while maintaining a suitable acoustic
radiation admittance. Tsai and co-workers [107] fabricated and tested
three- and four-element arrays on y-cut $LiNbO_3$, demonstrating overall 3-dB bandwidths of 358 and 680 MHz. In the latter case, the diffraction efficiency was found to be $\geqslant$ 8% at a total applied RF power
of 0.8 W throughout the 680-MHz bandwidth. The authors project an
eventual performance figure of 1 mW of electrical drive power per
megahertz of bandwidth in a device with a 50% diffraction efficiency and
a 1-GHz bandwidth. The maximum achievable bandwidth and diffraction efficiency will be limited by the facts that increased bandwidth
implies operation at higher frequency and that acoustic propagation
losses increase as the square of the frequency. Furthermore, the
acoustic wave becomes more tightly confined to the waveguide surface
with increasing frequency so that the degree of overlap between the
optical and acoustic beams will diminish.

12.4.5.2 Phased-Array Transducer

Generation of surface acoustic waves over broad frequency bandwidths
has also been implemented by means of a phased-array transducer.
This device embodies multiple ID elements having identical center frequencies and parallel propagation axes but with an incremental offset
in the direction of propagation between adjacent elements, as illustrated in Fig. 12.27 [108,109]. The offset introduces a phase shift
between adjacent waves which results in frequency-dependent interference effects in the resultant radiation patterns. In the case where
the offset is an odd number of half wavelengths at the center frequency,
the individual waves destructively interfere in the forward direction,
and most of the radiated energy goes into the first diffraction orders.
If the array is so oriented that one of the first-order lobes matches
the Bragg angle at the center frequency, then the tilting of the

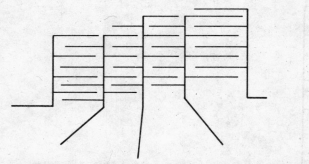

Figure 12.27 Broadband surface acoustic wave transducer consisting of four interdigitated transducers of identical frequency and propagation axes but with an incremental step height between adjacent elements to provide beam steering with varying frequency.

direction of propagation of this lobe with frequency serves to offset partially the error in matching the Bragg angle at other frequencies. This allows the large-aperture acoustic beam to provide a high diffraction efficiency over a much greater frequency range than would be possible in the absence of tracking of the Bragg angle.

Tsai [101] described a six-element phased-array transducer on a y-cut $LiNbO_3$ outdiffused waveguide. The elements were provided with an offset which yielded an electric phase shift of π rad between adjacent transducers. The frequency response was observed to be flat to within 3 dB over a bandwidth of 110 MHz. A similar six-element planar array without acoustic beam steering was measured to have a 3-dB bandwidth of only 19 MHz. In the case of the six-element phased array, 50% of the optical beam was diffracted with only 70 mW of RF drive power over the entire bandwidth of 110 MHz.

12.4.5.3 Chirped Frequency Transducers

A third type of broadband SAW transducer which shows considerable promise for IO applications, the tilted-finger chirped transducer, has been developed recently by Lee et al. [107]. This device can be envisioned as consisting of a large number of tilted, stepped-frequency elements with closely spaced center frequencies, with each element having only a single finger pair, and with small tilt angles between adjacent elements. If all these transducers should be placed one behind another and connected in parallel electrically, the result will be the chirped array pictured in Fig. 12.28.

SAW devices with varying finger spacing but with all fingers lying parallel had been known previously [111], but the incorporation of the varying tilt angle is an AO-related innovation which allows the resultant

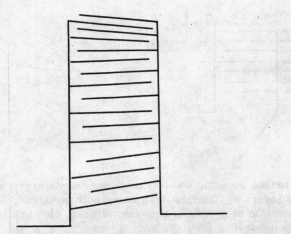

Figure 12.28 Broadband surface acoustic wave transducer with tilted fingers having varying finger spacing. Each finger pair can be looked upon as a separate stepped-frequency transducer, tilted to satisfy the Bragg condition at its center frequency.

SAW wave front to track the Bragg condition over the entire operational bandwidth. It is possible to achieve large AO bandwidth with a parallel-finger chirped transducer by using a very small aperture or finger overlap [112], but this approach spreads the acoustic energy over a large acoustic diffraction angular spread and trades off efficiency against bandwidth. This is undesirable because, in most AO devices, it is necessary to maintain low RF drive in order to avoid onset of acoustic nonlinearities.

The tilted-finger chirped transducer has been observed by Liao et al. [113] to provide a diffraction efficiency of 16% at a total RF drive power of only 100 mW throughout a 470-MHz bandwidth centered at 615 MHz. It has also been operated at a diffraction efficiency of 50% and with a performance figure of 1.4 mW of electrical drive power per megahertz of bandwidth.

12.4.5.4 Other Types of Transducers

Tsai [49] has also described two other forms of transducers which are offshoots of the tilted, stepped-frequency, and phased-array transducers. One of these is called a curved transducer, which can be pictured as a large number of tilted, staggered-frequency transducers placed side by side and joined to form a single transducer that is curved with respect to the optical beam. The other is a tilted phased-array transducer which combines the concepts of both the tilted-array and the phased-array transducers by having each element of the tilted array consist of a pair of phased-array transducers, thus allowing acoustic beam steering for each element. This device should, in principle, provide both the very large bandwidth attainable with the tilted array and the very high diffraction efficiency provided by the phased array, at the cost of a more complex design with its concomitant fabrication problems.

12.4.5.5 Relative Merits of Array Versus Single-Element Transducers

The single-element transducers of either the chirped or the curved type offer the advantage of elimination of the need for either power splitters or matching networks. This advantage comes, however, at the expense of a more complex, difficult-to-fabricate device which offers no flexibility should the response prove to be insufficiently uniform over the entire bandwidth of the device. The multiple-element arrays, including the tilted array, the phased array, and the tilted, phased array, occupy more area on the substrate and require a power splitter; however, they have the advantage that an individual attenuator may be placed in series with each transducer so that the response uniformity can be adjusted experimentally to any desired accuracy. This can prove to be of considerable value in cases where fabrication nonuniformities or defects in the acousto-optic material cause the measured uniformity to fall short of the designed value. The advantages and disadvantages of each approach weigh differently for each new application, and it is necessary, therefore, to consider flexibility, response uniformity, complexity, bandwidth, and diffraction efficiency as parameters in a tradeoff analysis before deciding upon a particular transducer design approach.

12.4.6 Sources for Integrated Optics

Double-heterostructure (DH) injection lasers, some of which are capable of producing mode-controlled CW (continuous-wave) power outputs of up to tens of milliwatts at room temperature, are nearly ideally suited to integrated optical applications. DH lasers based on various three- and four-element compounds of the III-V intermetallic series are under intense development, and commercially available devices now allow coverage of most of the wavelength spectrum between 0.8 and 1.5 μm. The most thoroughly developed among the DH lasers are those of the GaAlAs system which can be made to lase between about 0.92 μm (pure GaAs) and approximately 0.75 μm by controlling the Al content of the active layer. The GaAlAs DH laser is the most promising light source for near-term IO device applications.

The active region in a DH laser is a very thin layer sandwiched between two layers having somewhat higher aluminum content and lower optical index of refraction. The resultant structure forms a waveguide

which is capable of supporting only a single mode in the direction perpendicular to, or transverse to, the junctions. The various GaAlAs
layers can be grown on a suitable GaAs substrate by liquid phase
epitaxy (LPE), molecular beam epitaxy (MBE), or metal organic chemical vapor deposition (MO-CVD). The active layer is usually between
0.1 and 0.3 µm in thickness, but it can be thinner than 0.1 µm; the
lower-index layers are thicker but still only of the order of 1 µm in
thickness. Typical laser diode lengths range between 200 and 400 µm,
although lasers have been fabricated with lengths as short as 50 µm.

Several different approaches to achievement of mode control in the
direction parallel to the heterojunction planes (the lateral direction)
have been explored. The resultant lasers can in general be classified
as either gain-guided or index-guided structures, but there are also
some more complex structures which employ both gain and index guiding. In the simplest variant of the gain-guided device [114], a contact stripe placed over the active region serves to confine the injected
carriers to the area beneath the stripe, thereby producing gain only
within this region. The gain profile in the lateral direction serves,
through the complex part of the index of refraction, to produce waveguiding. When the stripe is sufficiently narrow, the waveguide sup-
ports only a single lateral mode. Since, however, the field intensity
and injected carrier density are greatest at the center of the stripe,
the stimulated recombination rate is also highest there, and this can
result in *hole burning* in the mode profile at high power levels. The
mode becomes unstable and can shift laterally between the peaks on
either side of the hole, as shown in Fig. 12.29. The hole-burning
effect can be eliminated by making the stripe sufficiently narrow, but
this also results in excessive lateral diffraction spread in the output
beam, and it can produce an output pattern which, while it appears to
be uniform in the near field, has two peaks, similar to the hole-
burnt profile, in the far field [115].

Index-guided lasers achieve lateral confinement by means of lateral
structure variations which produce an effective index of refraction
that is greater in the center than on either side. Such structures
form true lateral waveguides exhibiting greater mode control and output beam directional stability. Reinhart et al. first demonstrated [116]
index guiding through the use of anodic etching to form low-loss rib
waveguides with widths ranging between 5 and 20 µm and with rib
step heights of 0.1 to 1 µm. Structures which have received considerably greater attention for commercial purposes are the buried hetero-
structure (BH) and the channeled-substrate-planar (CSP) laser geome-
tries. The CSP structure, which has its active layers deposited over
an etched channel in the GaAs substrate, is shown in Fig. 12.30 [117].
Index guiding is also exhibited in the planoconvex waveguide laser in
which the active region is made thickest in the center so that the effective index will peak on axis and in structures which utilize an asymmetric aluminum content along with the gradual change in layer thick-

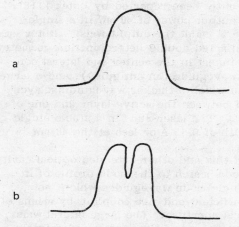

Figure 12.29 Carrier density distribution in a semiconductor diode laser (a) at or near threshold and (b) at higher current density where spatial hole burning has set in due to the higher recombination rate at the center where the local optical intensity is greatest.

ness. Most index-guided lasers also run in a single longitudinal mode over a considerable range of drive powers, and a laser linewidth of less than 40 MHz at current levels of 1.2 times threshold has been reported by Aiki et al. [117]. The same lasers are capable of delivering 3 to 5 mW of output per facet and now have expected lifetimes at these powers of 10^5 to 10^6 h.

A great deal of effort is currently being focused on the development of relatively high GaAlAs laser powers in larger output beams for both optical signal-processing and communications applications. Considerable

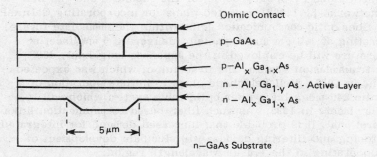

Figure 12.30 Channeled-substrate-planar (CSP) semiconductor diode laser structure in n-GaAs.

success in this direction has recently been reported by Botez [118],
who has achieved a single-facet output power of 40 mW in a single-
mode beam measuring 1.7 μm × 6.5 μm at the output waist. Botez employed a combination of the constricted double-heterojunction geometry,
in which the active layers are thinnest in the center and lateral confinement is achieved by a leaky waveguide (an antiguide), and a large
optical cavity (LOC) structure in which a thicker waveguiding layer
of intermediate index is inserted between the active layer and one of
the outer GaAlAs cladding layers. The laser runs in a stable single
longitudinal mode with a line width of 0.15 Å or less at the 40-mW
power level.

The large transverse waist of this and other extended optical cavity
devices provides an improved modal match to the mode profile of indiffused $LiNbO_3$:Ti and other single-mode waveguides which, as
Burns has shown [119], allows efficient end-fire coupling by means of
lenses of quite moderate numerical aperture. The large lateral waist,
moreover, reduces the diffraction spread of the beam coupled into a
planar waveguide and permits optical systems to be designed to operate
at relatively higher F-numbers where diffraction-limited imagery is
more readily achieved. The LOC-produced beam also contributes an
improved match to the mode profile of single-mode optical fibers. It
is thus conceivable that near-term technology will make possible the
coupling of powers approaching 50 mW into single-mode waveguides
and fibers.

In addition to GaAlAs lasers which can be hybrid-coupled into
optical waveguides, considerable research has been performed on distributed feedback and distributed Bragg reflector lasers which are
well suited to monolithic devices incorporating GaAs waveguide technology. This work has been surveyed in an excellent review paper
by Tien [120] and will not be discussed here.

The development of the GaAlAs CW, room-temperature laser has
occurred gradually over the past decade, but the pace at which the
III-V quaternary lasers are progressing is very much more rapid.
Recent presentations by spokespeople for the Japanese and the Bell
telephone networks [121,122] reported plans for incorporating GaInAsP
lasers into fiber optic communication links within the immediate future.
Diodes operating at 1.3 μm and capable of delivering 5 mW/facet at
room temperature will be employed in the Japanese long-haul, 400-
mega-bit/s transmission system, the first link of which was expected
to go on-line in 1982. Bell Telephone plans to initiate operation of a
trans-Atlantic 240-mega-bit/s fiber optic cable system which will
utilize similar lasers in 1985. As such fiber-based communication links
become operational, it is probable that increased demand for integrated
optical switching and filtering devices will stimulate development of
IO circuits operating in the 1.3-μm wavelength region.

Finally, it is necessary to consider the problems associated with the
butt coupling of a laser diode to an integrated optical waveguide. As

has been shown by Hall et al. [123], the most critical tolerance to be met for efficient coupling involves the alignment of the transverse waist of the laser beam to the mode profile of the waveguide. A technique has recently been described which allows this alignment to be effected by means of a relatively simple micromechanical fixture [124, 125]. It involves bonding of the laser diode to a large copper heat sink having an optically flat, specularly reflecting surface, measurement of the height of the active region above this surface by means of the Lloyd's fringes formed by interference between the direct and reflected laser beams, and highly accurate setting of adjustable spacers which, when placed between the heat sink and the top surface of the waveguide, position the laser waist with respect to the waveguide mode profile. This technique has been employed in the butt coupling of a GaAlAs DH laser to an IO RF spectrum analyzer [125].

12.4.7 Detectors for Integrated Optics

For most of the early years of the development of integrated optics, attention was focused upon waveguide structures, modulators, lenses, and other components to be employed in demonstrations of the feasibility of using guided light in signal management applications. Since solid-state integrated circuits technology was being advanced at an enormously more rapid rate than IO during this same period, it was generally assumed that detectors would be available for use with integrated optical systems when the need arose. Little effort was expended, therefore, toward the development of detector arrays specifically for coupling to an optical waveguide until it became apparent in the mid-1970s that commercially available arrays were unsatisfactory on several counts. A consequent surge of activity in this area has led to the development, first, of silicon detectors for use with waveguides sputtered monolithically onto the same silicon substrate [126,127] and, more recently, of detector arrays to be end-butt-coupled to LiNbO$_3$ waveguides [128-130]. Only with the advent of these new detector arrays has it become possible to begin to test integrated optical, as well as bulk optical, RF spectrum analyzers at data output rates approaching the capabilities of these AO devices. The development of photodetectors designed specifically for acousto-optic signal-processing systems has recently been reviewed by Borsuk [131].

Principal considerations in the design of photodetectors for use in integrated optical systems are size, response uniformity at a given spectral frequency, dynamic range, data rate, and cross talk. Small size is of importance because it has a controlling influence on the design of the optical systems and, thereby, on the overall size of the IO substrate. Since IO devices will in general operate in only a very narrow spectral region determined by the laser source, the spectral bandwidth of the detector is not a major consideration; response uniformity over the length of the array, however, is essential if the

accurate signal amplitude information required in most processing applications is to be provided. Certain nonuniformities, such as fixed
pattern noise on the array, can be corrected with suitable postdetection processing, but such processing should be held to a minimum in
order to simplify overall system performance.

Dynamic range is of extreme importance in most signal-processing
systems, with typical requirements for such devices as RF spectrum
analyzers, convolvers, and correlators being of the order of 50 dB in
input signal range. The various parameters of an integrated optical
device which limit its dynamic range will be discussed in Sec. 12.5.1,
which deals with the spectrum analyzer, but it is obviously necessary
that the detector exhibit a dynamic range of better than 50 dB if the
system in which it is utilized is to meet this requirement.

The output data rate depends on the particular type of IO signal
processor with which the detector is to be employed. Spectrum analyzers produce a completely updated report of signal activity within
their bandwidth during each acoustic transit time across the optical
beam (usually 2 μs or less), and a high data rate is essential in
order to make efficient use of the spectral information and to provide
accurate determination of time of arrival of a signal. This means that
each element should be read out as often as possible, and since large
numbers of elements are required to produce high resolution over a
large RF bandwidth, data rates therefore approach 100 MHz. On the
other hand, detectors to be used with time-integrating correlators
must have the capability of integrating signals for very much longer
durations. The design criteria employed in the development of high
data rate detectors where dark current is not generally a problem are
significantly different from those utilized in a long-integration-time
detector where high dark currents will seriously impair detector performance.

Cross talk in an integrated optical system can arise either from
electrical factors in the array or from optical factors in the optical
train. A major source of electrical cross talk is photons which are
not absorbed at the detector surface and penetrate to deeper levels.
The carriers created upon absorption at the deeper levels can migrate
laterally before being collected by a photodiode. Such lateral diffusion
gives rise to cross talk, and it is more prevalent at lower optical carrier frequencies where the absorption coefficient is lower. Thus, the
electrical cross talk in a silicon photodiode will be greater at GaAlAs
wavelengths (830 nm) than at He-Ne wavelengths (632.8 nm). To minimize photon penetration cross talk, a detector array fabricated for
use in a spectrum analyzer has had the N^+ photodiode elements isolated
in boron-doped tubs, made by ion implantation, which are regions of
opposite carrier concentration from that of the substrate material in
which the array was fabricated [131]. While this does effectively limit
the electrical cross talk, it also somewhat reduces the quantum efficiency of the detector so that a tradeoff between these two parameters becomes necessary.

The sensor array referred to above and shown in Fig. 12.31 is a self-scanned linear photodiode array consisting of 140 elements on a 12-μm pitch. For high-speed readout the array is divided into seven groups of 20 elements, with all groups being addressed in parallel by a 10-stage dynamic CMOS shift register. Each group has two electrometer output circuit channels, one handling the odd-numbered pixels while the other handles the even-numbered ones during each clock cycle of the shift register. Thus, 14 parallel samples are read out during every clock cycle. The maximum shift register clock rate is 5 MHz, resulting in an access time or integration time of 2 μs.

The individual elements are 12 μm wide and 360 μm long. The length was selected in order to provide sufficient charge-handling capacity to allow a dynamic range in excess of 50 dB. Despite the large active pixel area, the dark current is essentially negligible because of the 2-μs integration time. Of the 360-μm total length, all but the central 20 μm is masked in order to minimize spurious responses due to scattered or reflected light from the waveguide or the substrate. Measurements of the operational dynamic range have yielded a figure of 43 dB, but the array was being operated with postdetection circuitry which prevented observation of the calculated noise equivalent signal of 1000 electrons.

Another array developed specifically to be butt-coupled to an integrated optical waveguide consists of an MOS depletion-mode linear array photodetector which is accessed by parallel-input/serial-output CCD (charge-coupled device) shift registers [130]. It is divided into four groups of 25 pixels on an 8-μm pitch, and it has been designed to be read out either in four parallel channels with each channel addressing 25 elements or in two parallel channels with each channel addressing 50 elements.

Developmental effort is currently underway toward building the next generation of integrated optical sensor arrays which will include postdetection processing to analyze and sort, by amplitude, frequency, and time of arrival, wide-dynamic-range optical signals presented to its input plane [131].

12.5 INTEGRATED OPTICAL DEVICES

12.5.1 RF Spectrum Analyzer

Over the course of the past several years a considerable effort has been expended, at several industrial laboratories in the United States and Europe, toward the development of an integrated optical signal-processing device which would demonstrate both the capability of performing complex signal-processing functions in integrated optical format and the advantages which integrated optics has to offer over bulk optical or other processing means. The device chosen as an appropriate example was the integrated optical RF spectrum analyzer.

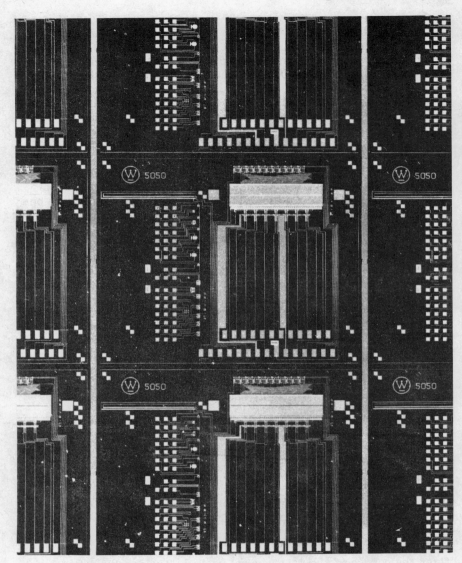

Figure 12.31 Self-scanned linear photodiode array of 140 active elements with 12-µm center-to-center spacing. This array was designed and fabricated specifically for use with the integrated optical RF spectrum analyzer shown in Figs. 12.32 and 12.34. (From Ref. 131.)

The principal goal established for the program was the development of a demonstration model which would serve as a credible first step toward a useful spectrum analyzer system. To this end the specifications were set at an RF bandwidth of 400 MHz, a nominal frequency resolution of 4 MHz, and an operational dynamic range of at least 30 dB. In addition, the readout time was to be consistent with the minimum integration and access time of the best available photodetector array.

Two waveguide-substrate systems were considered as candidates for the spectrum analyzer application, and much of the initial effort in the program was directed toward development of individual components for each of them. One system was silicon with waveguides of either Corning 7059 glass or Nb_2O_5 deposited by sputtering over a thermally grown buffer layer of SiO_2; the other was $LiNbO_3$ with waveguides formed by indiffusion of titanium. In addition to the differences in waveguide processing for these materials, they also require different approaches toward fabrication of SAW transducers and waveguide lenses as well as toward waveguide-detector coupling.

The silicon-based approach appeared to have several advantages. All the technology associated with integrated circuits was available to assist in processing. The refractive index of the sputtered glass waveguides is sufficiently low that many optical materials are available which can be deposited to form Luneburg lenses [132]. The detector array could be fabricated in the waveguide substrate, and techniques had been developed for coupling radiation from waveguides to such arrays [126,127]. Two major factors, however, eventually swung the decision in favor of $LiNbO_3$.

As noted previously, Si is nonpiezoelectric, and it is necessary to deposit a piezoelectric film on the waveguide in order to allow generation of SAWs. Mergerian et al. [104] developed a broadband transducer array covering a 268-MHz bandwidth centered at 400 MHz using the tilted, frequency-staggered array approach sketched in Fig. 12.26. The arrays were fabricated on 7059 waveguides on silicon by first evaporating a set of interdigitated electrode fingers and then depositing a film of ZnO over the fingers and tapering the ZnO film so as to launch the generated SAW onto the waveguide surface. Well-ordered ZnO films, which exhibited transduction efficiencies approaching theoretical limits, were obtained, but laser probe measurements using the method of Lean and Powell [133] showed SAW propagation losses on the ZnO which were about 38 dB/cm at 300 MHz and which increased approximately as the square of the frequency. To overcome such losses and launch useful SAW intensities onto the guide would require inordinately large RF input powers.

The other factor which rules in favor of $LiNbO_3$ was the development a short time later of the technology for producing near-diffraction-limited aspheric geodesic lenses in $LiNbO_3$ [89,93]. Until this major breakthrough, it was widely believed that aspheric surfaces of

adequate profile quality could not be generated in a practical manner
on a waveguide substrate, and the Luneburg lens appeared therefore
to be the only promising approach to the fabrication of waveguide
lenses. With the advent of the aspheric geodesic lens, $LiNbO_3$, with
its far superior acoustic properties, became the obvious choice as the
IO material to be employed in developing the spectrum analyzer. It
should be pointed out, however, that work on Luneburg lenses has
continued, and recent results reported by Boyd et al. [134], who
measured waveguide propagation losses as low as 0.01 dB/cm on laser-
annealed sputtered waveguides on SiO_2, could eventually result in
silicon-based waveguide technology again gaining favor, at least for
certain applications.

The basic layout of the IO spectrum analyzer (SA) is shown schematically in Fig. 12.32. It is a three-element hybrid assembly consisting of the laser source, the $LiNbO_3$ integrated optical substrate, and
the photodiode array. The system is designed for operation with a
butt-coupled GaAlAs laser diode emitting at approximately 0.83 µm,
but it can also be (and has been) operated, at some loss in AO performance because of Bragg angle mismatch, with focused, end-fire-
coupled He-Ne radiation. The detector array, which is butt-coupled
to the output end of the waveguide, is the 140-element, self-scanned
photodiode array discussed in the previous section.

The optical system will be discussed briefly. Although early pro-
posals for IO spectrum analyzers suggested the use of a three-lens
optical system [135], it can readily be shown that the beam spread from
either a butt-coupled injection laser or a He-Ne laser beam focused to
a spot size of a few micrometers is sufficient to obviate the need for a

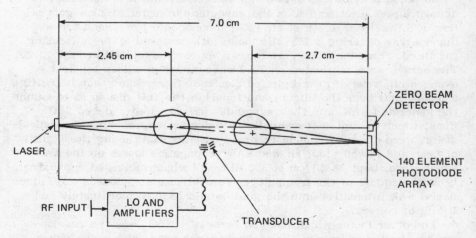

Figure 12.32 Schematic of the 400-MHz bandwidth integrated optical
RF spectrum analyzer. (From Ref. 5.)

divergent input lens. The focal length of the output (transform) lens is determined by the number N and the pitch p of the detector elements to be addressed and the total deflection angle $\Delta \theta$ to be provided by the 400-MHz Bragg cell. This angle is twice the difference between the maximum and minimum Bragg angles or

$$\Delta \theta = 2[\theta_B (max) - \theta_B (min)]$$

$$= 2\left(\sin^{-1} \frac{\lambda f_{max}}{2nv} - \sin^{-1} \frac{\lambda f_{min}}{2nv} \right)$$

$$\approx \frac{\lambda}{nv} \Delta f \qquad (12.46)$$

For $\Delta f = 400$ MHz and with $\lambda = 0.83$ µm, $n = 2.18$, and $v = 3.48 \times 10^5$ cm/s, $\Delta \theta = 0.043$ rad. By simple trigonometry the focal length becomes

$$f = \frac{N(p/2)}{\tan(\Delta \theta/2)} = 2.74 \text{ cm} \qquad (12.47)$$

The focal length of the collimating lens was calculated from the beam spread of the laser source and the optical aperture required to yield the desired resolution. The aperture was selected to allow the optical system to produce 100 spots overlapping at their $1/e^2$-intensity points even if the system operates at 1.5 times the diffraction limit; this set the gaussian waist in the AO cell at 1 mm. The laser chosen for design purposes was the Hitachi HLP-1400, which was reported to have an output spot width of 6 µm [117] (waist size = 3 µm). Using the expression for gaussian beam propagation, we find that the beam will grow to a waist of 1 mm after traveling 2.45 cm in LiNbO$_3$. The magnification of the optical system is the ratio of the output to input focal lengths, or 1.12; the design F-numbers of the lenses are both between F/12 and F/14. The separation between the lenses is not critical and was chosen to be approximately 2.5 cm for convenience in depositing the transducers.

The center frequency of 600 MHz was chosen because it is the lowest frequency which allows a 400-MHz bandwidth to be covered without exceeding a full octave. The stepped-frequency tilted transducer array approach was adopted, and a three-element array was originally selected. Subsequent analysis showed that a 3-dB bandwidth of nearly 400 MHz should be realizable with a two-element array, and it was decided to accept some response roll-off at the ends of the band in return for considerable simplification of the mask-making and transducer-deposition processes. The parameters of the transducer array are summarized in Table 12.3. Measurements of the acousto-optical diffraction efficiency taken on test samples of this array on LiNbO$_3$:Ti resulted in peak deflection efficiencies of 6% at 490 MHz and 5% at 700 MHz with 60 mW of RF drive power applied to the unmatched transducers.

Table 12.3 Two-Element Transducer Design: 400-MHz Total Bandwidth and 600-MHz Center Frequency

Center frequency	483 MHz	669 MHz
Number of fingers	5	5
Acoustic aperture	0.73 mm	0.36 mm
Finger widths	1.80 μm	1.30 μm
Finger pitch	3.60 μm	2.60 μm
Tilt to axis	1.52°	2.10°

Source: Ref. 125.

Initial tests of diamond-turned geodesic lenses were performed on y-cut LiNbO$_3$ wafers, and it was observed that the lenses had lowest attenuation coefficients for TE radiation propagating along the x direction, where it sees the extraordinary index of refraction. y-cut crystals of LiNbO$_3$ are not available, however, in the lengths of 6 to 7 cm needed for the layout shown in Fig. 12.32, and x-cut was therefore chosen. The width of the substrate was set at 2.5 cm for convenience in handling and mounting.

Considerable developmental work on all the components, as well as on edge-polishing techniques, was necessary following the selection of material and completion of the design. The performance of the two-lens optical system for an end-fire-coupled He-Ne input spot of 5-μm FWHM (full width at half maximum) is shown in Fig. 12.33. The system optical quality of 1.15 times diffraction-limited is considerably better than the 1.5 factor allowed for in the design. The work led to the successful operation of the first working spectrum analyzer in April 1980 [5].

The fabrication sequence followed in integrating all the components into a working IO SA begins with the polishing of the input and output edges of the substrate. Next, the aspheric depressions for the collimating and transform lenses are machined to the required depths and profiles to accuracies which are typically measured to be of the order of 1 μm; they are also positioned so that the center of each depression lies at a distance of exactly a focal length from the polished substrate edge nearer to it to accuracies of better than 1.5 μm. The samples are then cleaned, titanium metal is evaporated onto the surface, and the waveguides are formed by diffusion for 6 hr at 1000°C. The transducer arrays are deposited using standard photolithographic procedures, and leads are bonded from the transducers to standoffs which are glued to the nearby surface.

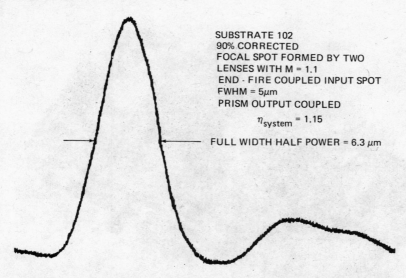

SUBSTRATE 102
90% CORRECTED
FOCAL SPOT FORMED BY TWO
LENSES WITH M = 1.1
END - FIRE COUPLED INPUT SPOT
FWHM = 5μm
PRISM OUTPUT COUPLED

η_{system} = 1.15

FULL WIDTH HALF POWER = 6.3 μm

Table 12.33 Far-field pattern produced by a pair of diamond-machined
integrated optical geodesic waveguide lenses on a LiNbO$_3$ substrate.
These lenses were corrected over 90% of their total apertures of 8 mm
and 8.8 mm, respectively, and provided an image spot size which was
1.15 times diffraction-limited. (From Ref. 5.)

The completed substrate is mounted face down in a Cer-Vit[†] fixture
which has been designed to serve as a miniature optical bench. The
photodiode array, mounted on a smaller Cer-Vit holder which rides on
the same optically polished surface as the substrate, is butt-coupled
to the output edge, at a coupling angle of 45° with respect to the waveguide plane in order to minimize reflective feedback to the waveguide.
The transducers are connected to the RF input ports, and the spectrum analyzer is ready for preliminary testing. Provision is made for
incorporation of a laser diode mounting fixture onto the overall assembly
on the Cer-Vit optical bench. A photograph of the completed device in
its Cer-Vit mount is shown in Fig. 12.34.

Much of the testing of the IO SA has been performed at He-Ne laser
wavelength because of the difficulty associated with the butt coupling
of a diode laser. The beam from a He-Ne laser is expanded and focused to a spot 6 to 7 µm in diameter precisely at the center of the input edge of the waveguide. Attenuators are placed in the beam to
limit the power provided in the spot to less than 400 µW in order to
prevent optical damage to the waveguide. The device has been ob-

[†]Trademark of Owens-Illinois Co.

Figure 12.34 Photograph of the integrated optical RF spectrum analyzer with its butt-coupled photodiode detector array in its Cer-Vit
mounting fixture. (From Ref. 124.)

served to operate over its full 400-MHz design bandwidth, but, since
the Bragg angles at 630 nm are only three-fourths of those at 830
nm, the frequency interval subtended by each detector element is increased from 4 to 5.3 MHz and only 75 detector elements are addressed
throughout the 400-MHz bandwidth. The response of a given detector
element to a scanning focal spot produced by a swept RF beam is depicted in Fig. 12.35, where it is shown that a total RF interval of approximately 8.5 to 9 MHz is represented from the point where the
leading edge of the spot begins to enter the detector until the trailing
edge passes out of the same element.

The dynamic range of the spectrum analyzer has been measured
using a frequency-swept RF input signal power of 40 to 80 mW applied
to the surface acoustic wave transducer through a calibrated attenuator
which can be varied in 1-dB steps. The signal from a single, arbitrarily chosen photodiode was passed through a sample-and-hold circuit
and displayed on an oscilloscope. Attenuation was inserted into the
line until the signal could no longer be distinguished from the noise
and then removed until the signal was equal to the noise. The RF
dynamic range determined in this manner varied between 18 and 22 dB.

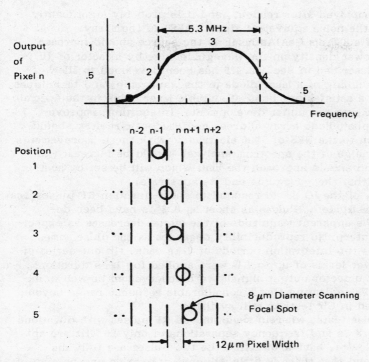

Figure 12.35 Response of a single pixel in the spectrum analyzer photodiode array to a swept RF input signal. (From Ref. 124.)

A second technique employed to determine the dynamic range compares the maximum observed signal from a given detector element to the minimum detectable signal. Maximum signal levels of up to 60 mV have been observed, and the minimum detectable signal appears to lie between 70 and 80 μV, thus providing an overall dynamic range of approximately 29 dB. The difference between the two measured values probably resulted from difficulty in maintaining optimal end-fire coupling efficiency over the time required to perform the initially described measurement.

The achievable dynamic range of this device is probably considerably greater than either of the above measurements would indicate. On the one hand, the peak output signal from the detector is limited by the optical input power which can be coupled into the waveguide at 0.63 μm without producing waveguide damage and by the RF power which can be applied to the transducer array without risking damage to the interdigitated fingers. At the same time, the minimum detectable signal quoted above is limited by the readout circuitry and the instruments employed after readout, and it is probably significantly greater than the noise equivalent signal (NES) of the array.

The use of a 830 nm GaAlAs laser as the source should increase the allowed power density on the waveguide edge by a factor of 10. The fixture described in Sec. 12.4.6 has been developed to allow efficient butt coupling of a laser diode to the waveguide, and techniques for achieving a satisfactory bond of suitable laser chips to the specially designed heat sink are under development. In addition, improvements in the photodiode array address and readout circuitry should allow operation to the NES of 1000 electrons. With these improvements the dynamic range of the spectrum analyzer should be increased to over 40 dB and should approach the limit which will be set by scattered light within the waveguide and its substrate.

The ability of the IO SA to respond to short-duration RF pulses has also been investigated. Pulses as short as 0.3 µs have been detected, but the apparent magnitude of the signal decreases as expected, and the interpulse reproducibility degrades as the pulse sometimes overlaps two integration periods of 2 µs each. In one series of tests, RF power levels of up to 1 W were applied for 1-µs durations, and resultant detector output signals were observed to be well in excess of 100 mV, indicating that a considerable response range beyond those observed in CW tests is still available.

Double-pulse tests, wherein simultaneous RF pulses with durations as short as 0.3 µs and frequency separations of only 20 MHz are applied to the device, have shown that the two pulses are fully distinguishable and that there is little evidence of overlap and no sign of intermodulation between the signals. Figure 12.36 shows the output of a single channel of the detector array when two such pulses of 1 µs are applied. The heavy traces in the figure are the output signals from neighboring pixels in the absence of light. The lighter traces above the sixth and eighth traces are the pulse detection outputs for input signals at 680 and 700 MHz, respectively. It is evident from the figure that the pixel between those two, which corresponds to approximately 690 MHz, is not excited.

A second integrated optical spectrum analyzer having essentially the same bandwidth and resolution specifications has been developed by Ranganath et al. [136]. Major differences lie in their use of a chirped transducer, of geodesic lenses fabricated by ultrasonic grinding, and of the 100-element MOS depletion-mode sensor array described at the end of Sec. 12.4.7.

12.5.2 Analog-to-Digital Converter

The use of integrated optical techniques to develop a high-speed electro-optic analog-to-digital (A/D) converter has been the subject of both theoretical and experimental investigations since it was first proposed by Taylor in 1975 [62]. This application is of special interest

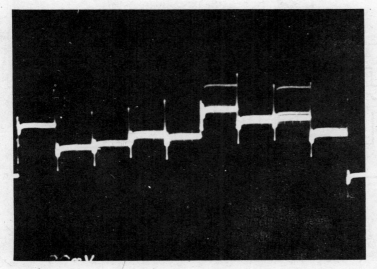

Figure 12.36 Oscilloscope trace showing detection of two simultaneously applied 1.0-µs RF pulses separated in frequency by 20 MHz. (From
Ref. 124.)

because the integrated optical device should be capable of performing
conversions at rates which far exceed those which can presently be
achieved with integrated circuit technology. An integrated optical
A/D converter, which should provide six-bit accuracy at rates of up
to one gigasample per second (GS/s), has been designed by Leonberger et al. [137].

The device is based on electro-optic modulator concepts proposed
by Martin [138] and Ohmachi and Noda [139]. The basic element of
the modulator is a channel-waveguide, Mach-Zehnder interferometer
with electrodes placed on either side of one arm, as shown in Fig.
12.19. When a field is applied across this arm of the interferometer,
the linear electro-optic effect will cause the phase velocity to be altered
with respect to that in the other arm. If the two arms are identical,
in the absence of a field the signals in each arm will recombine in
phase at the output to produce a maximum light level. If a field
which alters the phase velocity in one arm by π rad is applied, the
signals will destructively interfere to produce a null output. Taylor
et al. [63] have shown that a phase retardation of π rad can be achieved
with a voltage of 1.2 V for a TE mode and 3.1 V for a TM mode.

A schematic diagram of a combination of four interferometric modulators to realize a four-bit A/D converter is shown in Fig. 12.37 [137,
140] along with the output of the modulators plotted as a function of an
analog signal V applied in parallel to all four modulators. The digital

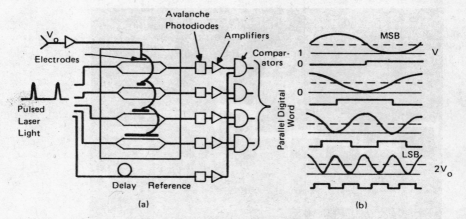

Figure 12.37 (a) Schematic diagram of a four-bit electro-optic analog-to-digital (A/D) converter; (b) intensity vs. voltage for a four-bit A/D converter with Gray code output. (From Ref. 137.)

code, in this case a Gray code, is obtained by comparing the modulator outputs of each of the photodiodes with a reference signal from the same light source used to excite the modulators. If the output intensity is above or below some threshold value I_t, a 0 or a 1, respectively, is generated. The sampling of the analog signal is performed using a series of short laser pulses at the desired sampling rate.

The electro-optic interaction length L_n for the nth modulator is determined by the electrode length and is given by

$$L_n = 2^{n-2}L_1 \qquad n = 2, 3, \ldots, N \tag{12.48}$$

The phase of light in one channel is retarded with respect to that in the other by an amount $\Delta\phi_n$, given by

$$\Delta\phi_n = 2^{n-2}KL_1V \tag{12.49}$$

where K is a constant determined by the electro-optic coefficients of the material, the waveguide parameters, and the electrode spacing. The intensity of light emerging from the nth modulator is

$$I_n = A_n \cos^2\left(\frac{\Delta\phi}{2} + \psi_n\right) \tag{12.50}$$

where ψ_n is a static phase shift obtained with a dc bias and A_n is the modulation amplitude. For an N-bit device a π phase shift in the Nth modulator, which represents the least significant bit, corresponds to a change of one quantization step q in the applied voltage and results in a one-bit change of the output code. For an applied signal

$$V = V_0(1 + \sin \omega t) \qquad\qquad (12.51)$$

and 2^N quantization steps, $q = V_0/2^{N-1}$ and $KL_1 = \pi/V_0$.

A Gray code is chosen to minimize errors since each quantization step results in a change in one bit channel, unlike the conventional offset binary code where multiple bits change at each quantization step. This Gray code output yields one more bit of precision than the offset binary code for a given set of electrode lengths and applied voltage.

In some recently published results Leonberger [141] reported operation of a modulator in which a Ti-indiffused $LiNbO_3$ waveguide with 5-μm-wide channels was used to demonstrate a 25-dB extinction ratio at a wavelength of 1.06 μm.

The electro-optic integrated optical A/D converter offers several advantages over other types of converters. One of these is the fact that a short laser pulse acts as a time window for performing a sampling operation; it therefore eliminates the need for a sample-and-hold device. Other features include a reduction in the number of electronic comparators required, lower electrical power dissipation, and the possibility of using mode-locked diode lasers to achieve very high-speed operation at rates of 2 GHz or more.

12.5.3 Time-Integrating Correlator

Temporal integration of an acousto-optically modulated signal, as opposed to spatial integration, can be utilized to realize extremely large time-bandwidth products. In particular, the time-integrating techniques permit operation on signals with very large time-bandwidths (TB) products without requiring storage of the entire temporal history as a spatial record [142,143]. As a result it is possible to perform certain two-dimensional algorithms without requiring two-dimensional spatial light modulators. The time-integrating correlator has been treated in earlier chapters of this text and will not be discussed here except to indicate that such a device could be implemented in an integrated optical format.

One version of a one-dimensional, integrated optical time-integrating correlator was suggested by Tsai [49] and is depicted in Fig. 12.38. The signal to be correlated, $S_1(t)$, is used to intensity-modulate a laser source which is coupled to the integrated optical waveguide. The light is then collimated by the first of three waveguide lenses and is diffracted by an amplitude-modulated surface acoustic wave produced by a transducer driven by an RF reference signal $S_2(t)$. The diffracted beam is then Schlieren-imaged onto a linear photodiode array where the intensity distribution in the image plane is proportional to $I_1(t)I_2(t - x/v)$, where x is the spatial dimension across the collimated optical beam and v is the acoustic wave velocity. This distribution is the correlation between the signal $S_1(t)$ and the

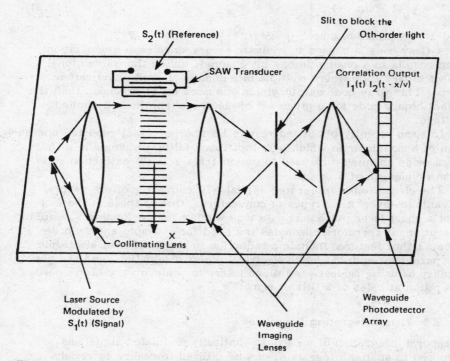

Figure 12.38 One version of an integrated optical, time-integrating correlator which uses a modulated laser source together with a surface acoustic wave and Schlieren imaging. (From Ref. 49.)

reference $S_2(t)$. The resultant output voltage from the ith detector in the array is given by

$$V\left(\frac{x_i}{v}\right) = \int_T I_1(t) I_2\left(t - \frac{x_i}{v}\right) dt \qquad (12.52)$$

where T is the integration time of the detector. The large value of the TB product results because the integration time is set by the timing of the CCD array used to read out the signal, and it can be made considerably longer than that of spatially integrating devices which is simply equal to the acoustic transit time.

This integrated optical time-integrating correlator is an incoherent device which either operates at low diffraction efficiency or uses an optical bias at high diffraction efficiency in order to achieve linear intensity modulation. It is also possible to fabricate an integrated optical version of the two-beam time-integrating correlator described by Berg et al. [144]. Such a device would again utilize a single laser, which in this case would be unmodulated. The output from the laser would be collimated by a waveguide lens and split into two equal-intensity beams by an integrated optical beam splitter, and each of these would interact with a surface acoustic wave propagating at the Bragg angle with respect to it. The interaction geometry is selected so that the resulting diffracted beams are made to be collinear and to interfere at the plane of a detector array. The intensity at each detector element will vary as a function of time depending on the relative amplitudes and phases of the two surface acoustic waves. The time-integrated output of the array contains the cross correlation of the signals applied to the two transducers, and the position of the correlation signal on the detector array is a measure of the time difference of arrival of the two signals. An interference pattern, which can be used to identify the frequency shift of the correlated signals from the center frequencies of the SAWs, will also be present. Furthermore, digital Fourier analysis of the detector array output waveform can be used to extract information concerning the modulation impressed upon frequency-hopped and other pulse-code-modulated signals.

The much greater TB products of integrated optical time-integrating correlators allow much finer frequency resolution than can be attained with the spatially integrating type of spectrum analyzer described in Sec. 12.5.1. Although time-integrating devices have not yet been demonstrated in an integrated optical format, significant developments in this area should be forthcoming over the next few years as natural outgrowths of the recent successes achieved in the fabrication of high-quality components for the IO spectrum analyzer.

12.5.4 High-Speed Optical Switching

A number of integrated optical-switching concepts which rely primarily upon the use of channel waveguides [134-135,141-142], with means for electro-optically altering the evanescent coupling conditions between the guides, have been proposed [138-139,145-146]. The proposed switches are generally relatively large, and they require high electric fields; they are therefore not suitable for use in applications which involve interconnecting a large number of channels on a single chip. Recently Peng et al. [147] reported the development of a 2 × 3 planar optical waveguide switch which features low switching voltages, low insertion and scattering losses, and good electrical isolation. In addition, it has the potential for extension to an N × M network suitable for use in computer communication lines. The device incorporates six Bragg electro-optical deflectors arranged in two rows and three columns, with those in different columns having different periodicities; a 4 × 4 version is depicted in Fig. 12.39. Separate pulsed light sources are collimated and fed to the two different rows. When a control voltage is applied to the Bragg electrodes in the ith column and jth row, a

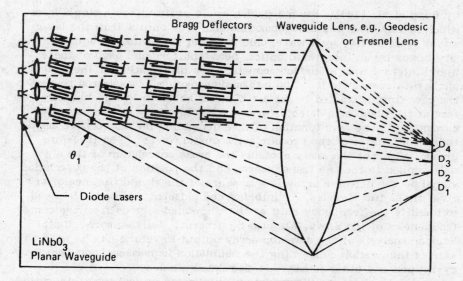

Figure 12.39 Planar waveguide optical switch featuring low switching
voltages, low insertion and scattering loss, and electrical isolation.
(From Ref. 147.)

fraction of the intensity in that beam will be deflected into the direction θ_i given by

$$\theta_i = 2 \sin^{-1}\left(\frac{\lambda}{2n_{eff}\Lambda_i}\right) \qquad (12.53)$$

where n_{eff} is the effective index of the guided mode and Λ_i is the
period of the ith deflector. This deflected beam will be detected by
the ith detector placed at the focal plane of a waveguide analyzing
lens. In a similar fashion the ℓth detector will receive signals deflected from the electrodes in the ℓth column which have a period Λ_ℓ
producing a deflection angle θ_ℓ.

This device, which has been developed to demonstrate the feasibility of the N × M switch concept, has an on-off switching ratio which
is greater in TM mode than in TE mode operation. In either case, the
switching ratio can be improved by the use of a smaller period on the
deflectors, by improvement of the alignment of the Bragg deflectors
relative to each other, and by the use of longer electrodes which
would produce a narrower angular spread of the deflected beam.

The switching can be produced at voltage levels of less than 10 V,
and the authors suggest that a 10 × 10 array should be achievable.

Integrated optical modulators and switches are expected to become important components of the single-mode fiber optical communication systems which are now under development. A serious problem with low-loss single-mode fibers is their rapid conversion of injected linearly polarized light into other states of polarization, and attempts to rectify this by including birefringence in the fiber have in general led to unacceptable losses. IO modulators and switches should therefore operate independently of the state of polarization, and, in fact, there are many applications in which a device capable of restoring a given polarization state would be valuable. Alferness has been involved in the development of high-speed, polarization-independent switches [148] and has recently described a novel polarization transformer which can convert an optical signal from any arbitrary polarization to any desired polarization state [149].

The device, which has been fabricated using a channel waveguide on $LiNbO_3$:Ti, utilizes his electro-optic TE $\leftrightarrow$ TM converter [61] situated between two electro-optically variable phase shifters. For arbitrary polarization transformation, the voltage on the first phase shifter is adjusted to set the phase difference between the TE and TM components at $\pm(\pi/2)$. With such a phase difference, the TE $\leftrightarrow$ TM converter acts as a voltage-controlled linear rotator which can deliver any desired ratio of TE to TM amplitudes. The second phase shifter serves, finally, to set the phase difference between the components in the output beam. It was shown experimentally that the process of setting the voltages on the three elements is a one-time sequential operation for a given input-output polarization pair.

REFERENCES

1. S. E. Miller, Integrated optics: An introduction, *Bell Syst. Tech. J. 48*:2059, 1969.
2. P. K. Tien, Light waves in thin films and integrated optics, *Appl. Opt. 10*:2395, 1971.
3. S. E. Miller, A survey of integrated optics, *IEEE J. Quantum Electron. QE-8*:199, 1972.
4. J. E. Goell and R. D. Standley, Integrated optical circuits, *Proc. IEEE* (special issue on optical communications) 58:1504, 1970.
5. D. Mergerian, E. C. Malarkey, R. P. Pautienus, J. C. Bradley, G. E. Marx, L. D. Hutcheson, and A. L. Kellner, Operational integrated optical RF spectrum analyzer, *Appl. Opt. 19*:3033, 1980.
6. E. Garmire, Semiconductor components for monolithic applications, in *Integrated Optics* (T. Tamir, ed.), Springer-Verlag, New York, 1975, pp. 243-302.

7. F. K. Reinhart and A. Y. Cho, Molecular beam expitaxial layer structures for integrated optics, *Opt. Commun.* *18*:79, 1976.

8. M. Born and E. Wolf, *Principles of Optics*, Pergamon, New York, N.Y., 1959.

9. N. S. Kapany and J. J. Burke, *Optical Waveguides*, Academic Press, New York, 1972.

10. D. Marcuse, *Theory of Dielectric Optical Waveguides*, Academic Press, New York, 1974.

11. H. Kogelnik, Theory of dielectric waveguides, in *Integrated Optics* (T. Tamir, ed.), Springer-Verlag, New York, 1975, pp 13-81.

12. E. M. Conwell, Modes in optical waveguides formed by diffusion, *Appl. Phys. Lett.* *23*:328, 1973.

13. R. D. Standley and V. Ramaswamy, Nb-diffused LiTaO$_3$ optical waveguides: Planar and embedded strip guides, *Appl. Phys. Lett.* *25*:711, 1974.

14. J. R. Carruthers, I. P. Kaminow, and L. W. Stulz, Diffusion kinetics and optical waveguiding properties of outdiffused layers in lithium niobate and lithium tantalate, *Appl. Opt.* *13*:2333, 1974.

15. J. P. Gordon, Optics of general guiding media, *Bell Syst. Tech. J.* *45*:321, 1966.

16. J. E. Goell, A circular-harmonic computer analysis of rectangular dielectric waveguides, *Bell Syst. Tech. J.* *48*:2133, 1969.

17. E. A. J. Marcatili, Dielectric rectangular waveguide and directional coupler for integrated optics, *Bell Syst. Tech. J.* *48*:2071, 1969.

18. E. A. J. Marcatili, Slab-coupled waveguides, *Bell Syst. Tech. J.* *53*:645, 1974.

19. C. Yeh, K. Ha, S. B. Dong, and W. P. Brown, Single mode optical waveguides, *Appl. Opt.* *18*:1490, 1979.

20. H. Furuta, H. Noda, and A. Ihaya, Novel optical waveguide for integrated optics, *Appl. Opt.* *13*:322, 1974.

21. M. Ohtaka, M. Matsuhara, and N. Kumagai, Analysis of the guided modes in slab-coupled waveguides using a variational method, *IEEE J. Quantum Electron.* *QE-12*:378, 1976.

22. R. M. Knox and P. P. Toulios, Integrated circuits for the millimeter through optical frequency range, *Proc MRI Symp. on Submillimeter Waves* (J. Fox, ed.), Polytechnic Press, Brooklyn, N.Y. 1970.

23. V. Ramaswamy, Strip-loaded film waveguide, *Bell Syst. Tech. J.* *53*:697, 1974.

24. G. B. Hocker, Strip-loaded diffused optical waveguides, *IEEE J. Quantum Electron.* *QE-12*:232, 1976.

25. G. B. Hocker and W. K. Burns, Mode dispersion in diffused channel waveguides by the effective index method, *Appl. Opt.* *16*:113, 1977.

26. E. A. J. Marcatili, Bends in optical dielectric guides, *Bell Syst. Tech. J. 48*:2103, 1969.

27. E. F. Kuester and D. C. Chang, Surface wave radiation from curved dielectric slabs and fibers, *IEEE J. Quantum Electron. QE-11*:903, 1975.

28. D. Marcuse, Radiation losses of parabolic-index slabs and fibers with bent axes, *Appl. Opt. 17*:755, 1978.

29. D. Marcuse, Length Optimization of an S-shaped transition between offset optical waveguides, *Appl. Opt. 177*:63, 1978.

30. H. F. Taylor, Power loss at directional change in dielectric waveguides, *Appl. Opt. 13*:642, 1974.

31. H. F. Taylor, Losses at corner bends in dielectric waveguides, *Appl. Opt. 16*:711, 1977.

32. L. D. Hutcheson, I. A. White, and J. J. Burke, Comparison of bending losses in integrated optical circuits, *Opt. Lett. 5*:276, 1980.

33. L. M. Johnson and F. J. Leonberger, Low-loss $LiNbO_3$ waveguide bends with coherent coupling, in *Third Int. Conf. Integrated Optics and Optical Fiber Communication*, Technical Digest, Optical Society of America, San Francisco, 1981, pp. 82-83.

34. P. K. Tien, R. Ulrich, and R. J. Martin, Modes of propagating light waves in thin deposited semiconductor films, *Appl. Phys. Lett. 14*:291, 1969.

35. L. Kuhn, M. L. Dakss, P. F. Heidrich, and B. A. Scott, Deflection of an optical guided wave by a surface acoustic wave, *Appl. Phys. Lett. 17*:265, 1970.

36. W. S. C. Chang, Acoustooptic deflections in thin films, *IEEE J. Quantum Electron. QE-7*:167, 1971.

37. T. G. Giallorenzi, Acoustooptical deflection in thin-film waveguides, *J. Appl. Phys. 44*:242, 1973.

38. (a) M. L. Shah, Fast acoustooptic waveguide modulators, *Appl. Phys. Lett. 23*:75, 1973. (b) M. L. Shah, Fast acoustic diffraction-type optical waveguide modulator, *Appl. Phys. Lett. 23*:556, 1973.

39. G. B. Brandt, M. Gottlieb, and J. S. Conroy, Bulk acoustic wave interaction with guided optical waves, *Appl. Phys. Lett. 23*:53, 1973.

40. R. W. Dixon, Acoustic diffraction of light in anisotropic media, *IEEE J. Quantum Electron. QE-3*:85, 1967.

41. L. Kuhn, P. F. Heidrich, and E. G. Lean, Optical guided wave mode conversion by an acoustic surface wave, *Appl. Phys. Lett. 19*:428, 1971.

42. R. V. Schmidt, Acoustooptic interactions between guided optical waves and acoustic surface waves, *IEEE Trans. Sonics Ultrason. SU-23*:22, 1976.

43. D. A. Pinnow, Elastooptical materials, in *Handbook of Lasers with Selected Data of Optical Technology* (R. J. Pressley, ed.), Chemical Rubber Co., Cleveland, 1971, pp. 478-488.

44. Y. Ohmachi, Acoustooptical light diffraction in thin films,
     *J. Appl. Phys. 44:*3928, 1973.

45. (a) J. Kushibiki, H. Sasaki, N. Chubachi, N. Mikoshiba,
     and K. Shibayama, Thickness dependence of the diffrac-
     tion efficiency of optical guided waves by acoustic surface
     waves, in *Proc. 1974 Ultrason. Symp.* (IEEE Cat. #74 CH0986-
     1SU, J. deKlerk, ed., IEEE, New York), p. 85. (b) J. Kushibiki,
     H. Sasaki, N. Chubachi, N. Mikoshiba, and K. Shibayama,
     Thickness dependence of acoustooptic diffraction efficiency in
     ZnO-film optical waveguides, *Appl. Phys. Lett. 26:*362, 1975.

46. (a) T. G. Giallorenzi and A. F. Milton, Light deflection in
     multimode waveguides using the acoustooptic interaction, *J.
     Appl. Phys. 45:*1762, 1974. (b) J. F. Weller, T. G. Gial-
     lorenzi, and A. F. Milton, Light deflection in single and multi-
     mode waveguides using the acoustooptic interaction, in *1974
     Topical Meetings on Integrated Optics,* Technical Digest, Optical
     Society of America, 1974, p. WA9-1.

47. K. W. Loh, W. S. C. Chang, and R. A. Becker, Convolution
     using guided acoustooptical interaction in As_2S_3 waveguides,
     *Appl. Phys. Lett. 28:*109, 1976.

48. See, for example, (a) C. S. Tsai, M. A. Alhaider, Le T.
     Nguyen, and B. Kim, Wideband guided-wave acoustooptic
     Bragg diffraction and devices using multiple tilted surface
     acoustic waves, *Proc. IEEE 64:*318, 1976; (b) B. Kim and
     C. S. Tsai, High-performance guided-wave acoustooptic
     scanning devices using multiple surface acoustic waves,
     *Proc. IEEE 64:*788, 1976; (c) Le T. Nguyen and C. S. Tsai,
     Efficient wideband guided-wave acoustooptic Bragg diffraction
     using phased-surface acoustic wave array in $LiNbO_3$ wave-
     guides, *Appl. Opt. 16:*1297, 1977.

49. C. S. Tsai, Guided-wave acoustooptic Bragg modulators for
     wide-band integrated optic communications and signal proces-
     sing (invited paper), *IEEE Trans. Circuits Sys. CAS-26:*1072,
     1979.

50. J. M. White, P. F. Heidrich, and E. G. Lean, Thin-film
     acoustooptic interaction in $LiNbO_3$, *Electron. Lett. 10:*510,
     1975.

51. C. Stewart, G. Scrivener, and W. J. Stewart, Guided-wave
     acoustooptic spectrum analysis at frequencies above 1 GHz,
     in *Third Int. Conf. Integrated Optics and Optical Fiber Com-
     munication,* Technical Digest, Optical Society of America, San
     Francisco, 1981, pp. 122-124.

52. G. S. Kino and R. S. Wagers, Theory of interdigital couplers
     on nonpiezoelectric substrates, *J. Appl. Phys. 44:*1480, 1973.

53. (a) W. R. Smith, H. M. Gerard, J. H. Collins, T. M. Reeder,
     and H. J. Shaw, Analysis of interdigital surface wave trans-
     ducers by use of an equivalent circuit model (invited paper),
     *IEEE Trans. Microwave Theory Tech. MTT-17:*856, 1969.

(b) W. R. Smith, H. M. Gerard, J. H. Collins, T. M. Reeder, and H. J. Shaw, Design of surface wave delay lines with interdigital transducers (invited paper), *IEEE Trans. Microwave Theory Tech. MTT-17*:865, 1965.

54. C. C. Tseng, Frequency response of an interdigital transducer for excitation of surface elastic waves, *IEEE Trans. Electron Devices ED-15*:586, 1968.

55. C. S. Tsai, I. W. Yao, B. Kim, and Le T. Nguyen, Wideband guided-wave anisotropic acoustooptic Bragg diffraction in $LiNbO_3$ waveguides, in *Int. Conf. Integrated Optics and Optical Fiber Communications*, Digest of Technical Papers, Tokyo, Japan, July 1977, p. 57.

56. R. J. Pressley, ed., *Handbook of Lasers with Selected Data of Optical Technology*, Chemical Rubber Co., Cleveland, 1971.

57. E. Hartfield and B. J. Thompson, Optical modulators, in *Handbook of Optics* (W. G. Driscoll and W. Vaughn, eds.), McGraw-Hill, New York, 1978, Chap. 17.

58. J. M. Hammer, Modulation and switching of light in dielectric waveguides, in *Integrated Optics* (T. Tamir, ed.), Spring-Verlag, New York, 1975, pp. 139-200.

59. I. P. Kaminow and E. H. Turner, Linear electrooptical materials, in *Handbook of Lasers with Selected Data of Optical Technology* (R. J. Pressley, ed.), Chemical Rubber Co., Cleveland, 1971, pp. 447-459.

60. J. M. Hammer and W. Phillips, Low-loss single-mode optical waveguide and efficient high-speed modulators of $LiNb_xTa_{1-x}O_3$ on $LiTaO_3$, *Appl. Phys. Lett. 24*:545, 1974.

61. R. C. Alferness and L. L. Buhl, Electrooptic waveguide TE $\leftrightarrow$ TM converter with low drive voltage, *Opt. Lett. 5*:473, 1980.

62. H. F. Taylor, An electrooptic analog-to-digital (A/D) converter, *Proc. IEEE 63*:1524, 1975.

63. H. F. Taylor, M. J. Taylor, and P. W. Bauer, Electrooptic analog-to-digital converter using channel waveguide modulators, *Appl. Phys. Lett. 32*:559, 1978.

64. P. S. Cross and R. V. Schmidt, A 1 Gbit/s integrated optical modulator, *IEEE J. Quantum Electron. QE-15*:1415, 1979.

65. (a) M. G. Cohen and E. I. Gordon, Electrooptic [$KTa_xNb_{1-x}O_3$(KTN)] gratings for light beam modulation and deflection, *Appl. Phys. Lett. 5*:181, 1964. (b) E. I. Gordon and M. G. Cohen, Electrooptic diffraction grating for light beam modulation and diffraction, *IEEE J. Quantum Electron. QE-1*:191, 1965.

66. R. V. Schmidt and I. P. Kaminow, Metal-diffused optical waveguides in $LiNbO_3$, *Appl. Phys. Lett. 25*:458, 1974.

67. H. Naitoh, M. Nunoshita, and T. Nakayama, Mode control of Ti-diffused $LiNbO_3$ slab optical waveguide, *Appl. Opt. 16*:2546, 1977.

68. J. Noda, N. Uchida, S. Saito, T. Saku, and M. Minakata, Electro-optic amplitude modulation using three-dimensional LiNbO$_3$ waveguide fabricated by TiO$_2$ diffusion, *Appl. Phys. Lett.* 27:19, 1975.

69. T. R. Ranganath and S. Wang, Suppression of Li$_2$O out-diffusion from Ti-diffused LiNbO$_3$ optical waveguides, *Appl. Phys. Lett.* 30:376, 1977.

70. B. Chen and A. C. Pastor, Elimination of Li$_2$O out-diffused waveguides in LiNbO$_3$, *Appl. Phys. Lett.* 30:570, 1977.

71. S. Myazawa, R. Guglielmi, and A. Carenco, A simple technique for suppressing Li$_2$O out-diffusion in Ti:LiNbO$_3$ optical waveguides, *Appl. Phys. Lett.* 31:742, 1977.

72. J. Noda, M. Fukuma, and S. Saito, Effect of Mg diffusion on Ti-diffused LiNbO$_3$ waveguides, *J. Appl. Phys.* 49:3150, 1978.

73. R. J. Esdaile, Closed-tube control of out-diffusion during fabrication of optical waveguides in LiNbO$_3$, *Appl. Phys. Lett.* 33:733, 1978.

74. W. K. Burns, P. H. Klein, E. J. West, and L. E. Plew, Ti diffusion in Ti:LiNbO$_3$ planar and channel optical waveguides, *J. Appl. Phys.* 50:6175, 1979.

75. R. Ulrich and R. J. Martin, Geometrical optics in thin-film light guides, *Appl. Opt.* 10:2077, 1971.

76. R. Shubert and J. H. Harris, Optical guided-wave focusing and diffraction, *J. Opt. Soc. Am.* 61:154, 1971.

77. F. Zernike, Luneburg lens for optical waveguide use, *Opt. Commun.* 12:379, 1974.

78. S. K. Yao and D. B. Anderson, Shadow sputtered diffraction-limited waveguide Luneburg lenses, *Appl. Phys. Lett.* 33:307, 1978.

79. G. E. Betts and G. E. Marx, Spherical aberration correction and fabrication tolerances in geodesic lenses, *Appl. Opt.* 17:3969, 1978.

80. P. R. Ashley and W. S. C. Chang, Fresnel lens in a thin-film waveguide, *Appl. Phys. Lett.* 33:490, 1978.

81. W. S. C. Chang, S. Zhou, Z. Lin, S. Forouhar, and J. M. DeLavaux, Performance of diffraction lenses in planar waveguides, *Proc. Soc. Photo-Opt. Instrum. Eng.* 269:105, 1981.

82. R. F. Rinehart, A solution of the problem of rapid scanning for radar antennae, *J. Appl. Phys.* 19:860, 1948.

83. K. S. Kunz, Propagation of microwaves between a parallel pair of doubly curved conducting surfaces, *J. Appl. Phys.* 25:642, 1954.

84. G. C. Righini, V. Russo, S. Sottini, and G. Toraldo di Francia, Thin-film geodesic lens, *Appl. Opt.* 11:1442, 1972.

85. D. W. Vahey and V. E. Wood, Focal characteristics of spheroidal geodesic lenses for integrated optical processing, *IEEE J. Quantum Electron* QE-13:129, 1977.

86. J. F. Weller and T. G. Giallorenzi, Indiffused waveguides: Effects of thin film overlays, *Appl. Opt. 14*:2329, 1975.

87. E. Spiller and J. S. Harper, High resolution lenses for optical waveguides, *Appl. Opt. 13*:2105, 1974.

88. G. E. Betts, J. C. Bradley, G. E. Marx, D. C. Schubert, and H. A. Trenchard, Axially symmetric geodesic lenses, *Appl. Opt. 17*:2346, 1978.

89. B. Chen, E. Marom, and R. J. Morrison, Diffraction-limited geodesic lens for integrated optics circuits, *Appl. Phys. Lett. 33*:511, 1978.

90. G. C. Righini, V. Russo, and S. Sottini, A family of perfect aspherical geodesic lenses for integrated optical circuits, *IEEE J. Quantum Electron. QE-15*:1, 1979.

91. S. Sottini, V. Russo, and G. C. Righini, General solution of the problem of perfect geodesic lenses for integrated optics, *J. Opt. Soc. Am. 69*:1248, 1979.

92. J. C. Bradley, E. C. Malarkey, D. Mergerian, and H. A. Trenchard, Theory of geodesic lenses, *Proc. Soc. Photo-Opt. Instrum. Eng. 176*:75, 1979.

93. D. Mergerian, E. C. Malarkey, R. P. Pautienus, and J. C. Bradley, Diamond-machined geodesic lenses in $LiNbO_3$, *Proc. Soc. Photo-Opt. Instrum. Eng. 176*:85, 1979.

94. B. Chen, E. Marom, and A. Lee, Geodesic lenses in single-mode $LiNbO_3$ waveguides, *Appl. Phys. Lett. 31*:263, 1977.

95. B. Chen, T. R. Ranganath, T. R. Joseph, and J. Y. Lee, Progress on the development of integrated optics spectrum analyzer, Technical Digest, IEEE-OSA topical meeting on integrated and guided-wave optics, *paper ME 3*, Optical Society of America, Incline Village, Nev., Jan. 1980.

96. D. Mergerian, J. C. Bradley, R. P. Pautienus, L. D. Hutcheson, A. L. Kellner, E. C. Malarkey, and G. E. Marx, Diamond turned aspheric geodesic waveguide lenses in $LiNbO_3$, Technical Digest, IEEE-OSA topical meeting on integrated and guided-wave optics, *paper ME 4*, Optical Society of America, Incline Village, Nev., Jan. 1980.

97. T. Y. Hsu and H. S. Tuan, Grating reflector for a thin-film Fabry-Perot laser, *Appl. Phys. Lett. 32*:481, 1978.

98. D. C. Flanders, H. Kogelnik, R. V. Schmidt, and C. V. Shank, Grating filters for thin-film optical waveguides, *Appl. Phys. Lett. 24*:194, 1974.

99. H. Kogelnik, Coupled wave theory for thick hologram gratings, *Bell Syst. Tech. J. 48*:2909, 1969.

100. S. Sottini, V. Russo, and G. C. Righini, Geodesic optics, new components, *J. Opt. Soc. Am. 70*:1230, 1980.

101. G. L. Tangonan, D. L. Persechini, J. F. Lotspeich, and M. K. Barnoski, Electrooptic diffraction modulation in Ti-diffused $LiTaO_3$, *Appl. Opt. 17*:3259, 1978.

102. W. T. Tsang and S. Wang, Thin-film beam splitter and re-
      flector for optical guided waves, *Appl. Phys. Lett. 27*:588,
      1975.

103. N. Chubachi, ZnO films for surface acoustooptic devices on
      nonpiezoelectric substrates, *Proc. IEEE 64*:722, 1976.

104. D. Mergerian, E. C. Malarkey, B. Newman, J. Lane, R.
      Weinert, B. R. McAvoy, and C. S. Tsai, Zinc oxide trans-
      ducer arrays for integrated optics, in *Proc. 1978 Ultrason.
      Symp.* (IEEE Cat. 78-CH1344-1SU, J. deKlerk and B. R. McAvoy,
      eds., IEEE, New York), pp. 64-69.

105. F. S. Hickernell, Zinc-oxide thin-film surface-wave trans-
      ducers, *Proc. IEEE 64*:631, 1976.

106. L. P. Solie, Piezoelectric waves on layered substrates, *J.
      Appl. Phys. 44*:619, 1973.

107. C. C. Lee, K. Y. Liao, C. L. Chang, and C. S. Tsai,
      Wideband guided-wave acoustooptic Bragg deflector using a
      tilted-finger chirped transducer, *IEEE J. Quantum Electron.
      QE-15*:1166, 1979.

108. C. S. Tsai, Le T. Nguyen, and B. Kim, Wideband guided-
      wave acoustooptic Bragg-diffraction using phased-surface
      acoustic wave array in $LiNbO_3$ waveguides, in *Proc. 1975
      Ultrason. Symp.* (IEEE Cat. 75-CHO-994-4SU, J. deKlerk and
      B. R. McAvoy, eds., IEEE, New York), pp. 42-43.

109. R. M. DeLaRue, C. Steward, C. D. W. Wilkinson, and
      I. R. Williamson, Frequency controlled beam steering of sur-
      face acoustic waves using a stepped transducer array,
      Electron. Lett. 8:326, 1973.

110. C. S. Tsai, Wideband guided-wave acoustooptic Bragg-devices
      and applications, in *Proc. 1975 Ultrason. Symp.* (IEEE Cat.
      75-CHO-994-4SU, J. deKlerk and B. R. McAvoy, eds., IEEE,
      New York), pp. 120-125.

111. W. R. Smith, H. M. Gerard, and W. R. Jones, Analysis and
      design of dispersive interdigital surface-wave transducers,
      IEEE Trans. Microwave Theory Tech. MTT-20:458, 1972.

112. M. K. Barnoski, B. Chen, H. M. Gerard, E. Marom, O. G.
      Ramer, W. R. Smith, G. L. Tangonan, and R. D. Weglein,
      Design, fabrication and integration of components for an inte-
      grated optic spectrum analyzer, in *Proc. 1978 Ultrason. Symp.*
      (IEEE Cat. 78CH1344-1SU, J. deKlerk and B. R. McAvoy, eds.,
      IEEE, New York), pp. 74-78.

113. K. Y. Liao, C. L. Chang, C. C. Lee, and C. S. Tsai,
      Progress on wideband guided-wave acoustooptic Bragg deflector
      using a tilted-finger chirp transducer, in *Proc. 1979 Ultrason.
      Symp.* (IEEE Cat. 79CH1482-9SU, J. deKlerk and B. R. McAvoy,
      eds., IEEE, New York, pp. 24-27.

114. F. R. Nash, Mode guidance parallel to the junction plane of
      double-heterostructure GaAs lasers, *J. Appl. Phys. 44*:4696,
      1973.

115. W. Streifer, R. D. Burnham, and D. R. Scifres, Current status of (GaAlAs) diode lasers, *Proc. Soc. Photo-Opt. Instrum. Eng. 269*:2, 1981.

116. F. K. Reinhart, R. A. Logan, and T. P. Lee, Transmission properties of rib waveguides formed by anodization of epitaxial GaAs on $Al_xGa_{1-x}As$ layers, *Appl. Phys. Lett. 24*:270, 1974.

117. K. Aiki, M. Nakamura, T. Kuroda, J. Umeda, R. Ito, N. Chinone, and M. Maeda, Transverse mode stabilized Al_xGa_{1-x} injection lasers with channeled-substrate-planar structure, *IEEE J. Quantum Electron. QE-14*:89, 1978.

118. D. Botez, CW high-power single-mode operation of constricted double-heterojunction GaAlAs lasers with a large optical cavity, *Appl. Phys. Lett. 36*:190, 1980.

119. W. K. Burns, Laser diode end-fire coupling into $Ti:LiNbO_3$ waveguides, *Appl. Opt. 18*:1536, 1979.

120. P. K. Tien, Integrated optics and new wave phenomena in optical waveguides, *Rev. Mod. Phys. 49*:361, 1977.

121. E. Iwahashi, First field trial of long-haul transmission systems using single-mode fiber cable at 1.3 μm wavelength, in *Third Int. Conf. Integrated Optics and Optical Fiber Communication*, Technical Digest, Optical Society of America, San Francisco, 1981, pp. 12-13.

122. P. K. Runge, Future transatlantic fiber optical communication systems, Paper MF1 (invited), in *Third Int. Conf. Integrated Optics and Optical Fiber Communication*, Technical Digest, p. 20.

123. D. G. Hall, R. R. Rice, and J. D. Zino, Simple Gaussian-beam model for GaAlAs double-heterostructure laser-diode-to-diffused-waveguide coupling calculation, *Opt. Lett. 4*:292, 1979.

124. D. Mergerian, E. C. Malarkey, R. P. Pautienus, J. C. Bradley, and A. L. Kellner, Advances in integrated optical spectrum analyzers, *Proc. Soc. Photo-Opt. Instrum. Eng. 269*:129, 1981.

125. D. Mergerian, E. C. Malarkey, R. P. Pautienus, J. C. Bradley, G. E. Marx, L. D. Hutcheson and A. L. Kellner, An integrated optical radio frequency (RF) spectrum analyzer, *Proc. Soc. Photo-Opt. Instrum. Eng. 239*:121, 1980.

126. G. E. Marx, M. Gottlieb, and G. B. Brandt, Integrated optical detector array, *IEEE Trans. Solid State Circuits, SC-13*:10, 1977.

127. J. T. Boyd, Integrated optoelectronic silicon devices for optical signal processing and communications, *Opt. Eng. 18*:14, 1979.

128. G. M. Borsuk, A. Turley, G. Marx, and E. Malarkey, Photosensor array for integrated optical spectrum analyzer systems, *Proc. Soc. Photo-Opt. Instrum. Eng. 176*:109, 1979.

129. G. E. Marx and G. M. Borsuk, Evaluation of a photosensor for integrated optics spectrum analyzers, Technical Digest IEEE, OSA topical meeting on integrated and guided wave optics, *paper ME6*, Optical Society of America, Incline Village, Nev., Jan. 1980.

130. J. Y. M. Lee and B. Chen, Detector array for an integrated optic spectrum analyzer, in *Extended Abstracts, Spring Meet. The Electrochemical Society*, Vol. 80-1, May 1980.

131. G. M. Borsuk, Photodetectors for acousto-optic signal processors (invited paper), *Proc. IEEE 69*:100, 1981.

132. D. B. Anderson and R. R. August, Progress in waveguide lenses for integrated optics, *Trans. Inst. Electron. Commun. Eng. Jpn, Sec. E (Jpn) E61*:140, 1978.

133. E. G. H. Lean and C. G. Powell, Optical probing of surface acoustic waves, *Proc. IEEE 58*:1939, 1970.

134. J. T. Boyd, S. Dutta, H. E. Jackson, and A. Naumaan, Reduction of the effects of scattering by laser annealing of optical waveguides and by use of integrated waveguide detection, *Proc. Soc. Photo-Opt. Instrum. Eng. 269*:125, 1981.

135. M. C. Hamilton, D. A. Wille, and W. J. Miceli, An integrated optical RF spectrum analyzer, *Opt. Eng. 16*:475, 1977.

136. T. R. Ranganath, T. R. Joseph, and J. Y. Lee, The integrated optic spectrum analyzer—a first demonstration, post-deadline paper in *Proc. 1980 Int. Electron. Devices Mtg.*, Institute of Electrical and Electronic Engineers, Washington, D.C. Dec. 1980, p. 843.

137. F. J. Leonberger, C. E. Woodward, and D. L. Spears, Design and development of a high-speed electrooptic A/D converter, *IEEE Trans. Circuits Syst. CAS-26*:1125, 1979.

138. W. E. Martin, A new waveguide switch/modulator for integrated optics, *Appl. Phys. Lett. 26*:563, 1975.

139. Y. Ohmachi and J. Noda, Electrooptic light modulator with branched ridge waveguide, *Appl. Phys. Lett. 27*:544, 1975.

140. H. F. Taylor, An optical analog-to-digital converter—design and analysis (invited paper), *IEEE J. Quantum Electron. QE-15*:210, 1979.

141. F. J. Leonberger, Guided-wave electrooptic analog-to-digital converter, *Proc. Soc. Photo-Opt. Instrum. Eng. 269*:64, 1981.

142. T. Turpin, Time integrating optical processors, *Proc. Soc. Photo-Opt. Instrum. Eng. 154*:196, 1978.

143. P. Kellman, Time integrating optical signal processing, *Opt. Eng. 19*:370, 1980.

144. N. J. Berg, J. N. Lee, M. W. Casseday, and I. J. Abramovitz, Acoustooptic processing of radar communications signals, *Proc. Soc. Photo-Opt. Instrum. Eng. 209*:57, 1979.

145. H. F. Taylor, Optical switching and modulation in parallel dielectric waveguides, *J. Appl. Phys. 44*:3257, 1973.

146. W. K. Burns, A. B. Lee, and A. F. Milton, Active-branching
      waveguide modulator, *Appl. Phys. Lett. 29*:790, 1976.
147. C. Peng, W. S. C. Chang, and R. J. Falster, An N × M
      optical waveguide switch for computer communications,
      Proc. Soc. Photo-Opt. Instrum. Eng. 269:34, 1981.
148. R. C. Alferness, Polarization-independent optical directional
      coupler switch using weighted coupling, *Appl. Phys. Lett.
      35*:748, 1979.
149. R. C. Alferness, Electrooptic guided-wave device for general
      polarization transformations, IEEE J. Quantum Electron.
      QE-17:965, 1981.

ADDITIONAL BIBLIOGRAPHY

Additional Bibliography

This additional bibliography is divided into two parts. The first part
consists of recent articles on acousto-optics which have appeared in
American journals. This part is divided into sections as per the text,
i.e., *basic acousto-optic theory and devices*, etc. The main purpose
of this part is to acquaint the reader with current activity in this
rapidly evolving field. More specifically, some new areas of endeavor
have very recently surfaced which consist of combinations of topics
covered separately in the text. An example of this is the area of
spectrum analysis (Chap. 4) using *coherent detection* (Chap. 5). This
topic is covered extensively in Refs. 10(a), 17, and 20(b) in the *frequency-domain signal-processing* section and Ref. 13(a) of the *time-
domain signal-processing* section.

The second part of the bibliography deals with articles on acousto-
optics appearing in English-language translations of Soviet journals,
published since 1976. It is not all-inclusive; however, we feel that it
is certainly representative. A large amount of research work is being
conducted in the Soviet Union on optical processing, and a text on
acousto-optic signal processing would not be complete without some
reference to this work. This part is divided into sections also, as per
the text sections. In addition, a very brief summary of each of the
Soviet articles is also included to aid the reader.

Bibliography of Recent American Literature

BASIC ACOUSTO-OPTIC THEORY AND DEVICES

1. D. L. Hecht, Multifrequency acoustooptic diffraction, *IEEE Trans. Sonics Ultrason. SU-24*:7, 1977.
2. N. A. Massie and R. D. Nelson, Beam quality of acousto-optic frequency shifters, *Opt. Lett. 3*:46, 1978.
3. Y. Imai and Y. Ohtsuka, Laser speckle reduction by ultrasonic modulation, *Opt. Commun. 27*:18, 1978.
4. *1979 IEEE Ultrasonics Symposium Proceedings* (79CH1482-9):
   (a) S. Fukuda, T. Shiosaki, and Kawabata, Acousto-optic interactions in piezoelectric semiconductor: Tellurium, p. 9.
   (b) D. L. Hecht, G. Petrie, and S. Wofford, Multifrequency acousto-optic diffraction in optically birefringent media, p. 46.
   (c) J. L. Dion, R. Simard, A. D. Jacob, and A. Leblanc, The acousto-optical effect in liquid crystals due to anisotropic attenuation: New developments and applications, p. 56.
   (d) Bill D. Cook, A procedure for calculating the integrated acousto-optics (Raman-Nath) parameter for the entire sound field, p. 90.
5. T. C. Poon and A. Korpel, Optical transfer function of an acousto-optic heterodyning image processor, *Opt. Lett. 4*:317, 1979.
6. R. V. Johnson, Temporal response of the acoustooptic modulator in the high scattering efficiency regime, *Appl. Opt. 18*:903, 1979.
7. H. P. Layer, Acousto-optic modulator intensity servo, *Appl. Opt. 18*:2947, 1979.
8. A. Korpel, Two-dimensional plane wave theory of strong acousto-optic interaction in isotropic media, *J. Opt. Soc. Am. 69*:678, 1979.

9.   *Proc. Soc. Photo-Opt. Instr. Eng. 180,* 1979:   (a) D. L. Hecht, Acousto-optic signal processing device performance, 150. (b) W. T. Rhodes, Acousto-optic devices applied to image processing, 143.

10. *1980 IEEE Ultrasonics Symposium Proceedings* (80CH1602-2): (a) M. Kohoshnevisan, R. L. Hall, E. Z. Sovero, E. Skurnick, and W. Davidian, Application of Tl_3AsSe_3, for long wavelength acousto-optic beam steering devices, p. 470, (b) D. L. Hecht and G. W. Petrie, Acousto-optic diffraction from acoustic anisotropic shear modes in gallium phosphide, p. 474. (c) D. G. Hawkins, Finite beamwidth effects in bulk acousto-optic interactions—theory and experiment, p. 497.

11. D. G. Hawkins, Resolution criteria for acoustooptic deflectors, *Appl. Opt. 19*:186, 1980.

12. Y. Imai and Y. Ohtsuka, Optical coherence modulation by ultrasonic waves 1: Dependence of partial coherence on ultrasonic parameters, *Appl. Opt. 19*:542, 1980.

13. E. H. Young and S. K. Yao, Design considerations for acousto-optic devices, *Proc IEEE 69*:54, 1981.

14. A. Korpel, Acousto-optics—a review of fundamentals, *Proc. IEEE 69*:48, 1981.

15. *1981 IEEE Ultrasonics Symposium Proceedings.* (81CH1689-9): (a) T. C. Poon and A. Korpel, Second order Bragg diffraction operation of acousto-optic devices, p. 751. (b) T. M. Turner and R. D. Claus, Dual differential interferometer for measurements of broadband surface acoustic waves, p. 384. (c) I. C. Chang, G. Petrie, and R. Cadieux, Wideband acousto-optic Bragg cells, p. 735.

16. A. E. Attard and B. L. Heffner, Diffraction of light by acoustic waves on a membrane, *Opt. Lett. 6*:225, 1981.

17. T. C. Poon and A. Korpel, Use of Laplace transforms in acousto-optic multiple scattering, *Opt. Lett. 6*:546, 1981.

18. D. Psaltis, Optical image correlation using acoustooptic and charge-coupled devices, *Appl. Opt. 21*:491, 1982.

19. A. Vander Lugt, Bragg cell diffraction patterns, *Appl. Opt. 21*:1092, 1982.

FREQUENCY-DOMAIN SIGNAL PROCESSING

1.   F. M. M. Ayub and P. Das, Fourier transform properties of acousto-optic lens, *Opt. Commun. 26*:161, 1978.

2.   J. H. Zablotney, Acousto-optic parallel channel wideband receiver concept, *Proc. Soc. Photo-Opt. Instrum. Eng. 180*:122, 1979.

3.   D. J. Granath and B. R. Hunt, Signal-detection tradeoff-analysis of optical vs. digital Fourier transform computers, *Appl. Opt. 18*:36; 1979.

4. T. R. Bader, Acoustooptic spectrum analysis: A high performance hybrid technique, *Appl. Opt. 18*:1668, 1979.
5. H. J. Babrov and M. M. Jacobs, Acoustooptic tunable filter performance in a staring IR sensor, *Appl. Opt. 18*:3901, 1979.
6. D. Psaltis and D. Casasent, Time- and space-integrating spectrum analyzer, *Appl. Opt. 18*:3203, 1979.
7. H. Sasaki and N. Mikoshiba, Collinear acousto-optic interaction in ZnO thin tilms and its applications to tunable optical filter and observation of frequency spectrum, *1979 IEEE Ultrasonic Symposium Proceedings* (79CH1482-9) p. 18.
8. M. Gottlieb, J. D. Feichtner, and J. Conroy, Programmable acousto-optic filter—a device for multispectral optical processing, 1980 International Optical Computing Conference, *Proc. Soc. Photo-Opt. Instrum. Eng. 232*:33, 1980.
9. A. Korpel, New ideas in acousto-optic signal processing using cavity resonances and Bragg imaging, 1980 International Optical Computing Conference, *Proc. Soc. Photo-Opt. Instrum. Eng. 232*:90, 1980.
10. A. Alippi, A. Palma, L. Palmieri, G. Socino, and E. Verona, Real time acousto-optical spectrum analyzer through unguided light-surface acoustic waves interaction, *Opt. Commun. 35*:37, 1980.
11. *1980 IEEE Ultrasonics Symposium Proceedings* (80CH1602-2): (a) J. N. Lee, N. J. Berg, M. W. Casseday, and P. S. Brody, High-speed adaptive filtering and reconstruction of broadband signals using acousto-optic techniques, p. 488. (b) E. A. Sovero and M. Khoshnevisan, A generalized method for designing acousto-optic tunable filters, p. 492.
12. T. M. Turpin, Spectrum analysis using optical processing, *Proc, IEEE 69*:79, 1981.
13. P. Kellman, H. N. Shaver, and J. W. Murray, "Integrating acousto-optic channelized receivers, *Proc. IEEE 69*:93, 1981.
14. G. Guidarelli, A. Palma, L. Palmieri, G. Socino, and E. Verona, Swept frequency acousto-optical spectrum analyzer, *Opt. Commun. 39*:15, 1931.
15. T. D. Black and V. A. Komtskii, Infrared detection using acousto-optic interaction with thermally induced grating in optical waveguides, *Appl. Phys. Lett. 38*:113, 1981.
16. D. Psaltis and B. V. K. Vijaya Kumar, Acousto-optical spectral estimation: A statistical analysis, *Appl. Opt. 20*:601, 1981.
17. A. Vander Lugt, Interferometric spectrum analyzer, *Appl. Opt. 20*:2770, 1981.
18. F. W. Freyre, Zero frequency shift Bragg cell beam deflection and translation, *Appl. Opt. 20*:3896, 1981.
19. G. Chin, D. Buhl, and J. M. Florez, Bulk and integrated acousto-optic spectrometers for radio astronomy, in Optical information processing for aerospace applications, *NASA Conf. Publ. 2207*, 1981, p. 85.

20. *1981 IEEE Ultrasonic Symposium Proceedings* (81CH1689-9):
     (a) M. C. Hamilton, Acousto-optic spectrum analysis for
     electronic warfare applications, p. 714. (b) M. L. Shah,
     J. R. Teague, R. V. Belfatto, D. W. Thomson, and E. H.
     Young, Wideband interferometric acousto-optic Bragg cell
     spectrum analyzer, p. 740. (c) J. P. Powers, D. E. Smith,
     M. Carmody, and W. Regan, A computer-based model of space-
     integration acousto-optic signal processing, p. 585.

TIME-DOMAIN SIGNAL PROCESSING

1.   J. D. Cohen, Ambiguity processor architectures using one-
     dimensional acousto-optic transducers, *Proc. Soc. Photo-Opt.
     Instrum. Eng. 180*:134, 1979.
2.   D. L. Huber, B. E. Adams, and J. C. Clegg, Wide-band fre-
     quency-modulation system using optical techniques, *Appl. Opt.
     18*:1249, 1979.
3.   D. Psaltis and D. Casasent, Space-variant ambiguity function
     processor, *Appl. Opt. 18*:1869, 1979.
4.   A. Alippi, A. Palma, L. Palmieri, G. Socino, and E. Verona,
     Acousto-optical processors based on light polarization discrim-
     ination techniques, in *1979 Ultrason. Symp. Proc.*, (79CH1482-9)
     p. 94.
5.   1980 International Optical Computing Conference, *Proc. Soc.
     Photo-Opt. Instrum. Eng. 232* (1980): (a) T. R. Bader,
     Coherent hybrid optical processors, 82. (b) W. T. Rhodes,
     Contrast in time-integration optical processing, 96. (c) N. J.
     Berg, M. W. Casseday, I. J. Abramovitz, and J. N. Lee,
     Radar and communication band signal processing using time-
     integration processors, 101.
6.   P. N. Tamura, J. J. Rebolz, and T. C. Lee, Ambiguity-func-
     tion generation using passive optical τ-shift technique, *Opt.
     Lett. 5*:401, 1980.
7.   D. Psaltis and D. Casasent, Spread spectrum time- and space-
     integrating optical processor, *Appl. Opt. 19*:1546, 1980.
8.   W. T. Rhodes, Acousto-optic signal processing: Convolution
     and correlation, *Proc. IEEE 69*:65, 1981.
9.   D. Psaltis, F. Caimi, and A. Goutzoulis, Decimal/residue
     conversion by time-integrating correlation, *Opt. Commun.
     36*:178, 1981.
10. L. Pichon and J. P. Hengnard, Dynamic joint-Fourier-trans-
     form correlator by Bragg diffraction in photorefractive $Bi_{12}SiO_{20}$
     crystals, *Opt. Commun. 36*:277, 1981.
11. L. K. Lam, T. Y. Chang, J. Feinberg, and R. W. Hellwarth,
     Photorefractive-index gratings formed by nanosecond optical
     pulses in $BaTiO_3$, *Opt. Lett. 6*:7, 1981.

12. J. P. Y. Lee, Acoustooptical spectrum analysis of radar signals using an integrating photodetector array, *Appl. Opt.* *20*:595, 1981.
13. *1981 IEEE Ultrasonics Symposium Proceedings* (81CH1689-2): (a) M. W. Casseday, N. J. Berg, and I. J. Abramovitz, Bragg cell signal processing advances, p. 731. (b) I. J. Abramovitz, N. J. Berg, M. W. Casseday, and J. J. Cecconi, Surface-wave acousto-optic cepstrum processor for characterization of wideband signals, p. 747.
14. Optical information processing for aerospace applications, *NASA Conf. Publ. 2207*, 1981: (a) A. Tarasevich, N. Zepkin, and W. T. Rhodes, Matrix vector multiplier with time varying single dimensional spatial light modulators, p. 61. (b) H. J. Caulfield, W. T. Rhodes, M. J. Foster, and Sam Horvitz, Optical implementation of systolic array processing, p. 53. (c) F. W. Freyre, A broadband RF continuously variable time delay device, p. 265.
15. D. Psaltis, Optical image correlation using acousto-optic and charge-coupled devices, *Appl. Opt.* *21*:491, 1982.

INTEGRATED OPTICS

1. *1978 IEEE Ultrasonics Symposium Proceedings* (78CH1344-1-SU): (a) F. S. Hickernell, R. L. Davis, and F. V. Richard, The acousto-optic properties of thin film Si_3N_4, Ta_2O_5, ZnO and 7059 glass on oxidized silicon substrates, p. 60. (b) D. Mergerian, E. C. Malarkey, B. A. Newman, J. R. Lane, R. W. Weinert, B. R. McAvoy, and C. S. Tsai, Zinc oxide transducer arrays for integrated optics, p. 64. (c) David W. Vahey, Corrected waveguide geodesic lenses for integrated acoustooptic spectrum analysis, p. 70. (d) M. K. Barnoski, B. Chen, H. M. Gerard, E. Maron, O. G. Ramer, W. R. Smith, Jr., G. L. Tangonan, and R. D. Weglein, Design fabrication and integration of components for an integrated optics spectrum analyzer, p. 74. (e) I. W. Yao and C. S. Tsai, A time-integrating correlator using guided-wave interactions, p. 87.
2. *1979 IEEE Ultrasonics Symposium Proceedings* (79CH1482-9): (a) K. Y. Liao, C. L. Chang, C. C. Lee, and C. S. Tsai, Progress on wideband guided-wave acousto-optic Bragg deflector using a tilted-finger chirp transducer, p. 24. (b) T. R. Joseph and B-U. Chen, Broadband chirp transducers for integrated optics spectrum analyzers, p. 28. (c) W. R. Smith, Design of Bragg cells for SAW/integrated optic signal processing devices, p. 98.

3. L. N. Bingh, J. Livingstone, and D. H. Steven, Tunable acousto-optic TE-TM mode converter on a diffused optical waveguide, *Opt. Lett.* 5:83, 1980.

4. *1981 IEEE Ultrasonic Symposium Proceedings* (81CH1689-9): (a) T. R. Joseph, T. R. Ranganath, and J. Y. Lee, Performance of the integrated optic spectrum analyzer, p. 721. (b) R. L. Davis and F. S. Hickernell, The IO spectrum analyzer: An emerging technology, p. 727.

5. C. M. Verber, R. P. Kenan, and J. R. Busch, Correlator based on an integrated optical spatial light modulator, *Appl. Opt.* 20:1626, 1981.

Bibliography of Recent Soviet Literature

BASIC ACOUSTO-OPTIC THEORY AND DEVICES

From *Soviet Technical Physics Letters*

1. A. G. Kuzin, Holographic correction of distortions of an acousto-optic deflector, 3(2):58, Feb. 1977. Describes technique for using hologram to correct for uncontrollable optical abberations of a deflector.
2. Yu M. Sosov, N. K. Yushin, and A. Yu. Kudzin, Radio-frequency acoustooptic properties of paratellurite crystals and optical information processing, 3(5):192, May 1977. Describes studies of AO properties of TeO_2 and shows that use of transverse elastic waves propagating in [001] direction will allow for usage as AO device up into microwave RF frequencies.
3. O. V. Shakin, A. G. Kuzin, S. V. Kulakov, V. V. Lemanov, V. P. Pikarnikov, E. V. Sinyakov, S. V. Akimov, M. Yu Lazovskii, I. V. Lesinkov, and N. F. Naryshkin, Lead moylbdate acoustooptic modulator for television systems, 3(6):202, June 1977. Describes design and construction of lead molybdate AO modulator with 45-MHz bandwidth to be used in television systems for recording and transferring images.
4. A. M. D'yakonov, Yu. V. Ilisavskii, I. I. Farbshtein, E. Z. Yakhkind, and I. A. Deryugin, Efficient tellurium acoustooptic modulator, 3(6): 231, June 1977. Study of tellurium for use as AO modulator in IR region; studies were done using both 50-MHz RF and microwave source.
5. A. N. Grishmanovskii, V. V. Lemanov, and M. Saltikulov, Acoustooptic interaction in lead molybdate and paratellurite crystals at high optical intensity, 4(6):233, June 1978. Study of AO diffraction efficiency with high-power laser pulses.

6. V. V. Kludzin, A. G. Kuzin, S. V. Kulakov, and V. A. Vinokurov, Parametric excitation in an acoustic interferometer with a TeO_2 crystal, 4(8):368, Aug. 1978. Study of parametric excitation by use of AO interaction in TeO_2.

7. V. V. Proklov, M. Ya. Mesh, and S. N. Antonov, Acousto-optical device with a TeO_2 volume-acoustic-wave generator, 4(11):547, Nov. 1978. Describes ultrastable AO deflector.

8. V. V. Proklov, S. V. Peshin, and S. N. Antonov, Optical diffraction by slow acoustic waves in TeO_2 with an arbitrary plane of incidence, 5(4):177, April 1979. Study of anisotropic AO scattering in TeO_2.

9. M. Ya. Mesh, V. V. Prokolov, and Yu. V. Gulyaev, Acoustic modulation of light in optical fibers, 5(4):204, April 1979. A study of the potential for modulating the transmission of light through optical fibers by sound.

10. A. A. Stashkevich, Acoustooptic diffraction at anomalously high values of Q, 6(3):141, May 1980. Experimental verification that nonlinear acoustooptic interaction of ultrasonic harmonics is markedly weakened for very high Q values.

11. A. P. Pogibel'skii, Time-ranging acoustooptic interaction at high light intensities, 6(5):274, May 1980. Numeric study of AO interaction at high light intensities and varying diffraction efficiencies.

12. I. A. Vodovatov, N. A. Esepkina, V. Pu Petrun'kin, and S. A. Rogov, Holographic method for compensating the divergence of ultrasound in multichannel acoustooptic devices, 7(3):157, March 1981. Describes technique of using hologram to compensate for overlapping output beams in multichannel AO modulator caused by divergence of acoustic waves.

From *Soviet Physics Technical Physics*

1. L. N. Magdin and V. Ya. Molchanov, Nonreciprocal phenomena in acoustooptic modulators, 22(5):637, May 1977. Experiments which demonstrate a nonreciprocal transmission of the leading and trailing edge of a light pulse in an AO modulator.

2. E. T. Aksenov, N. A. Esepkina, and A. S. Shcherbakov, High-frequency crystal acoustooptic deflectors, 22(2):213, Feb. 1977. Study of AO bulk-wave deflectors in 500 to 1500-MHz regime.

3. L. N. Magdick and V. Ya. Molchanov, Thermal distortions of the diffracted light in an acoustooptic modulator, 23(12):1486, Dec. 1978. Study of ways to reduce acoustothermal focussing, i.e., distortions in AO devices due to thermal heating of bulk-wave delay line by acoustic wave.

4. O. B. Gusev, S. V. Kulakov, V. A. Mel'zikov, N. S. Mirgorodskii, V. P. Pikarnikov, V. V. Soroka, and S. P. Fadeev, Multichannel acoustooptic modulator for real-time recording and

optical processing, *23*(1):99, Jan. 1978. Design study of multi-channel AO modulator.

5. S. V. Akimev, M. D. Volnyanskii, V. G. Monya, and E. F. Dudnik, Acoustooptic properties of certain crystals with the appatite structure, *24*(11):1405, Nov. 1979. Study of AO interaction efficiency of appatite structure in the 500-MHz range; M_2 = 43 to 48 are obtained, and attenuation is only 2 to 4 dB/cm at 500 MHz.

6. F. L. Vizen and L. A. Chernozatonskii, Simple method for increasing the bandwidth of an acoustooptic deflector, *24*(11):1344, Nov. 1979. Describes technique for obtaining broadband AO interaction by placing together separate deflectors.

7. A. G. Kuzin, S. V. Kulakov, A. M. Semenov, and V. V. Soroka, Use of a wide-band scattering in an anisotropic diffraction two-coordinate deflector, *24*(10):231, Oct. 1978. Describes how two TeO_2 delay lines can be used to obtain broadband (50-MHz) 2D deflection.

8. A. A. Stashkevich, Attenuation of a slow acoustic shear wave in TeO_2 crystals at high frequencies, *26*(4):530, April 1981. Study using AO interaction efficiency of the attenuation of TeO_2 slow shear wave at 500 MHz; results indicate that even at these frequencies time apertures of 1 to 2 μs can still be obtained.

9. Yu. A. Zyuryukin and V. M. Pushin, Imaging of acoustic transducers in a collinear Y-cut lithium niobate acoustooptic filter, *26*(5):627, May 1981. Technique for imaging the acoustic transducer in bulk-wave delay line by utilizing collinear AO interaction.

rom *Soviet Journal of Optical Technology*

1. A. G. Poleshchuk and A. K. Khimich, System for linear control and stabilization of laser radiation power by an acoustooptic modulator, *47*(9): 543, Sept. 1980. Describes AO modulator system which employs feedback control techniques to increase linearity of AO modulator by factor of 1000 and to decrease amplitude of laser power fluctuation by 100; operating frequency bandwidth is 0 to 250 kHz.

2. L. M. Vasil'era, O. B. Gusev, V. V. Kludzin, S. V. Kulakov, and V. P. Pikarnikov, Multichannel optoacoustic modulator, *48*(5):275, May 1981. Description of design of multichannel (N = 20), broadband (100-MHz) AO modulator.

rom *Soviet Journal of Quantum Electronics*

1. I. A. Deryugin, A. P. Pogibel'skii, M. A. Talalaev, and G. E. Teterin, Problem of constructing wide-band acoustooptic deflectors, *10*(5):649, May 1980. Study of multielement AO deflectors.

2. I. F. Gonchapova, L. S. Kornienko, M. V. Kravtsov, O. E. Nanii, and A. N. Shelaev, Competitive effects in a YAG:Nd^{3+} ring laser with acoustooptic mode locking, 11(6):811, June 198 Study of the competitive interactions of opposite light waves in a YAG:Nd^{3+} ring laser which has AO mode locking performed with the laser at rest and rotating.

FREQUENCY-DOMAIN SIGNAL PROCESSING

From *Soviet Technical Physics Letters*

1. E. T. Aksenov, N. A. Esepkina, and A. S. Shcherbakov, Acoustooptical filter with LiNbO$_3$ crystal, 2(3):83, March 1976 Tunable AO filter.
2. V. S. Bonderenko, N. A. Esepkina, V. Yu Petrun'kin, V. V Chkalova, and A. S. Shcherbakov, Acoustooptic TeO$_2$ RF spectrum analyzer with high resolution, 2(10): 367, Oct. 1976 Spectrum analysis.
3. N. A. Esepkina, B. A. Kotov, Yu. A. Kotov, N. F. Ryzhkov A. V. Mikhailov, S. V. Pruxx-Zhukovskii, and A. I. Shishkin Acoustooptic spectrograph for the RATAN 600 radiotelescope, 5(5):227, May 1979. AO spectrum analyzer used in radioastronomy.

From *Soviet Journal of Quantum Electronics*

1. V. I. Balakskii, V. N. Porygin, and Kh. A. Uparena, Feasability of recording the phase structure of an optical field by an acoustooptical method, 11(4):517, April 1981. Description of AO technique to allow observation of phase objects, i.e., objects which alter only phase of transmitted light.

TIME-DOMAIN SIGNAL PROCESSING

From *Soviet Technical Physics Letters*

1. A. E. Mandel and S. M. Shandorov, Production of a phase grating in an acoustooptic interaction in lithium niobate, 4(6):297, June 1978. Acoustophotorefractive storage effect using He-Ne illumination produced by interaction between zero order and second-order diffracted light.
2. N. A. Esepkina, V. Yu. Petrun'kin, N. A. Bukharin, B. A. Kotov, and Yu. A. Kotov, Acoustooptic correlation devices for processing interferometer signals, 5(2):74, Feb. 1979. Time-integrating AO correlator and applications.

3. V. V. Kludzin, S. V. Kulakov, and L. N. Preslenev, Collinear diffraction by oppositely directed acoustic beams in a calcium tungstate crystal, 5(3):125, March 1979. AO convolver using collinear interaction.

4. E. T. Aksenov and A. S. Shcherbakov, Acoustooptic correlator based on collinear nonlinear interaction of elastic waves in a lead molybdate crystal, 6(1):8, Jan. 1980. Correlator based on the nonlinear interaction between two contrapropagating acoustic waves with AO providing time-variable readout.

5. N. A. Esepkina, N. A. Bukharin, Yu. A. Koto, and A. V. Mikhailov, Hybrid optical-digital acoustooptic correlator, 6(1): 31, Jan. 1980. Time-integrating correlator interfaced with computer to obtain longer integration times with applications.

INTEGRATED OPTICS

From *Soviet Technical Physics Letters*

1. V. V. Lemanov, B. V. Sukharev, V. V. Kludzin, and S. V. Kulakov, Acoustooptic control of laser beams in lithium niobate optical wave guides, 2(6):208, June 1976. AO diffraction in a waveguide.

2. E. M. Zolotov, V. M. Pelekhatyi, A. M. Prokhorov, and E. A. Shcherbakov, Thin-film acousto-optic deflector and electro-optic modulator in $LiNbO_3$, 3(3):89, May 1977. Study of titanium indiffused waveguides in $LiNbO_3$ for use as AO deflector and electro-optic modulators.

3. G. A. Smolenskii, M. A. Garsia, S. A. Mironov, A. N. Aggev, B. P. Trubitsyn, and O. P. Obrubov, Diffraction of optical waveguide modes by standing surface elastic waves, 3(9):356, Sept. 1977. Study of diffraction of light in indiffused titanium waveguides by standing surface acoustic waves set up by two contratraveling surface acoustic waves; output observed at twice RF frequency; device can be used to construct AO convolver.

4. G. A. Smolenskii, M. A. Garsia, S. A. Mironov, and A. N. Ageev, Convolution of pulsed signals by acoustooptic interaction in a thin-shell waveguide, 3(9):364, Sept. 1977. Continuation of previous paper where AO convolution of two pulses is demonstrated.

5. D. V. Petrov, A. V. Tsarev, and I. B. Yukovkin, Acoustooptic mode conversion in a waveguide diffused on lithium niobate, 3(9):386, Sept. 1977. Studies of AO interaction in titanium indiffused waveguides which indicate either TE → TM or TM → TE mode conversion.

6. M. A. Garsia, S. A. Mironov, A. N. Ageev, T. A. Shaplygina, B. P. Trubitsyn, and T. V. Loding, 4(9):229, May, 1978. Study of titanium indiffused waveguides.

7. I. G. Voitenko and V. P. Red'ko, Light diffraction by opposit
    ly propagating surface acoustic waves in an optical waveguide
    4(6):282, June 1978. Study of Fe indiffused waveguide as
    possible AO convolver.

8. E. T. Aksenov, N. A. Esepkina, and A. A. Lipovskii, Diffus
    lithium niobate waveguides for acoustooptical signal processing
    4(11):530, Nov. 1978. Describes outdiffused waveguides and
    AO deflectors, convolvers, and correlators made on them.

9. Yu. A. Bykovskii, V. L. Smirnov, V. N. Sorokovikov, and
    A. V. Shmal'ko, Acoustooptic deflection and modulation of ligh
    by a stationary phase-grating structure in a thin-film wave-
    guide, 4(12):611, Dec. 1978. Deflection and modulation in
    As_2S_3 using combination of AO and a stationary phase grating

10. V. V. Kludzin, S. V. Kulakov, L. N. Preslenev, M. N. Vikh
    and G. O. Karapetyan, Acoustooptic interaction in a plane
    glass waveguide, 5(4):188, April 1979. Study of AO interac-
    tion in photochromic waveguides produced in plane glass sub-
    strates; only moderate diffraction efficiency was achieved;
    however, bandwidth was quite large.

11. E. T. Aksenov and A. A. Lipovskii, Optical-waveguide light
    modulator which uses Raman-Nath diffraction of a volume
    acoustic wave, 5(5):260, May 1979. AO interaction between
    waveguided light and bulk acoustic wave in glass prism.

12. E. T. Aksenov, N. A. Esepkina, A. A. Lipovskii, and A. V.
    Pavlenko, Geodesic lenses formed in diffusion-fabricated optic
    waveguides, 5(10):531, Oct. 1979. Study of geodesic lenses
    formed in glass substrates by optical grinding and polishing.

13. V. S. Bondarenko, S. A. Mironov, S. P. Rzhevskii, V. V.
    Chkalova, A. N. Ageev, and T. A. Shaplygina, Waveguide
    SAW acoustooptic convolver, 6(2):59, Feb. 1980. Improved
    integrated optic AO convolver which uses offset transducers
    to minimize reflections.

14. L. N. Deryugin, V. I. Anikin, A. I. Gudzenko, V. G.
    Dneprovskii, and V. F. Terichev, Mid-IR acoustooptic interac-
    tion in planar waveguides, 6(4):183, April 1980. AO interac-
    tion between SAW and CO_2 laser light ($\lambda = 10.6$ µm) in plana
    waveguides.

15. B. V. Sukharev and N. K. Yushin, Gigahertz-range planar
    acoustooptic modulator, 6(11):564, Nov. 1980. Demonstration
    of modulation of waveguided light by bulk elastic waves at 1
    GHz.

16. O. V. Borovkov and I. Ya. Kucherov, Controlling laser beams
    in diffused waveguides by normal elastic waves in the sub-
    strates, 6(12):654, Dec. 1980. Report shows that waveguided
    light can be deflected and modulated by normal elastic waves
    the substrate; advantages are simplicity and change of deflec-
    tion angle by variation of amplitude of sound (rather than fre

quency) and no frequency modulation of light transmitted through modulator.

17. V. M. Shanderov, Wideband acoustooptic interaction with mode conversion in titanium-diffused lithium niobate waveguides, 7(7):361, July 1981. Study of wideband AO interaction with TE_m–TE_n mode conversion in a $LiNbO_3$:Ti waveguide .

18. Yu. V. Gulyaev, Yu. M. Dikaev, Yu. L. Kopylov, I. M. Kotelyanskii, V. B. Kravchenko, E. N. Mirgorodskaya, and V. P. Orlov, Corrugated grating in $LiNbO_3$ for exciting surface waves in a diffused optical waveguide, 7(10):500, Oct. 1981. Report on first development and study in USSR of coupler for exciting SAW consisting of a corrugated grating on the surface of a diffused $LiNbO_3$ waveguide.

19. E. T. Aksenov, A. V. Kukharev, A. A. Lipovskii, and A. V. Pavlenko, Acoustooptic convolver using integrated-optics elements, 7(10):513, Oct. 1981. Acoustooptic convolver using combination of integrated optics waveguide, transducers, and geodesic lens with external He-Ne laser and PIN photodetector. Bandwidth achieved was 110 MHz, with about 2 microseconds time aperture.

20. E. M. Korablev. V. V. Proklov, V. A. Sychugov, and A. S. Andreev, Two-coordinate integrated-optics deflector using a Ti-diffused $LiNbO_3$ waveguide, 7(12):616, Dec. 1981. A two-dimensional AO spectrum analyzer using for the horizontal deflection the noncollinear interaction between a z-propagating SAW and an x-propagating guided light wave. The vertical deflection is obtained by the collinear interaction of the horizontally deflected light with an x-propagating SAW. This latter interaction deflects the light beam out of the waveguide. Depending on the phase-matching condition chosen for the collinear interaction, either 90 × 400 spot resolution with 1% diffraction efficiency or 90 × 250 spot resolution with 2% diffraction efficiency was obtained.

From *Soviet Journal of Quantum Electronics*

1. E. A. Kolosovskii, D. V. Petrov, and A. V. Tsarev, Frequency dependence of the acoustooptic interaction efficiency of TE modes in a diffused optical waveguide, 9(9): 1119, Sept. 1979. An algorithm is presented to calculate field distribution of TE modes in graded-index waveguides; then this algorithm is used to calculate frequency dependence of AO interaction efficiency.

2. K. W. Ziling, E. A. Kolosovskii, D. V. Petrov, and A. V. Tsarev, Use of generalized parameters to describe acoustooptic interaction in a diffused waveguide, 10(1):44, Jan. 1980. Analysis of AO interaction between TE modes in diffused waveguides; experimental measurements in 50- to 550-MHz range are included.

3. E. A. Kolosovskii, D. V. Petrov, and A. V. Tsarev, Influence
of the parameters of a diffused waveguide on the frequency dependence of the acoustooptic interaction efficiency, $10(8):998$,
Aug. 1980. Study of AO efficiency for different diffusion profiles in indiffused waveguides, viz., gaussian, exponential,
and parabolic.

From *Soviet Physics Technical Physics*

1. L. A. Osadchev, Efficiency of acoustooptic interactions in
polystyrene optical waveguides, $25(1):106$, Jan. 1980. Study
of AO interaction efficiency in polystyrene optical waveguides
deposited on quartz; efficiency is studied as function of baking
temperature.

Index